Henry Adams

American Political Thought

edited by

Wilson Carey McWilliams and Lance Banning

Henry Adams

The Historian as Political Theorist

James P. Young

UNIVERSITY PRESS OF KANSAS

Published by the University Press of Kansas (Lawrence, Kansas 66049), which
was organized by the Kansas Board of Regents and is operated and funded by
Emporia State University, Fort Hays State University, Kansas State University,
Pittsburg State University, the University of Kansas, and Wichita State University.

Library of Congress Cataloging-in-Publication Data

Young, James P., 1934–
    Henry Adams : the historian as political theorist / James P. Young.
        p. cm — (American political thought)
    Includes index.
    ISBN 0-7006-1087-1 (cloth : alk. paper)
    1. Adams, Henry, 1838–1918—Political and social views.   2. United
States—History—Philosophy.   3. United States—Politics and
government—Philosophy.   I. Title.   II. Series.
    E175.5.A2   Y68   2001
    973'.07'202—dc21   00-012522

British Library Cataloguing in Publication Data is available.

Printed in the United States of America

10 9 8 7 6 5 4 3 2 1

The paper used in this publication meets the minimum requirements of the
American National Standard for Permanence of Paper for Printed Library
Materials Z39.48-1984.

Once again for Gladys
and for
Jim, Ellen, Julia, and Allison
Sue, Drew, and Elizabeth

A teacher affects eternity; he can never tell where his influence stops.

At the utmost, the active-minded young man should ask of his teacher only the mastery of his tools . . . Once acquired, the tools and models may be thrown away.

— *Henry Adams*

CONTENTS

PREFACE AND ACKNOWLEDGMENTS

Henry Adams is a thinker more admired than read, though it is interesting to note that the Board of the Modern Library has placed *The Education of Henry Adams* at the top of a list of the best one hundred nonfiction books of the twentieth century published first in English. Nevertheless, I think my characterization remains true for political scientists and political theorists and probably others as well, even including historians. In this study, I suggest that while there is some material by Adams that is of little use and a smaller part that is utterly reprehensible, there is also much that is of value to political theorists, as well as to historians and to political scientists of a historical bent.

Because of the obscurity into which much of his work has fallen, I felt the need for more exposition than is usual in studies of historical figures in political theory, and because he is such a superb writer, I chose to develop the exposition in his own words to the greatest possible extent in the hope of conveying to the reader new to Adams a sense of his often scintillating style. He writes so brilliantly that it is no wonder that a large proportion of the work devoted to Adams is by literary scholars.

In quoting Adams, I have taken the liberty of modernizing a few spellings, usually archaisms or Anglicisms, such as substituting *clue* for *clew*. These changes are not frequent, and they may help keep the contemporary reader from getting distracted. In contrast, I retained Adams's sometimes unusual punctuation, notably his use of the semicolon where today we would use a comma.

I hope that this study will revive interest in the work of Adams. At this time, when political scientists have rediscovered the virtues of historical analysis, he has a lot to offer, both substantively and by the example of the way he worked. The *History of the United States during the Administrations of Thomas Jefferson and James Madison* is perhaps the greatest work of history ever written by an American and has been compared with Adams's model, Gibbon's *Decline and Fall of the Roman Empire*. This is a period crucial to the founding of the American nation; moreover, Jefferson is so central to the history of the United States that no one seriously interested in the American experience can afford to overlook Adams's seminal contribution to our understanding of this elusive leader. Another reason for attending to Adams is that he lived in a time much like ours, a time of great political corruption and extremely rapid technological development. Adams's journalism exploring the nexus between money and politics makes fascinating reading in our time, as do his reflections in the *Education.* So do his writings on science and technology, which become a major theme in the *Education* and are continued in some difficult and perplexing essays written late in his career. And his wonderful meditation on art, religion, science, and theology in *Mont Saint Michel and Chartres* deserves to be read not just for its ideas but for its sheer beauty as well. Also, the much too often neglected journalism Adams produced in the 1870s has great resonance in today's world of rampant financial speculation. Finally, though I have focused on Adams's published writings, his letters are a treasure trove of ideas and observations on nineteenth- and early-twentieth-century society in both the United States and Europe, not to mention his excursions to the South Seas. Out of this large body of work I think it is possible to derive a theory of American political development and a philosophy of world history. Neither is uncontroversial, but they demand to be read.

Beyond my endnotes, I wish to express a general debt to three major studies that were of inestimable help to me. All Adams scholars are reliant on the three-volume biography by Ernest Samuels. While I have differences with Samuels on a few matters of interpretation, his work has been of the greatest importance to me in understanding the setting of Adams's ideas. As a study of these ideas, J. C. Levenson's *The Mind and Art of Henry Adams*, after over forty years, is still a model of interpretation not equaled since. If anyone has come close to meeting the standard set by Levenson it is William Merrill Decker, whose *The Literary Vocation of Henry Adams* has not received the attention it deserves, perhaps due to the recent neglect of Adams's work.

While I was still at Binghamton University I had wonderful assistance in compiling the materials on which this study is based from two graduate students, Kimberly Maslin-Wicks and Michelle Barnello, who are now my friends and professional colleagues. I also benefited from the helpful staff of the Hatcher Library at the University of Michigan. At the University Press of Kansas it was a pleasure to work with Susan Schott and Melinda Wirkus. The director of the press, Fred Woodward, was a wonderful publisher, gently prodding me along while providing me with good conversation and constant support. I also owe a great debt to my computer guru son-in-law, Drew Schmidt, who managed to overcome my technological ineptitude and made it possible for me to get past the problems posed by recalcitrant programs and actually produce a manuscript.

Several friends and colleagues provided aid and comfort. Some early drafts were read by Tom Dumm and Josh Miller, who raised questions I tried to answer, though perhaps not to their satisfaction. Lance Banning brought his historian's mind to bear and made me reconsider a number of points. My greatest debts go to George Kateb and Wilson Carey McWilliams. As he has before, George Kateb provided encouragement, along with penetrating questions and observations. In particular, the discussions of *Mont Saint Michel and Chartres* and of technology were enriched by his ideas and his writings, though he bears no responsibility for the use I made of them. And if some parts of the book are clear, it is because his doubts pushed me to rewrite some previously incomprehensible passages. Carey McWilliams read through not one but two drafts and, to my great benefit, shared with me his vast knowledge of Adams, American political thought, and American history in general. Every writer needs the sort of warm encouragement he provided. My stubborn streak is well enough developed that I rejected or ignored some of the advice I received, but the fault is mine rather than my friends'.

My other debts are personal, but even more important. Years ago, in my first book I wrote that my wife Gladys performed all the traditional tasks of the traditional academic wife in the traditionally outstanding fashion. She still does. Without her there would be no book. As in everything I do, Jim and Ellen, Susan and Drew, are constantly in my mind. Last, but absolutely not least, are Julia, Allison, and Elizabeth, who provide so much joy. I look forward to the time they are old enough to read what I have written.

INTRODUCTION

Henry Adams is a lonely figure in American political thought. By any standard he is one of the finest, possibly the greatest, of American historians, and his "autobiography," however idiosyncratic, is one of the undisputed classics in the genre. His great multivolume history of the Jefferson and Madison administrations is also undoubtedly a masterpiece; he wrote some of the best political journalism of the nineteenth century; and he was the author of two novels that, while not the work of a truly gifted fiction writer, are nevertheless full of intellectual interest. He is the author of one of the deepest meditations on the difference between the medieval world and modern industrial civilization, the great creation through which he hopes to describe the trajectory of modern Western history. He also made a serious attempt to come to grips with the biological and physical sciences of his time. Not least, he poured out a body of letters of great literary distinction and sociopolitical interest. On the side, he was a competent amateur painter. In this vast flood there is embedded a theory of the development of America history and, still more broadly, a theory of Western history that can be interestingly compared with those of Karl Marx and Max Weber. It may be that this concern with the meaning of history is characteristically American. Richard Hofstadter once remarked, "While it is no doubt true to some degree everywhere that history doubles for political theory and has even in secular ages taken on some of the work of theology, it is perhaps more keenly true in the United States.[1] Therefore, to have such a theory of history is almost automatically to have a social and political theory as well, even when, as in the case of Adams, it is not formally developed.

And yet, while historians are very respectful of the massive history of the Jefferson and Madison presidencies, his work is probably more admired than actually read by any other than specialists on the early national period, and, interestingly, a large part of the commentary on his writing is by specialists in American literature. This is particularly true of his great late books, *Mont Saint Michel and Chartres* and *The Education of Henry Adams*. But even in literature, though he may be admired, he is not really of canonical status; he is not one of those writers who is perceived as essential to a literary education. Perhaps only the famous chapter on the Virgin and the Dynamo in the *Education* is widely known. Most surprisingly, political theorists, with a few exceptions, have slighted his work; he is certainly not part of the standard curriculum on American political thought. Of the writings by theorists that stand out, even so brilliant a reader as Judith Shklar seems so handicapped by her dislike of the subject that she has less than usual to contribute, though she is certainly not without insights.[2] Russell Hanson and Richard Merriman are closer to the mark when they suggest that Adams was the last of the civic republicans, a plausible designation, given Adams's hope for leadership dedicated to public as opposed to private interests, though at the time Adams wrote, that had become a rare species indeed.[3] These ideas are surely central to Adams's critique of his society, although they cannot be said to exhaust the complexities of Adams's position. Another useful theoretical contribution is by Henry Kariel, who has interesting and important things to say about Adams's deep concern with science and technology, as well as on the limits of historical positivism.[4] But there is not a great deal more from political theorists.[5]

Some of the neglect is probably fairly easy to explain. Adams is not always a particularly attractive character. He has a pronounced snobbish streak, and his "autobiography"—*The Education of Henry Adams*—is sometimes marred by excessive irony and a sense of self-pity that, in spite of the personal tragedy that marred his life, is almost entirely uncalled for, given Adams's social position and his proximity to the centers of American power. More seriously, there is a thoroughly nasty streak of anti-Semitism that often appears in the letters, though it does not erupt too often in his public writings. It is not, I think, central to his theories, but it still must be dealt with. Further, as he repeatedly observed, he had what he said was an eighteenth-century mind, which he claimed made him out of place in the twentieth century; yet at the same time, he was both attracted and repulsed by twentieth-century science and technology, so the matter is not so simple as he made it out to be. It is precisely this sense of distance and alienation, coupled, in a complex way, with his acute sense of personal, familial connection to American politics and culture, combined with his interest in science, that is a major source of his power and insight. In spite of his often acid criticism of American life and politics, he is clearly what Michael Walzer would call a "connected critic," even when the ties that bound him to the nation his family had done so much to shape were strained to the breaking point.[6] His was a lover's quarrel with his country. As William Merrill Decker says, he sought public influence, though it must be said that in the end he despaired of achieving it and chose publication forms that worked against it. Still, "although at times he seems to write to no end but to annoy, his work always betrays the wish to be dialogically placed in a purposive and sophisticated national discussion. It always reveals the hope (or the equally significant despair) that it may contribute to an American civilization that would vindicate the aspirations of the country's fathers, among whom an Adams had conspicuously figured."[7] It is important to understand that a connected critic is still a critic and that his discussion of his tradition may gain as much as it loses from the connection.

Other, more specifically intellectual factors may account for Adams's relative neglect. He was a master political historian, and this is a time when social rather than political history is dominant. His is also a history of the actions of elites, even when he despises them; there is little sense at all of the now fashionable history "written from the bottom up." And although he is fully aware of the difficulties, his initial goal is to write Rankean history *wie es eigentlich gewesen ist.* This is, or on the surface appears to be, positivist history with no trace of currently voguish notions that reality is somehow a matter of human invention. As he puts it in *The Education of Henry Adams,* "He had even published a dozen volumes of American history for no other purpose than to satisfy himself whether, by the severest process of stating, with the least possible comment, such facts as seemed sure, in such order as seemed rigorously consequent, he could fix for a familiar moment a necessary sequence of human movement."[8] In principle then, however difficult, there is a world out there whose sometimes inscrutable workings we can at least hope to understand.

Still, Adams by no means adheres rigorously to this positivist position in all his work, and even in the *History,* the mind of a critical moralist is clearly at work. Moreover, he was clearly aware that a historian's perspective influences what he sees, as is demonstrated by his letter to President Eliot of Harvard in support of a position in the history faculty for Henry Cabot Lodge. As he put it, Lodge's views, being "federalist and conservative," as opposed to his own, which "tend to democracy and radicalism," have an equal right to expression.[9] Moreover, in the *Education,* he begins to raise serious questions about the very idea of truth, though, at the same time, he fights against this temptation. Still, the attempt to understand requires a grip on reality, difficult to come by though that may be. And to understand also requires a theory of how the world works. The theory he advances is increasingly a critical theory. Adams transcends historical positivism through his literary power and sometimes rhapsodically poetic style, combined with an increasing sense of moral outrage at what he sees as the deterioration of his country that makes him a powerful scourge of American life in the post–Civil War era. As Clive Bush argues, his Rankeanism has limits and serves as the basis for a narrative strategy that is "biased toward value and point of view."[10]

Adams judges what he sees, and he judges harshly. The standards of judgment are those of a "New England conscience," a term I borrow from Austin Warren. For Warren, the term indicates a kind of "fussy and overactive conscience," a state of mind that often takes on pathological overtones and in which "pleasure, graciousness, joy, [and] love" are missing.[11] Warren understands that Adams is a somewhat atypical example of the type. Though his intellectual conscience is very strong, there is little examination of his "personal moral conscience," though there certainly *is* a great deal of self-examination of his own very active intellect. But Warren's term is useful anyway, because it suggests Adams's Puritan ancestry without identifying him specifically as a Puritan. To identify him so would overlook the fact that, though he might have wished otherwise, Adams lacks religious faith. But, in his way, Adams is trying to provide the *nation* with a New England conscience he sees to be sorely lacking. He writes in the great tradition of the Puritan Jeremiad. The Puritans were possessed by a sense that they were betraying the high calling that had brought them to New England, that they were falling away from their own very high moral and social standards.[12] The Jeremiad, a sermon that pointed out the huge gap between the shining ideal and the often ugly real, became one of the characteristic forms of American political rhetoric.[13] Adams is one of its late, great masters. The sense of betrayed ideals is a major theme of his history of the Jefferson and Madison administrations, and it permeates much of his other writing. And once he moves beyond the great *History* and the post–Civil War journalism, his work takes on a philosophical dimension that no purely positivist history could offer. At no point in his career is it possible to mistake his profound theoretical and moral concerns.

But even on its most positivist side, the *History* represents a great event in American historiography. Among Adams's greatest predecessors, Francis Parkman focused on the wilderness and the struggle between Britain and France for Canada, so that his main themes were at some remove from American national development. George Bancroft was an enthusiastic Jacksonian nationalist who could descend into "mindless patriotism," in spite of genuine historical ability.[14] And while lesser, or today at least less well known figures such as Francis Bowen and Richard Hildreth were more critical and skeptical, they were still men with a celebratory message. Many of the influential men who came of age during or after the Civil War were New England amateurs who had their differences but were still resolutely conservative nationalists especially anxious to defend property rights.[15] Adams shared many of these biases, but he was in every way more iconoclastic. He wrote in anything but a celebratory mode, and while he never came close to being a socialist, though he did flirt with it in some of his letters, he was bitterly critical of capitalism and the abuse of society by those with great accumulations of property. He could be very conservative, but he could also be profoundly radical, particularly in the Marxian sense of "going to the root." And any picture of Adams as some sort of antidemocratic ideologue is mistaken. It is necessary to consider seriously his own self-portrait in the letter to Eliot quoted earlier. As J. C. Levenson says of him:

> Since he did not always share the sentiments and ideas by which American democrats or radicals are conventionally classified, his statement of belief is often ignored or dismissed as insincere. He never idolized those who labor in the earth or in the shop, he only respected them as men. He never cherished a dream of the barricades, for to him the revolutionary impulse (which he too sometimes felt) was essentially anarchic. He seriously thought that in this country democracy had once and for all taken possession of the national government and that secession movements, after 1798, were right-wing revolutions, antidemocratic and antilibertarian in nature.

We need, Levenson goes on, to recapture this sense of "democratic nationalism" if we are to understand Adams.[16] Adams's sense of democracy may not be ours, and he certainly might be upset by some forms of contemporary democratic theory, but his claims cannot simply be dismissed. And surely he was right in his assessment of the secessionist movement, not an unimportant thing if one considers secession and the Civil War to be at the very center of American history. Finally, if, as Hofstadter suggests, all the great American historians present theories, this is above all true of Adams, though his ideas are sometimes masked by a facade of positivism in his earlier work and become overt primarily in the later, much more speculative writings.

Thus, I think, history as Adams understands it is a very complicated enterprise. Surely he would have subscribed to Kierkegaard's view that "Life is lived forward but is understood backward."[17] Equally surely, for all his nostalgia, he would have agreed with Clifford Geertz, perhaps not without some sorrow, that it is not possible to live in the past. Unlike Geertz, he may have believed that one can foretell the future from the past, at least in a general way, and he may have thought it possible to derive laws of social necessity from the past. At least he experimented, though with limited success, along these lines. But, in the end, I think he would endorse Geertz's view that the best we can derive from the past is the ability to perceive, "a bit less blankly, what is happening around one, reacting, a bit more intelligently, to what, in the event, swims into view."[18]

Insights into the exceedingly complex nature of this problem also come from an unexpected source. I think Adams would have agreed with his contemporary, the Russian composer Modest Mussorgsky, who wrote, "The past within the present—there's my task." But the musicologist Richard Taruskin, in his great book on Mussorgsky, accidentally refined the problem by transposing this comment to read "the present in the past."[19] For Taruskin, this fruitful misquotation captures the essence of Mussorgsky's historical operas better than the original statement. For the study of Adams, Taruskin's inadvertent error points to the complex way in which the relation of past to present in the study of history is reciprocal and therefore dauntingly complicated. This problem is central to the complex intertwining of past and present in Adams's thought. And Adams's approach, based as it is on tremendous narrative power combined with deep philosophical insight, is ideally suited to dealing with these problems. And writing along these lines can, as Shklar suggests, be a vital path to understanding both our past and our present: "Narrative history, informed by philosophical and social analysis and a critical spirit, remains our likeliest path to political understanding."[20] Surely if it is not the likeliest path, it is one of the most powerful.

An exploration of these problems involves some complex theory. And the complexity deepens because we are dealing with a writer often hidden behind a mask compounded of irony and self-deprecation. (That the latter is often merely a pose does not reduce its presence.) Moreover, for all his theoretical impulses, Adams does not write in the way political theorists, or even historical theorists, typically present their works. There is no real system. No ideal is specifically spelled out. There is no formal discussion of subjects such as power, authority, democracy, equality, or any of the other standard topics of the political theorist. The lack of a genuine system is itself a complicating factor. If Adams has a theory of history, in its artistry it is closer in style and, to some extent, in content to Tolstoy than to such social scientists as Marx or even Weber, though he shares many of the concerns of the latter two.[21] His work is saturated by ideas, but they are not stated in propositional, let alone testable, form. Adams is a humanist to the core. That is a large part of his quarrel with modernity, which, in spite of, or perhaps because of, his scientific interests, he sees as dominated by an antihumanistic scientific ethos. He is serious about his scientific concerns, however dated or even bizarre they now seem, so that there is a tension in his mind between his deep humanistic and his strong scientific leanings.

There is no need for another biography of Adams. Ernest Samuels has given us a superb life and letters in his magisterial three-volume study, and another equally massive study by Edward Chalfant is in progress.[22] Nor is there need for an exploration of Adams's relation to his illustrious family, surely one of the most distinguished in American history.[23] After all, his great-grandfather was John Adams; his grandfather was John Quincy Adams; and his father, Charles Francis Adams, was a congressman and held the vitally important post of ambassador to the Court of St. James during the Civil War. His brother Charles Francis, Jr., was also a member of Congress and later president of the Union Pacific Railroad, and another brother, Brooks, was a theorist of some interest, though not on a level with Henry. Such familial factors cannot be completely ignored, but it is important to remember that theory cannot be reduced to biography, however interesting. If we want to understand the theory, we must turn to the published works, which is surely where we will find the ideas Adams hoped to leave behind. Letters and biographical materials can assist this effort, but they are no substitute for it. This is not to denigrate the letters. They are often brilliant, witty, charming, gossipy, and full of interesting ideas; they can also be self-serving, disingenuous, and filled with the worst sort of prejudice. It is certainly possible that Adams believed that someday they would be published. In any event, they provide important clues to the works that were more immediately released to the public; it is these texts that receive the bulk of my attention here.[24]

Adams's later works are written in a mood of world-weary cynicism. But the cynicism is, I think, born of disappointment. The early Adams was almost flamboyantly idealistic, an ardent pro-Union nationalist possessed of a sense of the potential for greatness embedded in the American Republic. The letters of his early manhood are filled with a contempt worthy of John Quincy Adams for the slaveholding South. Moreover, there is an abiding belief in the superiority of American democratic institutions to the sclerotic conditions he perceived in Europe. These beliefs were certainly in no way altered by the duplicitous behavior of the English during the Civil War, when he served in London as private secretary to his father, the ambassador.

But the Union victory in the war turned hollow. It ended slavery and subdued the South, but it also ushered in a period of incredibly rapid social and industrial change, accompanied by a period of monstrous corruption, arguably matched in American history only by what we have seen in the last generation. And Adams was mesmerized, attracted, repelled, and almost paralyzed by the technological developments he saw as the driving force in Western history, another interesting parallel to the present. Under similar circumstances, some have turned to religion, and Adams was fascinated by an idealized medieval unity and a near enchantment with the Virgin Mary. Yet someone who could not submit to the authority of the Unitarian Church could hardly embrace Catholicism, so he became a pessimistic prophet compelled, so he claimed, to wander in the wilderness, surrendering to blind historical forces seemingly beyond human control. His interest in science and technology combined with his religious concerns led him to symbolize the movement of world history as a conflict between the Virgin and the Dynamo, and with some apparent reluctance, he perceived the Dynamo as the winner, though one must be very careful not to overestimate his rejection of technology or to see him as some sort of technophobic neo-medievalist.

The principal foci for this study are Adams's two interlocked theories of history. The first is his overview of the American experience, focusing on what he saw as the early betrayal of the original constitutional understanding by the Jeffersonians and the further debasement of American ideals by the rapid development of industrial and financial capitalism following the Civil War. One might even argue that his more speculative, more philosophical writings are warranted by the solid empirical foundations of his historical and journalistic work. The second theory takes off from the American experience and is closely linked to it. It is an almost Weberian lament for the decline of humane values in the wake of capitalist industrialization and the concomitant growth of technological power, a set of forces seen in their most advanced form in the United States. In the face of these changes, he bemoans the world lost to us with the decline of medieval unity and religious faith, but he is under no more illusions than Weber that such faith can be restored. Thus, his "system," if that is not too grandiose a term, ends on a note of tragic despair, though a despair sometimes lightened by brief rays of hope. These are ideas that may shed some light on contemporary problems, and even paradoxical ideas such as "conservative, Christian, anarchy," as developed in *The Education of Henry Adams*, may offer some clues for a democratic revival, particularly when combined with some of the themes that run through his monumental history of the Jefferson and Madison administrations. For now, we can leave open the question of whether he would approve of such a revival.

To explore such possibilities requires some subtle interpretation — if possible, as subtle as the author of the ideas themselves. Adams is not an easily accessible writer. The famous description he wrote of Thomas Jefferson might well apply to him: "Jefferson could be painted only touch by touch, with a fine pencil, and the perfection of the likeness depended upon the shifting and uncertain flicker of its semi-transparent shadows."[25] Adams's "autobiography," a term appended by his publisher to *The Education of Henry Adams* after his death, only complicates matters. All autobiographers present themselves as they wish to be seen, but in this case, the matter is more complicated than usual. To start with, the *Education* is written in the third person to convey a sense of detachment. And as Brooks Simpson writes, *"The Education* is part autobiography, part novel, part philosophy, and part social commentary, for Adams consciously shaped and distorted the facts of his life to fit larger themes concerning power, education, and knowledge."[26] Leaving aside Simpson's evident bias, the cautionary note is warranted. Adams is an elusive thinker, one all too often oversimplified in a vain effort to capture him with an easy label. To do justice to him, we must take into account his irony, the cynicism that clouds his idealism, and the change in his views over time. Beyond all this, he is, I think, a deeply divided thinker. He would like to have had religious faith but failed to achieve it. He worried about the effects of science and technology but nevertheless admired their achievements, and his mind was much influenced by them. And, contrary to much opinion, he was a believer in democracy, though he was often dismayed by the results it produced. The dilemmas he faced have not disappeared, and so I believe he remains an important voice for us today. It is time to revive interest in the whole body of his work, particularly the neglected history of the Jefferson and Madison administrations, which is arguably still his most successful work.

Part I

Theory of American History

Chapter 1

Foundations of the Early Republic

Though he does not offer anything remotely like a systematic theory of American history, nor is his an interpretation without historical gaps, taken together, Adams's formal historical writings, his journalism, and his autobiography, combined with some of his letters, provide a fairly comprehensive, if often rather grim, overview of the course of American democratic development. The early hopes, the basic problems, and the first wrong turning are set out in his massive and masterful history of the presidential administrations of Thomas Jefferson and James Madison, but the place to begin is with his early letters and journalism, written at the outset of the Civil War. These reveal a degree of unforced enthusiasm for a cause and for his country that is unexpected, given the seeming cynicism of his later work. Moreover, they are the earliest of Adams's mature writings, predating the *History* by approximately two decades.[1]

The Early Idealism of Henry Adams

For all the dour, sometimes cynical character of his mature work, the young Henry Adams was almost flamboyantly idealistic in his belief in the superiority of the North to the South—based on his and his family's long-standing hatred of slavery—and of the superiority of the United States to decadent Europe. And going beyond his feelings about slavery is the fact that his family had a long and often contentious relationship with the founders of southern thought—in the case of Thomas Jefferson, something close to a love-hate relationship. Adams, after all, was the great-grandson of John Adams, Jefferson's close colleague in the American Revolution. Although their relationship degenerated into enmity when Jefferson defeated Adams for the presidency in the election of 1800, it was revived in old age, a revival that led to one of the great bodies of correspondence in the history of American letters. That the younger Adams might have ambiguous feelings about the Jeffersonian subjects of his greatest historical work is entirely understandable. But the disunionist Southerners who followed Jefferson were, in his view, simply beneath contempt. They were "beyond all imagination demented,"

given "to the contemplation of fancies which were oriental in their magnifi-
cence."[2] Always the moralist, Adams, writing from London in his post as his
ambassador father's secretary, concluded that the slave power was offensive
"not only to the spirit of our Government but to that of our religion and
whole civilization."[3] Certainly any thought of Southern independence was
beyond the pale, since Adams, like his ancestors, was unionist to the core. As
the North's fortunes in the war rose and fell, so too did Adams's spirits. Thus
in the summer of 1864 he feared a Democratic victory over Lincoln that
would lead to a disastrous decline in the much desired influence of Northern "gentlemen" such as himself and his brother Charles.[4] But Lincoln's triumph revived him and elevated him to an effusive mood. While critics of
the American system of government saw the very fact of an election in time
of crisis as a significant constitutional weakness, in the event, it turned out to
be "in practice a great and positive gain and a fruitful source of national
strength." He continues, "After all systems of Government are secondary matters, if you've only got your people behind them. I never have as yet felt so
proud as now of the great qualities of our race, or so confident of the capacity of men to develop their capacities in the mass. . . . Europe has a long way
to go to catch us up."[5] And yet, with his usual sense of complexity, Adams is
certain that Europe *will* catch up. Once the English aristocracy and the
Roman Church, the two great influences holding Europe back, go down, as
will happen whether in ten or a hundred years, and when "all the world
stands on the American principle, [then] where will be our old boasts unless
we do something more."[6] Is this a source of the restlessness that characterizes
so much of American history? And, as Andrew Delbanco suggests, is this one
of the ironies Adams sees in America, this readiness "to conceive of American history as the dissemination of democratic energy to the world with a
consequent exhaustion at home?" When this was written, Adams still seemed
to believe that America could do that "something more." But, as Delbanco
says, this seems to anticipate Adams's late theories about the dissipation of
energy according to the second law of thermodynamics. There the conclusions are notably more pessimistic.[7]

For all their latent gloominess, these speculations may seem startling sentiments for one with a reputation for skepticism about democracy, but they
are not alone. Though certainly never a socialist, Adams nevertheless waxed
enthusiastic after attending a socialist meeting in London. Again, the language is striking. The gathering was "most threatening and dangerous to the
established state of things . . . as alarming here as a slave-insurrection would
be in the South . . . I never quite appreciated the 'moral influence' of Amer-

ican democracy, nor the cause that the privileged classes in Europe have to fear us, until I saw how directly it works . . . The lower orders . . . go our whole platform and are full of the 'rights of man.' The old revolutionary leaven is working steadily here in England. You can find millions of people who look up to our institutions as their model and who talk with utter contempt of their own system of Government."[8] In this time of high hopes, American institutions become for Adams something akin to the shining city on a hill of his Puritan ancestors. One must be careful. Adams was not a radical democrat, though on occasion he wrote and even acted like one, but he did not by any means hold a deep, natural hostility to democracy, as some of his critics seem to think. If, in later years, he was highly critical of the workings of American democracy, this was due to his disgust with the endemic corruption of the period after the Civil War. But, as is implied in his wartime letters, at the beginning of the American experiment he saw a potential for good that could transform the world. The best way to see this is to explore his famous view of the American scene in 1800.

The United States in 1800

The first six chapters of Adams's *History* of the Jefferson and Madison administrations, which portray the situation of the United States in 1800, are one of the great tours de force in the literature of American history. Devoted primarily to geography, economics, and culture, they illustrate a type of work far ahead of its time, and also in some contrast to the seemingly more conventional political, diplomatic, and military analysis that constitutes the bulk of Adams's huge study. Having said this is to take nothing from the brilliance of the remainder of the work, which is positivist history at the highest level, without ever quite abandoning a critical stance toward his subject. The *History* as a whole is superbly well researched, with Adams delving deep into primary sources, both domestic and foreign, to which he could gain access because of his family connections. Still, the opening six chapters are of great structural importance to the work as a whole. Together with the last four chapters at the conclusion of his study of the Madison years, they constitute a framework for the entire massive study. The questions at the end of the sixth chapter also provide a starting point for evaluation of the changes wrought by the two Virginians, and they raise a set of questions that the work as a whole purports to answer, only to be succeeded by a new set of problems at the conclusion of the final volume. The first six chapters in particular have been almost universally recognized as masterful, have been published as a separate volume, and, in fact, may well be the only part of the *History* still regularly read today.[9]

Apparently simple on the surface and presenting what purports to be a straightforward factual account of the conditions facing Thomas Jefferson as he took office, they are in fact more complex—and controversial—than they at first appear. On the whole, critics have looked to their obvious merits and taken them at face value and have turned their attention to other parts of the huge edifice created by Adams. However, they are central to the interpretation Adams offers of the course of American history and must be examined with more care than usual.

At the start, the situation he describes is not prepossessing. He begins with geography and economics. The population is small, 5,308,483 according to the census of 1800, and it is spread out over a narrow ribbon of land along the Atlantic coast. Discounting slaves, there were 4.5 million free whites, which meant less than a million able-bodied males. The land west of the Alleghenies was undeveloped and inhabited by only 400,000 to 500,000 people, "living in an isolation like that of the Jutes or Angles in the fifth century," a population in which Adams had little interest.[10] New York was "medieval in regard to drainage and cleanliness."[11] "The Saxon farmer of the eighth century enjoyed most of the comforts known to Saxon farmers of the eighteenth." Even Adams's beloved New England, where "the ordinary farmhouse was hardly so well built, so spacious, or so warm as that of a well-to-do contemporary of Charlemagne," was seriously backward, though one might suggest that the last comparison is almost flamboyantly unfair.[12]

Transportation and communication were rudimentary. Roads were poor, as were the inns, and stage travel was difficult. As Thomas Jefferson wrote of his frequent journeys from Monticello to the nation's capital, "Of eight rivers between here and Washington, five have neither bridges nor boats."[13] The union of New England with New York and Pennsylvania was difficult, but the union of New England with the Carolinas was "hopeless."[14] "Nature was rather man's master than his servant," and it "had decided that the experiment of a single republican government must meet extreme difficulties."[15] On top of all this, and especially surprising given later American innovations, Adams saw a great resistance to technological development. The paradigm case was the steamboat. John Fitch invented an early version, but his company failed because the public simply had no interest. In the end, "Livingston and Fulton, by their greater resources and influence, forced the steamboat on a skeptical public."[16] Beyond this, there was a hostility to banks and finance typified by, but by no means limited to, Thomas Jefferson.[17] More generally, there was neither a scientific nor a wealthy class to lead the way. Such habits of mind had to be overcome if the United States was to become a "speculating and scientific nation."[18] Not surprisingly, under these conditions commerce was hindered. "In becoming politically independent of England, the old thirteen provinces developed little more commercial intercourse with each other in proportion to their wealth and population than they had maintained in colonial days. The material ties that united them grew in strength no more rapidly than the ties which bound them to Europe. Each group of States lived apart."[19]

The geographic barriers no doubt contributed to the social, economic, and political characteristics that divided the new nation and in later years were to divide it still more. This was not a condition conducive to truly *national* development. "Only with diffidence," Adams comments, "could the best informed Americans venture, in 1800, to generalize on the subject of their own national habits of life and thought."[20] One could just barely discern the outlines of a nation in the complex mix of interregional, not to mention intraregional, animosities and peculiarities. This becomes apparent in the three chapters Adams devotes to the New England, the Middle Atlantic, and the Southern states.

Given the idea that Adams embodied the New England conscience, one might expect a more favorable view of his native region than he presents. His focus is on the New England intellect and the upper classes, and it is not an attractive picture. Massachusetts was divided sharply into two political camps, one Republican and the other, slightly larger group representing elites. The latter encompassed nearly all members of the professional and mercantile classes, thus including the wealth, social position, and educational leadership of the state. But the real strength of this group lay in the Congregational churches and "in the cordial union between the clergy, the bench and bar, and respectable society throughout the State." This was thus an oligarchy with deep roots, its power not soley dependent on retaining public office.[21]

The clergy, though no longer wielding the equivalent of police authority, nonetheless had enormous power, and that power was turned against the Jeffersonian Republicans and especially against their leader. And in this, "The temporal arm vigorously supported the ecclesiastical will. Nothing tended so directly to make respectability conservative, and conservatism a fetish of respectability, as this union of bench and pulpit." Thus democrats were simply seen to be not respectable, just no-accounts who could not be allowed into a Federalist house. "Every dissolute intriguer, loose-liver, forger, false-coiner, and prison-bird; every hair-brained, loud-talking demagogue; every speculator and atheist, — was a follower of Jefferson; and Jefferson was himself the incarnation of their theories."[22] These were the doctrines preached in the churches and published in the press. But, Adams says, these ideas were too extreme to be successfully maintained for any long period of time, particularly when, in the hands of a Fisher Ames, "they degenerated into a morbid illusion."[23]

Jefferson's victory in 1800 intensified these feelings. Listen to the lament of Ames: "Our country is too big for union, too sordid for patriotism, too democratic for liberty. What is to become of it, he who made it best knows. Its vice will govern it, by practicing upon its folly. This is ordained for democracies." Further, "A democracy cannot last. Its nature ordains that its next change shall be into a military despotism. . . . The reason is that the tyranny of what is called the people, and that by the sword, both operate alike to debase and corrupt." The sentiments of George Cabot were similar: "I hold democracy in its natural operation to be the government of the worst."[24] Though he was not a New Englander, the views of these leaders were perhaps best represented by Alexander Hamilton in his notorious remark, "Your people, sir—your people is a great beast."[25] To be sure, Cabot claimed to support a "democratic mixture," but it was based on a property qualification so high as to render his support meaningless, a fact that Adams fully recognized.[26]

Thus, politically speaking, the New England intellect was at a dead end. As Adams comments, given their history and experience, "They [the New England conservatives] were right as far as human knowledge could make them so; but the old spirit of Puritan obstinacy was more evident than reason or experience in the simple-minded, overpowering conviction with which the clergy and serious citizens of Massachusetts and Connecticut . . . sat down to bide their time until the tempest of democracy should drive the frail government so near destruction that all men with one voice would call on God and the Federalist prophets for help."[27] But of course, the help that these Federalists, the leaders of the separatist Essex Junto and mortal political enemies of the Adams family, wished for was not to come. The rule of these antiquated conservatives was near the end.

Only in popular literature was there some sign of hope, though even Boston was weak in literature and even poorer in science. Connecticut produced Timothy Dwight, but alas, Dwight was "a man of extraordinary qualities, but one on whom almost every other mental gift had been conferred in fuller measure than poetical genius."[28] But the Jeffersonian Dwight was positively "Miltonic" compared with Joel Barlow. Nonetheless, Barlow must be given "respectful attention," and the reasons are interesting. He was a progressive with ambitions above even those of Jefferson, Dwight, Barlow, and others even less well known today. His ideas had one important quality: "the boundless ambition which marked the American character." Whatever Adams may have thought of the limitations of the Jeffersonians, one thing was clear to him: there could be no progress along the lines of Fisher Ames. At least the poets opened the possibility that something worthy of respect might emerge from New England.[29]

New York and Pennsylvania present a different picture. According to Adams, a gap separated them from New England as great as the divide between England and Scotland. And, though Adams does not say so, the differences between New York and Pennsylvania seem as great as those in the motherland. Even more than New England, New York was the home of potential leaders from upper-class backgrounds. Had they lived in the section to the north, they probably would have united in defense of their class or left the country, but, as Adams wryly notes, being New Yorkers, they quarreled instead. Men like Alexander Hamilton and John Jay were Federalists, but George Clinton was a leader of Northern Republicans well before Jefferson emerged as a rival, and Robert Livingston's faction, "after carefully weighing arguments and interests, with one accord joined the mob of free-thinking democrats, the 'great beast' of Alexander Hamilton." By 1800, New York was aligned with the Jeffersonian Republicans.[30]

Tradition was weak, there was no established church, and intellectual life was not in good condition. As Adams astringently puts it, "The intellectual and moral character of New York left much to be desired; but on the other hand, had society adhered stiffly to what New England thought strict morals, the difficulties in the path of national development would have been increased."[31] The new nation needed innovation, and *that* New York was prepared to provide; New Yorkers had no interest in wasting time on the metaphysical subtleties that divided New England and Virginia. Thus came about the strange alliance between the Jeffersonians and Clinton, Livingston, and Aaron Burr, "in the hope of fixing the United States in a career of simplicity and virtue." Clinton actually believed the Jeffersonian verities, but Adams saw that, for the rest, the new political partnership "was from the first that of a business firm; and no more curious speculation could have been suggested to the politicians of 1800 than the question whether New York would corrupt Virginia, or Virginia would check the prosperity of New York."[32]

While Adams's Puritan conscience is clearly uneasy with the New Yorkers, he is very warmly disposed to Pennsylvania. According to Adams, this was the state with the most potent voice in the nation on all issues. If New England,

New York, and Virginia had disappeared in 1800, democracy would still have survived as long as Pennsylvania lived on. It was "the only truly democratic community then existing in the eastern States." There was no New England hierarchy, no great New York families, and no plantation oligarchy. Adams's true hero, Albert Gallatin, summed up: "In Pennsylvania not only have we neither Livingstons nor Rensselaers, but from the suburbs of Philadelphia to the banks of the Ohio I do not know a single family that has extensive influence. An equal distribution of property has rendered every individual independent, and there is among us true and real equality." Thus Pennsylvania became the ideal American state, "easy, tolerant, and contented."[33] It was not a state where genius or even cleverness flourished, nor was there much interest in politics. Adams suggests that the democratic instinct was so deep that Pennsylvanians did not know what to do with political power when they had it. Politics, it seemed, was in the peculiar position of being the province of the aristocracy in a state without an aristocracy. Again Gallatin represents the position and the ideas that flowed from it. His "celebrated financial policy carried into practice the doctrine that the powers of government, being necessarily irresponsible, and therefore hostile to liberty, ought to be exercised within the narrowest bounds. . . . Unlike Jefferson and the Virginians, Gallatin never hesitated to claim for government all the powers necessary for whatever object was in hand; but he agreed with them in checking the practical use of power, and this he did with a degree of rigor which has often been imitated but never equaled."[34]

Still, in spite of being the intellectual center of the nation, even in that regard it was not impressive. Here, as elsewhere in the United States, "the labor of the land had precedence over that of the mind," but if this was true in Philadelphia, "the traveler who wandered further toward the south felt still more strongly the want of intellectual variety, and found more cause for complaint."[35]

The famous remark of English humorist Stephen Potter that in every country the south is different from everywhere else is amply borne out by Adams's treatment of Virginia and the other Southern states. Of course, their great curse was the institution of slavery. The young William Ellery Channing admired the fact that Southerners loved money less than New Englanders, so that "their patriotism is not tied to their purse-strings." But still, he goes on, "Could I only take from the Virginians their sensuality and their slaves, I should think them the greatest people in the world. As it is, with a few great virtues, they have innumerable vices."[36]

Among the vices was domination by a plantation aristocracy. There were some reforms; primogeniture was abolished, and Madison led the way to a separation of church and state. But the reforms stopped short of slavery, though there were abortive attempts following the Revolution. Astute observers like George Washington knew that the practice could not long continue and that it was a brake on progress, but the planters had not liked the earlier reforms, and abolition of the slave system was not politically possible. One would have thought that an aristocracy "so lacking in energy and self-confidence" would easily succumb to reformist pressures, but the best efforts of Jefferson and Madison were to no avail. The result was that "Jefferson's reforms crippled and impoverished the gentry, but did little for the people, and for the slaves nothing."[37] And in 1862 Adams's position was clear, if more sanguinary than usual. Writing to his brother, he said:

> But one thing is clear to my mind, which is that we must not let them as an independent state get the monopoly of cotton again, unless we want to find a powerful and bitterly hostile nation on our border, supported by all the moral and social influence of Great Britain in peace; certain in war to drag us into all the European complications; surely to be in perpetual anarchy within, but always ready to disturb anything and everything without; to compel us to support a standing army no less large than if we conquer them and hold them so, and with the infinite means of wounding and scattering dissension among us. We must ruin them before we let them go or it will have to be done over again. And we must exterminate them in the end, be it long or be it short, for it is a battle between us and slavery.[38]

The deep-seated bitterness over slavery, doubtless fueled by family tradition, is clear. But there were other difficulties as well. Middle- and lower-class Virginians had many admirable qualities, but, in Adams's view, they, like the upper class, lacked a sense of self-restraint. In spite of Jefferson, schools were poor, and of course, Jefferson discouraged both manufacturing and urbanization. Collectively, the Virginians hoped to perpetuate "simple and isolated lives" and pursue an "idyllic conservatism." With no manufacturing, shipping, or domestic markets, Virginians were limited to agricultural pursuits. Intellectually, the sole concern was politics, but this preoccupation at least led to a distinctive body of ideas of great importance.[39]

In this field, the undisputed intellectual leader was Thomas Jefferson. And, Adams is forced to remark, "According to the admitted standards of greatness, Jefferson was a great man." No matter what his detractors said, his character "could not be denied elevation, versatility, breadth, insight, and delicacy." And yet he seemed ill at ease as a democratic leader. He was deeply reserved, did not appear in crowds, and had the instincts of a "liberal European nobleman." And to underscore his sectionalism, for the last thirty years of his life, he did not visit a single Northern city. He did not enjoy politics, and for him, the pursuit of happiness led him to the life of the mind.[40] Happiness was to be found in Monticello with his books, his inventions, his violin, his correspondence, and the enormous range of his other activities.[41] Never a natural politician and ineffective in debate, his natural bent was theoretical; thus he was "prepared to risk the fate of mankind on the chance of reasoning far from certain in its details." Echoing the most extreme Federalists, Adams quite unkindly remarks that Jefferson breathed "with perfect satisfaction nowhere except in the liberal, literary, and scientific air of Paris in 1789."[42] And certainly it is true, as Henry Adams's great-grandfather John perceived, that Jefferson liked better "the dreams of the future, than the history of the past."[43]

As Adams read them, Jefferson's aspirations reached beyond mere nationality and embraced universalistic ideals according to which America would provide a model for the world and lead mankind to a new era. War as an instrument of policy in the European manner was out of the question. But these ideas, which seemed irrationally utopian to Adams, were complemented by other views that "seemed narrower than ordinary provincialism." Here Adams refers to the famous passages in *Notes on the State of Virginia* in which Jefferson celebrates the agrarian life so that farmers are the "chosen people of God." By implication, this looks ahead to Jefferson's hostility to cities. This theory was not new, of course, and Adams shrewdly points out that it clashed with Jefferson's "intellectual instincts of liberality and innovation." But fortunately or unfortunately, none of the Virginians, not even Madison, showed much interest in carrying out these ideas until John Taylor of Caroline, and by the time he developed his system such views had been overtaken by events and had been rendered beside the point.[44]

The other Southern states get short shrift from Adams. He sees North Carolina as peaceful and somewhat backward, but still the healthiest and most democratic part of the South. South Carolina is less attractive. Though it has the advantage of a decent, if rather puritanical, city in Charleston, it is perhaps the least democratic of all the states in the Union and hence least likely to ally itself with the Jeffersonian cause. And South Carolinians, whether in the backcountry or in the tidewater, share a common hostility to change.[45]

Adams closes his introduction with a brilliant portrait of the American national character as he sees it. He is, of course, sophisticated enough to realize that "Of all historical problems, the nature of a national character is the most difficult and the most important."[46] The portrait he paints is fascinating and subtle. The United States faced many burdens. Except in a few towns, commerce was underdeveloped, art and literature did not flourish, and geographical separation was reinforced by differences in the theory and practice of politics. Fragmentation and separation of the sort that had made a slaughter house of Europe were imminent dangers. Moreover, slavery ate at the nation like a cancer. And yet Americans were filled with self-confidence, partly because of temperament, but also out of ignorance of the dangers they faced. Their ignorance led them to fantasize about the decrepitude of Europe, yet Adams is forced to concede that possibly they were right on that score. In some critical factors, Europe was a hundred years behind the United States as long as certain assumptions held:

> *If* they were right in thinking that the next necessity of human progress was to lift the average man upon an intellectual and social level with the most favored, they stood at least three generations nearer than Europe to their common goal. [Americans were staked] on the soundness of this doubtful and even improbable principle, ignoring or even overthrowing the institutions of church, aristocracy, family, army, and political intervention, which long experience had shown to be needed for the safety of society.[47]

But having expressed these doubts, Adams proceeds to show how American he himself is by conceding that, in fact, the Americans might be right. After all, in spite of his many animadversions, and with the major exception of slavery, America was "sound and healthy in every part." He grows almost rhapsodic: "Stripped for the hardest work, every muscle firm and elastic, every ounce of brain ready for use, and not a trace of superfluous flesh on his nervous and supple body, the American stood in the world a new order of man." Opportunities to attain power were everywhere, and, in an important reversal of the social order of the Old World, "the American stimulant [to acquire power] increased in energy as it reached the lowest and most ignorant class, dragging and whirling them upward as in the blast of a furnace." Penniless and homeless immigrants became capitalists with every action of an ax or hoe, and their children became gentlemen. And, in spite of his skepticism only a page earlier, Adams remarks that beside this new man Europe really was decrepit.[48]

Thus Europe was still inert, its conservative habits supported by power. And it is clear that in the Adams lexicon, *conservative* came very close to being a synonym for *antidemocratic*. Europe was not really enlightened; Voltaire and Priestly had not succeeded there. America, in contrast, was emerging as the land of the small capitalist. Europeans thought Americans rapacious and avaricious, but if Europeans and Americans were compared, then the Europeans were surely no better. What Adams saw, though he did not have the term for it, was the rise of what Isaac Kramnick calls bourgeois radicalism.[49] And though he was later to disapprove heartily of large-scale industrial capitalism, this early form of economic organization was one in which Adams saw real merit.

All this did not come without a price, so that Federalists could see nothing but "greed for wealth, lust for power."[50] These conservatives could perceive only destruction of the institutions and values that held society together. Insofar as democrats had an answer, it came from Jefferson, though his writings did not reveal the whole man, let alone the movement he led. Adams understands fully that Jefferson, though a man of many ideas, had no system. But besides his Virginia prejudices, Jefferson held to the Enlightenment belief in science, which led further to a belief in progress, a progress that would eventually be moral as well as intellectual—all of this, of course, without "a priesthood, a state church, or revealed religion." Conservatives responded as they always had, by attaching themselves to their own moral standards. The two parties could see little common ground. But already the conservatives were losing out. According to Adams, "The average American was more intelligent than the average European, and was becoming every year still more active-minded as the new movement of society caught him up and swept him through a life of more varied experiences. On all sides the national mind responded to its stimulants."[51]

Thus, in spite of the manifest difficulties in 1800, there were grounds for hope. At the same time, the hopes could turn out to be illusions, and the historical result was still in doubt. The problems facing American society at the turn of the nineteenth century and the beginning of the Jefferson era were these:

> Could it transmit its social power into the higher forms of thought? Could it provide for the moral and intellectual needs of mankind? Could it take permanent political shape? Could it give new life to religion and art? Could it create and maintain in the mass of mankind those habits of mind which had hitherto belonged to men of science alone? Could it physically develop the convolutions of the human brain? Could it produce, or was it compatible with, the differentiation of a higher variety of the human race? Nothing less than this was necessary for its complete success.[52]

What do we make of this portrait of the United States in 1800, of the staggering agenda with which Adams concludes, and of the thought of Adams as revealed in this discussion? Of course, it would be surprising if a hundred years of research had not challenged some of Adams's findings here and in the remainder of his huge study. Thus, Richard Hofstadter, in *America at 1750*, stresses the great growth in the eighteenth century, while Adams points to economic weakness. However, given Adams's emphasis on the enormous *potential* for growth, this does less to undermine Adams than Noble Cunningham suggests.[53] Still, though life, particularly on the frontier, could be harsh, Adams's picture of American life as a form of medieval misery is no doubt exaggerated. And contemporary historians do not see the inertia and conservative hostility to innovation portrayed by Adams.[54] But here too, Adams's stress on the restlessness of the "new man" goes some distance toward undercutting this criticism. Cunningham also argues that it was the Federalists who feared change and who charged Jefferson with being a revolutionary. But Adams is fully aware of this and ridicules them for their hysteria.[55] Instead, his argument in the body of the study, whether right or wrong, is that Jefferson's principles were revolutionary, though clearly nonviolent, but that in office Jefferson betrayed those principles and adopted much of the Federalist program. Cunningham rightly points out that the *History*'s treatment of the sections is truncated; the West is ignored, and the discussion of the South is essentially limited to Virginia and South Carolina.[56] It is also true that Adams has a lack of interest in the West amounting almost to prejudice, as illustrated by his apparent inability, in other writings, to grasp the greatness of Abraham Lincoln. But surely his failure to discuss Georgia and his perfunctory paragraph on North Carolina are justified by the subsequent development of American history. Even more to the point is the stress placed on sectional division rooted, more than anything, in slavery—perhaps the single most important factor in American history, one destined, as we all know, to lead to a gruesome catastrophe.[57]

As for the economy, Cunningham is probably right that there was more economic growth in the 1790s than Adams allows, though there were certainly powerful forces at work that retarded Southern development. And Cunningham is probably also importantly right that Adams overemphasizes American backwardness in 1800 in order to make dramatic change from 1800 to 1816 a major theme in the body of the study.[58] From this point of view, the portrait—say rather the sketch—of the United States in 1800 should be seen more as a theoretical device than as an empirical analysis.[59]

Cunningham's discussion of politics and political culture in his short

book is the most important part of his analysis of Adams. He is right that
Adams leaves electoral politics largely out of the study and that he seems to
miss the importance of the election of 1800.[60] At least in part, this is probably due to Adams's wish to minimize the extent to which he would have to
write about his ancestors, which would have been necessary since Jefferson's
opponent in that election was Adams's great-grandfather. Thus, he leaves out
the campaign, though he does not slight the scurrilous anti-Jefferson pamphlet literature as much as Cunningham suggests. A more complicated point,
which is discussed later in this book, is his complaint about Adams's claim
that the Jeffersonians took power as republicans opposed to monarchists
rather than as democrats opposed to oligarchy.[61] Certainly Jefferson had a
real obsession about allegedly monarchical opponents that was possibly somewhat exaggerated. However, both democracy and republicanism are "con-
tested concepts" and, moreover, are terms that Adams did not use with
complete consistency.[62] The two tended to merge in his mind. After all,
Adams wrote before the current revival of the theory of civic republicanism.
To be sure, the Jeffersonians proclaimed their democratic credentials, and it
may be that they earned them, but this cannot be taken for granted any more
than Adams's alleged antidemocratic views. For instance, why was it wrong,
as Cunningham suggests, for Adams to emphasize Jefferson's states' rights
views at the expense of his democratic commitments?[63] There is a clear tension between the two, and it is not surprising that in the aftermath of the Civil
War, Adams chose to stress this aspect of the very complex Jeffersonian ideology; surely he was not wrong to do so. This underlines Jefferson's complexity. No other figure in American history is more ambiguous than
Jefferson, and it is one of Adams's great merits to point this out.[64]

    But in the end, it is necessary to come back to one of Cunningham's
complaints. By avoiding the election of 1800 and then by distorting Jefferson's claim that the election of 1800 was a true revolution, Adams misses a
great opportunity. In his famous letter to Spencer Roane, Jefferson not only
says that the election was "as real a revolution in the principles of our government as that of 1776 was in its form" but goes on to say that it was "not
effected indeed by the sword but by the rational and peaceful instrument of
reform, the suffrage of the people."[65] A great deal of sad history shows us that
such a peaceful transfer of power in a postrevolutionary period is rare and
difficult. That it did occur peacefully, in spite of the real differences between
the Federalists and the Jeffersonian Republicans, suggests that there was an
element of rhetorical overkill in Jefferson's claim to have led a second revo-

lution, though the evidence on this point is complex. In any case, the emergence of a competitive party system, though for a time it would fall into desuetude, was a major event in the development of modern democracy. Adams's avoidance of electoral politics thus constitutes a real weakness.

But the power of Adams's analysis of the American scene in 1800 is such that it would be unfair to end on a negative note. First, if we look at *The Life of Albert Gallatin,* it is clear that Adams did in fact see the Federalist right as a genuine threat to democracy, which in turn justifies the idea of the election of 1800 as a revolution. Summarizing the Federalist position on creating an army and navy, which *both* sides saw as of possible use in domestic situations, Adams concludes, "To crush democracy by force was the ultimate resource of Hamilton. To crush that force was the determined intention of Jefferson."[66] In fact, the extreme Federalists hoped for an opportunity to use force to further their dreams of a more powerful executive.[67] For their part, the Republicans "believed, not without ground, that the federalists aimed at a war with France and an alliance with England for the purpose of creating an army and navy to be used to check the spread of democracy in America. . . . A collision between the two parties was imminent, and Virginia prepared for it on her side as the Federalists were doing on theirs."[68] The situation was explosive, and it is not hard to see that the Jeffersonians could plausibly look at the election of 1800 as an antiauthoritarian revolution, or that Adams was in substantial sympathy with their antagonism to the High Federalists. Obviously, these are important issues, and Adams's position on them is clear.

Second, to do justice to Adams, we must return to the questions raised in his discussion of American character, to his understanding of the American people, and to the enormous aspirations that lay behind his questions and his analysis. The national character he describes is deeply, essentially middle class and it also displays marked egalitarian leanings.[69] Of course, Adams is no fool, and he does not see total egalitarianism or a classless society. It is in comparison with England and western Europe that American bourgeois egalitarianism becomes apparent.[70] As Richard Hofstadter notes of the colonies in 1750, even then they were a middle-class world. Hofstadter and Adams are joined in their analysis by Adams's friend and contemporary, the novelist Henry James. In a much noted passage in his book on Nathaniel Hawthorne, James writes:

One might enumerate the items of high civilization, as it exists in other countries, which are absent from the texture of American life,

until it should become a wonder to know what was left. No State, in
the European sense of the word, and indeed barely a specific national
name. No sovereign, no court, no personal loyalty, no aristocracy, no
church, no clergy, no army, no diplomatic service, no country gentlemen, no palaces, no castles, nor manors, nor old country-houses,
nor parsonages, nor thatched cottages nor ivied ruins; no cathedrals,
nor abbeys, nor little Norman churches; no great Universities nor
public schools—no Oxford, nor Eton, nor Harrow; no literature, no
novels, no museums, no pictures, no political society, no sporting
class—no Epsom nor Ascot![71]

Though Adams gives every sign of welcoming what James describes with
evident sneering distaste—imagine life without Ascot—this provides a brief
summary of much of what Adams found in his examination of early America, minus, of course, any of the respect for the energy and willingness to
work that Adams so clearly admired. Here is Adams's own summary, terse
and perhaps less eloquent, but to the point: "War counted for little, the hero
for less; on the people alone the eye could permanently rest. The steady
growth of a vast population without the social distinctions that confused other
histories—without kings, nobles, or armies; without church, traditions, and
prejudices,—seemed a subject for a man of science rather than for drama-
tists and poets."[72] This is a picture of a society in which the traces of aristocracy are rapidly disappearing. It is, as Hofstadter said of the time fifty years
before, a middle-class society; indeed, Hofstadter's description is very similar
to James's, though entirely without the condescending tone.[73] And more
recent historical studies, such as Gordon Wood's study of the radical consequences of the American Revolution and Joyce Appleby's book on the generation of Americans born after the Revolution, though not so sharply focused
on 1800, point in the same general direction, emphasizing the rapid development of a commercial, capitalist, egalitarian democracy and a citizenry
made up of hard-driving, competitive individuals.[74] As Wood has said, "Not
only did they [the postrevolutionary generation], or at least the Northerners
among them, radically democratize politics and create a liberal, commercial
or capitalist market society of unparalleled scope and social influence, but
they also constructed the peculiar national identity of autonomous and enter-
prising individuals that came to characterize Americans throughout much
of their history." It was this generation that was the first to advance "an interpretation of the collective meaning of American democracy that made it difficult for the people of subsequent generations to set forth other identities
and other meanings of America."[75]

What emerged in this period is what one might call an "official ideology," in the sense the term is used by the legal theorist William Miller.

By "official" I mean to indicate a position that claims a certain privilege for itself independent of whether in fact that position represents an accurate description of motive or behavior. The official claims the ground of legitimacy often backed by public institutions. Its style is often aspirational, sometimes hortatory; it also claims for itself the realm of the moral as that is defined in the society's dominant institutions. Official discourse can be complacent in tone, the kind of thing we understand as represented by the paying of lip service. Yet it would be wrong to think of official as a kind of sham. The official represents those kinds of public statements in which a culture images itself, and as such it bears no small role in reproducing the culture that produces such official discourses.[76]

Adams's theory is a major contribution to this literature, a contribution rooted in his Northern perceptions. He clearly anticipates the consensus theory associated with Hofstadter and the political theorist Louis Hartz, which came to dominate the interpretation of American politics in the middle of the twentieth century. And behind Hartz, in particular, there is the looming presence of Alexis de Tocqueville's *Democracy in America*. It was Tocqueville, along with John Stuart Mill, who was hailed by Adams, writing to his brother, as the "patron saint of our movement."[77] And it was Tocqueville who insisted on the essential egalitarianism of this new and very strange nation. Not that Tocqueville thought that Americans were in fact perfectly equal, but that equality in America was a state of mind, and beyond that, Americans had been "born equal," rather than having to become so.[78] To this Hartz added a bit of Marx and pointed out that, in a new version of Trotsky's Law of Combined Development, the United States had skipped the feudal stage of history, just as Russia had supposedly skipped over capitalism.[79] The result, to both Hartz and Tocqueville, was a bourgeois, liberal, middle-class society. This consensus does not preclude conflict, nor does it imply a complete endorsement of American society. It is also important to remember, with Miller and Wood, that such a consensus is not just a sham and that it can capture a significant part of reality. Nor does the official preclude conflict. In spite of the consensual rhetoric of Jefferson's First Inaugural Address in 1801, Adams saw plenty of potential for sharp dispute, particularly had Jefferson fully pursued his principles. Moreover, no one can fail to see the critical edge in Adams's interpretation of American history. However, the conflict takes place within a powerfully middle-class consensus that Adams begins to outline in the early chapters of the *History*. These chapters provide a standard against which to measure the successes, and the failures, of American democracy. But more than that, Adams offers us a kind of democratic idealism that is too often overlooked in the stereotypical sketches of his work. In what follows, I try to outline Adams's theory more fully and to suggest the extent to which his standard was being met, and, where it was not, why not. Adams's career spanned a tumultuous time in American history, and he is one of the more powerful guides to explaining the wrenching transitions through which the United States passed during his lifetime. Moreover, it is clear that much of what he has to say is of continued value today. Many of his problems are still ours.

Chapter 2

The Jeffersonian Foundation

Thomas Jefferson, with all his contradictions, or arguably precisely because of them, is at the heart of the American experience. That experience is full of complexity and ambiguity, but so was Jefferson. A recent summation suggests that his was a "life of paradox. . . . A Virginia nationalist, a slaveholding *philosophe*, an aristocratic democrat, a provincial cosmopolitan, a pacific imperialist—the paradoxes, it seems clear, are of no ordinary variety, reaching far beyond the life of one man. They are as large in meaning and as portentous in significance as America itself."[1] And Henry Adams, though referring in this instance to Jefferson's visionary tendencies, had this same understanding of Jefferson as typifying American character. These qualities "seemed to be a national trait, for every one admitted that Jefferson's opinions, in one form or another, were shared by a majority of the American people."[2]

This, of course, is enough to make Jefferson, with all his contradictions, one of the central figures in American history. Jefferson is surely one of those to whom Martin Diamond referred when he wrote that the history of American politics is "the story of the American heritage and the fight among the heirs."[3] And Henry Adams in his monumental *History* is surely one of the heirs who has contributed most to the debate on the meaning of Jefferson and Jeffersonianism.[4]

Adams on Jefferson's Character

Adams's views are characteristically complex, highly nuanced, and the cause of nearly as much debate as is his subject. His attitude toward Jefferson was less than transparent, but an explanation of its complexities reveals a great deal about the intricacies of his own thought.[5] Sometimes the *History* has been called a pro-Federalist work, though Merrill Peterson, discussing this assessment, considers it unjust to Adams.[6] Just as commonly it has been classified as anti-Federalist, though having made this point, Ernest Samuels quickly points out that Adams was unmerciful in his exposure of the failings of the Jeffersonians.[7] William Jordy is unequivocal: "The *History* was virulently anti-Federalist."[8] If we consider the great contest between Jefferson and Alexander Hamilton, it is clear that Adams, for all his criticisms of Jefferson, in no way sided with Hamilton. Indeed, it is obvious that Adams intensely disliked Hamilton, pursuing a feud that went back to great-grandfather John Adams, who was a political enemy of Hamilton's and deplored his sexual morals as well. Adams comments on Hamilton's Napoleonic tendencies— far from a compliment, in his view—and notes that he was "equally ready to support a system he utterly disbelieved in as one that he liked."[9] Such interpretive tension seems to support the conclusion of Peterson: "The admirers of the *History* from the day of its appearance to the present have been unable to agree whether it is Jeffersonian or anti-Jeffersonian. In truth, it is neither, and both at once, which is the secret of its endless fascination and the mark of its distinction in American historiography."[10]

First it is important to consider the possible extent of Adams's psychological identification with Jefferson. Adams's Jefferson was an enormously subtle, complex creature, surely qualities Adams would have wished attributed to himself. Here it is only necessary to recall his famous account of the difficulty of characterizing the Virginian (quoted in the introduction), where he stresses the extreme delicacy of touch required to capture Jefferson, qualities also necessary to capture Adams.[11] And Jefferson the inveterate theorist might also have had an appeal, though one that had to be qualified. "His mind shared little in common with the provincialism on which the Virginia and Kentucky Resolutions were founded. His instincts led him to widen rather than narrow the bounds of every intellectual exercise." Again, these are qualities not unlike Adams's, though there were problems associated with this disposition, including a tendency to overgeneralize on the basis of superficial knowledge and his sense of omniscience, combined with a taste for radicalism, which, as we have seen, Adams sees as having Parisian roots.[12] The last point seems to echo the common Federalist charge that Jefferson was dedicated to the revolutionary principles that led to the Terror, but in general, Adams's analysis does not support this view, and he must surely have been charmed by the intellectualism that expanded the boundaries of any problem, a characteristic not far removed from his own style of thought. And one should recall Adams's skepticism about the near-hysterical denunciations of all things French that were at the heart of Federalist attacks on Jefferson.[13] Adams could be very hard on Jefferson, but not in the style of the High Federalists, whom he despised just as much as he did the most passionate Southern secessionists.

Finally there is this assessment of Jefferson's personality:

His tastes were for that day excessively refined. His instincts were those of a liberal European nobleman. . . . The rawness of political life was an incessant torture to him, and personal attacks made him keenly unhappy. His true delight was in an intellectual life of science and art. . . . [He] fairly reveled in what he believed to be beautiful, and his writings often betrayed subtle feeling for artistic form—a sure sign of intellectual sensuousness. He shrank from whatever was rough or coarse, and his yearning for sympathy was almost feminine. That such a man should have ventured into the stormy ocean of politics was surprising, the more so because he was no orator.[14]

Surely Adams saw in all this a spirit similar to his own, though he himself was never able to down his distaste for the political life to the extent of his great subject. Though he made a few forays into independent politics following the Civil War, for Adams, the chosen path of influence was through the pen. And perhaps he thought that one way to exert that influence was through an analysis of the foundations of American society and politics, which is the subject of his account of the Jefferson and Madison administrations.

However, whatever affinity Adams may have had with Jefferson's persona, his views of his thought and politics are complex and even convoluted. Some of Jefferson's ideas clearly seemed to him to lead to disunion, or at least a weak state, conclusions that Adams could not endorse. At the same time, he clearly thought that Jefferson was altogether too ready to abandon the principles he professed to hold. The great paradox of Adams's thought is that he disapproved of Jefferson's principles and then chastised him for setting them aside in favor of policies that moved in the nationalist direction supported by Adams and his entire clan. There is a major tension at work here that may be a key to the complexity of vision described by Merrill Peterson.[15] And yet, for all his animadversions against Jefferson and his colleagues, it is hard to escape the conclusion that Adams's final estimate is positive:

As their scheme existed in the minds of Mr. Jefferson, Mr. Gallatin, and Mr. Madison, it was as broad as society itself, and aimed at providing for and guiding the moral and material development of a new era,—a new race of men. . . . They failed, and although their failure was due partly to accident, it was due chiefly to the fact that they put too high an estimate upon human nature. . . . Yet, whatever may have been the extent of their defeat or of their successes, one fact stands out in strong relief on the pages of American history. Except those theories of government which are popularly represented by the names of Hamilton and Jefferson, no solution of the great problems of American politics has ever been offered to the American people. Since the day when foreign violence and domestic faction prostrated Mr. Gallatin and his two friends, no statesman has ever appeared with the strength to bend their bow, —to finish their uncompleted task.[16]

The First Inaugural Address

For Adams, the place to begin an analysis of Jefferson's thought was the First Inaugural Address of 1801.[17] This once popular document was now, he felt, unduly neglected, though it needed to be supplemented by other documents in order to have a full grasp of Jefferson's program. But time had not diminished the importance of the address, though Adams hints that the years may have imparted to it meanings not intended by the author.[18] Jefferson's first goal was political; that is, he wanted to calm the anxieties of his opponents, particularly the more extreme Federalists. It was to them that Jefferson spoke when he proclaimed that "every difference of opinion is not a difference of principle. We are all Republicans, we are all Federalists."[19] But, Adams comments, Jefferson did not—indeed, could not—really mean this, and in suggesting that he was in any way a Federalist, Jefferson did himself an "injustice." Any real harmony, Jefferson felt, would result from his own further triumph.[20] Thus Adams initially appears to take seriously Jefferson's private claim that the election of 1800 was a true peaceful revolution.

Whatever Federalists might fear, there was no doubt that republican government could be as strong as any on earth. And the implication that heretofore the Federalist administration had kept the new nation strong and free was a true compliment coming from one not accustomed to praising his opponents.[21] But fortunately, Americans had advantages in the effort to meet their challenges. A "wise and frugal government" restricted to keeping the peace would be up to the task. At this point, Adams observes, Jefferson launched into his only public gloss on the principles of republicanism beyond those suggested in the Virginia and Kentucky Resolutions. The text is sometimes problematic and even somewhat startling. Equal justice for all; peace, friendship, and commerce with all nations but no "entangling alliances"; states' rights, but with the preservation of the general government; the preservation of the right of election; "absolute acquiescence in the decisions of the majority"; a well-regulated militia; civil supremacy over the military; a frugal government, as already noted; the encouragement of agriculture; and the preservation of what are commonly called the First Amendment freedoms are the basic principles of republicanism.[22]

For the most part, none of this is strikingly original; indeed, they were the principles of President Washington and would have occasioned little notice had they been uttered by a Federalist. Coming from Jefferson, the words sounded a little unfamiliar, and "certain phrases seemed even out of place."[23] The most notable statement is the flat enunciation of the doctrine of absolute majoritarianism. Coming from one whose bedrock principles were stated in the Virginia and Kentucky Resolutions, this was indeed startling. As Adams says, "No principle was so strongly entwined in the roots of Virginia republicanism as that which affirmed the worthlessness of decisions made by a majority of the United States, either as a nation or a confederacy, in matters which concerned the exercise of doubtful power."[24] The central point of the resolutions was the first statement of the doctrine of nullification. The Jeffersonians were emphatically not majoritarians where the national government was concerned. They held "that freedom could be maintained only by preserving inviolate the right of every State to judge for itself what was, and what was not, lawful for a majority to decide."[25] And Adams might have observed, though he did not, that the First Amendment guarantees listed by Jefferson are opposed to majoritarian domination. Nor, of course, was Jefferson a simple majoritarian even at the level of the state legislature. Power must be divided to prevent majority abuses. As he put it in the *Notes on Virginia*, "It will be no alleviation that these powers will be exercised by a plurality of hands, and not by a single one. 173 despots would surely be as oppressive as one. . . . An elective despotism was not the government we fought for."[26]

And, Adams asks, in light of these ideas, what could it mean to pledge the preservation of the full vigor of the general government? A "bottomless gulf" divided the two parties in their constitutional theories. Still, until Federalist precedents had been explicitly repealed, they had to be treated as acts of the majority, even when in serious violation of Jeffersonian doctrine. How, for example, could Jefferson promise to preserve the powers assumed in the Alien and Sedition Acts, and how, given his deep distrust of the judiciary, could the Judiciary Act of 1789 go unchallenged? Surely, Adams contends, Jefferson did not literally mean what he said. Rather, "he meant no more than to preserve the general government in such vigor as in his opinion was Constitutional, without regard to Federalist precedents; but his words were equivocal, and unless they were to be defined by legislation, they identified him with the contrary legislation of his predecessors." But such legislation never appeared.[27] The Alien and Sedition Acts were simply allowed to expire rather than being challenged on principle, and the Judiciary Act was untouched even when the Republicans clearly had the power to repeal it. Thus Jefferson almost seemed anxious to prove that the revolution he proclaimed in private had not in fact occurred. In public, he preached a theory of consensus in which Federalists and Republicans became virtually one. In private, he harped on the theme that the Federalists were monarchists at heart.[28] Indeed, fear of monarchy was a lifelong obsession on his part.

The issue of monarchy raises another question. How do we classify Jefferson's own views on the forms of government, and, indeed, how do we classify those of Henry Adams? As we have seen, in Adams's view, "Jefferson and his Southern friends took power as republicans opposed to monarchists, *not* as democrats opposed to oligarchy. Jefferson was not in a social sense a democrat, and was called so only as a term of opprobrium. His Northern followers were in the main democrats, but he and most of his Southern partisans claimed to be republicans, opposed by secret monarchists."[29] Thus Jefferson saw a three-way conflict among Southern republicans, Northern democrats, and Federalist monarchists. Like the Puritans before him, whom he despised and doubtless misunderstood, he hoped to offer to the world an example, in his case, one of a decentralized, nonmonarchical republic. Centralization was the enemy, and in it he saw nothing democratic. The model he wished to establish was an enlarged Virginia dedicated to agriculture, with commerce as a handmaid and with manufactures and large cities discouraged.[30] Finally, banking must be recognized as a great villain; indeed, banks were "more dangerous than standing armies," involving a swindle of the future.[31] These ideas, Adams comments, were "republican in the Virginia sense, but not democratic; they had nothing in common with the democracy of Pennsylvania and New England, except their love of freedom; and Virginia freedom was not the same conception as the democratic freedom of the North."[32] Adams does not elaborate on this point, but there can be no doubt that this is a none-too-veiled reference to Southern slavery, a major preoccupation for generations in the Adams family. Nor can there be any doubt that Adams sided with the New England democrats.

However, Adams does not take an overt position on these forms of government at this stage in his argument. Bear in mind that for all his judgmental qualities, he was still presenting his work as scientific history. Still, his position is not hard to discern. He clearly despised the High Federalists, who were old family enemies, for being as willing to destroy the Union as were the most passionate states' rights Southerners. The Jeffersonian principles were also seriously flawed, and we are left to recall his warm feelings for the Northern democrats, particularly the Pennsylvanians, which he expressed in his brilliant analysis of the United States at the start of the nineteenth century. And we will see at the conclusion of the great *History* the extent to which the people as a whole emerge as the collective hero of his epic, often in spite of the ineptitude of their leaders. These are the marks of a writer whose sympathy for the ordinary citizens of American democracy is often underrated, while his distrust of all the organized political positions is deep.

A few more features of Adams's perception of the essentials of Jeffersonianism are important. The great danger to Jefferson's minimalist utopia was foreign war. His foreign policy was intimately connected to commerce. One of his deep beliefs was that Europe required peace and free trade with America. A properly regulated international trade provided "the machinery for doing away with navies, armies, and war."[33] Except for commerce, Americans should distance themselves from other nations. In Jefferson's theory of the Constitution, the states were to be independent in all things within themselves, but united in facing foreign nations. Thus, he wrote, "The federal is in truth our foreign government, which department alone is taken from the sovereignty of the separate states."[34] To Adams, these views show why Jefferson saw his rise to power as a true revolution. "His view of governmental functions was simple and clearly expressed. The national government, as he conceived it, was a foreign department as independent from the domestic, which belonged to the States, as though they were governments of different nations." Foreign policy was to be conducted by commercial restrictions, which he saw as a form of "peaceable coercion." And he added, "Our commerce is so valuable to them that they will be glad to purchase it, when the only price we ask is to do us justice."[35]

These, then, are Jefferson's principles, as Adams saw them. The *History* was explicitly designed to show how and with what success they were applied.

Jefferson, the Louisiana Purchase, and the Executive Power

We can examine only a small part of Adams's massive study.[36] I focus primarily, though not exclusively, on one great event from each term; the Louisiana Purchase from the first term, and the embargo from the second. Here we can see great success and enormous failure, combined sometimes with startling flexibility and sometimes with equally amazing inflexibility of principle.

First the flexibility. Republican ideology called for Jefferson to mount a frontal challenge to the Federalist-dominated judiciary. The Judiciary Act of 1789, a triumph of Federalist centralization, as Adams called it, had effectively made the state courts subordinate to the Supreme Court in cases in which the powers of the general government were at stake. The Judiciary Act of 1801, the last gasp of the Federalist administration, had increased the size of the judiciary and had created the circuit courts as a new level of the judicial system. Clearly the former was more threatening to the states, but it was the latter that Jefferson chose to attack.[37] It was not that Jefferson was unaware of the heart of the problem. He knew that the Federalists "have retired into the judiciary as a stronghold," an allusion to the famous midnight judicial appointments of John Adams as he was leaving office.[38] In his annual message of 1801, Jefferson proposed that the new courts did not have enough business and were hence unnecessary and therefore improper in constitutional terms. Moreover, they were uneconomical, and the act of 1801 should be repealed. The Federalists argued on the slightly higher ground that since judges were to hold their offices during good behavior, to abolish the courts was a violation of that principle. In any case, the debate, though often bitter, was conducted on what Adams pointed out was substantially a technical issue. The opportunity for a principled debate was lost. Though some came close to the edge, no true democrat argued for an elected judiciary or one that could be removed by the legislative branch. This would have been in no way improper, Adams comments somewhat surprisingly, and the Federalists greatly feared such a system, but in the end, the Virginians were timid, to their great cost in the long run.[39]

Jefferson's timidity was in some ways characteristic, although, given his forceful action in the acquisition of Louisiana and the imposition of the embargo, Adams may have exaggerated this point to a significant degree. Interestingly, it is during the discussion of the judiciary debate that Adams makes his famous remark about the need to portray Jefferson ever so subtly, touch by touch. Above all, he makes clear, Jefferson was not *simply* a dogmatic ideologue; there was never anything simple about Thomas Jefferson. Thus, Adams agrees with Alexander Hamilton when he said, "Nor is it true that Jefferson is zealot enough to do anything in pursuance of his principles which will contravene his popularity or his interest. He is as likely as any man I know to temporize, to calculate what will be likely to promote his own reputation and advantage; and the probable result of such a temper is the preservation of systems, though originally opposed, which, being once established, could not be overturned without danger to the person who did it. To my mind, a true estimate of Mr. Jefferson's character warrants the expectation of a temporizing rather than a violent system."[40]

But Jefferson left Republican principles behind in pursuit of policies in which his actions, while perhaps conscience stricken, were extremely bold.

When he felt the need to act, he did not temporize. And sometimes, Adams believed, principles were abandoned because Jefferson was moved by forces beyond his control. "Honest as Jefferson undoubtedly was in his wish to diminish executive influence," Adams writes, "the task was beyond his powers."[41] Paradoxically, this was in part a result of the weakness of the congressional Republicans. The Northern Jeffersonians could provide votes but no leadership. They lacked the habit of command and tended to fall back on the wishes of upper-class Virginians and New Yorkers. "[Congressmen] were thrust aside with more or less civility by their leaders, partly because they were timid, but chiefly because they were unable to combine under the lead of one among themselves."[42] John Marshall sensed what proved to be the dynamic of executive-legislative relations. He predicted that Jefferson would "embody himself in the House of Representatives, and by weakening the office of President" would "increase his personal power. He will . . . become the leader of that party which is about to constitute the majority of the legislature." Thus, according to Edward Corwin, Jefferson was the first example of a president who is primarily a party leader and only secondarily an executive.[43]

Jefferson's control over his party no doubt stood him in good stead in the drama of the Louisiana Purchase. The purchase itself was of dubious constitutionality, a fact that Jefferson fully realized. To deviate from the Constitution on such a matter was to place Jefferson's deepest principles at risk. As Adams tells us, "The principle of strict construction was the breath of [Jefferson's] political life. The Pope could as safely trifle with the doctrine of apostolic succession as Jefferson with the limits of executive power."[44] As Jefferson dramatically put it, "I had rather ask an enlargement of power from the nation, where it is found necessary, than to assume it by a construction which would make our powers boundless. Our peculiar security is in the possession of a written Constitution. Let us not make it a blank paper by construction."[45] Thus Jefferson's first thought was to amend the Constitution to legitimate the Louisiana Purchase when the great opportunity presented by the French arose.

But Jefferson was fully prepared to run these constitutional risks if necessary. The dangers he saw were remote and, as Adams remarked, he believed that the leadership he exerted was based on sympathy and love rather than command. Moreover, as Adams wryly comments, "there was never a time when he thought that resistance to the will of his party would serve the great ends he had in view." Perhaps it is not surprising that immediately after expressing his fear of the destruction of the Constitution, Jefferson went on to add, "If, however, our friends shall think differently, certainly I shall acquiesce with satisfaction, confiding that the good sense of our country will correct the evil of construction when it shall produce ill effects."[46]

Thus Jefferson and Madison embarked on a course that Jefferson himself believed would make blank paper of the Constitution and, at the same time, effectively tore up the Virginia and Kentucky Resolutions; unsurprisingly, their followers were no more principled than their leaders.[47] The result of the congressional debates was a foregone conclusion. Federalists and Republicans alike agreed that the United States had the right to acquire new territory by either conquest or treaty. The parties differed only on whether Louisiana belonged to the central government or to the states. The Federalists held that the territory could be governed as a colony but could not be admitted into the Union without the consent of the states. The Republicans thought that the new territory could be so admitted or otherwise disposed of, but that neither the people nor the states had anything to say about the matter. "At bottom," Adams continues,

> both doctrines were equally fatal to the old status of the Union. . . . The Federalist theory was one of Empire, the Republican was one of assimilation; but both agreed that the moment had come when the old Union must change its character. Whether the government at Washington could possess Louisiana as a colony or admit it as a State, was a difference of no great matter if the cession were to hold good; *the essential point was that for the first time in the national history all parties agreed in admitting that the government could govern.*[48]

This last point is in some ways an astonishing comment and requires further analysis.

However, before turning to this, there is another dimension of Louisiana politics that requires consideration. What powers did Congress hold over the newly acquired territory? The first possibility was to adopt a constitutional amendment admitting Louisiana to the Union—in effect, to follow Jefferson's first instinct. However, the Republicans feared casting doubt on the legality of the purchase, and the Northern Democrats cared little for Southern theoretical dogmas. Moreover, the Southern Republicans were jealous of central authority but were also, in general, "impatient of control and unused to self-restraint." In addition, counting as they did on their own goodwill, they saw no need for a curb on their power. Only Senator John Quincy Adams suggested such an amendment. James Madison demurred, and though Adams persisted, he was denied even the courtesy of a referral to committee for his proposal. This was the end of any talk about incorporating Louisiana by constitutional amendment.[49]

What followed was an act described by Adams as "an act of sovereignty so despotic as the corresponding acts of France and Spain. Jefferson and his party had annexed to the Union a foreign people and a vast territory, which profoundly altered the relations of the States and the character of their nationality." Federalists complained that the bill introduced pursuant to these positions gave unconstitutional powers to the president, while John Randolph, the great apostle of states' rights, defended it on grounds of necessity and argued that with respect to the new territory, the United States "possessed the powers of European sovereignty."[50] A territorial government was then created "in which the people of Louisiana were to have no say," pursuant to a bill introduced by Senator John Breckinridge, but probably drafted by Madison in consultation with the president.[51] Senator Adams, continuing in his role as gadfly, introduced three resolutions to the effect that no constitutional authority existed, in a familiar phrase, to tax Louisianans without their consent, but he was able to win only three supporters for his position.[52] Through these acts, his grandson acerbically observed, "Louisianans received a government in which its people, who had been solemnly promised all the rights of American citizens, were set apart, not as citizens, but as subjects, lower in the political scale than the meanest tribes of Indians, whose right to self-government was never questioned."[53]

For Adams, the effects of these actions on American constitutionalism were enormous. And on this subject, his air of historical detachment largely vanishes. There is still historical analysis, but perhaps because John Quincy Adams appears as an actor who can help speak for the family, Henry allows himself the luxury of direct criticism, partly stripped of irony. This reveals some of his deepest political impulses, though on close examination, those impulses are more complex than they appear at first and are perhaps tinged with some ambivalence. "A government competent to interpret its own powers so liberally in one instance," he writes, "could hardly resist any strong temptation to do so in others. The doctrines of 'strict construction' could not be considered as the doctrines of the government after they had been abandoned in this leading case by a government controlled by strict constructionists."[54]

This is arguably true enough, but then the argument takes a rather odd turn. Adams points out that in the *Dred Scott* case, whose basic holding Adams could not have endorsed, Justice Taney and his colleagues reviewed the acts surrounding the Louisiana Purchase and found them constitutionally wanting.

Territory might be acquired, argued Taney, but it could not be governed as a colony by a Congress possessing absolute authority. The central government cannot assume "despotic" powers that have been denied it by the Constitution. The clear implication is that in Taney's view, "all the Louisiana legislation was unconstitutional."[55]

In any event, the government, Adams contends, was changing profoundly, and he suggests an interpretation of American history claiming that "the government had at some time been converted from a government of delegated powers into a sovereignty."[56] In defending the Louisiana Treaty, Jefferson, writing to Breckinridge, who had introduced the Kentucky Resolution on his behalf, proposed an "appeal to *the nation*" and went on to add, "We shall not be disavowed by the nation, and their act of indemnity will confirm and not weaken the Constitution by more strongly marking out its lines."[57] Adams notices that Jefferson underscored the word *nation*, that ominous phrase, as he calls it. But this requires notice, because the word *nation* was unknown to the Constitution. Invariably the term used was *Union*, and of course, in the Virginian theory, Congress could not appeal to the nation at all, except in the sense of a nation of states.[58] What was occurring seemed to confirm what the anti-Federalists had feared—that the Constitution contained a centralizing dynamic.[59] The strange thing was that this dynamic was being furthered by Thomas Jefferson, in theory an avowed opponent of this tendency.

Justice Taney seems an odd ally for Adams in his critique of Jefferson's constitutional practices. Adams cannot have been comfortable in league with the author of *Dred Scott*, the most reviled decision in the history of the Supreme Court. But Taney is not alone in the ranks of strange bedfellows. In pursuing the idea that "the government had at some time been converted from a government of delegated powers into a sovereignty," Adams turns to John C. Calhoun in his "Address to the People of the Slave-holding States." There Calhoun declared, "The one great evil, from which all other evils have flowed, is the overthrow of the Constitution of the United States. The government of the United States is no longer the government of confederated republics, but of a consolidated democracy. It is no longer a free government, but a despotism."[60]

Adams is quick to point out the irony inherent in this strange statement. If even the strict constructionists believed that such an important change in the structure of American constitutionalism had occurred, then the only event in American history of sufficient magnitude to have brought it about was the Louisiana Purchase, of which the strict constructionists were the authors. Adams's critical summary is devastating and provocative:

> Even in 1804 the political consequences of the act were already too striking to be overlooked. Within three years of his inauguration Jefferson bought a foreign colony without its consent and against its will, annexed it to the United States by an act which he said made blank paper of the Constitution; and then he who had found his predecessors too monarchical and the Constitution too liberal in powers, . . . made himself monarch of the new territory and wielded over it, against its protests, the powers of its old kings. Such an experience was final; no century of slow and half-understood experience could be needed to prove that the hopes of humanity lay thenceforward, not in attempting to restrain the government from doing whatever the majority should think necessary, but in raising the people themselves till they should think nothing necessary but what was good.[61]

The rhetoric here is strong, and no one can doubt that Adams sees the Louisiana Purchase and the methods by which it was accomplished as a profound turning point in American history. He is revolted by the thought of absolute sovereign power unchecked by constitutional limitations, and his concern for the democratic rights of the people of the Louisiana Territory helps make the point that Adams was not the sour critic of democracy he is often portrayed as being. However, when his love of irony leads him to adopt the interpretation of American constitutionalism of Taney and Calhoun, he is aligning himself, however temporarily, with exponents of positions he detested. Surely he might better have paused to note the absurdity of Calhoun's claim that the United States had become not free but a "consolidated democracy." But of course, Adams knew that as long as slavery endured, a claim that the nation was any sort of democracy was untenable.[62] And he also cannot have endorsed the conclusions of the *Dred Scott* decision. He is using Taney and Calhoun to show that it was the defenders of states' rights that undermined their own position. This is, as I say, a temporary if perhaps slightly dangerous liaison.

But of course, this was a position he rejected as subversive of the Union, just as he rejected the secessionist leanings of Federalist extremists, the ancient political enemies of the Adams family. And certainly, nationalist that he was, he approved of the acquisition of the vast Louisiana Territory, though he would have preferred that it be ratified by a constitutional amendment.

Thus he agreed with the most basic result of Jefferson's policy, while, at the same time, in an access of residual Puritanism, he rejected what he took to be the completely unprincipled methods by which the policy was achieved.[63] But it should be said that the whole episode suggests the fragility of law when it conflicts with the perceived necessities of politics. This is an analysis that points to Adams's later emphasis on the dynamics of power and his sense of the declining force of principled action.

It is important to remember Adams's analysis of the bipartisan agreement on the basic need for the purchase, which indicated that for the first time all parties agreed that the nation could in fact be governed. It is difficult to believe that Adams did not join in this agreement. The very language of his discussion is approving. If this meant the end of the Union as it had existed, then so be it. The clear implication of Adams's position is that government under the original Union was impossible. A nation destined for greatness must be governable. Thus, in spite of the undermining of constitutional niceties, the end result was desirable. It also follows that the original Constitution, in spite of Adams's apparent obeisance to it, was not viable. This, in turn, is consistent with the earlier point about the tendency of expediency to triumph over law. The way was open for a democratic nation as opposed to a union of states, many of them disfigured by slavery and secessionist impulses. None of this is clearly stated, given Adams's surface commitment to a form of positivist history, but the implications are clear. Earl Harbert is right to say that, for Adams, no account of Southern politics in terms of Jeffersonian Republican principle was possible, because each principle could be abandoned if a "special case" like the opportunity to purchase Louisiana should arise. The older Adamses tended to obsolescence in clinging to their principles in a time of rapid change, while Jefferson and Madison became pragmatists *avant le lettre*. To a substantial extent, Henry Adams, however uncomfortably, was willing to join them.[64] Given the difficulties of making a system based on an extreme notion of states' rights work, it is hard to disagree. Most of American history moves along this line of development.

Finally, Adams's emphasis on raising people to the point that they sought only what was good is also of great theoretical importance. As J. C. Levenson suggests, one thing Adams held against Jefferson was his failure as a political educator. Adams thought that for Jefferson, "to have dropped the political theory of 1798 without constructing another in its place thus became an offence, not simply against the demands of rationality, but against the democratic principle."[65] Adams certainly did not mourn the passing of the principles of 1798, but he did wish for new justificatory principles. This reading lends support to the interpretation that Adams was one of the last of the civic republicans.[66] Certainly he hoped for a citizenry focused on the public good, a point he was to explore more fully in his didactic novel *Democracy*. My own reading is that the amalgam of Adams's thought is more complex and more modern than that, but surely there are lingering elements of the older ideology in his thinking. And finally, it is characteristically and appropriately ironic that Jefferson, the inveterate theorist, is accused by Adams of theoretical failure just when theory is most needed.

The nature of the theoretical failure should be further discussed. John P. Diggins makes much of a wonderful story recounted by Adams in the *Education*. When Adams was a six-year-old, he resisted going to school. His mother was about to give in when John Quincy Adams emerged in all his stern majesty from his library, took the recalcitrant boy by the hand, and, without saying a word, marched him the one mile to school. Adams comments that Locke and Rousseau must be revised, because here was an exercise of authority that did not stem from consent but rather from something, as Diggins puts it, "directly experienced without mediation of the reflective mind."[67] There is indeed such a form of authority, and Grandfather Adams certainly had it; as described, this sounds very much like a version of personal authority, akin to charisma, and surely based on force of personality blended with the traditional and legal authority theorized by Max Weber. But there is at least one other form of authority, and this seems to be what Adams is getting at in the *History*. Authority can stem from the leader's ability to give good reasons for his actions, so as to persuade citizens of the legitimacy of their deeds.[68] This is what Adams claims Jefferson conspicuously failed to do in his actions surrounding the Louisiana Purchase—a critical failing in a democratic leader, because it is possible to rely on personal force for just so long within the framework of a democratic system. Beyond that, the ability to make arguments, to give reasons that help establish legitimacy, is a vital need.

The Embargo and the Failure of Principle

If we leave questions of theory and principle aside, then the successful purchase of Louisiana was surely the major policy triumph of Jefferson's first term. Just as surely, the failed policy of the embargo dominated the second term. Almost as if a great triumph was the necessary prelude to disaster, the embargo followed Jefferson's enormous victory in the election of 1804, just when it appeared that Republicanism was everywhere in near-total control.

With the purchase, Jefferson felt that he was in "the harvest season of his life. His theories were proved sound, his system of government stood in successful rivalry with that of Bonaparte and Pitt; and he felt no doubt that his friendship was as vital to England, France, and Spain as all the armies and navies of the world."[69] Of course, this delight was premature, but it was certainly understandable. As Adams writes:

> Rarely was a Presidential election better calculated to turn the head of a President, and never was a President elected who felt more keenly the pleasure of his personal triumph. At the close of four years of administration, all Jefferson's hopes were fulfilled. He had annihilated opposition. The slanders of the Federalist press helped to show that he was the idol of four fifths of the nation. He received one hundred and sixty-two of one hundred and seventy-six electoral votes, while in 1801 he had but seventy-three in one hundred and thirty-eight; and in the Ninth Congress, which was to meet in December, 1805, barely seven out of thirty-four senators, and twenty-five out of one hundred and forty-one representatives, would oppose his will. He described his triumph, in language studiously modest, in a letter to Volney: "The two parties which prevailed with so much violence when you were here are almost wholly melted into one."[70]

In such a setting, Jefferson might well have thought that the consensus he pretended already existed in his Inaugural Address had actually arrived and on his own terms, just as he had hoped. This was the form Jefferson liked opposition to take. As Adams remarks with characteristic acerbity, "Jefferson resembled all rulers in one peculiarity of mind. Even Bonaparte thought a respectable minority might be useful as censors; but neither Bonaparte nor Jefferson was willing to agree that any particular minority was respectable."[71] But Jefferson's joy was based partly on illusion. Like so many leaders, he had convinced himself that his admirable situation was permanent, particularly since he was surrounded by flatterers who would offer him no challenge, while the electoral triumph outweighed even the subtlest flattery. No one, says Adams, dared question the means by which his popularity was achieved. No one spoke of states' rights or strict construction except the "monarchical Federalists, who were fit inmates for an asylum."[72]

Yet again Adams returns to his main theme. "After nearly four years of Executive authority more complete than had ever been known in American history, Jefferson could see in himself and in his principles only a negation of Executive influence. What had become of the old radical division of parties . . . ? In this fusion his own party had shown even more willingness than its opponents to mix its principles in a useful, but not noble, amalgam."[73] This is a politics based on illusion and self-deception, and of course it did not last. No such politics can. Still, it must be repeated that while Adams saw through the illusions and the betrayal of principle, in his own guarded way, behind the constitutional jeremiads, he accepted the *utility* of what Jefferson had done, even while denying it any quality of nobility.

But the ironies continue to accumulate, for in the crisis over the embargo on foreign trade, Jefferson followed Republican dogma in the most principled possible way, with results that were disastrous for his personal popularity and the nation's economy. "The essence and genius of Jefferson's statesmanship," Adams writes, "lay in peace. Through difficulties, trials, and temptations of every kind he held fast to this idea, which was the clue to whatever seemed inconsistent, feeble, or deceptive in his administration."[74] He firmly believed that European nations, particularly Britain, could be controlled through the exercise of America's growing commercial power. "Jefferson felt sure that England could not afford to sacrifice a trade of some forty million dollars, and that her colonies could not exist without access to the American market. What need to spend millions on a navy, when Congress, as Jefferson believed, already grasped England by the throat, and could suffocate her by a mere turn of the wrist!"[75]

Apparently this was not as clear to the English as it was to Jefferson. As Adams sees it, in European affairs, America was little more than an appendage to England. Almost all the manufactured products consumed by Americans were British. English ships blockaded New York and Chesapeake Bay; they were impressing American seamen and interfering with French and Spanish commerce, all with little regard for American dignity.[76] Perhaps worst of all was the *Chesapeake* affair, in which the British man-of-war *Leopard* fired on the American frigate *Chesapeake*, producing for the first time in American history, as Adams sees it, a truly national emotion,[77] though it has to be added that the emotion proved to be impermanent.

But in spite of this event, Jefferson continued to have faith in his theory of peaceable coercion, to the extent that Adams believes "that he would hardly have thought his administrative career complete, had he quitted office without being allowed to prove the value of his plan."[78] One of the early fruits of his policy was the Non-Importation Act of 1806, which, taking effect in December over the protests of the merchants, banned the import of all articles from Britain. Two days after the law went into effect, Madison received a document dated October 17, in which the king issued a proclamation requiring British naval vessels to exercise the right of impressment over neutral

merchant ships.[79] A precedent dating from 1794 suggested the imposition of
an embargo for a short, fixed period—thirty to ninety days at most—which
would have allowed time to ascertain British and French intent. Jefferson responded to the king with a draft embargo message addressed to Congress.
Madison offered a revision that skirted around the fact, ignored by Jefferson,
that the official British impressment proclamation had not been received, but
a proposal by Secretary of the Treasury Gallatin that the embargo be limited
in time was ignored.[80]

The message was quickly sent to Congress, where it was just as quickly
passed by an overwhelming majority that included J. Q. Adams of Massachusetts, a vote later used against him by his Federalist enemies in his home
state. The House then conducted its debate in secret session, an unfortunate
fact, since "no private citizen ever knew the reasons which Congress considered sufficient to warrant a strain of the Constitution so violent as a permanent embargo implied." The bill passed overwhelmingly.[81]

Once again, Adams allows himself the luxury of open criticism, a criticism that gives a sense of his understanding of democracy:

> Thus the embargo was imposed; and of all President Jefferson's feats
> of political management, this was probably the most dextrous. On
> his mere recommendation, without warning, discussion, or public-
> ity, and in silence as to his true reasons and motives, he succeeded
> in fixing upon the country, beyond recall, the experiment of peace-
> able coercion. His triumph was almost a marvel; but no one could
> fail to see its risks. *A free people required to know in advance the
> motive which actuated government, and the intended consequences of
> important laws.* Large masses of intelligent men were slow to forgive
> what they might call deception. If Jefferson's permanent embargo
> should fail to coerce Europe, what would the people of America
> think of the process by which it had been fastened upon them? What
> would be said and believed of the President who had challenged so
> vast a responsibility.[82]

This case is clearly different from the Louisiana situation. Here, Jefferson
held to his republican principles on the immediate question, though he violated basic concepts of democratic theory, to use a term Adams does not, in
pursuing them. And here too, Adams returns to the theme of his analysis of
the Louisiana Purchase: a government that does not explain the principles
underlying its actions threatens to undercut its own legitimacy. This theoretical failure is arguably worse to Adams than the disastrous policy or the de-

fective principle on which it rests. This is the view of a man who takes democratic principles seriously.

However, also unlike the Louisiana case, where the policy was a success, in the embargo controversy, the policy itself proved to be a huge mistake. But in spite of the fact that Jefferson, in the pursuit of his policy, "trampled upon personal rights and public principles" in the belief that "a higher public interest required the sacrifice," Adams somewhat oddly concedes that the embargo was "an experiment in politics well worth making."[83] Implicitly, then, it was useful to learn that the policy of peaceful coercion as a substitute for war, intended to spare the United States the evils that had disfigured European history, would not work. A sense of international realism had to be learned the hard way.

In an irony that no doubt pleased Adams, the Republican dread of war stemmed not so much from its waste and destruction as from the effects war would have on the institutions of government, which led Jefferson to pursue a policy more destructive to "the theory and practice of a Virginia republic than any foreign war was likely to be." And Adams adds, "Personal liberties and rights of property were more directly curtailed in the United States by embargo than in Great Britain by centuries of almost continuous foreign war. . . . If American liberties must perish, they might as well be destroyed by war as be stilled by non-intercourse."[84]

The economic costs were somewhat more difficult to measure. However, Adams contends in a brief and somewhat speculative analysis that, "If long continued, embargo must bankrupt the government almost as certainly as war; if not long continued, the immediate shock to industry was more destructive than war would have been."[85]

But in Adams's worldview, the *moral* cost was greater than the economic cost. The brutality of war corrupts and debauches society, but "the peaceable coercion which Jefferson tried to substitute for war was less brutal, but hardly less mischievous than the evil it displaced."[86] Of course, the impact of "brute force and brutal methods corrupted and debauched society." But beyond that:

> The embargo opened the sluice-gates of social corruption. Every citizen was tempted to evade or defy the laws. At every point along the coast and frontier the civil, military, and naval services were brought in contact with corruption; while every man in private life was placed under strong motives to corrupt. Every article produced or consumed in the country became an object of speculation; every form of industry became a form of gambling. The rich could alone

profit in the end; while the poor must sacrifice at any loss the little they could produce.[87]

Adams then adds a comment that is especially interesting in light of the still recent Civil War. Perhaps it is the remark of a victor not likely to be uttered in the South, perhaps the product of a romantic, almost medieval, somewhat European sense of the costs and benefits of war, and certainly it is the thought of a thinker briefly under the influence of Darwinism.

> If war made men brutal, at least it made them strong; it called out the qualities best fitted to survive in the struggle for existence. To risk life for one's country was no mean act even when done for selfish motives; and to die that others might more happily live was the highest act of self-sacrifice to be reached by man. War, with all its horrors, could purify as well as debase; it dealt with high motives and vast interests; taught courage, discipline, and stern sense of duty. Jefferson must have asked himself in vain what lessons of heroism or duty were taught by his system of peaceable coercion.[88]

No doubt Adams is at least partly right about the usually deeply hidden but perhaps sometimes salutary effects of war. Still, in the twenty-first century, it is much harder to praise them than it was for Adams. Had he written after the horrors of World War I, perhaps he would have been more reserved on the subject.[89]

Though the constitutional, economic, and moral damage of the embargo was great, it was perhaps surpassed by the political carnage it left in its wake. Oddly, though Adams admits that the economic cost of the embargo was hard to calculate, most of his assessment of its political damage is based on its economic impact on the different sections of the country. For instance, it struck like a thunderbolt in New England, "where foreign commerce and shipping were the life of the people" and "the ocean," as Pickering said, "was their farm." But in spite of that, the region was better able than most to withstand the rigors of the embargo, and in fact, the Northeast emerged with a monopoly on the market for domestic manufacturing. Pennsylvania also felt a similar economic stimulus, and as a result, the embargo was less unpopular there than elsewhere. Wheat and livestock growers in the middle states were more damaged as the market for their products collapsed. Ironically, the states that were hit hardest were in the South, especially in Virginia. Embargo or not, "Four hundred thousand Negro slaves must be clothed and fed, great establishments must be kept up, the social scale of living could not be reduced, and even bankruptcy could not clear a large landed estate without creating new encumbrances in a country where land and Negroes were the only forms of property on which money could be raised."[90]

The description of the economic havoc may not seem an adequate justification for the political upheaval that followed, but upheaval there was. Jefferson, Madison, and the Southern Republicans had no idea of the consequences of their policy. Jefferson woke from his dream to find his political fortunes in ruins. In the contemporary parlance, he and his collaborators were clueless: "Except in a state of society verging on primitive civilization, the stoppage of all foreign intercourse could not have been attempted by peaceable means. The attempt to deprive the laborer of sugar, salt, tea, coffee, molasses, and rum; to treble the price of every yard of coarse cottons and woolens; to reduce by one half the wages of labor, and to double its burdens,—this was a trial more severe than war."[91]

In the South, few were prepared to oppose a system that was so much a Southern invention, but in the North, there was a political conflagration, one of the early victims of which was John Quincy Adams, who paid the price for his support of Jefferson by losing his Senate seat in the spring of 1808. Under these circumstances, one might have expected a Republican defeat in the election of 1808, but due to their opponents' inability to consolidate their opposition and the peculiarities of the electoral system as it was then structured, James Madison was able to eke out a victory and continue the Virginia dynasty in office. However, the Republican majority in the electoral college was greatly reduced, as were Republican seats in the House. Moreover, many of the Northern Republicans were as hostile to the embargo as were the Federalists. The Congress that emerged was without policy and leaderless. Thus, politically, for Jefferson, the costs were "the fruits of eight years painful labor for popularity," while the Union was "brought to the edge of a precipice."And finally, of course, the policy failed to achieve its end of peaceable coercion.[92] The War of 1812 still had to be fought to settle the maritime issues that had precipitated the crisis.

Adams makes two other notable points. The first is an early attempt to apply physical laws to political affairs. If, Adams reasoned, we think of an embargo as a force less violent than war, then to succeed, it must be applied for a longer time than a war in order to generate an equivalent amount of energy. Wars could last years, and it was only natural that embargoes would have to last longer if they were to succeed. But the price of such an attempt, on the evidence of the short experience of Jefferson's embargo, could only be the destruction of the Union.[93] Although it is interesting, perhaps, this sort

of precise calculation seems so hard to make as to be almost delusive. Nonetheless, as a heuristic device, it is of some interest; certainly it is clear that if
the embargo had not been repealed at the end of Jefferson's term, the stability of the Union might have been undermined.

Finally, there is a more important observation that contributes to one of
the long-standing debates about the nature of American history.

> Under the shock of these discoveries Jefferson's vast popularity van-
> ished, and the labored fabric of his reputation fell in sudden and gen-
> eral ruin. America began slowly to struggle, under the consciousness
> of pain, toward a conviction that she must bear the common burdens
> of humanity, and fight with the weapons of other races in the same
> bloody arena; that she could not much longer delude herself with
> hopes of evading laws of Nature and instincts of life; and that her new
> statesmanship which made peace a passion could lead to no better
> result than had been reached by the barbarous systems which made
> war a duty.[94]

The debate in question is the idea of American exceptionalism, or, more
specifically, the question of the end of American exceptionalism.[95] In his
vision of an egalitarian, hardworking, middle-class society freed of the limitations of aristocracy, Adams clearly subscribes to a form of the exceptionalist
thesis, whose roots go back at least to his intellectual mentor Tocqueville.
Here, however, he anticipates a theme often suggested in the twentieth century, namely, that America could not maintain an isolationist stance and hold
itself aloof from world affairs, and further, to the extent that this was so, the
United States must necessarily lose its innocence and play by the same rules
as other powers. For Diggins, Adams's observations look ahead to the teach-
ings of Max Weber and Reinhold Niebuhr, who criticized pacifists "who
would cling to their ethical integrity regardless of consequences." This is true,
I think, though the matter is even more complicated than Diggins makes it.
Jefferson was willing to compromise his principles over Louisiana with hardly
a backward glance, but in foreign affairs, he held to the essence of his policy
of peaceable coercion long after it was realistic to do so. His policy was the
policy of a pacifist. Diggins is close to the mark. Thinking of Louisiana, he
writes, "Jefferson succeeded in politics by ceasing to practice philosophy."[96]
Thus, in this point of view, Jefferson might have done better had he abandoned his principled philosophy in foreign relations as he did in making the
Louisiana Purchase. But Adams sharply attacks him for abandoning principle in his great Louisiana success and then, perhaps more importantly, for

failing to justify this departure. Conversely, Jefferson's great failure was in foreign relations, and there Adams attacks him precisely for following principle, especially since the very implementation of the embargo policy forced him to resort to an intrusive government that also, paradoxically, *was* in violation of Jeffersonian principles. Thus, Jefferson learned the lesson of what international relations theorists call "realism" in his conduct of domestic affairs, but in foreign affairs, the lesson was still to be understood. The embargo did not solve his policy problem. As James Madison was to learn, mere trade sanctions could not avert war in the effort to protect American shipping, though in his own rather inept way, Madison solved his problem.

Out-Federalizing the Federalists?

The most general, and most famous, interpretation offered by Adams in the *History* is his thesis that Jefferson out-federalized the Federalists, a position implicit in the previous discussion of the Louisiana Purchase. "If," Adams writes, "Jefferson's favorite phrase was true,—that the Federalist differed from the Republican only in the shade more or less of power to be given to the executive,—it was hard to see how any President could be more Federalist than Jefferson himself." Writing of the conduct of foreign affairs, he adds, "of all Presidents, none used these arbitrary powers with more freedom and secrecy than Jefferson."[97] This is very much a Federalist, even Hamiltonian, approach to executive power, though arguably it is not inconsistent with Jefferson's constitutional theory. David Mayer contends that although Jefferson anguished over the problem, in political economy and foreign relations he was a nationalist. In these areas he resorted to a Hamiltonian use of the necessary and proper clause. Here he considered himself to have wide discretionary powers as president. Thus, Mayer goes so far as to say that although Jefferson was deeply concerned with the apparent constitutional problem inherent in the purchase, his actions involved a mere "technical problem."[98] Perhaps this is true, but the stress on Jefferson's anguish undercuts this point to a considerable extent. In any case, whatever his constitutional scruples, Jefferson's actions revealed a capacity for the exercise of sweeping presidential power, a precedent that, though not consistently followed until the twentieth century, pointed the way ahead. Adams's remark that it was now clear that the United States could in fact govern itself indicates a willingness to accept this new dispensation, though, like Jefferson, he would have preferred it to be ratified by a constitutional amendment. Adams's constitutional purism could be as flexible as Jefferson's.

When it comes to executive authority, then, Adams's claim that Jefferson's constitutional practice was much like that recommended by his Federalist enemies seems quite sound. However, if one considers the whole range of public policy, the idea of Jefferson in thrall to Federalist policies holds up less well. Though it should be stressed that Adams's claims relate to the federal system and the use of executive power, a broader consideration of Jefferson's administration reveals a greater consistency between theory and practice. As Joyce Appleby points out, "In office, the Jeffersonians carried out their mandate with remarkable fidelity. Direct taxes were repealed, the national debt was quickly retired, revenues were applied to internal improvements, and the size of the federal government was scaled down despite the enlargement of national territory. International free trade was pursued with a vengeance and land sales jumped astronomically." This, she says, "should lay the ghost" of Adams's interpretation.[99] There is something to be said for this point of view, but not quite enough to dispose of Adams. Appleby is convincing that Jefferson did indeed pursue his own theoretical notions and implemented them in policy, but it remains true that he conceived of executive power much more expansively than his political thought might suggest. And the argument that he pursued free trade with a "vengeance" must be qualified by pointing to the embargo. Thus, in its broad outlines, a qualified version of Adams's interpretation holds up fairly well.

What Adams and Appleby share is a belief that Jefferson was right to think of his administration as a revolutionary force. As Appleby puts it, "The revolution came from the defeat of aristocratic values in American politics."[100] What they both see is the emergence of a commercial, inventive, democratic society, a society that Adams saw as a major advance over anything Europe had to offer, though not, of course, free of problems.

But Adams appears to exhibit some real theoretical tensions in his thinking about Jefferson. It is not an easy argument to criticize Jefferson for abandoning principle in one arena and clinging to it in another. Perhaps because of his own self-limiting positivism, however inconsistently held, and perhaps because of his own philosophical uncertainty, Adams might appear to leave an unresolved tension at the heart of his critique of Jefferson. But perhaps the tension is more apparent than real. No doubt part of the difficulty is that Adams, since he writes as a historian rather than a philosopher, is unwilling to provide an explicit normative critique of Jefferson's policy. Moreover, his own position is complex, though the outline is clear. Implicitly, in Adams's analysis, one must ask two questions: Were Jefferson's principles viable? and Did he meet his obligation to provide explanations of his policies that would establish their democratic legitimacy? In the case of Louisiana, Jefferson's radical decentralist principles were untenable, and Jefferson did well to abandon them, but his justification for doing so was inadequate and thus did not meet the test required of a democratic leader who needed to provide civic education. Nor did he ever admit that his original theories were inadequate. As for the embargo, he held to his untenable principles, and the result was political and economic disaster. In both cases he was dishonest with the public and probably with himself as well. He refused to admit that his doctrines were wrong or, in the case of the embargo, to accept, until it was too late, that his policies too were disastrous. Adams's position on the relation of principle to practice is complex, though not more so than required by the situation he describes. No Adams could doubt that principles were important, but if the principles were unsound, then policies pursuant to them were likely to encounter difficulties. And, just as important, the abandonment of principles in the pursuit of policy had to be justified by the enunciation of new principles in order to meet the basic requirements of democratic political legitimacy.[101] And, of course, the matter is further complicated by the extent to which Adams seems to have admired Jefferson's temperament and the fact that, while he thought some of Jefferson's ideas to be mistaken, he still preferred the second president's egalitarian democratic principles to those of the Federalist opposition. (Perhaps this is why he admired Albert Gallatin so much. Here was a democrat without Jefferson's quirky Virginian views.)[102] As is often the case in the vast body of Adams's work, there is a deep ambivalence in his thought. His was a mind too complex to advance simple interpretive solutions. This is why he remains elusive to this day.

Chapter 3

The Madisonian Continuation

Henry Adams was clearly fascinated by Thomas Jefferson, however frustrating the results of his observations. Though equally frustrated with James Madison, Adams seems to have had very little interest in Madison as a person and held his presidential career in low esteem. Madison simply lacked the charm that helped make Jefferson so interesting to Adams.[1] Adams, with his usual gift for portraiture, offers a somewhat condescending description. "Madison had a sense of humor, felt in his conversation, and detected in the demure cast of his flexible lips, but leaving no trace in his published writings. Small in stature, in deportment modest to the point of sensitive reserve, in address simple and pleasing, in feature rather thoughtful and benevolent than strong, he was such a man as Jefferson, who so much disliked contentious and self-asserting manners, loved to keep by his side."[2] Later he offers a somewhat more complex picture. Madison is described as a man "incapable of surprising the world by reckless ambition or lawless acts." Yet he "paid surprisingly little regard to rules of consistency or caution." Citing Madison's Virginia Resolutions, his role in the Louisiana Purchase, his embargo policy, and numerous other foreign policy actions, Adams says, "he ignored caution in pursuit of an object which seemed to him proper in itself; nor could he understand why this quiet and patriotic conduct should arouse tempests of passion in his opponents, whose violence, by contrast, increased the apparent placidity of his own persistence."[3]

But in spite of this reckless streak, Jefferson and Madison made a near ideal pair. As Joseph Ellis writes, "Jefferson orchestrated the strategy and Madison implemented the tactics. Jefferson could afford to emphasize the broadest contours of a political problem because Madison was silently handling the messier specifics. (If God was in the details, Madison was usually there to greet Him upon arrival.)"[4] And yet, as even Ernest Samuels concludes, doubtless reflecting Adams, "the very materials of Madison's first administration defied enlivening. . . . After the greater Jefferson left the stage, . . . the colorless Madison was pure anticlimax."[5]

For Adams, Madison represented a mediocre continuation of Jeffersonian-

56

ism. His necessary historical role was to "retrieve the failures of Jefferson," but the utter "conventionality" of his thought betrayed itself in his First Inaugural Address. Dismayingly, "Madison seemed to show his contentment with the policy hitherto pursued, rather than his wish to change it,"[6] though in fairness to Madison, given the political circumstances and his close partnership with Jefferson, it was all but necessary to proceed as he did. And for the great tasks before him, "Madison's cabinet," in Adams's evaluation, "was the least satisfactory that any President had known," with the exception of Albert Gallatin. So weak were they that they hardly had strength enough to support two sides of an argument.[7] To have such an administration at such a time was potentially dangerous. Faction was rife. Jefferson had strained his authority to the breaking point, and the result was social as well as political disorder. And yet, in spite of Adams's perception of Madison's incompetence, and "dark as the prospect was within and without," the president was able to calm the situation temporarily, not least because in New England the economic stimulus to manufacturing and shipping interests provided by the embargo generated a need for order felt by the most militant Federalists.[8] And in spite of his animadversions against the embargo, Adams was forced to admit that, "in truth, the manufactories of New England were created by the embargo, which obliged the whole nation to consume their products or go without."[9] From a Jeffersonian point of view, the results were ironic and painful, while it must be said that the New Englanders were more than a little hypocritical:

> The Yankee, however ill-tempered he might be, was shrewd enough to see where his profit lay. The Federalist leaders and newspapers grumbled without intermission that their life-blood was drained to support a Negro-slave aristocracy . . . , but they took the profits thrust upon them; and what they could not clutch was taken by New York and Pennsylvania, while Virginia slowly sank into ruin. Virginia paid the price to gratify her passion for political power; and at the time, she paid it knowingly and willingly. . . . American manufactures owed more to Jefferson and Virginians, who disliked them, than to northern statesmen, who merely encouraged them after they were established.[10]

One begins to see here the strong sense that history rarely moves according to the plans of historical actors, a theme that must be explored more fully, since it assumes a large place in Adams's work and becomes a major component of his general philosophy of history.

Even though a temporary improvement in relations with England raised Madison to great heights of equally temporary popularity that placed him on

a par with Jefferson at his greatest height, the basic trajectory of his administration turned downward. Adams sums up his critique in a series of three devastating chapters whose titles sum up the indictment: "Executive Weakness,"
"Legislative Impotence," and "Incapacity of Government." According to
Adams, Madison derived all the power he possessed from British misman-
agement of foreign policy.[11] But what power he had did not lead to any consistent policy. Francis Jackson, retiring as the English ambassador in March
1810, wrote, "At Washington they are in a state of the most animated confusion, the Cabinet divided, and the Democratic party going various ways. . . .
Their foreign policies embarrass them even more than their home ones. One
moment they want another embargo, the next, to take off the restrictions;
then, to arm their merchantmen; and next to declare war. In short, they do
not know what to be at."[12] At last, reflecting Madison's distrust of unrestricted
commerce that was so deeply ingrained in Jeffersonian republican principles, a new Non-Intercourse Act was passed in March 1809, with the same
dismaying consequences as the earlier measures.[13]

> Ingenuity [Adams claims], could hardly have invented a system less
> advantageous for the government and people who maintained it. The
> government lost its revenue, the shipping lost much of its freight, the
> people paid double prices on imports and received half-prices for their
> products; industry was checked, speculation and fraud were stimu-
> lated, while certain portions of the country were grievously wronged.
> Especially in the Southern States all articles produced for exchange
> were depressed to the lowest possible value, while all articles imported
> for consumption were raised to extravagant rates.[14]

Thus, once again, the pursuit of a misguided principle created havoc, which
affected most dramatically the region represented by the perpetrators of the
policy. In fact, a fundamental problem of the Jeffersonians seems to be that
principle and policy were rarely in alignment, a condition that a stern moralist such as Adams inevitably found disturbing. The experiment of "peaceable
coercion" may have been worth making during the Jefferson administration,
but clearly the idea had been invalidated by the time Madison reached the
White House and should have been abandoned due to the noxious consequences that flowed from it. Bad principle makes for bad policy, and there is
no credit to be had from adhering to it. In contrast, to abandon principle,
even in pursuit of a policy whose long-run consequences were beneficent,
as in the case of Louisiana, was also deplorable because of the damage done

to constitutional integrity. The Jeffersonians could hardly win when caught in this intellectual vise.

But worse was to come. The failure to make American shipping safe on the high seas led to the War of 1812, which not only destroyed Madison's popularity but also strained the Union close to the breaking point.

And yet, in Adams's view, the war need not have been fought. Madison's speech asking Congress for a declaration of war against Britain revealed the deficiencies of his thinking. He charged the British with continuing the policy of impressment of American citizens on the high seas and also with violating the peace of the coasts while harassing commerce. Both charges were true and, according to Adams, "warranted war." To these complaints were added two others, also involving depredations against American shipping in the form of blockades, particularly those deriving from the British orders in council.[15] But true and demonstrable though the charges were, Adams was still not satisfied by Madison's *justification* for war. It was, in his view, a war fought at the wrong time and against an only partially identified enemy.[16] In particular, in his message, Madison ignored what Adams took to be the offenses of the French that were as great as or greater than those of the British.[17]

The various wrongs cited had long been endured because it seemed expedient to do so as an alternative to war. In fact, Jefferson believed that war, however just, was always inexpedient. Moreover, the British, though not the French, showed signs of yielding on the issues. In Adams's view, "In June, 1812, the reasons for declaring war on Great Britain were weaker than they had been in June 1808 or in January 1809." In 1807, England would have welcomed war, but in 1812, it wanted peace and was willing to surrender a good deal to get it. On the other side, in 1808, the United States was ready for war; in 1812, the people were divided, the government weak, and the treasury empty.[18]

The war was unpopular even from the start, when one often expects a conflict to win broad public endorsement. Madison's support in both the House and the Senate was seriously eroded. None of this was made better by what Adams took to be Madison's incompetence, which sapped half the energy of the American people and enabled the New England Federalists to persuade themselves that "Jefferson and Madison were sold to France."[19]

At times, the military disasters were truly humiliating, as when Madison was ignominiously forced to flee the burning capital city. But Adams's greatest rage seems to have been aroused by the fall of Fort Detroit. The president ordered a court-martial of William Hull, the garrison commander. He was

charged with treason, cowardice, neglect of duty, and "unofficer-like" conduct. The president, who had a deep interest in Hull's conviction, so as to shift
the blame from himself, then blundered by making General Dearborn, whose
own war record was also at stake, the president of the court-martial, thus in-
stalling in power another with a vested interest in seeing a conviction. This
evident "impropriety" seemed lost on Madison; Hull was sentenced to be shot,
with Madison approving but then remitting the sentence. Adams was outraged: "That someone should be punished for the loss of Detroit was evident,
and few persons were likely to complain because Hull was the selected victim"; but "many thought," Adams tells us, "that if Hull deserved to be shot,
other men, much higher than he in office and responsibility, merited punish-
ment; and the character of the court-martial added no credit to the government, which in effect it acquitted of blame."[20] Precisely what Adams intended
by this sally is not altogether clear. Peter Shaw, always ready to attribute to
Adams the harshest possible judgments on Jefferson and Madison, contends
that this suggests that the president, having failed to prepare the nation for
war, "should have been tried and executed for criminal incompetence."[21] This
may be so, since Adams often argues by indirection. However, there is room
for interpretation, because there are other superiors short of the president who
might have been tried, and Adams is not explicit as to the target of his wrath.
Nor is execution explicitly mentioned, perhaps due to the fact that Hull's sentence was never carried out. Moreover, criminal incompetence is not pun-
ishable by death. However, Madison was the commander in chief and hence
the bearer of the ultimate responsibility. It is certainly true that Adams's analysis drips with contempt for Madison not only on grounds of incompetence
but also for his poor judgment in choosing a deeply interested party to preside over the fate of Hull. Certainly the episode was not one of the luminous
moments in the history of the Madison presidency.

But military disasters were not the only troubles in the war. Political disaffection was widespread, not least in Adams's native New England. Here the
issue of separatism, which so troubled him when it appeared in the South,
seemed to be an even more immediate political threat to the Union the
Adams family had so long defended. As the war neared its end, a large part
of the "most intelligent citizens" feared the worst in the impending battle of
New Orleans and also worried that the peace negotiations in Ghent would
fall apart. The enemies of the government in New England were certain that
these events would lead to the collapse of the national government.[22] Already
the Hartford Convention, made up of New England dissidents, was meeting
to assess the situation. Federalist ultras were ready to make major concessions

to the British in order to secure peace and were prepared to establish a new constitution encompassing "either the whole or a portion of the actual Union."[23] Adams was by no means friendly to the New England Federalists and asserts that it was quite possible that "much was said that verged on treasonable conspiracy," but in the end, when Harrison Gray Otis caused the official journal of the convention to be published, it was evident that the delegates had behaved with some circumspection, which "proved that nothing was done or formally proposed which contradicted the grave and the strained attitude maintained in [the leader's] public expression."[24] So too did George Lodge, who was chosen to preside. It appears on Adams's evidence that the delegates were in fact more conservative than their constituents. Secession was in the air, but the convention report states that "a severance of the Union by one or more States against the will of the rest, and especially in time of war, can be justified only by absolute necessity." But having made this plea for moderation, the report then closely followed the Virginia Resolution in claiming "the right and duty of a State to 'interpose its authority' for the protection of its citizens from infractions of the Constitution by the general government."[25] In the eyes of an Adams writing in the post–Civil War period, this position could hardly qualify as moderate, whatever the protestations of the authors and however more restrained than that of the public and the press in New England. In effect, such provisions as the states being given a "reasonable" portion of taxes collected within the state and the rejection of conscription so that the states could assume their own defense clearly moved toward the establishment of a New England Confederation. Because of the urgency of the situation, these provisions were to be accepted immediately.[26] Besides these matters of pressing concern, seven constitutional amendments, which Adams oddly does not specify in detail, were proposed.

The proposed amendments were clearly aimed at the South and at Virginia in particular. From today's perspective, the first, which called for abolition of the three-fifths clause of the Constitution, seems totally unexceptionable, though in its time it was politically explosive. The second required a two-thirds vote to admit new states; the third and fourth placed restrictions on embargoes and the interdiction of commerce; the fifth required the concurrence of two-thirds of both houses of Congress to declare war or "authorize acts of hostility," except in self-defense; the sixth precluded naturalized citizens from serving in the House or Senate, or even from holding civil office; and the last imposed a one-term limit on the president and proclaimed that the president could not be elected from the same state two times in succession, an obvious slap at the Virginia Dynasty.[27]

These resolutions may have been "moderate" in the overheated atmosphere of the time, but they were certainly well calculated to upset supporters of the Republican administration. In this the Republicans were perhaps not entirely wrong, even though on the interposition matter they were, in effect, being given a dose of their own medicine. At least one newspaper, the *Boston Centinal*, claimed that the old Constitution was no more. Addressing the convention, it editorialized, "At your hands, therefore, we demand deliverance. New England is Unanimous. And we announce our irrevocable decree that the tyrannical oppression of those who at present usurp the powers of the Constitution is beyond endurance. And we shall resist it." With heavy irony, Gouverneur Morris wrote to Senator Pickering, "The traitors and madmen assembled at Hartford will, I believe, if not too tame and timid, be hailed hereafter as the patriots and sages of their day and generation."[28]

In later times, Adams observes, the Hartford Convention was often defended on the ground that popular opinion was more extreme than the convention's. Adams gives considerable credence to this view: "The tone of the press and the elections bore out the belief that a popular majority would have supported an abrupt and violent course." Threats of civil war were frequent, and there was talk of coercing Madison into retirement. It was certainly the belief of the Republican Party that the convention could only lead to a New England Confederation.[29]

But the Republicans were not alone in this estimate. George Ticknor, a twenty-three-year-old Federalist, loved to tell of his meeting with the elderly John Adams, who declaimed to him in a loud and excited voice: "Thank God! Thank God! George Cabot's close-buttoned ambition has broke out at last: he wants to be President of New England, sir."[30] Here Henry Adams's true feelings about the secessionist tendencies in his native region appear, and once again his view is validated by one of his distinguished ancestors. Whether he wanted it or not, Cabot was in danger of becoming what John Adams had predicted, having been forced into a position from which there was no escape. It was hard for either people or leaders to retreat. Once taxes were sequestered, "the establishment of a New England confederation could hardly be matter of choice."[31] The danger was real. The anticipated fall of New Orleans would have been the signal to demand Madison's resignation. Henry Adams did not believe that it would come to this. However, the fall of both Washington and New Orleans would have destroyed the president's authority. To resign was impossible, but "the alternative was a collapse of government," and in this crisis, "the least probable solution was that England would consent to any tolerable peace."[32] Perilous times indeed! An incompetent government generated secessionist pressures that were anathema to a devoted nationalist, and there had been serious national humiliations.[33]

And yet the worst did not happen. Andrew Jackson won a famous victory at New Orleans, which had the effect of choking off the Hartford initiatives. The peace talks at Ghent did not founder, though they were resolved only when Madison gave up the demand for an end to impressment, which had been the principle casus belli. Essentially the war ended with a return to the status quo ante, though the number of incidents of British impressment declined sharply. In the conduct of the war, however inept it had been, even Adams found some cause for celebration, most notably the triumphs of American gunnery, particularly at sea, the remarkable quality of American warships, and the outstanding skills of the American rifleman. There had been signs of this sort of technological achievement as early as August 17, 1807, when Robert Fulton took the steamship *Clermont* on its first voyage up the Hudson River. This was a day that separated "the colonial from the independent stage of growth." Thus, "for the first time America could consider herself mistress of her vast resources."[34]

This leads Adams to an important reflection:

> The unfailing mark of a primitive society was to regard war as the most natural pursuit of man; and history with reason began as a record of war, because, in fact, all other human occupations were secondary to this. The chief sign that Americans had other qualities than the races from which they sprang, was shown by their dislike for war as a profession, and their obstinate attempts to invent other methods for obtaining their ends. . . . Desperate physical courage was the common quality on which all great races had founded their greatness; and the people of the United States, in discarding military qualities, without devoting themselves to science, were trying an experiment which could succeed only in a world of their own.[35]

This triumphant remark reflects Adams's delight in the American success in overcoming the backward state of technology lamented in the discussion of the United States in 1800. It also suggests that the picture of Adams as a simple technophobe so commonly based on a reading of his late writings is overdrawn and in need of revision. It points toward the United States becoming a world power through technological innovation and suggests one of the attributes of American exceptionalism, in that Adams clearly alludes here to the emergence of a distinctive American identity.

The war proved American superiority in a number of technically based areas. In spite of Adams's delight in the success of Robert Fulton, which was the most striking success in the application of science, "it was neither the most original nor the most ingenious of American efforts, nor did it offer the best example of popular characteristics." Other inventions such as the torpedo, the screw propeller, and perhaps above all the fast sailing schooner with a pivot gun deserved that honor.[36] In any case, the Americans developed surprising skill in naval affairs. Even according to the British newspapers, American cruisers "threatened to overthrow England's supremacy on the ocean." And battle after battle showed that American gunnery at sea was superior to England's. The American rifle fired by American soldiers was felt to be unequaled, partly because every American learned to shoot from childhood. And finally, the war gave tremendous impetus to the development of scientific engineering.[37] All this demanded great ingenuity, but what Adams thought it said about the level of either intelligence or morality is a subject to which we must return.

In spite of these important successes, there is no doubt that much of the war seemed a disaster to Adams. Nor was the incompetence limited to the Madison administration. Adams wryly remarks that "readers who have followed the history here closed, have been surprised at the frequency with which the word *imbecility* has risen in their minds in reading the proceedings of the House." He continued:

> So strong was the same impression at the time, that in the year 1814, at the close of the war, every earnest patriot in the Union, and many men who were neither earnest nor patriotic, were actively reproaching the House for its final failure, at an apparent crisis of the national existence, to call out or organize any considerable part of the national energies. The people in truth, however jealous of power, would have liked in imagination, though they would not bear in practice, to be represented by something nobler, wiser, and purer than their own average honor, wisdom, and purity. They could not make an ideal of weakness, ignorance, or vice, even their own; and as they required in their religion the idea of an infinitely wise and powerful deity, they revolted in their politics from whatever struck them as sordid or selfish.[38]

What we see here is a complex sense of the difficulties of representative democracy. The instincts of the people are good, perhaps for the best, though they distrust the idea of strong government. But their leaders betray them, a problem first glimpsed in the Jefferson administration, when the president eroded his authority through his methods of imposing the embargo and thereby failed in his responsibility to elevate the people through his leadership.

In the end, in spite of many serious complaints, Adams offers a very nuanced verdict on the outcome of the war and of the Jeffersonian years in general, if not on the quality of the leaders. Certainly there were major economic benefits. The doubts that had accompanied the nation's birth were put to rest. Population and wealth were steadily increasing. Every immediate foreign or domestic peril had disappeared, so that the society could devote itself to whatever it pleased. The way was open for rapid economic progress. "The continent lay before [the people] like an uncovered ore-bed."[39]

Given his animadversions against both president and Congress, it makes considerable sense to say that Adams's real hero is the collective people. William Jordy is characteristically terse in his account: "All but leaderless," as Adams saw it, "the people redeemed the blunders of their statesmen and stumbled through the War of 1812."[40] Peter Shaw puts the thesis well: "Madison's war was saved only by the real hero of the *History*, the American people, whose nascent pride and heroism, though Madison was temperamentally incapable of recognizing them, salvaged his fortunes and those of the incompetent generals he had appointed." Thus the real strength of the American nation was proved.[41] This is close to Adams's view, which is more vivid and more nuanced.

> Only by slow degrees the country learned to appreciate the extraordinary feat which had been performed, not so much by the people as by a relatively small number of individuals. Had a village rustic, with one hand tied behind his back, challenged the champion of the prizering, and in three or four rounds obliged him to withdraw the stakes, the result would have been little more surprising than the result of the American campaign of 1814.[42]

But even with Adams's qualification, this is a great tribute to the people. The victory belonged not to aristocrats, for there were none, and certainly not to the political leadership, and still less to the generals. If the victory was not due to the people en masse, it certainly could be attributed to enough of them drawn from the ranks of ordinary citizens to warrant a faith in the viability of democracy.

Perhaps the clue to the final Adams family judgment on the war comes from great-grandfather John. "Mr. Madison's administration must be accorded by the historians, notwithstanding all the errors, blunders, confusions, distractions, disasters, and factions with which it has been tarnished, as the most glorious period of the history of the United States,"[43] a position that seems suggestive, though certainly hyperbolic. Henry's own view is more complex but, in the end, perhaps not entirely different. Referring to the attempt to induce Britain to renounce the right to impressment, Adams writes:

> The experiment was worth trying, and after the timidity of the American government in past years was well suited to create national character, if it did not destroy the nation; but it was not the less hazardous in the face of sectional passions such as existed in New England, or in the hands of a party which held power by virtue of Jefferson's principles. That the British government should expressly renounce its claim to impressment was already an idea hardly worth entertaining; but if the war could not produce that result, it might at least develop a government strong enough to attain the same result at some future time. If a strong government was desired, any foreign war, without regard to its object, might be good policy, if not good morals; and *in that sense* President Madison's war was the boldest and most successful of all experiments in American statesmanship, though it was also among the most reckless; but only with difficulty could history offer a better example of its processes than when it showed Madison, Gallatin, Macon, Monroe, and Jefferson joining to create a mercenary army and a great national debt for no other attainable object than that which had guided Alexander Hamilton and the Federalists toward the establishment of a strong national government fifteen years before.[44]

Interpreting this comment is somewhat tricky. Shaw contends, "The passage could easily be read as ironical about history and sympathetic toward Madison, where actually it was ironical toward Madison and pleased with the ironies of history."[45] Given Adams's cast of mind, this distinction may be smaller than Shaw believes, but certainly he is right that there are ironies. Madison was not a partisan of strong government, so that for someone like Adams who was, the experiment was, ironically, a success, even if inadvertent. But it seems less clear than it does to Shaw that Madison's hope that the British would abandon the principle of impressment was foolish. After all, principle or not, the *practice* was largely abandoned.[46] And given the state of preparedness of the United States, the war surely could be called reckless, though it is less certain that Adams found it immoral, particularly given his sense of the possible benefits of war. As always, Shaw reads Adams in a way that makes him maximally critical of Madison, and Jefferson too, for that matter. But that raises complex issues about the extent to which any historical actors have real influence over the course of history. These issues are part of Adams's emerging philosophy of history, and to them it will be necessary to return more than once.

Before turning to these problems however, Adams's political conclusions about the War of 1812 should be considered. These too have a bearing on one of his lifelong philosophical concerns: the relations between unity and diversity. About the end of the war, Adams writes:

> Until 1815 nothing in the future of the American Union was regarded as settled. As late as January, 1815, division into several nationalities was still thought to be possible. Such a destiny, repeating the usual experience of history, was not necessarily more unfortunate than the career of a single nationality wholly American; for if the effects of a divided nationality were certain to be unhappy, those of a single society with equal certainty defied experience or sound speculation. One uniform and harmonious system appealed to the imagination as a triumph of human progress, offered prospects of peace and ease, contentment and philanthropy, such as the world had not seen; but it invited dangers, formidable because unusual or altogether unknown. The corruption of such a system might prove to be proportionate with its dimensions, and uniformity might lead to evils as serious as were commonly ascribed to diversity.[47]

Adams's sense of the uniqueness and the difficulties of the American system is clear. However new it might be, Americans no longer doubted that the path they were to take would not follow European models; Adams says, "the American in his political character, was a new variety of man."[48] Late in life, Adams as a philosopher desperately pursued unity. Here he is more ambivalent. He sees the advantages of unity and hopes for the best, but looking back after the Civil War, he can see the troubles that will arise. The question is, as John Patrick Diggins says, "Are we to emphasize the *pluribus* or the *unum*, the many or the one?"[49] This dilemma is a permanent factor in American history, perhaps now more than ever.

The United States in 1817

The entire structure of Adams's magnum opus points to the last four chapters on the Madison years, which close the frame of the whole work begun with the six chapters on the United States in 1800. Here Adams assesses the results of the tumultuous events of the Jefferson and Madison administrations. He begins with a discussion of the economy. The analysis of the beneficial development of technology has already been described. Beyond this, population growth was so rapid as to produce a doubling in twenty-three years. In spite of this, the war led to a check on the growth of cities. Economic and population growth were distributed somewhat unequally, with the Middle Atlantic states growing faster than New England or the South,[50] but in general, there was cause for optimism. To repeat, the continent lay open to the people. "With almost the certainty of a mathematical formula, knowing the rate of increase of population and of wealth, they could read in advance their economical history for at least a hundred years."[51]

One could not be so optimistic about the world of literature and art. The situation was rather like the prevailing political mood, in that just as society showed an interest in discussing political or religious dogma but had no interest in being subjected to it, it also "touched here and there, with a light hand, the wide circuit of what was called *belles lettres*, without showing severity in either taste or temper."[52] Except for the work of Washington Irving, little remains of what Adams described, so it is enough to note his closing comment, which is entirely consistent with the general theme of his work as a whole. The Americans, he says, were not artistic and had little sense of beauty, "but their intelligence in its higher as in its lower forms was both quick and refined." Literature and art showed qualities similar to those that produced the great schooners. "If the artistic instinct weakened, the quickness of intelligence increased."[53] Presumably, this would not lead to a great culture, but as a frame of mind for a rapidly growing commercial republic, it had clear advantages.[54]

In spite of this, it is perhaps not surprising that Adams found the movement of political and religious thought more interesting than either economics or literature, though it must be said that he was not very impressed by the quality of that thought. One should bear in mind the dramatic change brought about by the end of the war, in particular the explosion of commerce and navigation following the cessation of hostilities. "The ease and rapidity of this revolution not only caused the war to be quickly forgotten, but also silenced political passions. For the first time in their history as a nation, the people of the United States ceased to disturb themselves about politics or patronage. Every political principle was still open to dispute, and was disputed, but prosperity put an end to faction."[55]

Adams is not terribly impressed by religious thought, which was characterized primarily by the decline of rigorous dogma, seen largely in the rise of Unitarianism and the relative decline of Calvinism. By offering a qualified rejection of the Trinity and offering what they thought to be a more plausible view of Christ's divinity, the theologians "subverted an essential doctrine of the Church, and opened the way to heresy."[56] Across the country, the debate seemed more emotional than intellectual, with the partial exception of Boston. There, the Unitarian claim advanced by William Ellery Channing—that the doctrine of the Trinity would suffice if only it were intelligible—led Adams to say, "Calvinists could not be blamed for thinking that their venerable creed, the painful outcome of the closest and most strenuous reasoning known in the Christian world," was entitled to more respect than to be called, as Channing put it, "little else than a mystical form of the Unitarian doctrine."[57] On the one hand, Adams is somewhat troubled by this cavalier attitude toward Calvinist theology, but he is forced to concede that the early stage of Unitarianism was of interest because "it marked a general tendency of national thought." On the other hand, he is not unimpressed by the new theology. "No such display of fresh and winning genius had yet been seen in America as was offered by the genial outburst of intellectual activity in the early days of the Unitarian schism." It might also be observed that even Adams, when writing about medieval theology, most notably including the Trinity, was more than a little heretical himself. Finally, he notes approvingly that the Unitarians in particular and the other popular religions in general were marked by "high social and intellectual character" and also by a "humanitarian tendency."[58]

In this complex situation, the Congregationalists made a political mistake. "Driven to bay by deistic and utilitarian principles of Jefferson's democracy, they fell into the worldly error of defying the national instinct, pressing their resistance to the war until it amounted to treasonable conspiracy. The sudden peace swept away much that was respectable in the old society of America, but perhaps its noblest victim was the unity of the New England Church."

False though this ecclesiastical self-confidence might have been, the political theorists were notably less confident. The first sixteen years of the new century were "singularly barren of new political ideas." After the great flowering of ideas in the last quarter of the eighteenth century, Americans seemed interested only in the practical workings of their institutions rather than in developing the principles of their government. "The same tendency which in religion led to a reaction against dogma, was shown in politics by a general acquiescence in practices which left unsettled the disputed principles of government. No one could say with confidence what theory of the Constitution had prevailed. Neither party was satisfied, although both acquiesced."[59] In fact, constitutional law stood almost still for a time; John Marshall's great decisions such as *McCulloch v. Maryland*, the Dartmouth College case, and *Cohens v. Virginia* still lay ahead, outside the time frame of Adams's work. Still, *Fletcher v. Peck* and *Martin v. Hunter's Lessee*, the latter by Justice Story, solidified the power of the Supreme Court over the states. In the *Martin* case, the Court importantly held that the Constitution could in fact "operate on States in their corporate capacity."[60]

In the face of such decisions, Jefferson still clung to his states' rights principles, returning to his old theme that "the national and state governments were 'as independent, in fact, as different,' and that the function of one was foreign, while that of the other was domestic." For Madison's part, he still believed that Congress could not build internal improvements such as roads; when Congress did so, Madison responded with a veto. Adams concludes, "In politics as in theology, the practical system which resulted from sixteen years of experience seemed to rest on the agreement not to press principles to a conclusion."[61]

No really new political ideas were put forward. Old and incompatible ideas continued to exist together like theological dogmas, but there was a difference between the movement of political and religious thought. "The Church showed no tendency to unite in any creed or dogma, — indeed, religious society rather tended toward more divisions; but in politics public opinion slowly moved in a fixed direction." Jefferson might protest and Madison might veto internal improvements, but the movement was real. "No one doubted that a change had occurred since 1798. The favorite States-rights dogma of that time had suffered irreparable injury. For sixteen years the national government in all its branches had acted, without listening to remonstrance, on the rule that it was the rightful interpreter of its own powers. In this assumption, the Executive, the Legislature, and the Judiciary had agreed."[62] This meant in fact, if not in theory, that the Jeffersonians had accepted the Federalist theory of the Constitution, even down to rechartering the Bank of the United States, a point that is probably the most famous of the generalizations of the *History*. The only major theoretical work of the time was produced by John Taylor of Caroline, a voice crying in the wilderness, whose theory was historically obsolete as soon as it appeared. Even Taylor saw this, as he recognized that the Virginia school, while admiring the theory, did not follow its tenets.[63] In all except theory, the Jeffersonian tradition appeared exhausted, and even the theory was beside the point.

Be that as it may, it is clear that for Adams, the changes in national character that took place during the Jefferson and Madison years were more important than those that occurred in politics. As late as January 1815, division into several nationalities still seemed possible. The effects of division would certainly have been unpleasant, but no one at that time could imagine a single society on a continental scale, however much it might appeal as a sign of progress. And, Adams comments somewhat ominously, not to say prophetically, "The corruption of such a system might prove to be proportionate with its dimensions, and uniformity might lead to evils as serious as were commonly ascribed to diversity."[64]

War had proved to be a severe test, but in spite of the strange course of the struggle with England, the United States emerged more unified than before. Perhaps more importantly, the differences from other societies were better defined.

Already in 1817 the difference between Europe and America was decided. In politics the distinction was more evident than in social, religious, literary or scientific directions; and the result was singular. For a time the aggressions of England and France forced the United States into a path that seemed to lead toward European methods of government; but the popular resistance, or inertia, was so great that the most popular party leaders failed to overcome it; and no sooner did foreign dangers disappear than the system began to revert to American practices; the national government tried to lay aside its assumed powers.

The result was peculiar. Public opinion and practicality drove the nation toward a European standard of sovereignty, but the form that sovereignty assumed "diverged from any foreign type." To repeat, "The American," says Adams, "in his political character, was a new variety of man."[65]

The dynamic of society was changed and also decided. The gap between Europe and America grew, while interest in Europe lessened. France no longer affected American opinion, and the British generated less alarm. The influence of New England was reduced, and the social cachet of close ties to England eroded. Ocean commerce became more balanced, and the South and West produced "a character more aggressively American than had been known before." Again Adams turns prophetic, claiming, "That Europe, within certain limits, might tend toward American ideas was possible, but that America should under any circumstances follow the experiences of European development might thenceforward be reckoned as improbable. The American character was formed, if not fixed."[66]

This clearly is a statement of American exceptionalism, however much Adams seems to move toward the view that, at least in the realm of foreign policy, America would have to adopt a form of European realism according to which it would have to act as did other great powers. In spite of this, it is the difference from European society that Adams stresses. Just as Tocqueville claimed that a new science of politics would be required for the new nation, Adams sees the need for a new form of "scientific" history, a history able to cope with the economic development of a great democracy. The history of Europe had been a history of fierce struggle that made permanence scarce and exalted the heroic individual. In Europe, as Adams sees it, great men were more interesting than their societies, a fact that may account for the brilliance of his portrait of Napoleon. But, overlooking the Civil War that occurred between the period Adams studied and the time he wrote about it, American history looked able to avoid such turbulence. Of course, since Adams knew full well the massive upheaval that was to come, one must presume that he refers to the feelings of the American people in 1817. The Americans were not entirely happy with this placid condition. They felt the need for heroes precisely because they lived under conditions that made them unnecessary. "Instinctively they clung to ancient history as though conscious that of all the misfortunes that could befall the national character, the greatest would be the loss of the established ideals which alone ennobled human weakness."[67] (Obviously Adams would not easily be persuaded by Bertolt Brecht's remark that happy is the nation that needs no heroes. That may be too much to expect from one who came from such a distinguished lineage.)

But there might be compensation. "In a democratic ocean science could see something ultimate. Man could go no further. The atom might move, but the general equilibrium could not change." Adams could not completely commit himself to this idea, however, saying that whether the scientific or heroic view of history prevailed, the chief object of study remained the national character. Whether as heroes or types, the figures of history must represent the people. "American types were especially worth study if they were to represent the greatest democratic evolution the world could know. Readers might judge for themselves what share the individual possessed in creating or shaping the nation, but whether it was small or great, the nation could be understood only by studying the individual. For that reason, in the story of Jefferson and Madison individuals retained their old interest as types of character, if not as sources of power."[68]

The principal trait of the people was antipathy to war; such a people could hardly be expected to develop great administrative skill, and yet "the Americans prided themselves chiefly on their political capacity." Even the abundant evidence of the war did not remove this delusion. In spite of that, "That incapacity in national politics should appear as a leading trait in American character was unexpected by Americans, but might naturally result from their conditions."[69]

As has already been discussed, where Americans did shine was in their technological abilities, particularly when adapted to warfare. But these national traits told little about whether the native intelligence of Americans was of a high order or whether it led to a high morality. "Probably the political morality shown by the government and by public men during the first sixteen years of the century offered a fair gauge of social morality. . . . Time alone would decide whether it would result in a high or a low national ideal."[70]

Adams then sums up. "A vast amount of conservatism still lingered among the people; but the future spirit of society could hardly fail to be intelligent, rapid in movement, and mild in method." And then ominously, once more echoing Tocqueville, Adams adds, "If at any time American character should change, it might as probably become sluggish as revert to the violence and extravagances of Old-World development. The inertia of several hundred million people, all formed in a similar social mold, was as likely to stifle energy as to stimulate evolution."[71]

But this is not the end. As at the start, Adams has questions to ask, questions that, as Levenson says, were unanswerable by science and unanswered by history.[72] These questions conclude Adams's magnum opus:

The traits of American character were fixed. . . . They were intelligent, but what paths would their intelligence select? They were quick, but what solution of insoluble problems would quickness hurry? They were scientific, and what control would their science exercise over their destiny? They were mild, but what corruptions would their relaxations bring? They were peaceful, but by what machinery would their corruptions be purged? What interests were to vivify a society so vast and uniform? What ideals were to ennoble it? What object, besides physical content, must a democratic continent aspire to attain? For the treatment of such questions, history required another century of experience.[73]

The importance of these questions is obvious, but at the same time, they are more than a little disingenuous. Adams published them in 1891, seventy-four years after the time about which they were raised. They had, in fact, been at least partially answered by history. Adams knew more than a little about the corruptions that would afflict Americans and how they would deal, or not deal, with them. His thoughts on this subject are considered in the next chapter, but first it is important to consider the philosophy of history that began to emerge out of his great study of the Jefferson and Madison administrations.

Toward a Philosophy of History

It is only later in his career that Adams develops a full-scale philosophy of history. However, the germs of that theory are evident in the pages of his accounts of Jefferson and Madison: the decline of the heroic individual shaping history by force of will; the idea that in democratic societies, only science can account for the important role of the collective people; and a growing, though still muted, interest in evolution. The discussion of the impact of Darwin and Spencer on his thought can best be left aside for the time being, though a few words of summary can be offered on the other topics.

The interest in science is evident early on. In 1862 he wrote to his brother Charles, "Man has mounted science, and is now run away with. I firmly believe that before many centuries more, science will be the master of man. The engines he will have invented will be beyond his strength to control. Some day science may have the existence of mankind in its power, and the human race commit suicide, by blowing up the world."[74] A little over a year later, again writing to Charles, his scientific speculations grow more specific. "The truth is everything in this universe has its regular waves and tides. Electricity, sound, the wind, and I believe every part of organic nature will be brought someday within this law . . . [and] as I entertain a profound conviction of the littleness of our kind, and of the curious enormity of creation, I am quite ready to receive with pleasure any basis for a systematic conception of it all. . . . I look for regular tides in the affairs of man, and, of course, in our own affairs."[75]

Given this cast of mind, it is not surprising that Adams's interpretation of American history concludes with a sharp focus on the national character, which he takes to be the proper object of analysis in any democratic society. A large number of people provides a sufficient N, as statisticians call it, to be able to make scientific generalizations of the sort Adams wanted. That said, large statistical samples have hardly brought the scientific advances that modern social analysts hoped for. And as for Adams, the pull of the humanist was very strong throughout all his work, even, or perhaps especially, when the force of science loomed particularly large. The compromise for Adams in the *History* is the idea that great men serve as types representative of the nation's people, though even this does not fit easily into Adams's schema. In his eyes,

Madison is certainly small enough to be treated as a mere type, but since the people emerge as so much greater than he, one wonders how he could be truly representative. As for Jefferson, almost the reverse is true. Regardless of his failings, he towers over the first half of the *History*, so that there can be no way to avoid the conclusion that Adams sees him as a great man and possessed of a character deeply fascinating to the sensitive observer. Yet even Jefferson could not control history. Its tides, particularly in a democratic society, were too strong. After all, even Napoleon, in corrupt old Europe—a setting Adams considered more conducive than democracy to heroic leadership—failed in the end. The failure of Napoleon is an apt comparison, because it suggests the theory of history expounded in Tolstoy's *War and Peace*.[76] In Tolstoy's novel, neither Napoleon nor the Russian leaders have any real control over events. Those who think they know the most are more foolish than the rest. History is determined by forces beyond the control of leaders. The heroes of Tolstoy's great novel are the simple Russian peasants symbolized by Platon Karataev; stolid, phlegmatic General Kutuzov, who has the sense to wait for Napoleon to destroy himself; and the saintly Pierre Bezukov. The only truly wise characters are those who do not pretend to know what they do not know. The general outline of Adams's view is similar to Tolstoy's, though there are significant differences. Tolstoy is a devoted Rousseauian, deeply dedicated, despite his riches, to the simple life; hence the love for Platon displayed in the novel. But Adams is anything but a simple lifer, nor did Rousseau appeal to him. And Tolstoy would adamantly reject all of Adams's pretensions to science, however qualified. Moreover, Tolstoy is that strange being, an anti-intellectual intellectual. By no standard could this apply to Adams, in spite of what a reader of *Mont Saint Michel and Chartres* might think, though he would surely have taken malicious delight in Tolstoy's hilarious burlesque of standard historical accounts centered on the hero.[77] What Adams does share with Tolstoy is a sense of the overwhelming complexity of human life. It is not ill will that causes Jefferson to betray his principles. To a great extent, Jefferson is redeemed in spite of his many flaws because he means well. But goodwill is not enough to master the forces of history. This is why even a highly principled leader, let alone one sometimes beset by character weaknesses, will find it difficult, if not impossible, to implement his ideals.

As William Merrill Decker suggests, the fact of moral failure is frequently evident, but its inevitability does not break out too often in the book. However, Adams draws out the scientific, deterministic lessons of his history more explicitly in his letters, perhaps revealing more clearly there how frustrated he is by the failure of the Jeffersonians to elevate the people they led. Writing to Samuel Tilden, Adams says, "I am at times almost sorry that I ever undertook to write their history, for they appear like mere grass-hoppers, kicking and gesticulating, on the middle of the Mississippi River. There is no possibility of reconciling their theories with their acts, or their extraordinary foreign policy with dignity. They were carried along on a stream which floated them after a fashion without much regard to themselves." More theoretically, he adds, "My own conclusion is that history is simply social development along the lines of weakest resistance, and that in most cases the line of weakened resistance is found as unconsciously by society as by water."[78]

But Adams, like most writers who profess some form of determinism, is unable to accept fully the logic of his own theory. This accounts for the full treatment received by true heroes, for good or ill, such as Napoleon or even Jefferson, and it allows him to slight "mediocrities" such as Madison. As Decker brilliantly suggests, this may be why Adams ends the last volume of the series with a set of questions to be answered in the future, rather than a more resounding conclusion. "It is thus," he argues, "that Adams suspends what had been his problem all along: his practical inability to treat human history as the amoral, dehumanized force field it is required to be by the inquiry he prophesies but never practices."[79] This also is his way of trying to escape Tolstoy's dilemma, the dilemma, in Isaiah Berlin's terms, of a fox consumed by his boundless knowledge of the frailties inherent in the human condition but who wanted to be a hedgehog, able to find one great idea that would allow him to reconcile his vast store of information with some moral ideal.[80] It remains to be discussed whether Adams succeeded in avoiding this problem throughout the rest of his long career.

It is also important to see that Adams's disappointment at the failure of Jefferson and Madison to elevate the people is much less a move to disparage the people than it is a comment on the failings of their upper-class leaders. And the Jeffersonians, however inept, devious, cowardly, or mendacious, get off lightly compared with their ultra-Federalist opponents, their ancient enemies, and also, of course, the Adams family foes. Commenting on the Burr conspiracy, Adams notes that the Federalists, who constituted almost the whole of fashionable society, professed disbelief in the existence of the conspiracy. And well they might, because "Burr's conspiracy, like that of Pickering and Griswold, had no deep roots in society, but was mostly confined to a circle of well-born, well-bred, and well-educated individuals, whose want of moral sense was one more proof that the moral instinct had little to do with social distinction."[81] No argument that Adams was an antidemocratic misanthrope can stand against comments like these. At most, Adams shows a skepticism about human nature, perhaps a residual Puritanism, that applies to all classes. It emerges, in Adams's narrative, when he considers the most virulent forms of behavior in upper-class leaders who are likely to be in a position to do harm. But Adams, in spite of his skepticism, is ever the moralist with the New England conscience, a conscience easily visible behind the facade of positivist history and always ready to pass judgment. Surely this is part of the greatness of the *History*.

Chapter 4

Secession, Capitalism, and Corruption

In the *History*, Adams lays a massive empirical and theoretical foundation for the interpretation of American development and begins to grope toward a more general philosophy of history. However, the period from the end of the Madison administration until after the Civil War receives comparatively little attention in Adams's published writings. Perhaps this is because he felt, as he claims in the *Education*, that between his friend John Hay's biography of Lincoln and his own history of the Jefferson and Madison administrations, most of the American history worth writing had been written.[1] There are passing comments on the presidency of Andrew Jackson and some discussion of the evils of slavery and secession, but there is no sustained analysis until the postwar journalism on politics and finance and the remarks on those subjects in the *Education*; the novel *Democracy* is also interesting from the perspective of political theory, though as a novel it leaves something to be desired. (His second novel, *Esther*, is also of interest in connection with the relation of science to religion and with his general philosophy.) The journalism is selective in its coverage but is of a very high standard and is worth reading to this day, both for historical information and for Adams's mordant commentary and the often highly polemical, sometimes over-the-top style, which reveals a good deal of his political thought. Of course, one can also learn a great deal from the *Education*, but by the time he wrote it, Adams had abandoned history as such and offers instead a highly introspective, not to say idiosyncratic, commentary not just on events but even more on the life of his own very complex mind. In the *Education*, we can see a speculative interpretation of American history, as well as speculation on the fate of the world, but without the massive supporting evidence presented in the multiple volumes on Jefferson and Madison. Perhaps, in some sense, Adams has earned our trust with the massive *History*. In any case, we should not miss the supporting empirical structure in the *Education*, since the result is one of the great masterpieces of American thought and literature. And, for all the sketchiness of his post-Madison historical writing, there are still many points worthy of note. While he offers no general theory or systematic history of the United States after 1817, he does offer interesting ideas about the relation of the slave power to the Civil War, the emergence of large-scale industrial capitalism with its attendant corruption, and the rise of empire. This important material reflects a well-developed worldview.

From Madison to the Civil War

Andrew Jackson claimed to be a successor of Jefferson, but he receives none of the indulgence Adams sometimes allowed his great predecessor. If Jefferson was an old Adams family friend, Jackson was an old family enemy. There was great bitterness in the relations between John Quincy Adams and Jackson, growing out of Adams's disputed victory over Jackson in the election of 1824 and the triumph of Jackson in 1828. Moreover, Jackson stood for much that the Adams family found deeply distasteful. The principal commentary on Jackson appears in an odd form, namely, a review of a lecture by the German historian Gustav von Holst that consists almost entirely of quotes from its subject.[2] Since Adams allows von Holst to speak for him, one is tempted to assume that he must have endorsed von Holst's very harsh conclusions. Noting that Jackson had won a plurality of both the popular and the electoral vote in the 1824 election, von Holst points out that Jackson's contention was that in choosing John Quincy Adams as president, the House of Representatives had "presumed to trample upon the will of the people," a point loudly echoed by those same people. But, he continues, the more fundamental will of the people lies in the Constitution. Jackson's position "demanded the subordination of the well-considered popular will, which had been fixed as a permanent fundamental law, to the momentary wish of the people, which in part could only be ascertained by unsafe conjectures." Thus the *considered* will of the people, von Holst contended, was for indirect election, with the House of Representatives deciding in the case of failure to win a majority. For von Holst, it followed that since the people had established the Constitution, any charges of an undemocratic system must be laid at the feet of the people themselves. And, even more contentiously, if Jackson's election four years later was a triumph of true democracy, "it was a victory of the people over their own self-appointed provisions,"[3] an argument that makes no sense, since Jackson won the election of 1828 via the procedures prescribed by the Constitution.

The president's character is treated with similar sharpness. "Since Louis XIV, the maxim *l'etat c'est moi* has hardly found a second time so naively complete expression as in Andrew Jackson." And combining his animosity toward Jackson with his derisive attitude toward the American people, von Holst goes on, "As Washington was the incorporation of the best traits of the people, Jackson was the incorporation of *all* its typical traits."[4] Not surprisingly then, von Holst had particular scorn for the Jacksonian idea of the president as tribune of the people. No one had conceived the possibility that the president might become the defender of the Constitution against Congress. That role was reserved to the judicial branch. "The Constitution knows a President only as a bearer of the executive power; of a 'direct representative of the American people' it knows nothing. Hence, too, it knows nothing of a choice of President 'by the people.'"[5]

However, in spite of appearances, it is unwise to conclude too easily that Adams's mode of presentation implies endorsement of von Holst's strictures. Von Holst's argument certainly reflects Adams's constitutional purism, discussed in more detail later, and doubtless no member of the Adams clan felt any warm regard for the old general. Still, as is already clear from the *History*, Adams displays none of the hostility to the American common man that is evident in von Holst's essay. If anything, in the *History*, Adams argues that it is political elites who have failed the people. Thus, the strange "review" of von Holst's pamphlet remains a mysterious anomaly. Probably we should see the piece as a straightforward report on the content of von Holst's remarks, for whatever they are worth, and be wary of reading very much of Adams's own beliefs into it. Given the absence of any commentary by Adams, this seems the safest course.

The Civil War

It is a pity we have so little else from Adams on the period from the end of the Madison administration to the end of the Civil War. That Adams had a hearty dislike of the slave system and the Old South, always with the somewhat partial and grudging exception of Jefferson, is already clear. The political influence of the "slave power" did not admit of any "defense or palliation." The great curse was that "slavery warped the Constitution itself in a manner that for the time amounted to absolute perversion."[6]

The closest Adams comes to a systematic treatment of the events leading to the war is in his brief, and very polemical, biography of John Randolph, published in 1882. This book gives an early look at one of the central theses of the *History*, the idea that the Jeffersonians capitulated to the Federalist idea of centralization, though they did so, ironically, as the Federalists embraced decentralization and secession. Adams clearly thought that Southern leaders such as Randolph bore a heavy burden of responsibility for this development and for the outbreak of war, a process in which Randolph is cast in a particularly villainous role. According to Adams, Randolph was behind the perversion of the essentially sound doctrine of states' rights, which in 1800 was a mere "fragment of republican dogma."[7] Oddly, for a nationalist member of a strongly nationalist family, Adams pays lip service to the states' rights doctrine. Initially, the Jeffersonians were at least sincere in their beliefs. "The constitution of the republican party was the federalists constitution read backward, like a medieval invocation of the devil; and this was in many respects and for ordinary times the best and safest way of reading it," though it was quickly abandoned as anything other than a party shibboleth.[8] Of course, one should be skeptical of Adams's apparent endorsement of Jeffersonian constitutional theory. Given his propensity for irony and his apparent rejection of those ideas in the *History*, it is probable that Adams should not be taken literally on this issue.[9] But, be that as it may, Adams takes seriously the Virginian's claim that the election of 1800 marked a new era. Adams writes that in Jefferson's mind, "what had gone before was monarchism; what came after was alone true republicanism. However absurdly this doctrine may have sounded to northern ears, and to men who knew the relative character of New England and Virginia, the still greater absurdities of leading federalists lent some color of truth to it."[10]

Nevertheless, as Adams saw it, the Jeffersonian reforms remained largely on the surface, leaving the legislative and executive branches substantially unchanged and fearing to make basic constitutional change, thus leaving in place the "terrible" necessary and proper clause.[11] Once again, though he delivers this judgment in the most straightforward way, it is hard to read this without suspecting irony.

But the Jeffersonians quickly threw away their principles when they welded the slave power and states' rights together. When these doctrines were combined, the slave power became dominant, and the list of its triumphs was long: "The slave power, when in control, was a centralizing influence, and all the most considerable encroachments on states' rights were its acts. The acquisition and admission of Louisiana; the embargo; the war of 1812; the annexation of Texas 'by joint resolution;' the war with Mexico, declared by the mere announcement of President Polk; the Fugitive Slave Law; the Dred Scott decision," all these destroyed the "very memory of states' rights as they existed in 1789."[12] This was a "prostitution" of states' rights "begun by Randolph, and only at a later time consummated by Calhoun." Thus, "Randolph organized the South. Calhoun himself learned his lesson from the speeches of this man."[13] In this perhaps somewhat hyperbolic formulation, the slave power emerges as the principal force behind much of American historical development in the first half of the nineteenth century.

It is no accident that the chapter in the *Education* dealing with 1860–1861 is called simply "Treason."[14] A brief summary of Adams's views appears in his *Life of Gallatin:*

> In fact, the politics of the United States from 1830 to 1849 offered as melancholy a spectacle as satirists ever held up to derision. Of all the parties that have existed in the United States, the famous Whig party was the most feeble in ideas and the most blundering in management; the Jacksonian democracy was corrupt in its methods; and both, as well as society itself, were deeply cankered with two desperate sores: the enormous increase of easily acquired wealth, and the terribly rapid growth of slavery and the slave power.[15]

This passage gives a good idea of the depths of the midcentury crisis. But although Adams offers some interesting brief comments in an essay published in 1876, we have from him no really deep analysis of the causes of the war, other than his deep dislike of the "slave power conspiracy," nor even any careful assessment of Abraham Lincoln. This last omission is particularly strange. To an extent, this may be due to the fact that throughout the war, Adams was in London as secretary to his ambassador father and so did not see Lincoln up close, in action, as president. It may also reflect his prejudice against the West from which Lincoln sprang. But there may be a more directly personal reason for his near-total silence on Lincoln. In spite of his somewhat feeble attempts as an activist, Adams had no love for politics, while Lincoln, in addition to his other qualities, was a great master of the political arts. Moreover, Lincoln's political concerns once intruded directly on a meeting between Lincoln and Henry's father, Charles Francis Adams. The senior Adams had not supported Lincoln for president, though he did campaign for him. Still, he was horrified when, on seeing the president in connection with his appointment as ambassador to the Court of St. James, Lincoln told him that he could thank William Henry Seward for the honor and, turning to Seward, began to discuss a post office appointment in Chicago.[16] This was hardly politics as the often self-righteous Adams family understood it, and the incident no doubt created a bad impression of the new president.

Early on, I discussed the high idealism of the young Henry Adams. In this he participated in a family tradition of long standing. To the Adamses, mere political expediency was a mortal danger. As Charles Francis Adams wrote:

The first and greatest qualification of a statesman in my estimation, is the mastery of the whole theory of morals which makes the foundation of all human society: The great and everlasting question of the right and wrong of every act whether of individual men or collective bodies. The next is the application of the knowledge thus gained to the events of his time in a continuous and systematic way. . . . The feebleness of perception and the deliberate abandonment of moral principles in action are the two prevailing characteristics of public men. . . . No person can ever be a thorough partisan for a long period without sacrifice of his moral identity. The skill consists in knowing exactly where to draw the line.[17]

This attitude toward political morality pervades the entire Adams family throughout its four generations of prominence, and the point about the moral danger of partisanship looks ahead to the character of Silas Ratcliffe in Adams's novel *Democracy*. Clearly it fosters a strong sense of independence and a ready willingness to defy party discipline, which influenced the thought of Henry Adams as well as his brief and not very successful interventions into the political world.[18] It is also an attitude that makes a political career difficult for someone who sees politics as merely "the systematic organization of hatreds."[19] A tender-hearted idealist cannot help but recoil from such an understanding of the political life, particularly given the fact that all too often it is accurate enough.

This deeply ingrained moralism created another dilemma for the members of the Adams family, or at least those of the third and fourth generations. The problem was that along with this fierce judgmental streak, which led, quite understandably, to the condemnation of slavery, came an equally deep faith in the Constitution. Though this faith stopped "this side of idolatry," there was still a belief in the system of separation of powers, checks and balances, and federalism that dated from the time of John Adams, the founding patriarch. This led Henry's father to oppose militant abolitionists such as William Lloyd Garrison, who had denounced the Constitution as a "covenant with death and an agreement with hell." But surely Garrison was not entirely wrong in calling attention to the constitutional compromises with slavery; moreover, the Adamses' attempt to fuse these two moral imperatives failed, and the family members left the Republican Party when leaders they took to be extremists assumed control.[20] The irony is that, had they understood Lincoln's position better, they would have realized that the president's goal was to preserve the Constitution while fighting the expansion of slavery, in the expectation, right or wrong, that slavery would be extinguished if it could be contained within the territory where it already existed. Given this, Lincoln should have been one of their best allies. Indeed, it was Lincoln's political savvy that helped hold the fragile Northern coalition together in pursuit of the end of the slavery that both he and the Adams family despised.[21] It is odd, then, that even in describing his family's policy toward slavery, Adams does not recognize the similarity to Lincoln's approach. He comments on the differences between the radical and moderate Republican opponents, saying: "The policy of the one wing led to a violent destruction of the slave-power; perhaps by war, perhaps by a slave insurrection. The policy of the other wing was to prevent a separation in order to keep the slave-power more effectually under control, until its power for harm should be gradually exhausted and its whole fabric gently and peacefully sapped away." The latter position was essentially Lincoln's, though, as it turned out, even under Lincoln's leadership, great violence was necessary to bring an end to the primal curse of American history. It should also be pointed out that Adams is prescient in summarizing the moderate position in the same discussion where he foresees that the outcome of Civil War might cause the slave power to be "restored to its old position, perhaps at the expense of the northern tier of states."[22]

But even the Adams family split over questions of principle. Looking on the Civil War scene from London in 1862, Henry and his father, with characteristic idealism, supported the proposal of General Hunter to enlist freedmen in the Union army. Charles Francis, Jr., from his position at the front, disagreed sharply, expressing deep-seated feelings about what he took to be the racial inferiority of the slaves. George Fredrickson contends that in this, Henry and his father did not in fact have a serious disagreement with Charles Francis, Jr. Rather, "his military experience had narrowed his perspective" while giving him contact with poor, uneducated Negroes, which "brought out the latent snobbishness and horror of equality which upper-class New Englanders living in the safety of Boston or London did not have to acknowledge." Fredrickson goes on to add that "the war was shaping a generation that would have little respect for the broad enthusiasms of their elders."[23] The last point is essentially true. After the war, the political emphasis shifted to economic expansion, political corruption, and the emergence of empire; Reconstruction was not the only problem facing the Union after the war, though the downplaying of the position of the former slaves was to have lasting and tragic consequences. Still, *during* the war, Henry Adams did, in fact, support arming the slaves, and we should not be too quick to deny him his bona fides at this stage in his career.

The Postwar Revolution

And yet, in spite of his clear detestation of the slave power and his almost apoc-
alyptic pronouncements on the need for its root-and-branch destruction,
Adams rapidly lost interest in Reconstruction. As Brooks Simpson says,
"Adams quickly abandoned earlier notions of revenge, military rule, and treason trials in favor of reconciling the wayward white brothers of the defeated
Confederacy." In particular, "Never did he display the slightest awareness, let
alone concern, about the plight of American blacks. When he spoke of minority rights, he meant the right of white Southerners to home rule. . . . The deepest evil of Reconstruction was not the violence against blacks in the South,
but the alleged violence done the constitution by Republicans seeking to protect those blacks."[24] Thus he could write, in this context, that "my blood boils"
thinking about Reconstruction.[25] This concern for a form of constitutional
purism is characteristic of much of Adams's thought, which sometimes leads
to a rather narrow view of politics. This sense that slavery, once abolished,
would cease to be a problem lies at the heart of a shrewd observation by Judith
Shklar: "It never occurred to Adams that slavery was more than a wrong to be
undone once and for all, that it was an ineradicable curse that would not be
ended in a battle but would haunt future generations and poison the body
politic."[26] This narrowly constitutional view of an important issue is a subject
to which it will be necessary to return. Here, however, it must be said that this
is a serious moral and political blind spot and is perhaps the greatest single
weakness in Adams's interpretation of the overall course of American history.

Adams offers little in the way of a systematic interpretation of the latter
part of the nineteenth century, though he makes many interesting observations, and the general outline of his position is clear enough. He believes that
the war touched off a seismic change in American life and politics, but the
nature of that upheaval is not spelled out in detail. At least twice he alludes
to the idea that the war resulted in a revolution. Writing from the perspective of 1868, he notes that the revolution of 1861 was "nearly complete" and
states proudly that "for the first time in history, the American felt himself
almost as strong as an Englishman."[27] Shortly after, and more obliquely, he
notes that by then, nine-tenths of his education was useless "and the other
tenth harmful," thus signifying a tremendous change that rendered previous
conceptions of politics and society obsolete. In this, Adams saw himself as
typical of his time. "All parties were mixed up and jumbled together in a sort
of tidal slack-water. The Government resembled Adams himself in the matter of education. All that had gone before was useless, and some of it was

worse."[28] This is somewhat cryptic, but if one examines his writings after the war, several things of momentous significance stand out.

There was a wave of corruption, both political and financial, that swept across the nation and was the focus of his attention for several years. This was, in Adams's view, not merely routine chicanery but rather the symptom of a profound constitutional derangement in which the all-important balance between the legislative and executive branches was upset. There was also the emergence of corporate capitalism and the social upheaval associated with it and, not least, the explosive growth of industrial technology. Later he would fear the great wave of late-nineteenth-century immigration. Closely related to all this was a crisis of democratic constitutionalism, discussed first in a brilliant essay occasioned by the bicentennial of the Constitution and then, a few years later, by the penetrating if excessively didactic novel *Democracy*. And then the movement of nineteenth-century history was climaxed by the sudden development of an empire, alluded to in the remark about the growing parity between the United States and Great Britain. The result is a sense of the emergence of inchoate, uncontrolled, and, in the end, uncontrollable change:

> Society in America was always trying, almost as blindly as an earthworm, to realize and understand itself; to catch up with its own head, and to twist about in search of its tail. Society offered the profile of a long, straggling caravan, stretching loosely toward the prairies, its few score of leaders far in advance and its millions of immigrants, Negroes, and Indians far in the rear, somewhere in archaic time. It enjoyed the vast advantage over Europe that all seemed, for the moment, to move in one direction, while Europe wasted most of its energy in trying several contradictory movements at once; but whenever Europe or Asia should be polarized or oriented toward the same point, America might easily lose her lead.[29]

Though their basic insights are not necessarily more acute, several contemporary scholars have conceptualized more concisely the momentous changes that occurred in the wake of the Civil War. Barrington Moore, along with Charles Beard, sees the Civil War and its aftermath as the last great capitalist revolution.[30] And of course, war and Reconstruction brought about, through the Thirteenth, Fourteenth, and Fifteenth Amendments, a profound constitutional change that still reverberates and is clearly one of the great watersheds of American history, a revolution that transformed, and is still transforming, the relations of nation, state, and individual. Although it took a very long time to work out the full implications of this, the question became not whether the rights of sovereign states trumped individual rights but which individual rights were so fundamental as to require national protection.[31] For Robert Wiebe, what characterizes this period is the search for order in a world in which old communities were crumbling under the force of the organizational revolution wrought by the emergence of the giant industrial corporations.[32] For Howard Mumford Jones, this is the age of energy, not just the tremendous release of tamed physical energy but, even more, the explosive creative energy, employed for better and worse, of all manner of Americans, including the builders of the giant organizations described by Wiebe. Thus, Jones writes, by this idea "I mean the discovery, use, exploitation, and expression of energy, whether it be that of personality or of prime movers or of words."[33] But no one has summarized the problems that emerged more concisely than Sidney Fine:

> The United States of 1900 was quite a different place from the United States of 1860, for during the intervening years America was transformed from an agricultural society into an industrialized, urbanized society. In 1860 the total capital invested in manufacturing was something over one billion dollars; by 1900 the figure had jumped to almost ten billion dollars. During the same period the number of wage earners increased from approximately 1,300,000 to about 5,300,000. By 1900 the total value of the products of manufacturing industries was almost two and one-half times as great as the total value of farm products. And whereas 16.1 per cent of the American people lived in cities of 8000 inhabitants or more in 1800, by 1900 the proportion living in such communities had increased to 32.9 per cent.
>
> Industrialization and urbanization intensified old problems and brought with them a host of new ones. The American people had to decide what to do about slums and tenements, public health, the wages, hours, and working conditions of standard and sub-standard labor, unemployment, and increased inequalities in the distribution of wealth, railroads, and industrial combinations. Although, for the most part, the intervention of government was required for the solution of these issues, existing theories with respect to the role of the state constituted an intellectual barrier to the development of any realistic program of state action. Jeffersonian-Jacksonian liberalism was already an anachronism in the America of the years after the Civil War.[34]

Clearly this was not the America into which Henry Adams had been born. It is little wonder that he seems to have experienced something like what we call culture shock or that his theory of American history in his time was a little sketchy. Perhaps it is more remarkable how much he did manage to see. And, for the sake of perspective, one might raise the question, how sure can *we* be of the long-term historical significance of the events of our *own* time?

Many, though not all, of the themes mentioned here were intertwined in Adams's work, even if in an unsystematic way. And the problems he did not take up are revealing about the nature and limitations of his thought. Perhaps it is best to consider his relevant writings more or less in chronological order, since his developing thought was closely linked to political and economic issues of his time. In some sense, like one of Michael Walzer's connected critics, in his historical and critical writing in the decades after the Civil War, Adams does not, for all his brilliance, emerge very far from the cave so wonderfully described by Plato. His preoccupation was with the here and now rather than with developing some independent standard of political morality. The starting point for much of Adams's concern is his disappointment, not to say disgust, with the Grant administration.

President Grant was a huge disappointment for men like Henry Adams who had supported his election and had hoped for good things from his administration. Presumably, given the disaster of Andrew Johnson's presidency, there was indeed reason for hope, yet Adams's brief remarks on Johnson reveal a characteristically quirky perspective. Recalling his one meeting with Johnson in the White House, Adams suggests that the president seemed utterly commonplace, and Adams felt no wish to see him again, "for Andrew Johnson was not the sort of man whom a young reformer of thirty, with two or three foreign educations, was likely to see with enthusiasm." Yet years later, he writes that he was "surprised to realize how strong the Executive was in 1868—perhaps the strongest he was ever to see."[35] Today this seems a decidedly odd perspective, given the disaster that was the Johnson presidency, though it highlights how hapless Adams felt Johnson's successors to be. In any case, Adams felt that he had every reason to be hopeful about Grant. Exploring the parallel with George Washington, Adams reasoned that a general who had organized huge numbers of men on the battlefield must know how to administer. There might be confusion in the old slave states and about the currency, "but the general disposition was good, and everyone had echoed the famous phrase: 'Let us have peace.'"[36]

But disillusionment soon set in, with Adams reflecting that someone as young as he was could be easily deceived. "Had Grant been a Congressman one would have been on one's guard, for one knew the type." Warming to his subject, Adams begins a vituperative set piece of the sort that often appeared in the journalism of the period. Recounting that he had once urged patience on a cabinet member in his dealings with a congressman, the secretary had exploded, "You can't use tact with a Congressman! A Congressman is a hog!" Adams professes to find this rather too harsh but is not deterred from raising the question, "If a Congressman is a hog, what is a Senator?" And he adds,

> Even Adams admitted that Senators passed belief. The comic side of their egotism partly disguised its extravagance, but faction had gone so far under Andrew Johnson that at times the whole Senate seemed to catch hysterics of nervous bucking without apparent reason. Great leaders, like Sumner and Conkling, could not be burlesqued; they were more grotesque than ridicule could make them; even Grant, who rarely sparkled in epigram, became witty on their account; but their egotism and factitiousness were no laughing matter. They did permanent and terrible mischief, as Garfield and Blaine, and even McKinley and John Hay, were to feel. The most troublesome task of a reform president was that of bringing the Senate back to decency.[37]

Adams saw little hope that a career politician could accomplish such a Herculean task; thus his support for Grant. Here Adams saw a role for himself, though one that seems more than a little cavalier for a constitutional purist. "He was eager to join in the fight which he foresaw as sooner or later inevitable. He meant to support the Executive in attacking the Senate and taking away its two-thirds vote and power of confirmation, nor did he much care how it should be done, for he thought it safer to effect the revolution in 1870 than to wait till 1920."[38]

But by simply announcing the membership of his cabinet, Grant dashed Adams's hopes. Adams was to become inured to poor cabinet choices, but "Grant's nominations had the singular effect of making the hearer ashamed, not so much of Grant, as of himself. He had made another total misconception of life—another inconceivable false start." About these nominees, "Senators made no secret of saying with senatorial frankness that . . . [they] betrayed his intent as plainly as they betrayed his incompetence. A great soldier might be a baby politician."[39] Doubtless Adams's disappointment was intensified by the fact that Grant's choices made it clear that there would be no place for men of Adams's type in the new administration. But the ambitions of Henry Adams aside, no one can claim that the Grant administration was a great success, and Adams unleashed a torrent of criticism, sometimes intemperate, but usually justified, starting with the person of the president himself.

To begin with, Adams thought the president's cabinet to be, for the most part, not only inimical to an Adams but of a quality whose only real virtue was that it promised to make his life as a literary figure cheery, since it would be an ideal object for ridicule. In particular, the name of Treasury Secretary George Boutwell suggested a "somewhat lugubrious joke." One could only look to the president and hope for the best. Still, Adams is willing to concede that Grant intended reform and that he aimed to put his administration above politics. Therefore, the main hope lay in assessing Grant's character.[40]

But the results of this investigation were deeply discouraging. Adams accepts the judgment of his friend, journalist Adam Badeau, that Grant "appeared as an intermittent energy, immensely powerful when awake, but passive and plastic in repose." And when Badeau took him to the White House to meet the president, Adams's own judgment was even harsher. Of the twelve presidents he had known, Grant struck him as the most "curious," noting that "a single word from Grant satisfied him that, for his own good, the fewer words he risked, the better." To drive home the point, he adds that for Grant, like Garibaldi, "the intellect counted for nothing; only the energy counted. The type was pre-intellectual, archaic, and would have seemed so even to the cave-dwellers. Adam, according to legend, was such a man." The products of Grant's mind tended to be vacuous commonplaces. His irritation rising, Adams continues that Grant "had no right to exist. He should have been extinct for ages." And to nail down the point, he puts the matter into the framework of the then fashionable theory of evolution, though not at all to the benefit of the theory: "That, two thousand years after Alexander the Great and Julius Caesar, a man like Grant should be called—and should actually and truly be—the highest product of the most advanced evolution, made evolution ludicrous. One must be as commonplace as Grant's own commonplaces to maintain such an absurdity. The progress of evolution from President Washington to President Grant, was alone evidence enough to upset Darwin."[41]

It is hard to overestimate the disappointment Adams felt in all this. He plaintively declares that all he wanted was someone to support; he did not even ask for office. In this, alluding to his closeness to John Hay, who was to be secretary of state in the McKinley and Theodore Roosevelt cabinets, Adams says that he was fifty years ahead of his time.[42]

It was in this mood that much of Adams's most important journalism was conceived. For him, the Grant administration was a turning point in American history and in his personal political hopes. In these brilliant, if often vituperative, political essays, there is no doubt that Adams deliberately planned to make his mark by rocking the boat as hard as his formidable talent for invective allowed. Certainly this is the most colorful writing in Adams's career. He sees the combination of political and financial chicanery so characteristic of the period as having its roots in the Civil War. It produced a new system out of the chaos, and the chaos bred life rather than the habit that comes with order, a life perhaps not unlike the release of energy seen by Howard Mumford Jones[43] and, of course, a life not always directed to the highest ends. Part of this energy was produced because "the Civil War in America, with its enormous issues of depreciated currency and its reckless waste of money and credit by the government, created a speculative mania such as the United States, with all its experience in this respect, had never before known."[44] It was probably this wave of speculation that lay behind the intense dislike of the banking industry that was so marked in Adams's work. Speaking of Hugh McCulloch, Johnson's secretary of the treasury, he commented:

> He was a banker, and towards bankers Adams felt the narrow prejudice which the serf feels toward his overseer; for he knew he must obey, and he knew that the helpless showed only their helplessness when they tempered obedience by mockery. The world, after 1865, became a banker's world, and no banker would ever treat one who had deserted State Street, and had gone to Washington with purposes of doubtful credit, or of no credit at all, for he could not have put up enough collateral to borrow five thousand dollars of any bank in America. The banker would never trust him, and he would never trust the banker.[45]

It was in this mood that Adams made his first sally into the field of contemporary politics and finance. This was his article "The Legal Tender Act," published in April 1870 in the *North American Review*, which he proudly described as "a piece of intolerably impudent political abuse."[46] Here he looked back to what he saw as the origin of much of the postwar troubles. His target was the 1862 issuance of Treasury notes as legal tender, as opposed to hard currency, in violation of what Adams took to be the natural laws of economics.[47] In his view, it was this weakening of government credit that opened the door to the speculative abuses that were to follow.[48] But as important as these consequences were, they were perhaps no more serious to Adams than what they revealed about the quality of political leadership. Military disasters might have been expected, but 200 years of experience should, in his view, have insured against the political mistakes that were made. Sadly, however, "Among the leading statesmen then charged with responsibility, not one was by training well fitted to perform the duties of finance minister, or to guide the financial opinions of Congress." The disaster was particularly the fault of the House of Representatives and, above all, of Thaddeus Stevens, chairman of the Ways and Means Committee. Justifying his claim to impudence, Adams comments that "Mr. Stevens was as little suited to direct the economical policy of the country at a critical moment as a naked Indian from the plains to plan the architecture of St. Peter's or to direct the construction of the Capitol, expresses in no extreme language the degree of his unfitness. That Stevens was grossly ignorant of all economical subjects and principles was the least of his deficiencies." To these had to be added dogmatism, a hot temper, and an "overbearing will."[49]

In addition to the deficiencies of Stevens, those of Elbridge Spaulding, chairman of an influential Ways and Means subcommittee dealing with national currency, loans, and Treasury notes and bonds, had to be considered. Spaulding did have experience and was proud to be both a banker and a legislator. But for Adams, his distrust of banks surfacing, this very qualification was part of the problem. "Had he not been a banker as well as a legislator, the Legal Tender Act might never have been enacted."[50] An uneducated Congress led by incompetent men was a dangerous thing; this was the problem. The oddity is that those who backed the act claimed to be protecting the people from bankers and brokers by creating paper money, "which has always been and always will be the most efficient instrument ever discovered for the purposes of this very class of men." But even Adams admits that the bankers could have replied to the abuse heaped on them by pointing to the inconsistencies that disfigured the legislative arguments on behalf of the act, particularly the use of the plea of necessity to

> exculpate themselves from what, without exculpation, was the wickedest vote the representatives of the people could ever give,—a vote which delivered labor to the mercy of capital; a vote which forced upon the people that as money which in no just sense was money; a vote which established as law one of the most abominable frauds which law could be prostituted to enforce,—[such legislators] were not qualified to judge of other men's patriotism, honesty, or good sense.[51]

Regrettably, it must be said that Adams did not often display such solicitude for labor or for the people as a whole. But the problem lay deeper than even the disasters sketched here. As Adams saw it, there was, first of all, a constitutional problem, at least in the minds of some legislators. Whether a strict interpretation of the Constitution allowed the issuance of paper money was not the major issue for him, which may be just as well, since *McCulloch v. Maryland* seems to have settled that point.[52] Rather, the real issue lay "beneath the letter of the Constitution,—to the principles upon which all government and all society must ultimately rest. This is the sum-total of the argument against legal tender; and this argument rests on the maxim that the foundation of law is truth."[53] And this meant, in the words of Senator William Pitt Fessenden, that paper money "encourages bad morality" and "must inflict a stain upon the national honor."[54] Two things stand out here. One is obviously the characteristically stern Adams morality. The other is the faith in the soundness of orthodox economics,[55] which, ironically, became one of the foundational claims of the plutocracy Adams so detested, thus opening a contradiction in Adams's critique of politics and finance that he never quite succeeded in overcoming.

With this assessment of the Civil War roots of the postwar disorder in mind, we can turn to Adams's notable article "The Session" and its sequel "Civil Service Reform," both published in 1869. Adams consciously modeled these articles on those discussing Parliament published annually in London by Lord Robert Cecil. Adams hoped that his yearly article would be "a power in the land," a power that he hoped would exercise "a distinct influence on public opinion by acting on the limited number of cultivated minds." And, in another display of self-congratulation, Adams proclaims that, "For once I have smashed things generally."[56] In some ways foreshadowing a more vituperative Theodore Lowi excoriating contemporary interest-group politics, Adams writes:

> the boiling and bubbling of this witches cauldron, into which we have thrown the newt and toe of frog and all the venomous ingredients of corruption, and from which is expected to issue the future and more perfect republic,—in short the conflict and riot of interests, grow more and more overwhelming; the power of obstructionists grows more and more decisive in the same proportion as the business to be done increases in volume; the effort required to accomplish necessary legislation becomes more and more serious; the machine groans and labors under the burden, and its action becomes spasmodic and inefficient. The capacity of our government to reconcile these jarring interests, to control refractory dissentients, and to preserve an appearance of governing, is already tested to the utmost.[57]

The late congressional session Adams discussed revealed to him that the flaws in the system were structural and that the legislative machinery itself must be reformed. The major issues before the country were simply not being addressed. Of these, Reconstruction had to come first, but far too optimistically, Adams believed that it was losing much of its salience because the general prosperity, combined with the results of the 1868 election, was causing the South to turn its attention to more profitable things. Though there was little in the Fifteenth Amendment to which he could object, he thought that it would be of little importance. Its major danger lay in the possible incentive for Congress to abuse its powers in enforcing it.[58]

More serious, in Adams's view, was the threat to executive power posed by the egregious Tenure of Office Act, which allowed the Senate to interfere with the president's power to remove executive officers. The Senate, though then not a popularly elected body, was in a position to do great damage to the separation of powers system by attempting to capitalize on the mistakes of the other branches of government.[59] But mere repeal would not be enough. Clearly the executive branch would have to put its house in order. And, as already noted, the most troublesome task was to bring the Senate to heel.

But the tariff issue was at least as important. The tariff was economically wasteful, but the nation was young and strong enough to withstand the loss, as well as the fact that under it the rich were getting richer and the poor were getting poorer. Again, the real danger was not the economic consequences but "the debauching effect of the system upon parties, public men, and the morals of the State." Adams continues with a ringing indictment:

> The condition of parties precludes the chance of reform. The "rings" which control legislation—those iron, or whiskey, or Pacific Railway, or other interests, which have their Congressional representatives, who vote themselves the public money—do not obtain their power for nothing. Congressmen themselves, as a class, are not venal, it is true. Perhaps not more than one member in ten of the late Congress ever accepted money. But though Congress itself has still a sense of honor, party organizations have no decency and no shame. The "rings" obtain their control of legislation by paying liberally towards the support of these party organizations, Republican or Democratic, as the case may be.[60]

In these conditions, the power of parties grows "dictatorial."[61]

The article "Civil Service Reform," published in the October 1869 issue of the *North American Review*, is a direct extension of "The Session." Had it not been for the fact that the resulting piece would have been too long, the two articles would have been published together. Once again, the analysis is concerned with what Adams took to be a structural problem. The focus is again not on corruption but on the Constitution, or rather the derangement of constitutional powers in the postwar period. The basic principle being violated is to be found in the Massachusetts Constitution, written, as Adams does not say, by his great-grandfather. "In the government of this Commonwealth, the legislative department shall never exercise the executive and judicial powers, or either of them; the executive shall never exercise the legislative and judicial powers, or either of them: *to the end it may be a government of laws and not of men.*"[62]

When Grant took office, Adams was willing to concede that he intended a nonpartisan administration. Indeed, in his first cabinet appointments, Grant attempted to build a group that was free of political entanglements. But this attempt failed, and he was forced to reconstruct, though even here, only one member was chosen more for his representation of Republican Party interests than of the Republic as a whole. Where Grant capitulated—though, Adams concedes, not without struggle—was in the inferior cabinet appointments.[63]

But, Adams argues, this was not always the practice followed in the history of American government. From Washington to Jackson's time, "The President represented not a party, nor even the people either in a mass or in any of its innumerable divisions, but an essential part of the frame of government; that part which was neither legislature nor judiciary; a part in which the nature of society must of necessity exist,—which in the United States was intentionally and wisely made a system by itself, in order to balance the other parts of the structure."[64] Even Jackson's spoils system did not destroy this essential balance, because in his attitude toward the Senate, he upheld the rights of the executive.

However, weaker men did less well. Adams sees an unwritten law according to which the Senate is the "nervous system of the great extra-constitutional party organizations." The Senate became the seat of party intrigue, "and when the party organizations discovered that their power would be greatly increased by controlling the executive patronage, the Senate lent its overruling influence to effect this result, and soon became through its individual members the largest dispenser of patronage."[65] Adams says that this nefarious practice reached new heights in the recent administration of Andrew Johnson and concludes that we must "confront face to face the bald and disgusting fact that members of Congress cannot be honest with such a power in their hands."[66]

Adams's great theme is the necessity to restore the proper balance between the legislative and executive branches. No particular way out is clear to Adams. His major suggestion reflects some real confidence in the people, since it is essentially populist in character. "Nothing remains but to act outside all party organizations, and to appeal with all the earnestness that the emergency requires, not to Congress nor to the President, but to the people, to return to the first principles of government, and to shut off forever this source of corruption in the state."[67] And this faith in average voters is restated near the conclusion of the essay. "If the President is weak, it is merely because public opinion is silent and support is not to be found. Arouse this, and there will be no danger that the President will prove indifferent to the duty of protecting the purity of his administration, or that politicians within Congress or elsewhere will assume an authority which belongs not to a man nor to any body of men, but to laws alone."[68] And yet again, to hammer home the point, Adams proclaims, "the true policy of reformers is to trust neither to Presidents nor to senators, but appeal directly to the people."[69] Not for the first time, it must be remarked that these are decidedly not the words of an antidemocratic snob. The Republic can be saved if only the people can be mobilized.

But if Adams's argument on civil service reform is made on the high level of principle, his 1870 discussion of the attempt by Jay Gould and James Fisk to corner the gold market goes right to the inside of a sordid conspiracy reaching deep into the Grant administration. Here Adams's language in his assault on the conspirators was so flamboyant as to force him to publish the results of his investigation in England, for fear of running afoul of the libel laws; even in London, some publishers were hesitant to put the article in print. Gould and Fisk, the two "malefactors of great wealth," to borrow Theodore Roosevelt's famous imprecation, were in control of the Erie Railroad. Gould was a broker, and "a broker is almost by nature a gambler, — perhaps the last profession suitable for a railway manager. In character he was marked by a disposition for silent intrigue . . . he had not a conception of a moral principle. The class of men to whom he belonged understood no distinction between right and wrong in matters of speculation." Fisk was "still more original in character. He was not yet forty years of age, and had the instincts of fourteen. . . . Personally Fisk was coarse, noisy, boastful, ignorant, the type of a young butcher in appearance and mind."[70] And of the two together, Adams writes, "Over this wealth and influence, — greater than that directly swayed by any private citizen, greater than is absolutely and personally controlled by most kings, and far too great for public safety either in a democracy or in any other form of society, — the vicissitudes of a troubled time placed two men in irresponsible authority; and both these men belonged to a low moral and social type."[71]

Once again the root of the trouble was in the speculative mania unleashed by the Civil War.[72] The details are of considerable complexity and need not detain us. Suffice it to say that "the effects of President Grant's character showed themselves. They were startling—astounding—terrifying." And through these defects, "Gould was led by the change at Washington into the belief he could safely corner gold without interference from the Government."[73] Though the scandal did not touch the president directly, it did reach deep into his administration and into his family as well. Congressman Garfield, a good friend of Adams, conducted a congressional investigation, but the committee

> took a quantity of evidence which it dared not probe, and refused to analyze. Although the fault lay somewhere on the Administration, and could lie nowhere else, the trail always faded and died out at the point where any member of the Administration became visible. Everyone dreaded to press inquiry. Adams himself feared finding out too much. He found out too much already, when he saw in evidence that Jay Gould had actually succeeded in stretching his net over Grant's closest surroundings, and that Boutwell's incompetence was the bottom of Grant's calculation. . . . The ways of Wall Street were dark and double.[74]

But scandal aside, even including the discussion of Gould's ties to Boss Tweed's Tammany, the corruption of judges, and the bribes offered, what is theoretically most interesting in Adams's article is his tracing the root of the problem to the emergence of the modern corporation. What he feared was the creation of "a system of quiet but irresistible corruption, [which] will ultimately succeed in directing government itself. Under the American form of society no authority exists capable of effective resistance." Adams concludes, "The corporation is in its nature a threat against the popular institutions spreading so rapidly over the whole world. Wherever a popular and limited government exists this difficulty will be found in its path; and unless some satisfactory solution of the problem can be reached, popular institutions may yet find their existence endangered."[75] To this day, in spite of much effort since Adams's time, no solution has been found. As Charles E. Lindblom concludes, democracy and the corporation simply do not fit.[76] As is so often the case, Adams is dismayingly prescient.

Adams's final foray against the Grant administration is in the second of his "Session" articles, published in the *North American Review* for July 1870. As usual, Adams hoped to make a splash, and this time succeeded. This piece was reprinted by the Democratic Party as a campaign pamphlet in the 1872 presidential election and earned him a response from Senator Timothy Howe of Wisconsin, who, along the way, called him a "begonia," a flower notable, says Adams, for "curious and showy foliage; it was conspicuous; it seemed to have no use or purpose; and it insisted on standing always in the most prominent positions. Adams would have greatly liked to be a begonia in Washington."[77] Elsewhere he rejoiced, "To be abused by a Senator is my highest ambition, and I am now quite happy. My only regret is that I cannot afford a Senator to abuse me permanently. That, however, might pall in time."[78]

In spite of the political uses of the second "Session" article, Adams's piece is less flamboyant than others of the same period. The most important subject he considers is yet again the profound constitutional derangement that he felt was firmly in place by the early days of the Grant administration. The starting point of the discussion is a comparison of European and American ideas on sovereignty. European thinkers such as Blackstone had long argued that all governments must rest on a supreme, final, absolute, and uncontrolled authority. Americans, in contrast, denied this principle, believing that there was no need for a supreme power and that none could be allowed to exist, for such a power was inimical to freedom. Liberty depended on "denying uncontrolled authority to the political system in its parts or in its whole." It was this that led to the reservation of certain powers to the states and, within the national government, the elaborate system of separation of powers with checks and balances to deter the abuse of power. Perhaps the purposes of the Framers were chimerical, and "the hopes then felt were almost certainly delusive":

> Yet persons who grant the probable failure of the scheme, and expect the recurrence of the great problems in government which were then thought to be solved, cannot but look with satisfaction at the history of the Federal Constitution as the most convincing and the most interesting experiment ever made in the laboratory of political science, even if it demonstrates the impossibility through its means.[79]

The Civil War had virtually "obliterated" the Constitution as originally conceived, but as noted before, Adams felt that there was reason for hope in a Grant presidency, though these hopes were rudely dashed almost at once. We hear again a litany of Grant's intellectual deficiencies. He was a president with a very limited sense of presidential duties, which he thought consisted largely in faithful administration, honest tax collection and disbursement of funds, and rigorous obedience to the law, whether good or bad, especially insofar as it was expressed by congressional enactments. He thought, in other words, like the commander in chief of an army in peacetime. But a president, in Adams's view, needed to offer more. He must be able to see a connection between ideas and acts, in other words, to have a *policy*. Merely to proclaim "Let us have peace" was not enough.[80]

The result, necessarily, in Adams's view, was not a policy but a *nonpolicy* of drift. The basic structural problems of the system were not being addressed:

> The steady process by which power was tending to centralization in defiance of the theory of the political system; the equally steady tendency of this power to accumulate in the hands of the Legislature at the expense of the Executive and the Judiciary; the ever-increasing encroachments of the Senate, the ever-diminishing efficiency of the House, all the different parts and processes of the general movement which indicated a certain abandonment of the original theory of the American system, and a no less certain substitution of a method of government that promised to be both corrupt and inefficient,—all these were either to be fixed upon the country beyond recall, or were to be met by a prompt and energetic resistance.[81]

Adams concludes in an outburst of constitutional despair. Somewhat surprisingly for one with his nationalist proclivities, he worries that the powers once reserved to the states will now be granted them only on good behavior and with the consent of Congress. It is clear to him that "the original basis of reserved powers on which the Constitution was framed has yielded and is yielding to natural pressure," to an extent that "there is little doubt that the great political problem of all ages cannot, at least in a community like that of the future America, be solved by the theory of the American Constitution." The second great lesson he draws is that "the system of separate responsibility realized in the mechanism of the American government as a consequence of its jealous restriction of substantial powers, will inevitably yield, as its foundation has yielded, to the pressure of necessity. The result is not pleasant to contemplate." And in a great anticlimax that is, unfortunately, not uncharacteristic of Adams, he adds that "it is not here intended to suggest principles of reform."[82]

This is perhaps the darkest expression of constitutional depression in this period of Adams's career. But in 1876, only six years after his deeply pessimistic last "Session" article, in his finale as a political journalist, he takes a more benign view of the broad outlines of American constitutional history. In the final issue of the *North American Review* published under his editorship, he offers two articles. One is his first sustained attempt to generalize about the course of American history, and the other is a commentary on the role of independents in politics. Once again, the German scholar Gustav von Holst appears on the scene, this time in the form of Adams's lengthy review of the first volume of von Holst's history of the United States. Written with his student Henry Cabot Lodge, Jr., as an assistant, the conclusion of the essay constitutes what Adams referred to as his Centennial Address. Along the way, he roams through a good deal of American history, anticipates some of the themes of his great work on Jefferson and Madison, and answers some of von Holst's harsh criticism of the United States.

Von Holst's first major point is that the American revolutionary statesmen were unclear in their ideas of what constituted a nation. Aside from Alexander Hamilton, who saw the inevitable failure of a confederation, the nature of a state was a deep mystery to the Framers. Thus the failure of the Articles of Confederation was inevitable, a situation that led to the Constitution of 1787. And of that Constitution von Holst writes, "The historical fact is, that the Constitution had been 'extorted from the grinding necessity of a reluctant people.' "[83]

Yet, in spite of this, von Holst points out that the Constitution became an object of worship for Americans.[84] As Adams notes, von Holst gives no analysis of the Constitution, though it is clear that he sees fundamental problems in it. The essence of his view, as Adams sees it, is the perception that, "in the process of converting the Confederacy into a nation, the Constitution made a convenient battle-ground on which the two old parties, States-rights men and Nationalists, could fight out their battle within a sort of self-imposed limit, much in the manner of a tournament. Under cover of the fetish worship, the old tendencies lived and throve, merely interpreting the Constitution to suit their fixed ideas."[85]

According to von Holst, the particularist tendencies were mostly quiet or gathering strength during the Washington administration. Disturbances such as the Whiskey Rebellion were suppressed by Hamilton with a firm hand. However, the departure of Thomas Jefferson from the cabinet and the inauguration of John Adams as president released the old provincial jealousies. The Virginia and Kentucky Resolutions were the classic symptoms of this development.[86]

But fortunately, from von Holst's point of view, Jefferson was too ambitious to follow his own interpretation of the Constitution, which he read as if the Constitution were perhaps even looser, and certainly no more tightly woven together, than the Articles. In fact, in a discussion that anticipates Adams's *History*, Jefferson emerges as a great centralizer during his presidency, while the Federalists became particularists and flirted with secession, thus leading to the

Hartford Convention.[87] There follows a discussion of slavery as treated in the Constitution and in subsequent policy that is roundly condemnatory and with most of which Adams can only agree. "The recapitulation of all the successive concessions to the slave power, all the steps by which the power slowly converted the national government into an instrument of its own will, is a terrible one. It is with a shudder that one turns the last page of this tremendous indictment, and yet the volume ends at the threshold of the antislavery struggle; the worst humiliations are not yet touched."[88]

Most of the preceding discussion is simply a summary of von Holst's argument, with much of which Adams clearly agrees. However, he is by no means uncritical of the German scholar, and the grounds of his criticism shed considerable light on Adams's constitutional theory, his understanding of American history, and his ideas about the potential of the democratically organized people.

Adams sees that von Holst understands the basic problem facing American statesmen. "That problem was how to weld thirteen 'sovereign states' into a nation without appealing to force."[89] Having said this, Adams notes that von Holst suffers from the European difficulty of perceiving confusion in the American mind on the subject of the state. But Americans deny that confusion, says Adams; they see the thirteen colonies as separate entities believed to be good in and of themselves. American statesmen were not doctrinaires, and they saw clearly that the distinctiveness of the states was a simple fact that had to be dealt with. Of necessity, the constitutional compromise had to be tentative and subject to adjustment when the extent of the sacrifice required of the state governments became clear. American leaders were not confused in their ideas; it was the facts they had to deal with that were confused. Happily, they did not approach the problem from an abstractly theoretical point of view. Even Hamilton, so much admired by von Holst, refused to break with the American past. Hamilton understood that the notion that "two supreme powers cannot act together is false. They are inconsistent only when aimed at each other or at one indivisible object." The question, then, was whether the practical solution adopted to deal with the intractable realities of American society worked.[90]

Von Holst understood that nullification and secession were not the product of slavery "but run through the whole century of our history as its particular ear-mark." What he did not understand was that this was not the fault of the Constitution. "Had there been no particularist feeling, there would have been no need of a closer union; the task of the Constitution would have been already performed." Again, the real question was how well the Constitution had worked. It is true, says Adams, that the Jeffersonians switched places with the Hamiltonians, but the real concern cannot be with the inconsistencies of individuals but with the effect of these inconsistencies on government. The central thing for Adams is this:

> What was established as law by Washington was respected as law by Jefferson. The precedents established as law by the Federalist administrations were accepted and enlarged by the Republican administrations. That Jefferson should have exercised as President powers more questionable than any of those which he had triumphantly assailed his predecessors for wielding, may prove that Jefferson was an unscrupulous politician, but it also proves, what is of far more consequence to the world, that the American political system was stronger than the individual, and that the Constitution vindicated its energy in its working. That J. Q. Adams should have been driven from power nominally because he advocated the application of national money to internal improvements, and that the application of national money to internal improvements should have continued with accelerated pace from that day to this, is only another instance of the operation of the same law.

Von Holst's charges against the Jeffersonians thus rest on the assumption that they "consistently carried out the national theory of the Constitution, at the expense of their own private consistency." But in fact, the Jeffersonian theory made no difference; *whoever* was in power, the authority of the executive branch increased.[91]

Moreover, Adams continues, the power of the legislative branch has also expanded continuously for eighty years, to an extent that began to justify the fears of anti-Federalist critics of the Constitution such as George Mason and Patrick Henry, as well as critical supporters such as Thomas Jefferson, all of whom European theorists insisted "upon branding as blockheads, because they thought they saw in the State organisms a protection against the uncontrolled despotism of the central government." If anything, the executive and legislative branches worked together almost too much to create a "more perfect union." Thus, even starting from von Holst's own position, the Constitution must be seen as a practical success because it did prevail in forming the thirteen states into one nationality.[92]

But this analysis contains an obvious difficulty that Adams is forced to consider—the collapse of the Constitution in the crisis leading to the Civil War. Von Holst believes that the tension between nationalism and particularism is the clue to an understanding of American history. Adams does not really disagree, but he believes that the Framers and their successors were, in fact, on their way to forming a "more perfect union," but for the development of the "slave power." Had they contemplated that development, they would have abandoned their task in despair, for "the Constitution was not intended to be subjected to such a strain." But this problem was not the fault of the Framers. Even von Holst understands, says Adams, that "the great development of the slave power in politics was due to economical causes which were of later origin, and the original concession made to the slaveholders in the Constitution was made on the theory that if there was any truth in the fundamental principles of human liberty, that truth was sure to vindicate itself by steadily undermining and destroying slavery." In spite of being subjected to the full force of states' rights tendencies, nationalism, under very unfavorable conditions, was not only gaining ground but actually conquering particularist tendencies. However, anticipating his study of John Randolph, Adams writes:

> Suddenly, under the guidance of Calhoun, the slave power seized upon the old and almost exploded theory of State rights, vamped it up, gave to it a superficial varnish of logic, and so breathed into it a new life. But that life was not due to the "inherent defect" in the Constitution in countenancing State rights, but to the unexpected development of the cotton industry. What Calhoun really defended was, not State rights, but the slave power; and what the North really had to fear was, not State rights, for if Calhoun had become President he would in all probability have been as strong a centralizer as Jefferson, but the perversion of the Constitution to the interests of slavery instead of those of freedom.[93]

Paradoxically, though it is not clear that he sees the paradox, Adams contends that the concessions of the North to slavery show the strength of the Constitution in forming a more perfect Union. While it was true that, as time passed, political principle was often sacrificed to nationalist passions, the Constitution nevertheless continued to do its work as it became the only instrument for preserving the Union against "colossal" peril. In his rather sanguinary view, "the Constitution did its work and . . . the nationality it created was so tremendous a force that at the first moment the slave power ventured to raise its hand against it, that moment the North suffocated the slave power in its own blood." For this reason, the veneration bestowed on it is deserved. Thus, the Constitution has done its work. It has, in fact, made a nation.[94]

The problem with von Holst's analysis, according to Adams, is that he cannot shed his European blinders when examining the United States and that, though it may be incongruous for an Adams to remark, he set "an absolute standard so high that no people of any age or country have ever approached it."[95] But, more importantly, von Holst missed something very deep:

> If the historian will only consent to shut his eyes for a moment to the microscopic analysis of personal motives and idiosyncracies, he cannot but be conscious of a silent pulsation that commands his respect, a steady movement that resembles in its mode of operation the mechanical action of Nature herself. As one stands in the presence of this primitive energy, the continent itself seems to be the result of agencies not more unlimited in their power, not more sure in their processes, not more complete in their result, than those which have controlled the political system. [And if we can agree with Bismarck that sovereignty must be "the sovereignty of law,"] then the history of the United States during its first century is surely entitled to the credit of having developed that principle with a rigor and on a scale which is not without its majesty and pathos.[96]

This remarkable statement contains at least two aspects that should be noted here but must be more fully discussed later. One is the intense patriotic nationalism displayed by Adams. The other is a determinist theory of forces beyond human control, which, as we have already seen, was to become a major theme, as well as a source of great intellectual tension, both in the *History* and in Adams's later works.

The review of von Holst, written in contrast to the many papers detailing the constitutional crisis of the Grant administration, is the high point of Adams's celebration of the potential of American constitutionalism. But at exactly the same time, in an article on the role that independents should play in the presidential campaign of 1876, Adams is notably less sanguine. If the Constitution was thriving, or at least had the potential to thrive, the party system was a disruptive force. Neither the Republican nor the Democratic Party was at all appealing. The issue of slavery had held the Republicans together. In the loyal states, "it numbered among its leaders or in its ranks a very considerable preponderance of the political virtue and intelligence, and of the disinterested public spirit of the community." Unfortunately, it also had "its train of camp followers and stragglers and adventurers . . . who were as loud-mouthed and repulsive a set of political vagabonds as ever canted about principles or hungered after loaves and fishes." This wing of the party was now in the ascendancy. "Accordingly, about the time when those who never knew what a principle was had pushed their way to the front and were confidently appealing to a glorious record, those who had made the party and inspired its policy through its years of active life found themselves pondering over new issues and striking out in independent action."[97]

The Democratic Party suffered from different defects. Adams believed that the completeness of the Republican destruction of slavery deprived the party of its occupation while re-creating that of the Democrats. Historically, the Northern branch had been the ally of the "slaveholding oligarchy." "Into it had naturally drifted the great mass of the political ignorance, corruption, and venality of the free States, and, throughout the Rebellion, it constituted simply a cowardly and traitorous opposition." A political lifetime spent under these conditions had unfitted the party for independent political action.[98]

However, the election of 1874 had made it clear that the South was becoming a political power again, a power motivated by a desire to throw off the rule of freed slaves, which it had been the goal of Reconstruction policy to prevent. But the policies imposed by the Republicans lacked "moderation and wisdom," as tends to be the case, in Adams's view, with the victors in civil wars. In its attempt to "reconstruct" the South, he believed that the party had "fairly overstepped the bounds of moderation, and went to work to reorganize a thoroughly disorganized social, political, and industrial system on preconceived theories which were wholly at variance with actual facts. By more than accomplishing their own work they thus made work for their opponents." The South was in great need of repair, and it was the role of the Democratic Party to carry out this task. For the Republicans, it remained to "see that in the process the great results [presumably the destruction of slavery] of the war [are] not disturbed."[99] (Adams is so critical of Reconstruction that it is important to keep in mind this last point on the role of the Republicans. He obviously has no desire to restore the status quo ante.)

Adams assumed—much too optimistically, as we look back from our perspective—that the great political issues of the preceding twenty years were no longer of much importance. His analysis would have been more rounded had he expanded the time frame from the preceding twenty years to the entire nineteenth century, during which, of course, his family had been so active in the struggle against slavery. This might have enabled him to focus on the centrality of race and slavery in the American experience. Had he done so, he might have seen the falsity of his assertion that peace, quiet, and goodwill were restored precisely in proportion to the passage of those states into Democratic control. He even dismisses the idea that the Southern states would deprive the freed blacks of their civil rights as a conjurer's trick.[100] Instead of recognizing this danger, Adams holds the view that political leaders were continuing to manufacture side issues out of old and dated struggles.

The result, in his view, was that the number of people who wanted to take action independent of the established parties would inevitably grow.[101] As he saw it, the major parties were exhausted, so it was time to go outside them to search for leaders who would address the central issues of the postwar period; the debates surrounding Reconstruction had no bearing on these new problems.

To make this point, he examines the Republican and Democratic platforms for the election of 1876 and, finding both empty, concludes that there is no real difference between the parties.[102] He is condescending to Rutherford Hayes, the Republican candidate, a man of "good purposes, fair talents, and high character," but insists that more than that is required to advance beyond mere local service. Thus Hayes is on the level of Franklin Pierce and John C. Frémont and far below the level of Lincoln when he was nominated for the presidency.[103] This is faint praise indeed, considering the disastrous performance of Pierce in office. And Samuel Tilden running for the Democrats did not offer much more, though to the party's credit, it had nominated the "most distinguished reformer in its ranks."[104] For the electorate and, above all, the independent-minded voter, what counted was the position of the two candidates on the key issues of the time, namely, currency reform through the resumption of specie payments, free trade, and the reduction of tariffs and, of course, civil service reform leading to appointments "during good behavior" of administrative officials below the cabinet level.[105] Taken together, the aim of all these efforts is political purification, since the aim of all reformers is "to overcome the tendency of our political system to corruption."[106] With this as a guide, no blame would attach to any civil service reformer who chose to vote for Tilden. And no matter who won, the reformers must hold the victor to the highest standard, in effect moving into the opposition, where they could do the most good.[107] What we see then is a Constitution capable of providing the framework for good government but seriously distorted by the Senate. Thus, the deep aim of all reform is a restoration of the proper "forms and formalities" according to the Constitution as it was understood in earlier and better times, before it was debauched by Andrew Jackson.[108] Whether this sort of formalism is enough to achieve Adams's ends is a question to be discussed later. But first, Adams's views of democracy must be considered. Here, when we might hope for a theoretical discourse, we get a novel.

Chapter 5

Democracy and Empire

The observation that Adams wrote a novel rather than a theoretical treatise is not really intended as a complaint, though the latter would certainly have been interesting. Adams's *Democracy*, published anonymously in 1880, while perhaps not very compelling as a work of fiction, is of considerable interest for its ideas; it was widely read in both Washington and England amidst a great deal of speculation about its authorship. Though it does not take the form, it has some of the characteristics of a philosophical dialogue, in which several different positions are advanced with considerable power. It is also a roman à clef in which the several characters are modeled on public figures or on friends of Adams and his wife Clover.[1]

The Novel as Theory

The protagonist is a wealthy young widow, Madeleine Lee, who doubtless represents both his wife and Adams himself and probably exhibits characteristics of others of their friends as well. She moves to Washington and establishes a fashionable salon in which she encounters the corrupt Senator Silas Ratcliffe, whose romantic interest in Madeleine precipitates a moral crisis for the idealistic young woman. Mrs. Lee had left New York, which she thought boring, since she had no interest in stock prices and little in the men who bought and sold them. "She had," the narrator tells us, "become serious," too serious, apparently, for the banalities of finance and commerce. Europe was exhausted, in her view, and she had come to realize that she was totally American, though by no means uncritically so, and she intended "to get all that American life had to offer, good or bad." She was well read in American history and literature, not to mention other contemporary writings. And, like the Adamses, she was entirely ready to defend American society against European snobbery:

> Society in America? Indeed there is society in America, and very good society too; but it has a code of its own, and newcomers seldom under-

107

stand it. I will tell you what it is, . . . and you will never be in danger
of making any mistake. "Society" in America means all the honest,
kindly-mannered, pleasant-voiced women, and all the good, brave,
unassuming men, between the Atlantic and the Pacific. Each of these
has a free pass in every city and village, "good for each generation
only," and it depends on each to make use of this pass or not as may
happen to suit his or her fancy. To this rule there are *no* exceptions.[2]

"She wanted," the narrator tells us, "to see with her own eyes the action
of primary force; . . . She was bent upon getting to the heart of the great
American mystery of democracy and government." Deeper still, "What she
wished to see, she thought, was the clash of interests, the interests of forty millions of people and a whole continent, centering at Washington; guided, restrained, controlled, or unrestrained or uncontrollable, by men of ordinary
mould; the tremendous forces of government, and the machinery of society,
at work. What she wanted, was POWER." But even more important, in the
midst of an intense discussion, she admits to a strange and probably impossible goal, redolent of the Adams family creed; "I must know whether America is right or wrong."[3] This is a question that can be asked only by a severe
moralist; the issue is not whether the citizens are happy or public policy is
sound or individual rights are protected or the country is safe from attack, or
even whether the Constitution is being followed. Instead, the question is entirely a moral one, reflecting Adams's New England conscience as clearly as
anything ever did.

With this mind-set Madeleine Lee conducts her brilliant and fashionable
salon, one that mirrors the one over which Henry and Marian "Clover" Adams
presided in Washington. There is not a great deal of action in the novel, but
there is much fine talk in which a considerable range of attitudes toward
democracy is displayed. The themes discussed are those raised in the essays
collected in *The Great Secession Winter*, "power, democracy, reform, party,
the Presidency."[4] Adams as narrator puts one dimension of the problem very
sharply, if a little cynically: "Democracy, rightly understood, is the government of the people, by the people, for the benefit of Senators,"[5] a point that
clearly echoes his journalism. It is the villainous Senator Ratcliffe, standing
in for Senators James G. Blaine and Roscoe Conkling, who, in the course of
a discussion about reform and corruption, responds to Baron Jacobi, representing Old World cynicism. Taking what he assumes to be a "realistic" position, he says, "No representative government can long be much better or
much worse than the society it represents. Purify society and you purify the

government. But try to purify the government artificially, and you only aggravate failure."[6]

The baron responds with a major salvo:

I declare to you that in all my experience I have found no society which has had elements of corruption like the United States. The children in the cities are corrupt, and know how to cheat me. The cities are corrupt and also the towns and the counties and the States' legislatures and the judges. Everywhere men betray trusts both public and private, steal money, run away with public funds. Only in the Senate men take no money. And you gentlemen in the Senate very well declare that your great United States, which is the head of the civilized world, can never learn anything from the example of corrupt Europe. You are right—quite right. I do much regret that I have not yet one hundred years to live. If I could then come back to this city, I should find myself very content—much more than now. I am always content where there is much corruption, and *ma parole d'honneur!* . . . the United States will then be more corrupt than Rome under Caligula; more corrupt than the Church under Leo X; more corrupt than France under the Regent.[7]

Senator Ratcliffe, himself more than a little tinged by corruption, makes no response and leaves the room. It falls to Nathan Gore, a brilliant if perhaps somewhat stuffy historian and diplomat, to offer a defense of democracy not unlike the views of Henry Adams articulated at the height of his youthful idealism, as well as in the *History*, which was still a work in progress when he wrote *Democracy*.

I believe in democracy. I accept it. I will faithfully serve and defend it. I believe in it because it appears to me the inevitable consequence of what has gone before it. Democracy asserts the fact that the masses are now raised to a higher intelligence than formerly. All our civilization aims at this mark. We want to do what we can to help it. I myself want to see the result. I grant it is an experiment, but it is the only direction society can take that is worth its taking; the only conception of its duty large enough to satisfy its instincts; the only result that is worth an effort or a risk. Every other step is backward and I do not care to repeat the past. I am glad to see society grapple with issues in which no one can afford to be neutral.[8]

Mrs. Lee challenges his position, asking what will happen if "society destroys itself with universal suffrage, corruption, and communism?" And

Gore replies with a declaration of faith: "faith in human nature; faith in science; faith in the survival of the fittest."[9] In spite of the fact that some think that Adams is hostile to democracy, here Gore clearly speaks for the author. Irving Howe, a democratic socialist surely not in thrall to Adams's ideas, is on the mark when he says that Gore's speech reflects "a deep bias of Adams' mind." And Ernest Samuels notes that it "came from the depths of Adams's heart, that it spoke the irreducible dogmas of his proud inheritance."[10] And so too, and just as surely, does Madeleine Lee's hymn speak to the egalitarianism of American society. Adams had good reason to be critical of the condition of democracy in the United States during the 1880s, but this need not be translated into a general critique of democracy itself. Rather, in the words of J. C. Levenson, here at least he speaks in a tone of "prudent hopefulness."[11] The hope was to make a deeply corrupted democracy work better. Though at the end of the novel Adams pulls back from saying so, one conclusion implicit in the discussion is one that Henry James attributes to Clover Adams: "She tried to devote her life to defining what was *best* in her country, in a political situation where she often found herself among the *worst*."[12]

But Nathan Gore does not even come close to having the last word in this discussion. Before that can come, it is necessary to deal with Senator Ratcliffe. Ratcliffe is a Mephistophelean or, better perhaps, a Machiavellian figure whose great advantage in this discussion of democracy is actually having had political experience, however depraved it might have been. It is this experience, as Howe says, that makes Ratcliffe so vital a figure, posing arguments "too good for the figure he is supposed to cut."[13]

In what little real action is depicted in the novel, Ratcliffe is struggling to win the hand of beautiful, rich, sophisticated Madeleine Lee. To do so, he must overcome her suspicion of his ethics in which the end justifies any and every means. His position is expressed with fearless openness. He proclaims that fidelity to his party is superior to everything but the national interest. He is contemptuous of philosophical politics and takes great pleasure in wielding political power.[14] John Carrington, representing war-battered Southern aristocracy, simply dismisses him for being "blindly ignorant of morals,"[15] a comment that is rather graceless coming from a Southerner who presumably fought for slavery, while Ratcliffe is identified with the antislavery party. Thus Ratcliffe is more complex than Carrington suggests. He is, the narrator tells us—perhaps ironically, but only partially so—"a great statesman." His great talent as a legislator is to bring together so many hostile interests, always a valuable skill in the kaleidoscope of American politics. "The beauty of his work consisted in the skill with which he evaded questions of principle." The real issues were not of principle but of power. The guiding idea "must be the want of principles."[16] And Ratcliffe is even more Machiavellian when he delivers his apologia, or credo. Somewhat disingenuously, he says that he is not one who is happy in political life; it is simply "the trade I am fittest for." And he goes on, "ambition is my resource to make it tolerable. In politics we cannot keep our hands clean. I have done many things in my political career that are not defensible. To act with entire honesty and self-respect, one should always live in a pure atmosphere, and the atmosphere of politics is impure."[17] The Machiavellianism is clear. Ratcliffe would certainly have fully understood the force of Jean-Paul Sartre's play *Dirty Hands,* in which corruption is a natural companion of political activity.[18]

Thus Ratcliffe can admit, almost proudly and certainly with little or no remorse, that, in the crisis of the Civil War, he had fixed the contest for president in the state of Illinois, thereby saving the election and, as he saw it, preserving the Union.[19] Mr. Carrington is shocked, but Adams, again as narrator, notes that he has missed Ratcliffe's point, saying, "The man who has committed a murder for his country, is a patriot and not an assassin, even when he receives a seat in the Senate as his share of the plunder. Women cannot be expected to go behind the motives of that patriot who saves his country and his election in times of revolution."[20] But Mrs. Lee, unlike Carrington, is not shocked by Ratcliffe, or at least is not shocked enough to turn away his attentions. Only at the climax of the novel, when Ratcliffe is accused of accepting a bribe to support a piece of legislation, does she reject him. The senator admits to the bribe with some shame, though he insists that the money went to the party's National Committee rather than to himself. But even here he admits regret for "not the doing, but the necessity of doing." And he points out to Madeleine one of the deep truths of politics that every realist knows: "There are conflicting duties in all the transactions of life, except the simplest."[21] Even Henry Adams at his most idealistic understands this.

Madeleine is understandably disturbed, since she had been in danger of marrying someone who had committed a major felony. But her reaction goes beyond Ratcliffe to democratic politics as a whole. Proclaiming that "democracy has shaken my nerves to pieces," she concludes that, in the narrator's words, "She had got to the bottom of this business of democratic government, and found out that it was nothing more than government of any other kind."[22] There is nothing left, she thinks, but to return to the true democracy of her private charitable work, though it should be insisted that democracy is quite different from other forms of government, even though it is impure.

Madeleine's abandonment of politics is a disturbing conclusion. The difference between democracy and antidemocracy or nondemocracy is much more than the difference between Tweedledum and Tweedledee. Democracy may share attributes—such as the use of political power—with other forms of politics. And of course, sometimes democracies, like other political systems, may become corrupt or abuse power or reach stupid decisions. But democratic government itself offers the best remedy to such situations. Adams knows this with at least part of himself when he speaks through Nathan Gore and also through Madeleine Lee when she enthuses about democratic society. Adams's well-justified revulsion for the deep-seated corruption in late-nineteenth-century America sometimes blinds him to the power of the democratic ideas that he himself has advanced in constructing the debates that form the intellectual substance of his novel. His is a failure of nerve. He builds up a strong structure of debate, which he undermines when Madeleine capitulates so easily to her more moralistic impulses. He would have done better to stick with the wisdom of his wife when, as Henry James suggested, she continued to look for the best even in the midst of the worst.

However, to return to Howe's point, Ratcliffe's ideas cannot be dismissed as easily as they are in the denouement of Adams's novel. Senator Ratcliffe is not an attractive character, and his arguments may be advanced too bluntly for our comfort, not to mention Adams's, but his thought cannot simply be brushed aside. Tacitly Adams seems to recognize this fact. Only after she learns that Ratcliffe has actually accepted a bribe does Madeleine reject her suitor. But by this time, she has already heard his harsh pronouncements on political morality and she knows that he has rigged an election, but these facts do not lead her to turn him away. Only what she takes to be a still greater crime can accomplish that. Perhaps what we see here is a "flirtation with pragmatism,"[23] a pull toward the less absolutist world of his friend William James or even, perhaps, to the world of Machiavelli. It is notable, as Michael Colacurcio points out, that "Adams refuses to let the battle between Ratcliffe and Mrs. Lee be fairly joined on theoretical grounds." And he adds, "perhaps successful government does depend on the rather free use of power by men more honest than Ratcliffe but less scrupulous than Adams."[24] But to see this clearly would require Adams to be much more a *Homo politicus* than he was, in spite of his not very successful forays into independent politics and his hope that his vigorous journalism would bring him some measure of power. Like his heroine, he saw much, but what he saw shook his nerves to pieces also. In the end, neither Adams nor Madeleine Lee can accept pragmatic arguments. Philosophically they yearn for absolute truths. And like Madeleine, when Ratcliffe asks her to assume responsibility by giving him moral guidance, Adams seems to say, with her, "No, no! . . . no responsibility. You ask more than I can give."[25] In the end, both Madeleine and Adams opt out of politics. As Colacurcio says, "Mrs. Lee's experience seems to be Adams's recognition that, for *him*, private integrity and public power were incompatible."[26]

What Adams displays is an example of the classic Mugwump sensibility.[27] In his brilliant sketch of these reformers, Richard Hofstadter might well have had Adams in mind. In general, the Mugwumps were New Englanders who had trouble finding a place for themselves in the rapidly emerging postwar society. They typically ignored or accepted the often terrible conditions of the working class and rigidly adhered to the principles of laissez-faire economics, along with tariff and civil service reform. What influence they had was derived from sheer brain power and social position, but they were cut off from any base of mass support. Only when this isolation ended at the turn of the century could the Progressive movement become a real force in American politics.[28] Adams fits this picture almost perfectly. He is brilliant in political criticism, and his insights remain useful today in a world that exhibits forms of corruption all too close to those he endured. But he was temperamentally ill suited to engage in the political action that might have been able to come to grips with the situation of his time. And when the time came, and though he knew Theodore Roosevelt well, he never engaged with the Progressives. By then, his always restless mind had moved on to other things.

In particular, Adams had little grasp of the role of political parties in democratic politics. This is understandable in part, since the parties of his time were deeply corrupt, and this corruption went hand in hand with the similarly deep corruption of American finance and the emerging industrial system.[29] Nevertheless, the parties, even in their debased condition, performed useful functions that Adams could not see. (Perhaps not until the twentieth century could anyone achieve the perspective necessary to see them.) Among other things, they helped to socialize new immigrants and served as a much-needed social welfare agency for them. In exchange, they cast their ballots as they were told, sometimes, as the old saw has it, voting early and often.[30] But the socially useful functions of the machines were below Adams's notice, though he was certainly not wrong to be bothered by the corruption of the urban organizations and of much else in American society as well.

But underneath the apparent surface moral simplicity of Adams's novel there is a much more complex argument. He would like to be able to offer simple, absolutist, moral answers to the political issues of his time, but he is too intellectually sophisticated to be entirely satisfied with them, as is revealed by the range of opinion offered in the pages of *Democracy*. Silas Ratcliffe is too powerful an enemy to be easily dismissed. So too is Baron Jacobi, for that matter.[31] One is reminded of Plato's *Republic*, where the initial argument of Thrasymachus is merely shoved aside rather than defeated. The whole dialogue is the "true" answer, and when we have the whole dialogue, Plato's own position is notoriously unclear. Of course, one way to read Plato is that he desires a system in which a superbly educated elite would rule in the interest of the whole. Adams is also tempted by this sort of thinking, as when he comments, "The great problem of every system of Government has been to place administration and legislation in the hands of the best men. We have tried our formula and find that it has failed in consequence of its clashing with our other fundamental principle that one man is as good as another."[32] Perhaps, in this sense, Adam's *Democracy* is also undemocratic, given its pessimistic conclusion, though the abrupt and underargued ending more clearly opens him to the charge of "premature closure."[33] In this view, the great theorists understand the open-ended nature of political argument and refrain from dogmatic conclusions. But, particularly with this in mind, if the views expressed by Nathan Gore and Madeleine Lee are combined with Adams's celebration of the American people in the contemporaneous *History*, any picture of Adams as just another antidemocratic misanthrope is too simple by far. The "closure" of *Democracy* is not really earned through the arguments presented. Adams falls far short of having viable answers for the new social problems of his time, but still he cannot easily be dismissed as an antidemocrat. It is much closer to the point to say that Adams was in some internal tension on this basic issue, as he recognized the power of the democratic idea, argued for in the novel by Nathan Gore and Madeleine Lee, but observed its shortcomings in the era of the Great Barbecue.

Before turning to some more general conclusions, a few other aspects of late-nineteenth-century American history should be noted. Two of these factors can best be addressed in the discussion of Adams's general philosophy of history. One is his growing xenophobia, particularly taking the form of anti-Semitism, which begins to appear after roughly 1890. There is no escaping this deplorable side of Adams's work; it is frequently vicious, but as I said in the introduction, it does not seem to be central to his theories and is, for the most part, confined to his letters. In any case, I believe that it is more appropriate to discuss it in the context of his reflections on the development of Western history. The second major theme, which also can best be handled later, is of enormous importance: his growing fascination with technology and his clear sense of its centrality not only to the history of the United States, but to the whole world as well. On this matter, Adams is a major prophet, and an extensive discussion is needed.

The third theme does require some comment here. That is the emergence of the United States as an imperial power. Adams has relatively little to say in his public pronouncements about this gigantic phenomenon; by then, his mind was fixed on more cosmic concerns. However, in his letters he reveals a good deal.[34] Since Adams's best friend John Hay was ambassador to the Court of St. James and then secretary of state under Presidents McKinley and Roosevelt, he had an insider's view of events, and since Hay viewed Adams as an expert on foreign affairs, Adams may well have been a significant influence on policy, though not everything went his way.[35] As Adams wrote to Hay, assessing his own role, "One has a right . . . to know what one's friends think. I never advise; I only diagnose, but it comes to the same thing."[36] Again, it is useful to recall the Mugwump sensibility: fiercely nationalistic; filled with foreboding about the fate of the world; hating big business, bankers, and trusts; fearing immigrants and workers; and often exhibiting anti-Semitism. In these thoughts, they were often at one with their apparent antithesis, the Populists.[37] Some of this description doubtless applies to Henry Adams, though it is a closer fit when applied to his brother Brooks. In any case, Henry sometimes emerges as a more flexible and more sympathetic figure than Hofstadter's general discussion of the Mugwumps might suggest.

Certainly, many of Adams's views turned out to be startlingly prescient. As early as 1898, he foresaw the cataclysm of World War I as English power declined. Like his mentor de Tocqueville, he saw the emergence of Russia as a great power, as well as a revolutionary upheaval in that country that made him "half crazy with fear." He also foresaw the rise of Japan, China, and the Pacific Rim. In response, he wanted an "Atlantic system," ranging from the Rockies to the Elbe, with an Anglo-American rapprochement at the center. As David Contosta points out, "Despite exaggerations and downright mistakes in judgement, Adams anticipated nearly every major shift in the international balance of power during the twentieth century, including those that transpired long after his death. That it turned out to be an American century would not have surprised him at all."[38] And in the *Education*, he sees something not at all unlike the structure of the contemporary political economy: "This was the instinct of what might be named McKinleyism; the system of combinations, consolidations, trusts, realized at home, and realizable abroad."[39] Unsurprisingly, Adams was not an admirer of McKinley. As Samuels writes, "He disliked McKinley's methods and saw in him only 'a very subtle and highly paid agent for the crudest capitalism,'" but at least his temperament was more palatable than that of his successor, Theodore Roosevelt: "From the beginning neither Adams nor Hay had been able to take Roosevelt's candidacy seriously." In spite of long years of friendship with Roosevelt, Adams worried. In the *Education* he comments, "Power when wielded by abnormal energy is the most serious of facts, and all Roosevelt's friends know that his restless and combative energy was more than abnormal." He was "pure act," a characteristic hardly likely to be attractive to so contemplative and cerebral a man as Adams.[40]

As for empire, though in the end Adams supported war with Spain, he worked hard for a peaceful resolution leading to Cuban independence, and he strongly opposed the annexation of the Philippines, using his influence in Congress and the McKinley administration to try to stop it. Annexation was contrary to America's national revolutionary heritage and "contrary to every profession or so-called principle of our lives and history."[41] These are certainly not the positions of a jingoistic radical so common at the time.

The Crisis of the Late Nineteenth Century

Henry Adams looked very deeply into some of the main currents of American life and politics in the late nineteenth century. At times his views were jaundiced and dyspeptic, but more generous impulses were at work too, and many of his diagnoses of the pathologies of his time were on the mark. There *was* a constitutional imbalance between Congress and the presidency. Woodrow Wilson, in an early attempt to get behind the paper text of the Constitution, looked at the American system as it operated in fact and saw a system of congressional dominance, though he did not share Adams's intense dislike for the Senate. And James Bryce, in his great work on American politics, was led to speculate on why great men did not become president.[42] Moreover, there was surely a need for some sort of civil service reform. Here, in spite of the impression one might get from reading the *Education*, Adams's polemics contributed to the passage of the Pendleton Act, though that legislation certainly did not meet with the success the reformers had hoped for.[43] It hardly needs to be added that the corruption of the urban machines and the financial system was as broad, deep, and genuinely scandalous as Adams said. Industrial capitalism had taken firm control of the nation's destiny. Looking back at the results, he wrote:

> [Adams] had stood up for his eighteenth century, his Constitution of 1789, his George Washington, his Harvard College, his Quincy, and

his Plymouth Pilgrims, as long as anyone would stand up with him. He had said it was hopeless twenty years before, but he had kept on, in the same old attitude, by habit and taste, until he found himself altogether alone. He had hugged his antiquated dislike of bankers and capitalistic society until he had become little better than a crank. He had known for years that he must accept the regime. . . . The matter was settled at last by the people. For a hundred years, between 1793 and 1893, the American people had hesitated, vacillated, swayed forward and back, between two forces, one simply industrial, the other capitalistic, centralizing, and mechanical. In 1893, the issue came on the single gold standard, and the majority at last declared itself, once and for all, in favor of the capitalistic system with all its necessary machinery. . . . Of all forms of society or government, this was the one he liked least, but his likes or dislikes were as antiquated as the rebel doctrine of State rights.

Continuing in the same vein, Adams says that such a society must be run by capital and capitalistic methods so that the populist idea of ruling the system by a coalition of Southern and Western farmers with urban laborers was doomed to fail, just as it had in 1800 and 1828. He concludes with some surprise and not a little acerbity:

Such great revolutions commonly leave some bitterness behind, but nothing in politics ever surprised Henry Adams more than the ease with which he and his silver friends slipped across the chasm, and alighted on the single gold standard and the capitalistic system with its methods; the protective tariff; the corporations and the trusts; the trades-unions and socialistic paternalism which necessarily made their compliment; the whole mechanical consolidation of force, which ruthlessly stamped out the life of the class into which Adams was born, but created monopolies capable of controlling the new energies that America adored.[44]

However, Adams's insights, while often deep, were also often narrow. He seems to have hoped for a return to some form of eighteenth-century constitutionalism, in which not only the balance between the branches of government but also the balance between the nation and the states would be restored. But this is to take a narrowly institutionalist position suggesting that the proper constitutional arrangements were the key to everything, a surprising point of view for one who was so sensitive to the momentous changes in the social and economic factors that shaped the Constitution during his lifetime. In this time of a healthy neo-institutionalism in political science, few today would argue that institutions are of little importance; consider only the impact of constitutional structures and Senate rules in the impeachment proceedings against President Clinton. But institutions are clearly affected by extraconstitutional forces.[45] And after all, as Adams contends in the *History*, as early as the Jefferson administration the original Constitution had been torn into so much scrap paper. Even if that is written off as an exaggeration, the Civil War certainly wrought a profound transformation of the constitutional structure; it was no longer possible to doubt that membership in the Union was permanent, and the Thirteenth, Fourteenth, and Fifteenth Amendments, while of regrettably little immediate effect other than the enormously important abolition of slavery itself, made possible the mid-twentieth-century struggles for civil rights.[46] And surely the tremendous economic changes following the war, of which Adams was so deeply aware, forced equally large alterations in constitutional politics. In addition to all this, it is evident from contemporary debates that discovery of the "intent of the Framers," even if desirable, is next to impossible,[47] so that an attempt to return to a presumably pristine earlier order is to pursue a chimera.

But the problem with Adams's view goes deeper than his well-intentioned constitutional purism. For all his intellectual acuity, he simply did not quite grasp some of the major events of his time. I have already commented on the first, namely, his inability to see the importance of a genuine Reconstruction of the former slaveholding states in the Old South. Partly, this was due to a limitation of his vision, tinged as it no doubt was by the sort of racism that was pervasive in nineteenth-century America and is all too common to this day, even if in altered forms. But more than this, as his paper "The Independents in the Canvass" shows, Adams was unable to imagine that the gentlemanly leaders of the plantation South would systematically deny the civil rights of the former slaves if they were returned to power. Perhaps this was due to the lingering sympathy of a Northern aristocrat for his Southern counterparts, in spite of the violent falling out over slavery. If only the latter could be destroyed, thought Adams, a happy and prosperous Union could be restored. Thus, early on, he bought into the mythology of black-dominated legislatures, carpetbaggers and scalawags, and a downtrodden South suffering under the heel of Northern occupiers. But now, of course, the commonly accepted historical view is that Reconstruction failed not because it was too harsh but because it did not go far enough, that it did not establish the conditions for a democratic politics that included the ex-slaves, now citizens in form but hardly in practice.[48]Adams was in tune with the thought of his time, but on this issue, that thought was destructively off the mark.

Ironically, the end of Reconstruction was signaled by the agreement that concluded the dispute over the election of 1876, in which Democrat Samuel J. Tilden won the popular vote and came within one vote of a majority in the electoral college but lost out to Rutherford B. Hayes in a deal between Northern Republican business interests, particularly those of the railroads, and conservative white Southerners. This compromise became the prototype for a coalitional form that assumed enormous power in American politics for the better part of a century.[49] One wonders if Adams understood the link between the sort of sectional peace he favored and the growing industrial-capitalist power he detested. As for those powers, Adams made many potent criticisms of those who held them and the institutional distortions their position caused. But his focus was largely limited to political and economic elites, and he displayed little concern for the impact the new economic system had on those at the bottom of the new economic order. Even in an increasingly urban, industrial society, and in spite of his expressed admiration for Karl Marx, he had no use for socialism and was not part of the intellectual movement toward the welfare state whose first stirrings could be observed in many of his contemporaries. Nor did he show much interest in the possibilities of government regulation of the new power centers.[50] In fact, his attachment to laissez-faire economics may have been enough by itself to deter him. Thus, his was a powerful voice, but it was largely critical, though usefully so, rather than constructive.

Adams was writing at a historical juncture where new forms of state organization were needed to deal with the new concentrations of financial and industrial power that developed with such explosive force after the Civil War. Although in the next decades the United States was to move toward increasingly powerful, centralized state forms, this was contrary to earlier American traditions in which, from a European point of view, the nation, as one of the attributes of its "exceptionalism," could hardly be said to have had a "state" at all.[51] In a long, complex process, the American "state" was first patched and then, during the Progressive movement, reconstituted. This took place, as Stephen Skowronek notes, "through political struggles rooted in and mediated by preestablished institutional arrangements."[52] It is fair to assume that intellectual-ideological conflicts were part of this process. Some members of the upper class, certainly including Adams, doubtless suffered from what Hofstadter called "status anxiety," a deep-seated perception that a once secure position of power is slipping away. One can easily see it in the lament quoted earlier. However, others were part of a newly developing reformist, professional elite of social scientists. As Skowronek puts it, "the institutional reform movements of the late nineteenth century represent a linkage between an older patrician style of deference politics and a new professional style based on expertise."[53] Adams was obviously one of those patricians, though, to repeat, his offerings were more critical than constructive, even though in foreign policy and finance he had a good deal of expertise to offer. Still, aside from his long and somewhat quixotic fight against Republican orthodoxy, he displayed little interest in the newer currents of reform.

Around 1890, Adams's career took a decided change in direction. With the completion of the *History*, he ceased to be a historian in any ordinary sense, though he did have some status as an elder statesman within the profession. And he had already left journalism behind long before. Thereafter, his interests turned to often very high-level speculation, even if in the guise of a study of medieval thought and architecture or his formally idiosyncratic "autobiography." Therefore, perhaps this is an appropriate time to make a preliminary assessment of the "historian as political theorist," at the end of this more orthodox phase of his career, though this obviously cannot be the last word on the subject, which is reconsidered in the final chapter.

To say *orthodox* certainly implies no criticism, nor does it suggest that Adams's work in the early and middle phases of his career was not powerfully critical or deny the strong theoretical impulse that ran through it. However, placing Adams in the eddying currents of American thought is not simple. It is *almost* conventional wisdom to follow Louis Hartz and define the American political tradition as liberal in its essence, with its emphasis on laissez-faire, individual rights, competitiveness, distrust of government, and so forth. Adams himself was inclined to identify his own position as liberal as well as democratic, which makes good sense, given his embrace of a putatively liberal Constitution and his devotion to liberal economics. Yet in the past thirty years, the hegemony of liberalism over the American mind has been challenged by a form of thought labeled *republican*, a concept just as difficult to pin down as liberalism. Perhaps the central idea of republicanism is virtue, whether in the form of a virtuous citizenry or virtuous leaders. In any event, both citizens and leaders need to be on guard against the nemesis of sound republicanism, namely, corruption, the subordination of the public good to special interests. Republicanism also includes an important warning that there is a tension between virtue and commerce. Until the late 1960s, the American Revolution was assumed to be liberal, deeply under the influence of John Locke. However, the new republican reading of revolutionary history challenged the theory of the Revolution as liberal by suggesting that what really set off the Revolution was fear of corruption as a threat to republican virtue, stemming from the corruption of the British Empire itself. By now, almost no one believes that liberalism can be replaced in American history by republican theory, as some seemed to believe at the high tide of what came to be called the "republican synthesis." When the revolutionaries spoke of republicanism, they referred first of all to the absence of a king, and though they did indeed fear corruption in the republican sense, they also were devoted to the preservation of a highly liberal set of individual rights. For example, one need only consider the well-known language of the Declaration of Independence. Nor did any of the Founders spend time debating the fine points of liberalism versus republicanism, since they were much too busy making a revolution and writing a constitution to debate the sort of theoretical niceties recent political theorists have enjoyed discussing. And after much debate, a lot of it quite fruitful, students of American thought have come to see the ideas of the founding period as a complex mix of liberal and republican ideas. The real question is how early liberalism emerged as the dominant force it is—or at least was, until recently.[54]

In the perspective of this history, Adams is a very interesting case. There are surely important liberal components in his thought, but there is a lot to be said for the position of Russell Hanson and Richard Merriman that Adams was one of the last, if not *the* last, of the civic republicans.[55] He himself would not have discussed his position in terms of liberalism versus republicanism, and it is also clear that his devotion to laissez-faire was liberal and perhaps deeply antirepublican in its implications. One could claim that the Constitution to which he was so committed was also liberal, even though defectively so, given its acceptance of slavery. And later, it will be necessary to take into account Adams's doubtless ironical but still provocative presentation of his position as that of a conservative Christian anarchist. But that is a subsequent development in his thought. At least for the first phase of his career, there is much to support the republican interpretation.

Adams's frequent remark that his was an essentially eighteenth-century mind ill at ease in his own century is at the heart of the republican component of his thought. He had a powerfully developed sense of the tension between virtue and commerce or, in the terms of Hanson and Merriman, "wealth and commonwealth."[56] He was drawn to the eighteenth century because then it was still possible to escape the determinism that he saw as such a powerful force as early as the years covered in the *History*. This is one of the reasons why Albert Gallatin was his favorite American statesman. Gallatin was a man of the highest ideals who had the chance to act, free of the powers that shaped policy and that soon began to spin out of control. "The early history of the republic was to a significant degree open to human intervention. The fate of the young republic was not predetermined." Yet even then, men like Gallatin had to wrestle with forces they themselves did not create.[57] As the end of the nineteenth century drew near, Adams could only warn through the powerful medium of his historical and journalistic writing, as well as his novel *Democracy*. This is history written in something like a classically republican mode, in which an effort is made to recall an errant, increasingly corrupt republic back to its founding principles. It is a history of statesmen, soldiers, and virtuous citizens. Increasingly, it takes the form of a lament, or, to revert to the language of Adams's Puritan ancestors, of the Jeremiad. But by 1890, Adams seems to have felt that there was no more audience for such sermons. The problem was not the worthlessness of the Constitution or of democracy. Rather, it was that these ideals had been corrupted by the subversive forces of industrial capitalism. Surely there was reason for Adams to mourn the condition of late-nineteenth-century democracy, just as there was reason to worry about the condition of late-twentieth-century democracy for many of the same reasons. This is why we, and particularly those engaged in the republican revival or its close cousin, the communitarian movement, may still be able to learn from Adams.[58] He does not always make it easy, with his retrograde attitudes on Reconstruction and his dated attachment to the dogmas of laissez-faire, but surely he is worth more attention than he receives from students of American political thought.

And yet, as important and revealing as the republican hypothesis is, it cannot fully capture the complexity of Adams's multifaceted thought. Another possibility is simply to absorb him into the conservative tradition, as suggested by Russell Kirk.[59] But Kirk, doubtless among others, seems to have been deceived by Adams's posthumously published collection of essays, originally edited by his brother Brooks and assigned by him the title *The Degradation of the Democratic Dogma*. In fact, this collection has precious little to do with either democracy or politics and not very much more to do with history as ordinarily understood. The title reflects more of Brooks's eccentric views than those of his older brother, while the essays themselves deal with Adams's fruitless search for a genuinely scientific theory of history rooted in physics. And if Henry Adams was in some sense what we call a conservative, then what do we make of the fact that he has been widely admired by such mainstream liberal historians as Henry Commager and Arthur Schlesinger,

Jr., as well as liberal literary critics such as Alfred Kazin?[60] Or still further away from Kirk, what about his influence on Martin Sklar, a writer often associated with the New Left and the theory of corporate liberalism?[61] Thinkers of a wide range of persuasions have clearly found inspiration in the work of Adams, no doubt a tribute to the protean character of his work.

But for whatever reason, perhaps out of sheer despair, Adams turned his attention to more speculative ventures as he tried to understand the role of religion in human life, particularly as played off against the wonders of science and technology and the dynamics of Western capitalism, while at the same time trying to chart the evolution, as well as the stops and starts, of his own remarkably capacious mind. Though his later writings can hardly be labeled history as ordinarily conceived, we can learn from them a great deal about the course of American development and of the Western world's as well. These works are a remarkable, if sometimes quirky, intellectual edifice in which Adams engages in a very American, very individualistic attempt to create a portrait of his own unique and often eccentric self.

Part II

The Philosophy of History

Chapter 6

Religion, History, and Politics

Adams's two great late books, *Mont Saint Michel and Chartres* and *The Education of Henry Adams*, form a pair; each complements the other. Both are concerned with the relation of politics and history to religion, science, and technology, and the development, one might even say creation, of Adams's sense of self. And central to much of this discussion is the role of women in society. On most of these questions Adams held unconventional, even iconoclastic views.

This was nowhere more true than his thinking on religion. I remarked earlier that, in spite of his Puritan ancestry, Adams could submit himself to the discipline of no church. In the *Education*, he tells us that as far as Boston was concerned, the Unitarian clergy had solved the problems of the universe, thus, in effect, leaving them with nothing to do.

> Of all the conditions of his youth which afterwards puzzled the grown-up man, this disappearance of religion puzzled him most. The boy went to church twice every Sunday; he was taught to read his Bible, and he learned religious poetry by heart; he believed in a mild deism; he prayed; he went through all the forms; but neither to him nor to his brothers or sisters was religion real. Even the mild discipline of the Unitarian Church was so irksome that they all threw it off at the first possible moment, and never afterwards entered a church.[1]

It is not even clear whether Adams was ultimately an atheist. Yet his most aesthetically beautiful book centers on the Virgin Mary. It is a veritable hymn of praise, a very joyful hymn at that. And it is highly personal, seemingly not rooted in any theology, least of all Roman Catholic theology. His Mariolatry was of a piece with his general adoration of women, though the adoration was always practiced, after the tragic death of his wife, from a safe distance. But to understand Adams on religion it is necessary to come to grips with his views on women.

Early in the *Education*, Adams lays down a "general law of experience—no woman had ever driven him wrong; no man had ever driven him right."[2] More specifically, he claims that "the American woman of the nineteenth century was much better company than the American man."[3] And in perhaps the most striking of all his generalizations, he proclaims, "The proper study of mankind is woman, and by common agreement since the time of Adam, it is the most complex and arduous."[4] His first general foray into the topic of women was a lecture given at the Lowell Institute in 1876, though it was not published until 1891.[5] In many respects, "Primitive Rights of Women" is an astonishing essay that exhibits considerable learning and a great historical sweep, ranging from North American Indians to ancient Egypt, Greece, and Rome, to the Scandinavian sagas, to the development of Christian ideas about the social role of women. Defining his interest, Adams tells us, "As he grew older, he found that Early Institutions lost their interest, but that Early Women became a passion. Without understanding movement of sex, history seemed to him mere pedantry."[6] In his paper, Adams is particularly concerned to show that his friend Sir Henry Maine was wrong to adopt the position that the early place of married women was one of slavery, with the husband wielding despotic power over his wife, just as he did over his children.[7]

Adams examines the social place of women in societies ranging from simple communal systems, where all things were owned in common, to the more complex ancient societies and on into early Christianity. In all the early societies he finds that women had a great deal of freedom to marry or divorce and that in these societies there was space for strong women to flourish as well. For instance, Homer's Penelope was besieged by suitors because of her power position, in spite of the fact that she was a good deal older than most of those who sought her hand.[8]

But this happy situation was not to last. The villain of the piece is Christianity. Christian theologians "adopted the Trinity, and in adopting it, dethroned the woman from her place." But Adams anticipates *Chartres* by noting, "Yet even then, notwithstanding this degradation, the irresistible spread of Mariolatry, the worship of the Virgin Mother, proved how strongly human nature revolted against the change."[9]

But worse was to come:

> Next to the purification of morals, and indeed as one of the principal means toward it, the Church felt with most intensity the necessity of discipline and obedience in society, and taught that lesson with only too much earnestness and success. The rise of Christianity marked the diminution of women's social and legal rights.[10]

Put bluntly, "the Church was the principal agency in degrading the status of women."[11] Church doctrine came to focus more on the duties of women than on their rights. The "legal and temporal" aspects of marriage tended to be subordinate to the moral aspect and religious meaning of the contract. A new ideal of femininity developed, displacing the "proud, self-confident, vindictive woman of the German tradition." The new woman was to be "meek and patient, the silent and tender sufferer, the pale reflection of the Mater Dolorosa, submissive to every torture her husband could invent, but more submissive to the Church than to her husband." Under these conditions, "the family, like the State, took on the character of a petty absolutism." Thus, neither the church nor the state could rest the claim to authority on consent.[12] Obviously, this is not the foundation for a conventional nineteenth-century view of either women or religion.

In Adams's New England context, perhaps the most notable aspect of this discussion of women's rights is the absence of any mention of women's suffrage. Ernest Samuels observes, "Henry Adams doubtless shared James Russell Lowell's amused contempt for the perspiring crusaders who proclaimed the New Jerusalem in strident treble voices. Entirely beneath notice were the unseemly activities of Susan B. Anthony, Elizabeth Cady Stanton, and Lucretia Mott, and their National Woman Suffrage Association." But perhaps there was some mitigation for Adams's position. In his view, Samuels goes on, "Women's suffrage did not touch the basic question: How to establish the dignity of women as co-equals with men. In his judgement mere legislative enactments did not face the question al all."[13]

This position cannot just be dismissed out of hand. Dignity and equality with men are surely worthy goals. And one could certainly argue that the adoption of women's suffrage has not solved all women's problems by any means. Yet from another point of view, Adams's position is more than a little strange. He was, after all, a member of the fourth generation of perhaps the most important political dynasty in American history. And surely he must have been aware of his great-grandmother Abigail's famous injunction to her husband John Adams to "remember the ladies." Nor could it be said that he did not treat women's political views seriously; for example, some of his most interesting letters from a political standpoint were sent to his dear friend Elizabeth Cameron, the estranged wife of Senator Simon Cameron of Pennsylvania. One can only assume that he was so caught up in the manners and mores of Victorian America that he simply failed to see the anomaly in his thought. But the flaw is significant. Perhaps in elevating women to an almost mystical level and in stressing motherhood, as he did, he could not see that the equality, if not the superiority, he sought for women could be furthered by granting them the suffrage. Here, as elsewhere in his career, Adams shows a weakened sense of politics and the political. As Clive Bush comments, "A sexual, or indeed sexist, bias then enters the picture. An opposition emerges between female-oriented institutions which are basically apolitical and male-oriented states which are fully political. As a symbolic narrative this opposition reflects a certain conservatism at a time when women in the United States were pressing for the vote."[14]

There is, as William Merrill Decker says, an undercurrent of reaction in this early paper by Adams. But perhaps to compensate for that, "he has elevated the woman to the status of historical subject," and while women play no role in the *History*, they can be studied in the freer form of the novel.[15] Thus, in spite of the suffrage problem, his paper on early women's rights is in some ways a remarkable performance. The range of learning Adams displays is genuinely impressive, though I would not venture to say how well the scholarship holds up today; it is the normative import of his position that is interesting.[16] Still, it can be argued that the work is that of a genuine pioneer. In her fine article "Henry Adams's Anthropological Vision," Eugenia Kaledin compares his work with that of Joan Wallach Scott and Natalie Zemon Davis. Thus Adams, like Scott, was interested in "looking at the way women's presence gave a richer 'meaning to the organization and perception of historical knowledge.'" And Kaledin suggests that Adams matches Davis's position on the role of gender studies, the goal being "to discover the range in sex roles and in sexual symbolism in different societies and periods and how they functioned in the social order to promote its change."[17] Pioneer or not, in Adams's worldview, women are surely central, as is absolutely clear in his second novel of ideas, *Esther*, published in 1884 under the pseudonym Frances Snow Compton.[18]

Faith, Science, and Organized Religion

Esther occupied a central place in Adams's mind and heart. As he wrote to Elizabeth Cameron, "I care more for one chapter, or any dozen pages of *Esther* than for the whole *History*, including maps and indexes."[19] The source of his deep feeling is that this is another roman à clef, closely modeled on his most inner circle of friends and, above all, on his wife Marian, who inspired the title character, with, as in the case of Madeleine Lee, elements of the author's mind and personality included in the portrait.[20] And of course, having exposed some of her deepest feelings, that meaning was even more precious to Adams after the suicide of his wife.

The plot of the novel is essentially simple, and the philosophical argument is clear, though not without complexity. Adams's heroine, Esther Dudley, loves and is loved by the Reverend Stephen Hazard. But she cannot share Hazard's religious faith and so, in an unhappy ending, rejects him because she feels that her lack of belief would be a hindrance to his ministerial career. The heart of the book is an intense series of conversations about religion and science with the active participation of geologist George Strong, who is so impressed by Esther's spirited defense of her ideas and beliefs that he too wishes to marry her. But he also is rejected because of Esther's love for Hazard.

Esther is perhaps the only character in either of Adams's novels who emerges as anything like a fully characterized person. She is very intelligent, quick-minded in discussion, and has a sure sense of herself that she is extremely reluctant to violate. She is introduced to us by Strong, modeled partly on Adams and primarily on Adams's dear friend, the distinguished geologist Clarence King.[21] Strong calls Esther "the sternest little Pagan I know."[22] Mr. Wharton, an artist based on another family friend, John La Farge, recalls Henry James's comment on Clover Adams when he refers to Esther as "one of the most marked American types I know."[23] And Wharton adds some interesting testimony on the nature of Esther's mind:

> She gives one the idea of a lightly-sparred yacht in mid-ocean; unexpected; you ask yourself what the devil she is doing there. She sails gaily along, though there is no land in sight and plenty of rough water coming. She has never read a book, I believe, in her life. . . . She picks up all she knows without an effort and knows nothing well, yet she seems to understand whatever is said. Her mind is as irregular as her face, and both have the same peculiarity. I notice that the lines of her eyebrows, nose, all end with a slight upward curve like a yacht's sails which give a kind of hopefulness and self-confidence to her expression. Mind and face have the same curves.[24]

Esther has a well-developed will and likes to have her own way. Also, like Madeleine Lee, not to mention Henry Adams, "She had the instinct of power, but not the love of responsibility."[25] She is also very strong. As her father lies dying, she fends off the concerns of her suitor, Reverend Hazard, saying, "Do not feel alarmed about me. Women have more strength than men."[26] It is also interesting and perhaps a little puzzling, in view of Adams's later attraction to the Middle Ages, that the painter Wharton pays her tribute by saying, "There is nothing medieval about her. If she belongs to any besides the present, it is to the next world which artists want to see, when paganism will come again and we can give a divinity to every waterfall."[27] And above all, she has no use for organized religion. Regarding church services: "By the time the creed was read, she could not honestly feel that she believed a word of it, or could force herself to say that she ever could believe it." In her words, "I can't be respectable and believe the thirty-nine articles. I can't go to church every Sunday or hold my tongue or pretend to be pious."[28]

This aversion to religion precipitates the dramatic crisis of the novel. She is loved by Hazard, an Episcopalian minister in New York, who is based on Adams's second cousin Philips Brooks. Throughout his courtship of Esther, Hazard and Strong are engaged in a struggle for her soul, or perhaps, given Esther's irreligious nature, one might better say for her sense of self. By representing himself to some extent in the characters of both Esther and Strong, Adams places himself in the heart of the discussions at the center of the novel. J. C. Levenson shrewdly observes that "as the spokesman for unromantic liberalism, he occupies the far point in the lover's triangle and, in his relation to Esther, he makes possible a dialogue between personifications of two aspects of Henry Adams."[29] The discussions among the three characters encapsulate much of the debate between science and religion in the nineteenth century.[30] And, as in *Democracy*, the discussions, in part due to Adams's limitations as a writer of fiction, take on some of the characteristics of a philosophical dialogue, with little genuine novelistic impact.

The heart of the problem is laid out early in the novel. Stephen Hazard preaches a sermon in which he claims that "the church now knows with the certainty of science what she once knew only by the certainty of faith," that behind all thought and matter lies one idea, "an idea which the church has never ceased to embody." That idea is "I AM." This idea is both the starting point and the goal of both metaphysics and philosophy, but "the church alone has pointed out from the beginning that the starting-point is not human but divine. The philosopher says—I am, and the church scouts his philosophy. She answers: No! You are NOT, you have no existence of your own. You were and are and ever will be only a part of the supreme I AM, of which the church is the emblem." As narrator, Adams adds sardonically, "In this symbolic representation of his right to property in their souls and bodies, perhaps the preacher rose a little above the heads of his audience." This gloss on Descartes is certainly not how the congregation identifies itself.[31]

But the sermon hardly seems over Esther's head, though she cannot be said to have been convinced. "I thought it very entertaining," she says, and a little later adds, in conversation with her freethinking father, "I am charmed. . . . Only it certainly does come just a little near being an opera house. Mr. Hazard looks horribly like Meyerbeer's Prophet. He ordered us about in a fine tenor voice, with his eyes, and told us that we belonged to him, and if we did not behave ourselves he would blow up the church and us in it."[32]

Therein lies the problem of the novel. Esther scorns the doctrine but rapidly comes to love its messenger. The stage, as I have said, is set for a number of spirited discussions of science, religion, and the relations among the three characters as Hazard tries to sweep aside Esther's qualms about his religion and Strong weighs in with his understanding of science. Strong argues from a slightly odd, almost pragmatic position, because he believes "that since the Church continued to exist, it probably served some necessary purpose in human economy, though he could himself no more understand the good of it than he could comprehend the use of human existence in any shape."[33] But Strong has no particular wish, or need, to impose his beliefs on others. In fact, his skepticism is so strong that he feels he cannot ask anyone else to accept them. Though at one point he says to Hazard that "science alone is truth,"[34] in general, he is a skeptic about even that. As he says later in another context, "Mystery for mystery science beats religion hollow. I can't open my mouth in my lecture room without repeating ten times as many unintelligible formulas as ever Hazard is forced to do in his church."[35]

It is in a discussion with Esther that Strong gives his fullest statement on the nature of science. Esther begins the dialogue by asking whether religion is true. Strong begs off answering and says, "Ask me something easier! Ask me whether science is true!" And of course Esther, being close kin to Madeleine Lee and the Adams family, does indeed ask, "Is science true?" Strong answers no.

> "Then why do you believe in it?"
> "I don't believe in it."
> "Then why do you belong to it?"
> "Because I want to help in making it truer. . . . There is no science which does not begin by requiring you to believe in the incredible."
> "Are you telling me the truth?"
> "I tell you the solemn truth that the doctrine of the Trinity is not so difficult to accept for a working proposition as any one of the axioms of physics. The wife of my mathematical colleague, to my knowledge, never even stopped to ask whether it was true that a point has neither length, breadth nor thickness."

Esther explodes that Strong is not being honest and asserts, "You don't care whether geology is true or not." And Strong answers that he really does not very much. But of course this does not satisfy Esther, who has a desperate need to know the truth of the claims of religion, because if she cannot accept them, she cannot marry Hazard, since her disbelief would damage him with his congregation. And Strong replies, "The trouble with you is that you start wrong. You need what is called faith, and you are trying to get it by reason. It can't be done. Faith is a state of mind, like love or jealousy. You can never reason yourself into it." But a moment later, Hazard tells her that if she has enough faith in *Hazard* she can accept the church and submit. And Esther's final outburst is, "I want nothing of the church! Why should it trouble me? Why should I submit to it? Why can't it leave me alone?"[36]

We have already encountered Esther's resistance to organized religion, and her love for Hazard develops in spite of what starts out to be his very orthodox position, so orthodox that he would rather face equally strong opponents because he is "never afraid of pure atheism; it is the flabby kind of deism that annoys me, because it is as slippery as air."[37] Indeed, his orthodoxy is his strongest point. "Of all weaknesses he most disliked timid and half-hearted faith. He would rather have jumped at once to Strong's pure denial, than yield an inch to the argument that a mystery was to be paltered with because it could not be explained."[38] Echoing the possessiveness claimed for the church in his sermon, Hazard extends it to Esther: "I am tyrannical. I want your whole life and even more. I will be put off with nothing else. Don't you see that I can't retreat."[39]

Given Esther's personality and beliefs, this is a very unlikely path to success for Hazard. Sensing this, he makes a strategic retreat and offers a version of Pascal's wager. Saying that even he has doubts and that every nontheistic question can be answered by a tenet even more inconceivable than that of the church, he goes on to ask, "What do you gain by getting rid of one incomprehensible only to put a greater one in its place, and throw away your only hope besides? The atheists offer no sort of bargain for one's soul. Their scheme is all loss and no gain. At last both they and I come back to a confession of ignorance; the only difference between us is that my ignorance is joined with a faith and hope."[40] Hazard then goes on to point out, still in his Pascalian, "pragmatic" mode, that there are scores of clergymen who are little more than skeptics, having made the same wager, in effect, exercising something akin to William James's "will to believe."[41] But orthodoxy triumphs; Hazard cannot long remain in the pragmatic mood, even in his desperate desire to win Esther. Asked whether he truly believes in the resurrection of the body, he answers that he does, to which Esther replies that the very idea is "shocking." And when Hazard challenges her by asking if she can imagine a future in which she would not see her loved ones again, she bursts out, "Why must the church always appeal to my weakness and never to my strength! . . . What is the use of appealing to my sex? The atheists at least show me respect enough not to do that!"[42]

With this Hazard admits defeat and leaves the scene. Strong has overheard Esther's defense of her principles and is so moved that he also proposes. He too is rejected, with Esther saying, "But George, I don't love you, I love him."[43] But of course, this is more than a simple sad romance come to a bad end. In rejecting both Hazard and Strong, Esther has rejected both science and religion. Levenson puts it with characteristic acuity: "Esther declares the emotional bankruptcy of both science and religion, the great contesting forces in the nineteenth-century struggle of belief."[44] Strong has told her that he believes in nothing but mind and matter and that he has no wish to convert anyone to his beliefs. In fact, he goes so far as to say, "I prefer almost any kind of religion. No one ever took up this doctrine who could help himself."[45] And though her position is certainly closer to Strong's than to Hazard's, this is not enough for Esther's ideals. Perhaps only the pagan world imagined for her by the painter Wharton can meet her needs. As it is, she can neither compromise her beliefs for the apparent satisfactions of pragmatism nor fit her conscience to the requirements of a church incapable of engendering her faith. She is the embodiment of the New England conscience stripped of religion.[46]

Just as Madeleine Lee cannot accept Senator Ratcliffe's pragmatic compromises with the absolutist morality she believes in, so too must Esther Dudley reject a religion weakened by pragmatism and a science focused only on mind and matter.[47] Just like an Adams, she must have something more permanent on which to stand. *Mont Saint Michel and Chartres* may be read as an attempt to discover such a standard.

The Ideal Female

Mont Saint Michel and Chartres occupies a special place in Adams's work. As he explains in the *Education*, he sought to measure man as a force by its motion starting from a fixed point. He looked for the point in history "when man held the highest idea of himself as a unit in a unified universe." Years of study led him to think that that point might be the century from 1150 to 1250. Then, "Setting himself to the task, he began a volume which he mentally knew as 'Mont-Saint-Michel and Chartres: a Study of Thirteenth Century Unity.' From that point he proposed to fix a position for himself, which he could label; 'The Education of Henry Adams: a Study of Twentieth Century Multiplicity.' With the help of these two points of relation, he hoped to project his lines forward and backward indefinitely, subject to correction from anyone who should know better."[48] Thus the two works cannot really be separated; they complement each other, and it is only for the sake of expository clarity that they are not treated together.

Chartres is something altogether remarkable and, I think, sui generis. Surely there is nothing else quite like it in American letters. Completed in 1904 but, like the great *History* and the *Education*, printed in a private edition for his friends, it was not available to the public until 1913. With the possible exception of *Esther*, it is Adams's most personal book.[49] Clearly it touches something very deep within him that inspires a work of great artistic beauty. It is a happy book, a jeu d'esprit, lacking the irony, bitterness, and cynicism that are characteristic of so much of his other writing. Adams has succeeded in heeding his own warning: "The man who wanders into the twelfth century is lost, unless he can grow prematurely young."[50] His friend William James, not always so sympathetic to Adams's work, caught this spirit: "I can't help sending you a paean of praise. From beginning to end it reads as from a man in the fresh morning of life, with a frolic power unusual to historic literature." And clearly, as Samuels says, James saw the book as an abandonment of both vulgar positivism and "arrogant intellectualism,"[51] in favor of an essentially aesthetic approach.

That is no doubt true. It certainly is not a book of history in anything like the usual sense, and its scholarship, from an orthodox point of view, is excessively personalized, not to mention sometimes quite derivative. What Adams offers is essentially a myth; referring to the central character in Adams's book, John McIntyre writes, "*His Virgin is a fiction and should be treated as such.*"[52] Edward Saveth is quite right to treat Adams's Virgin as another character along with Madeleine Lee and Esther Dudley.[53] The myth he constructs is a very pretty picture indeed, though his view of the Middle Ages is certainly highly selective. As Alfred Kazin says: "In his American histories he had shown himself the most demanding student of social and economic facts. There was nothing like these in the thirteenth century—he took no interest in how the Church spellbound and controlled the masses; there were no tiresome wars of tribute; no looting Crusaders; no murders in the cathedral or disease raging outside it."[54]

Though *Chartres* has some partially buried political implications, Adams leaves politics and economics, in any modern sense, almost completely out of the picture he is painting, though one might argue that in the medieval world, politics and perhaps even economics were religious in some fundamental way. If one does take them directly into account, it is hard to find the unity Adams attributes to the medieval world. Samuels sums up more fully than Kazin:

> The politics of the time were a trackless jungle in which feudal monarchs and nobles stalked each other in a ceaseless contest for territory and power, a contest in which the rival ambitions of great priests and prelates were inextricably confounded. Serfs and peasants were hustled off to fight and die in a thousand nameless quarrels or stayed home to be plundered with savage ferocity by lawless marauders. Whole populations were decimated in the hysterical frenzies of the Crusades. . . . It was a society in which barbarous superstitions were maintained by a penal system whose tortures confront us in countless paintings. It was also a world undergoing an immense transformation as commerce rapidly expanded, dotting the landscape with thriving towns, developing manufactures, and encouraging science.[55]

Ignoring these factors in order to focus on a unity of religion and art is to pay a high historical price. The result is a work that stands in marked contrast to the complex mix of politics, economics, and culture that was characteristic of the *History*.[56]

Of course, Adams was fully aware of these lacunae. After all, he had introduced the seminar method to Harvard in his teaching of medieval history. And in the *History*, he was quite scathing in his remarks about the medieval period. Thus Napoleon, the great villain of the *History*, had a "moral sense which regarded truth and falsehood as equally useful modes of expression— an unprovoked war or secret assassination as equally natural forms of activity— such a combination of qualities as Europe had forgotten since the Middle Ages." Between them, Napoleon and Pitt had renewed "the bigotry and despotism of the Middle Ages."[57] Given this, it is clear that Adams knew that he was not writing any kind of standard history but rather a work that is, for the most part, a prose poem.

It can hardly be said that when Adams tried to find a fixed, unified starting point for his interpretation of Western history he cared much for historical precision. As he said of Eleanor of Aquitaine, her "real nature in no way concerns us." And he states, "For us the poetry is history, and the facts are false."[58] What Adams sought was less a real-world starting point than an ideal against which to measure the development of history and the condition of twentieth-century civilization.[59] *Mont Saint Michel and Chartres* is an exceedingly rich book, and it is necessary to bypass much that is of great interest. I have no qualifications to evaluate what Adams says about the architecture of the great cathedrals or medieval literature. Also, I cannot enter into a discussion of the merits of Adams's ideas on medieval thought. Instead, I focus on Adams as an early-twentieth-century figure who was deeply concerned with the dynamics of his own society and sought to understand his own century by contrasting it with a particular and very personal image of the medieval worldview. The subject, then, is Adams and not medieval France.

One final comment should be made before discussing Adams's fascinating book. In spite of its subject matter, *Mont Saint Michel and Chartres* is in no sense a religious or devotional book. As Levenson says, "He had no desire to teach faith, which he thought was unteachable and knew he had not earned,"[60] a position that is entirely consistent with the views of Adams as expressed by George Strong in *Esther*.

Adams begins dramatically with Saint Michael, the patron saint of Mont Saint Michel: "The Archangel loved heights. . . . The Archangel stands for Church and State, and both militant. He is the conqueror of Satan, the mightiest of all created spirits, the nearest to God."[61] But note that these are intensely masculine images, and it is women that concern Adams much more profoundly, not just in the medieval world, but in his own time too.

Thus, *Chartres* clearly begins in a masculine mode, a mode that is the first part of a tripartite structure. According to one view, the whole argument of the work is a stepping down from the archangel's heights to the end of the discussion of Thomas Aquinas in the last chapter of the book. This is not altogether fanciful when the book as a whole is considered, but it overlooks the still greater heights reached in the central chapters, which deal with women in general but above all with the place, the sheer force, of the Virgin Mary's role in medieval society.[62]

Thus, *Chartres* may begin with Saint Michael, but the heart of the book is the colorful, iconoclastic, some might say heretical portrait of Mary, spelled out in detail over several chapters focused on Chartres Cathedral. As R. P. Blackmur has written, the discussion of Mont Saint Michel was "Romanesque and military," while the description of Chartres was "Gothic and intuitive; the one was a matter of struggle and survival, the other a matter of understanding and aspiration. But Adams' interest is in the second rather than in the first."[63] For Adams, "The Virgin was a real person, whose tastes, wishes, instincts, passions, were intimately known." Writing about her almost as if she were the subject of a standard scholarly biographical literature, he claims, "Enough of the Virgin's literature survives to show her character, and the course of her daily life. We know more about her habits and thoughts than those of earthly queens."[64] At the very least, his treatment of her is unorthodox. The best way to approach it is by quoting from it at length. To the extent that Mary is near the center of Adams's thought, we can understand a significant part of his social, historical, and political thought through his picture of her. Interestingly, but surely not coincidentally, she seems to share some of Adams's quirks and ideas. Perhaps this is because his portrait of Mary is a direct descendant of his picture of Esther Dudley and, by extension, of Marion Adams.[65] And unfortunately, like Adams, "She had many of the failings and prejudices of her humanity. For example, in spite of her own origin, she disliked Jews, and rarely neglected a chance to maltreat them," though here, in contrast to some of his other writings, Adams has the grace to suggest that this was a failing on the part of his heroine. Again like Adams, "Mary never loved bankers."[66] But more importantly, I think, she shared with Clover Adams her sprightly and iconoclastic nature, though of course not her motherhood or her ability to work miracles. Surely here, as elsewhere, Adams created a heroine who suited his political and historical purposes.

But to begin more systematically, "She was the greatest artist, as she was the greatest philosopher and musician and theologist, that ever lived on earth, except for her Son, who, at *Chartres*, is still an infant under her guardianship. Her taste was infallible; her sentence eternally final."[67] Notice that in Chartres Cathedral, the Son is decidedly in second place, reduced to an afterthought.

She was surrounded by people begging her for favors "mostly inconsistent with law," a theme that arises often in different variations.[68] In general, she was a problem for those in authority, not least those in the church, who "never quite accepted the full claims of what was called Mariolatry." Nor were bourgeois capitalists or medieval schoolmen really at ease with her.

The *bourgeois* had put an enormous share of his capital into what was in fact an economical speculation, not unlike the South Sea Scheme, or the railway system of our own time; except that in one case the energy was devoted to shortening the road to Heaven; in the other to shortening the road to Paris; but no serious schoolman could have felt entirely convinced that God would enter into a business partnership with man, to establish a sort of joint-stock society for altering the operation of divine and universal laws. The bourgeois cared little for the philosophical doubt, if the economical result proved to be good, but he watched this result with his usual practical sagacity and [satisfied] himself that relics were not certain in their effects; that the Saints were not always able or willing to help; that Mary herself could certainly not be bought or bribed; that prayer without money seemed to be quite as efficacious as prayer with money; and that neither the road to

Heaven nor Heaven itself had been made surer or brought nearer by
an investment of capital which amounted to the best part of the wealth
of France.[69]

Continuing with the theme of investment, Adams notes, "Illusion for
illusion,—granting for the moment that Mary was an illusion,—the Virgin
mother in this instance repaid to her worshipers a larger return for their
money than the capitalist had ever been able to get, at least in this world,
from any other illusion of wealth which he had tried to make a source of
pleasure and profit."[70] Perhaps in this passage we hear an echo of Pascal's
wager, already raised in *Esther*. Is this another flirtation with pragmatism?

As for the clergy, they fair no better than the bourgeoisie. "The Virgin
had the additional harm to the public that she was popularly supposed to
have no very marked fancy for priests as such; she was a Queen, a Woman,
and a Mother, functions, all, which priests could not perform."[71] Nor did she
have any taste for the metaphysics of theology. Chartres Cathedral is wholly
given over to the Mother and the Son; the Father does not often appear, and
the Holy Ghost even less. "Chartres represents, not the Trinity, but the identity of the Mother and Son. The idea is not orthodox," Adams continues, "but
that is no affair of ours. The Church watches over its own."[72] So much for the
bourgeoisie and the church, even with all its theological trappings.

The Virgin was more favorably disposed to those less well placed in society than were the clergy and the bourgeoisie. She was prejudiced against neither prodigal sons nor even prodigal daughters. Indeed:

She was rather fond of prodigals, and gentle toward the ladies who
consumed the prodigal's substance. She admitted Mary Magdalen
and Mary the Gypsy to her society. She fretted little about Aristotle so
long as the prodigal adored her, and naturally the prodigal adored her
almost to the exclusion of the Trinity. She always cared less for her
dignity than was to be wished. . . . Among the peasants she liked to
appear as one of themselves; she insisted on lying in bed, in a stable,
with the cows and asses about her, and her baby in a cradle by the
bed-side, as though she had suffered like other women, though the
Church insisted she had not.[73]

She was hardly at home in "polite" society. In fact, according to Adams,
"in no well-regulated community, under a proper system of police, could the
Virgin feel at home, and the same thing may be said of most other saints as
well as sinners. Her conduct was at times undignified. . . . She condescended

to do domestic service, in order to help her friends, and she would use her needle." She did not worry about such things because she was, in effect, a law unto herself. "The Virgin cared little for criticism of her manners or acts. She was above criticism. She made manners. Her acts were laws. No one thought of criticizing in the style of a normal school, the will of such a Queen; but one might treat her with a degree of familiarity, under great provocation, which would startle easier critics than the French."[74]

But while Mary's word was law, other authorities received less support from her. "Intensely human, but always Queen, she upset, at her pleasure, the decisions of every court and the orders of every authority, human or divine; interfered directly in the ordeal; altered the processes of nature; abolished space; annihilated time." And though she showed a "marked weakness for chivalry," she had little knowledge of political economy, and "her views on the subject of money-lending or banking were so feminine as to arouse in that powerful class a vindictive enmity which helped to overthrow her throne."[75] Common moneylending practices displeased her greatly, "because she knew too well how easily the banker of good credit, could arrange with the officials of the Trinity to open the doors of paradise for him." Unfortunately, the administration of heaven was much like that of France, but since her sentiments inclined toward pity rather than justice, "she shut her eyes to much she could not change." Thus she directed her miracles to those who needed them most, who were "rarely the well-to-do."[76]

Such attitudes did not sit well with ecclesiastical authorities, as one might expect:

> Mary concentrated in herself the whole rebellion of man against fate; the whole protest against divine law; the whole contempt for human law as its outcome; the whole unutterable fury of human nature beating itself against the walls of its prison house, and suddenly seized by a hope that in the Virgin man had found a door of escape. She was above law; she took feminine pleasure in turning Hell into an ornament; she delighted in trampling on every social distinction in this world and the next.[77]

But Mary is presented in terms even more radical, so that she is in conflict with the established religion. Adams explains that "the Church itself never liked to be dragged too far under feminine influence, although the moment it discarded feminine influence it lost nearly everything of any value to it or to the world, except its philosophy." Mary's tastes were simply too popular, which was a great loss for the church.

The convulsive hold which Mary to this day maintains over human imagination,—as you can see at Lourdes,—was due much less to her power of saving soul or body than to her sympathy with people who suffered under law,—divine or human,—justly or unjustly, by accident or design, by decree of God or by guile of Devil. She cared not a straw for conventional morality, and she had no notion of letting her friends be punished to the tenth or any other generation, for the sins of their ancestors or the peccadillos of Eve.

"So Mary filled Heaven with a sort of persons little to the liking of any respectable middle-class society." In effect, she created a church of her own "so effective that the Trinity might have perished without much affecting her position."[78]

This dilemma also spread to Protestantism, leading Adams to take a hearty swing at his ancestors. Mary's treatment of the respectable, law-abiding people who could get into heaven through ordinary channels was so irritating that "three hundred years later the puritan reformers were not satisfied with abolishing her, but sought to abolish the woman altogether as the cause of all evil in heaven and on earth. The puritans abandoned the New Testament and the Virgin in order to go back to the beginning and renew the quarrel with Eve."[79]

One final characteristic of the Virgin is of great significance and eventually exposes a significant problem in Adams's argument. He begins his case with typical boldness, making a point of such breathtaking "political incorrectness" that few today would dare utter the thought, though Adams clearly intends it as praise of women rather than denigration. Adams asserts, "that the Virgin was by essence illogical, unreasonable and feminine, is the only fact of any ultimate value worth studying, and starts a number of questions that history has shown itself clearly afraid to touch."[80] Today we resist the conclusion that to be feminine is to be illogical and unreasonable, but to focus on this is to miss a larger point. Adams propounds a list of unanswered questions:

No one has ventured to explain why the Virgin wielded exclusive power over poor and rich, sinners and saints alike. Why were all the Protestant churches cold failures without her help? Why could not the Holy Ghost,—the spirit of love and grace,—equally answer their prayers? Why was the Son powerless? Why was Chartres Cathedral in the thirteenth century—like Lourdes today—the expression of what is in substance a separate religion? Why did the gentle and gracious

Virgin Mother so exasperate the Pilgrim Fathers? Why was the
Woman struck out of the Church and ignored in the State? These
questions are not antiquarian or trifling in historical value; they tug
at the very heart-strings of all that makes whatever order is in the cosmos. If a Unity exists, in which and toward which all energies center,
it must explain and include Duality, Diversity, Infinity, — Sex![81]

The question of sex is considered later, though Adams does not dwell on
it at length, since his main interest in his pre-Freudian world is femininity. He
develops these themes most generally in the *Education*. However, first we
need to consider the source of Mary's popularity in the Middle Ages, which
is not, in Adams's view, sexual. She was supported by all classes, as Adams sees
it, because men did not want justice or equity but rather favor. Since all men
were sinners, no one wanted to face strict justice. Individuality penetrated
society from top to bottom. "The individual rebelled against restraint; society
wanted to do what it pleased; all disliked the laws which Church and State
were trying to fasten on them. They longed for a power above law, — or above
the contorted mass of ignorance and absurdity bearing the name of law." Like
children, men yearned for "protection, pardon, and love."

> This was what the Trinity, though omnipotent, could not give. What-
> ever the heretic or mystic might try to persuade himself, God could
> not be Love. God was Justice, Order, Unity; Perfection; he could not
> be human and imperfect, nor could the Son or the Holy Ghost be
> other than the Father.

Then Adams continues with what, in the context of his larger argument or
what is generally taken to be his larger argument, is a strange contention.
"The Mother alone was human, imperfect, and could love; she alone was
Favor, *Duality, Diversity*." Under any religion, Adams argues, duality must
find its place somewhere. If, in the Middle Ages, it could not be embodied
in the Trinity, then it must be in the Mother. "If the Trinity was in essence
Unity, the Mother alone could represent whatever was not Unity; whatever
was irregular, exceptional, outlawed; and this was the whole human race. . . .
In Mary's eyes, all were subjects for her pity and help."[82] In this connection,
William Merrill Decker makes an important point, namely, that in his celebration of Mary's willful, illogical nature, Adams "develops a recognition that
he had made years before in 'Primitive Rights of Women,' that Mary served a
popular need that could not be satisfied by the Holy Ghost, the abstraction

with which the misogynist church fathers replaced the eternal woman when they assimilated the Egyptian Trinity into Christian doctrine, manifesting a reflex later to reappear in the Anglo-American Puritan."[83]

I have presented this argument in great detail because it seems to open up a large hole in the structure of Adams's thought as conventionally interpreted. If his goal is to find unity in the face of multiplicity, then, based on his apparent rejection of the source of unity in favor of the diversity represented by his heroine, the Virgin, we must at least question his commitment to the unity he claims to seek. At the most, his apparent rejection of his own century from the depths of his eighteenth-century mind may be less firm than he wants us to believe. Always remember that Adams is not a notably straightforward writer. To return to an earlier discussion (see chapter 3), perhaps Adams, like one of Isaiah Berlin's hedgehogs, appears to be seeking (as did Tolstoy) a single theory to explain all of history but is really a fox in disguise, one who recognizes the irreducible multiplicity of history in spite of his longing for a more orderly view of the world.

It is necessary to consider that theme again in the context of the *Education*, but it is possible to see in Adams's image of the Virgin the origins of the theory of conservative Christian anarchy that he begins to toy with in his letters and treats somewhat more directly in the *Education*. Mary is certainly Christian, though not in any orthodox way, and her disregard for convention, her uneasiness with established authorities (whether legal or clerical), and her sympathy for the underdog may well lead toward some form of anarchism, though it is hard to see the conservatism. In any event, it is unclear how even the perceived domination of medieval society by a woman of such unsettling characteristics could last.

Adams is too far removed from writing conventional history to offer any account of the downgrading of Mary in the medieval world. At the end of the chapter on Nicolette and Marian, he hints at what is to come. Between 1250 and 1300, according to him, "the Woman and the Rose became bankrupt. Satire took the place of worship. Man, with his usual monkey-like malice, took pleasure in pulling down what he had built up." And then, in conclusion, he adds, "For the first time since Constantine proclaimed the reign of Christ, a thousand years, or so, before Philip the Fair dethroned him, the deepest expression of social feeling ended with the word: Despair."[84]

Samuels offers a considerably more circumstantial account of the displacement of the Virgin from her place of eminence. Taking up the political, social, and economic history that Adams avoids, and following Adams's favorite architectural authority Viollet-le-Duc, Samuels notes that the erection of cathedrals became a duty because it was a protest against feudalism. "The popular support for the Virgin of Majesty had therefore a revolutionary character, becoming in fact one of the instruments for the overthrow of the feudal system." But ironically, this did not work to the Virgin's advantage. In place of Adams's imaginative account, Samuels argues that church building was not just the expression of a simple faith. It was the work of powerful priests "whose ambition marvelously energized their piety." They competed with one another to build the most magnificent edifices. As society grew more secular, the kings provided better protection than the Virgin, while the levies imposed by the great bishops were resisted more and more. "The Virgin of Majesty had indirectly achieved her revolutionary purposes."[85] But given her enemies, this was at the cost of her special position.

As a result of the decline of the Virgin, in the final three chapters of *Chartres*, Adams returns to a world of men: Pierre Abelard, the mystics, and Thomas Aquinas. What distinguished Abelard was his relentless logic, beautifully illustrated in the dialogue that Adams constructs between him and William of Champeaux on that favorite topic of medieval philosophy—universals and particulars. It is not to the point here to reconstruct Adams's brilliant set piece. It is necessary only to note that Abelard wins the debate by making a reductio ad absurdum argument that leads to the conclusion that realism always leads to pantheism.[86] Abelard's logic then turns to the Trinity. Adams tells us, "No human being was so stupid as not to understand that the Father, Mother and Child made a Trinity." The difficulty comes when the church tries to identify the Mother with the Holy Ghost. It is this concept that Abelard insists on subjecting to his logic. Adams explains the problem in biting nonphilosophical terms. The difficulty is that "common people like women and children and ourselves could never understand the Trinity; naturally intelligent people understood it still less, but for them it did not matter; they did not need to understand it provided their neighbors would leave it alone."[87] But the mass of men wanted the Mother, who was nearer to them than either Father or Son. The substitution for the Mother was inadequate because the Holy Ghost was feared rather than loved. The church went on the defensive, realizing that to inquire into this mystery risked discrediting the whole Trinity, "under the pretense of making it intelligible." But "precisely this license was what Abelard took, and on it he chose to insist. He avoided open heresy and treated the idea with great respect, but he refused to let it alone."[88]

It was this style of thought that frightened the church. As Saint Bernard, Abelard's major opponent, understood the problem, "Pure logic admitted no contingency; it was bound to be necessitarian or ceased to be logical; but the result, as Bernard understood it, was that Abelard's world, being the best and only possible, need trouble itself no more about God, or Church, or man,"[89] a result obviously unsettling for the religious establishment.

Given his praise of Mary's irrationality in the heart of the book, one might expect Adams to be hostile to Abelard, the great logician. Indeed, this is what R. P. Blackmur takes to be his position, or at least the implication of his position. Abelard "saw little comfort or grace in any mind but his own. His function was that of irritant, innovator, anarchist as rebel, and his power was that of the unaided intellect everywhere passionately equal to itself, everywhere calamitously unequal to the world in which it found itself." In fact, he was rather like John Randolph, despised by Adams as brilliant, but erratic and unstable.[90] And later Blackmur comments, "Abelard, a philosopher who dealt with theology as if it were a part of the study of law, seems to have resented the human need for the Virgin," a need that Adams certainly saw to be essential.[91] And it is also true that Adams is briefly rather harsh in his characterization of Abelard's style of argument. Throughout his career, he tells us, Abelard "made use of every social and personal advantage to gain a point with little scruple in manner or in sophistry." The form of logic he preferred was the reductio ad absurdum, a weapon "Socrates abused" and of which Abelard was the "first French master"; however, "neither State nor Church likes to be reduced to an absurdity, and on the whole, both Socrates and Abelard fared ill in the result."[92] But this suggests only that Socrates and Abelard courted danger, which they certainly did, but not necessarily that they were wrong, since the problems they dealt with remain unsolved.

None of this is implausible, but it is hard to read the chapter on Abelard without feeling a real sense of Adams's sympathy for his subject. I suggest that Adams's feelings about Abelard are rather like those he had toward Thomas Jefferson—critical, but not uncomplicated, and with a certain admiration for a kindred, even if misled, spirit. I think Robert Mane is right to say that in the medieval drama, "Abelard will certainly not appear as the villain of the play; indeed he rather seems to act the part of a hero, not unlike Hamlet, who makes *catharsis* possible. It is easy to understand how Adams could—more or less consciously—identify himself with this man, 'well-born,' whose chief crime was to be more intelligent than his contemporaries."[93]

Through all this, something significant about the mind of Adams is emerging. He is critical in important ways about twentieth-century rationality and is drawn to the medieval aesthetic, as well as to the "irrationality" of the Virgin and to mystics such as Saint Francis, who is considered next. But he is not prepared to give up logic, even logic as corrosive as Abelard's. His is a divided mind, trying to encompass a wide range of thought that might help critics of the twentieth century adjust to their world.

The internal church debate, in his view, had reached a dead end and created a dilemma:

> The schools argued, according to their tastes, from Unity to Multiplicity or from Multiplicity to Unity, but what they wanted was to connect the two. They tried Realism and found that it led to Pantheism. They tried Nominalism and found that it led to Materialism. They attempted a compromise in Conceptualism which begged the whole question. Then they lay down exhausted.[94]

The search for a solution to these conundrums led Adams to Italy for a consideration of Saint Francis, "the ideal mystic Saint of western Europe."[95] The "immense popular charm" of both Francis and the Virgin lay in their heresies. "Both were illogical and heretical by essence;—in strict discipline, in the days of the Holy Office, a hundred years later, both would have been burned by the Church, as Jeanne d'Arc was, with infinitely less reason, in 1451." But in the twelfth century, "the Church drew aside to let the Virgin and Saint Francis pass and take the lead—for a time. Both were human ideals too intensely realized to be resisted merely because they were illogical. The Church bowed and was silent."[96]

But, Adams says, "What the Church thought or thinks is its own affair." What is important is what Francis and Mary thought. "Saint Francis was even more outspoken than the Virgin. She calmly set herself above dogma, and with feminine indifference to authority, overruled it. He, having asserted in the strongest terms the principle of obedience, paid no further attention to dogma, but, without the least reticence, insisted on practices and ideas that no Church could possibly permit or avow."[97]

Of course, the guiding principle for Saint Francis was the universal brotherhood of all living things, indeed, of all creation. "If Saint Francis made any exception from his universal law of brotherhood it was that of the schoolmen, but it was never expressed." Even so, at a meeting of several thousand of the schoolmen, he chided them for their excessive intellectualism and placed them below the devils, who were, in his scheme of things, God's wardens.[98]

Some lines are being clearly drawn here. No one, says Adams, was to blame for the contradictions between the saint and the scholars. "The schoolmen saw their duty in one direction; Francis saw his in another; and apparently, when both lines had been carried, after such fashion as might be, to their utmost results, and five hundred years had been devoted to the effort, society declared both to be failures." And here, for once in this work, Adams makes an explicitly political deduction. The universal church has no choice but to move with caution, while Francis, who acted only for himself, could operate on the basis of a simple, childlike faith. Faced with this dilemma, Adams declares: "The two poles of social and political philosophy seem necessarily to be organization or anarchy, man's intellect or the forces of nature."[99] Adams clearly lays out the alternatives as he sees them, and it is equally clear that he is torn between them. He lacks faith, though he would like to have it, and he is skeptical of the power of intellect, but like most powerful thinkers, he is reluctant to simply dismiss it. It is to Thomas Aquinas, an apostle of both faith and intellect, that Adams turns to see whether these tensions can be worked out.

Adams clearly attached great importance to the chapter on Aquinas that concludes *Chartres*. Adams said that he was most proud of this part of his study, even though, as Samuels has written, for years he thought of the work as a whole as his "Miracles of the Virgin." But, Mary drops completely out of sight in the chapter on Saint Thomas, as does the masculine-feminine dichotomy that to this point is omnipresent in the work. Samuels puts it bluntly: "Adams intends the emphasis of omission. Aquinas' solution not only dethroned the Virgin, it ignored her."[100]

There is a degree of oddity in Adams's approach to the Angelic Doctor, particularly given his insistence on the importance of Aquinas. He remarks that the twenty-eight quarto volumes of the *Summa* "must be closed books," for only Dominicans dare interpret him. For others, too many intricate problems are entailed.[101] However odd, this approach is consistent with his practice. He never refers to the *Summa* in his correspondence, nor were any of its volumes in Adams's library. Undoubtedly, what he knew about Aquinas was derived from secondary sources.[102] Some sense of the spirit in which he approached his subject can be gleaned from a letter to Charles Milnes Gaskell. "All day long I read metaphysics, and study Saint Thomas Aquinas. It is as amusing as Punch, and about as sensible. St. Thomas is frankly droll, but I think I like his ideas better than those of Descartes or Leibnitz or Kant or the Scotchmen, just as I like better a child of ten that tells lies, to a young man of twenty who not only lies but cheats knowingly. St. Thomas was afraid of being whipped. Descartes and the rest lied for pay."[103] And yet, in spite of this lighthearted stance, Adams wrote, "I care more for my theology than for my architecture, and should be much mortified if detected in an error about Thomas Aquinas, or the doctrine of universals."[104]

The problem Adams chooses to tackle is narrow, given the huge range of Thomas's work. He does not write of the politics, ethics, or theory of natural law, which interest us so much today.[105] Still, what he does cover is undoubtedly theologically important. Granting that God is a concrete thing rather than an idea, "He [Aquinas] admitted that God could not be taken for granted." This was a bold and dangerous move, because "God must be proved as a true cause in order to warrant the Church or the State in requiring men to worship him as a Creator." A churchman wants to be "assured that Thomas succeeded in his proof, especially since he did not satisfy Descartes and still less Pascal."[106] And, of course, the very demand for proof tends to undermine faith; for Adams, as he makes clear as early as *Esther*, faith cannot be reached by reason.

The proof Adams discusses is well known: "'I see motion,' said Thomas:— 'I infer a motor!' The reasoning, which may be fifty thousand years old, is as strong as ever it was; stronger than some more modern inferences of science; but the average mechanic stated it differently. 'I see motion,' he admitted:—'I infer energy. I see motion everywhere; I infer energy everywhere.'"[107]

But however adequate or inadequate is Aquinas's proof, Adams's treatment of it leaves something to be desired. As Michael Colacurcio says, it sounds quite reasonable to move from the idea of motion to the idea of a motor. But this is not exactly what Aquinas wrote. Colacurcio says, "At the risk of seeming pedantic one may point out that Thomas' Latin for that which does the moving is *movens*; it has always been translated *mover* rather than *motor*." The distinction may appear small, but in the common philosophical language, *mover* suggests a being capable of producing change or motion, while *motor* has a clear materialist and mechanical bias, which is contrary to Thomas's sense of God as a spiritual act but consistent with Adams's place as a twentieth-century man with a deep interest in physics. This substitution continues throughout the discussion of Thomas's proof.[108]

On this foundation, Thomas builds his gigantic intellectual structure. The Trinity is restored to its place, though Adams insists once again "that no one may even profess to understand the Trinity,"[109] with the result that Mary is removed from her exalted throne. Deep down, this conclusion must have been a disappointment to Adams, but this is merely a theological issue, and Adams tells us, with considerable insouciance, that we need not be concerned:

About Saint Thomas's theology we need not greatly disturb ourselves; it can matter now not much whether he put more Pantheism than the law allowed, or more Materialism than Duns Scotus approved,—or less of either—into his universe, since the Church is still on the spot,

responsible for its own doctrines; but his architecture is another matter. . . . Neither the Church nor the architect's Church was a sketch,
but a completely studied structure.

Adams goes on to add that in Aquinas, "Science and art were one." And still
further, "Both the *Summa Theologiae* and Beauvais Cathedral were excessively modern, scientific, and technical, marking the extreme points reached
by Europe on the lines of scholastic science. This is all we need to know."[110]

In this connection, the change from mover to motor discussed by Colacurcio is not at all pedantic. Rather, it is a significant indicator of where Adams
stands. Also, it should be remarked that the treatment of the Virgin is much
the same as that of Aquinas. The motor stands for a physical force, and so do
the activities of the Virgin, though it must be said that her force might be
interpreted as spiritual. But Adams understands her as "only a capacity to get
work done."[111] Thus, in the construction of Chartres Cathedral, "the inspiration of the art proves the Virgin's presence." As he puts it, "Every day, as
the work went on, the Virgin was present, directing the architects."[112] Deep
down, his is not an eighteenth-century mind so much as a twentieth-century
mind with a considerable, if seriously ambivalent, commitment to science.
And in spite of his assurances, "Adams takes for granted his readers' ready
agreement that 'metaphysics were a medieval absurdity.' "[113] Of course, the
matter is more complex than this suggests. Adams did not write a long book
on medieval art, religion, and culture out of mere whimsy, and his constitutional purism has a decidedly eighteenth-century cast to it. But one ought
not to portray him simply as a technophobe in revolt against his own time.
Rather, he is a sophisticated critic of that time for whom a highly artificial
contrast model of medieval unity is a useful device. One ought not to leap to
the conclusion that the loving care devoted to this model necessarily means
that he fully embraces it or totally rejects his own century. And certainly he
is aware that it is not possible to return to the conditions of medieval France,
even if it were desirable.

In the discussion of Saint Thomas, the physical imagery continues. The
restoration of the Trinity creates a problem in the balance of forces. Church
theologians did not like to look deeply into the subject, on which they were
philosophical realists. They did not want to admit "that the third member of
the Trinity contained multiplicity, because the Trinity was a restless weight
on the Church piers, which, like the central tower, constantly tended to fall,
and needed to be lightened. Thomas gave it the lightest form possible, and
there fixed it."[114]

Aquinas was also concerned with the social balance of forces. "Saint Thomas was working for the Church and the State, not for the salvation of souls, and his chief object was to repress anarchy."[115] (Where this would leave the conservative Christian anarchy that was beginning to germinate in Adams's mind is not clear.) Mankind, Adams says, cannot admit an anarchic or multiple universe. "The world was there, staring them in the face, with all its chaotic conditions, and society insisted on its Unity in self-defense." But it also insists on free will, which raises deep, fundamental problems. Thomas tried to resolve the problem by admitting that while unity was the rule, it was "full of defects," which might even prove beneficent. This was a huge concession, but Thomas

> still needed a means of bringing into the system one element which vehemently refused to be brought, that is, Man himself, who insisted that the universe was a unit, but that he was a universe; that Energy was one, but that he was another energy; that God was omnipotent but that man was free. The contradiction had always existed, exists still, and always must exist, unless man either admits that he is a machine, or agrees that anarchy and chaos are the habit of nature, and law and order its accident. . . .
>
> No one has ever seriously affirmed the literal freedom of will. Absolute liberty is absence of restraint; responsibility is restraint; therefore the ideally free individual is responsible only to himself. This principle is the philosophical foundation of anarchism, and for anything that science has yet proved, may be the philosophical foundation of the Universe; but it is fatal to all society and is especially hostile to the State.[116]

In his own way, Adams here discusses one of the basic problems of political theory, and one that has generated perhaps more than its fair share of recent American debate, in the form of extended discussions of the relation of the individual to the community or society. His analysis is a little puzzling, since he simply skips over the liberal theory of the responsible person and leaps to a critical view of anarchism, a formulation that is peculiar, in that Adams had already clearly identified himself as a liberal and was, as *Chartres* was being written, well on his way to his own unique, though ambiguous, form of anarchism. Whether the discussion of the latter in *The Education of Henry Adams* resolves these problems will have to be put aside until the next chapter.

But Adams and Aquinas are still troubled by the problem of free will. Adams presents an argument that is very dense and requires detailed elaboration. He tells us that the church never admitted free will, nor did Thomas. Adams discusses Aquinas's solution in his characteristic way by "translating his school-vocabulary into modern technical terms." God—the "Prime Motor"—supplies all the energy of the universe and "acts directly on man . . . moving him as a mechanical motor might do." But man, since he is more complex than other creatures, has a capacity to reflect, "which enables him within certain limits to choose between paths; and this singular capacity is called free choice or free-will." But the reflection is not *really* a choice, since without an energy impelling us to act, we would never, in fact, make up our minds to choose. Adams then quotes Aquinas as saying, "We must therefore recur to the intervention of an exterior agent who shall impress on our will a movement capable of putting an end to its hesitations:—That exterior agent is nothing else than God." And Adams concludes, "The scheme seems to differ little from a system of dynamics as modern as the dynamo."[117]

Thus Aquinas is converted into a modern scientist, or perhaps an electrical engineer. Of course, this analysis has important implications for science, religion, and the relations between the two. "Modern science, with infinite effort, has discovered and announced that man is a bewildering complex of energies, which helps little to explain his relations with the ultimate Substance or Energy or Prime motor whose existence both Science and the Schoolmen admit; which Science studies in laboratories and Religion worships in churches." But in spite of the similarities between science and religion that many believe exist to this day, "Modern science, like modern art, tends, in practice, to drop the dogma of organic unity. Some of the mediaeval habit of mind survives, but even that is said to be yielding before the daily evidence of increasing and extending complexity."[118]

But it is not at all clear, contrary to common interpretations, that Adams views this conclusion as a disaster.

> The fault, then, was not in man, if he no longer looked at science or art as an organic whole, or as the expression of unity. Unity turned itself into complexity, multiplicity, variety, and even contradiction. All experience, human and divine, assured man in the thirteenth century that the lines of the universe converged. How was he to know that these lines ran in every conceivable and inconceivable direction, and that at least half of them seemed to diverge from any imaginable centre of unity![119]

At least three things are striking here. In this passage, Adams, having returned from the thirteenth century, seems much more concerned with the empirical evidence of contemporary science than he was with empirical evidence about the medieval world. Nor does he seem terribly concerned about these findings. He even admits, "Art had to be confused in order to express confusion; but perhaps it was truest, so."[120] And finally, he makes a telling remark about Scholastic philosophy, Gothic architecture, and their connection to modern science. To repeat a point already made in a slightly different context, "Both the *Summa Theologiae* and Beauvais Cathedral were excessively modern, scientific, and technical, marking the extreme points reached in Europe on the lines of scholastic science. This is all we need to know. If we like, we can go on to study, inch by inch, the slow decline of the heart. The essence of it,—the despotic central idea—was that of organic unity both in the thought and the building. From that time, the universe has steadily become more complex and less reducible to a central control."[121]

The reference to Beauvais Cathedral is a particularly arresting image, for Beauvais is contrasted throughout with Chartres. The latter was still solid, while Beauvais, though it survived, "after a fashion" was a "towering fragment" that was "poorly built from the first, which has broken down oftener than most Gothic structures, and seems ready to crumble again, whenever the wind blows over its windy plains."[122] Given the elaborate parallel Adams draws between the Church Intellectual of Saint Thomas and the Church Architectural, the implication that both are unstable structures does not seem to bode well for the Thomistic philosophy. In this connection, Blackmur adds a telling comment. There is not much use in this lesson on instability, he says,

> unless we think of it in terms of something Adams was well aware of but which he hardly touched on in his book—namely, the ferocious and single-minded brutality which was the complement of every aspiration in the balance. The brutalities balanced too: those done for God, for Church, for simple aggrandizement, or for their own sake were somehow of equal weight and pressure in the general turbulence of society. [Further] man is most violent in asserting and imposing order when his society is least capable of receiving it.[123]

Once again, Adams pays a price for his aestheticized, depoliticized view of medieval life. He paints a gorgeous portrait but without a real-life model.

According to Adams, one idea controls both Gothic architecture and Saint Thomas's church. "The method was the same for both, and the result was an art marked by singular unity, which endured and served its purpose until man changed his attitude toward the universe." Unity dissolves through no fault of the art or the architecture. "Granted a Church, Saint Thomas's

Church was the most expressive that man has made, and the great gothic Cathedrals were its most complete expression."[124]

But it is not clear that Adams was really prepared to grant a church, and if he was, it is also not clear, in view of his celebration of the Virgin Mary, in all her irrationality, that that church really would be or should be the Church Intellectual of Saint Thomas. In any case, the church, on Adams's own showing, had ceased to be viable. At the end of chapter 10, Adams takes leave of Chartres Cathedral, and the discussion of architecture begins to recede into the background. His conclusion at that juncture is more than a little grim: we can "safely leave the Virgin in her Majesty, with her three great prophets on either hand, as calm and confident in their own strength and in God's providence as they were when Saint Louis was born, but looking down from a deserted heaven, into an empty church, on a dead faith."[125]

The praise of Saint Thomas turns out to be faint praise indeed. Both architecture and philosophy reveal an "apparent instability." As Adams puts it, "The equilibrium is visibly delicate beyond the line of safety; danger lurks in every stone." Everything rests on faith. "The peril of the heavy tower, of the restless vault, of the vagrant buttress; the uncertainty of logic, the inequalities of the syllogism, the irregularities of the mental mirror, — all these haunting night-mares of the Church are expressed as strongly by the gothic Cathedral as though it had been the cry of human suffering, and as no emotion has ever been expressed before or is likely to find expression again." But it would not do to end this exposition on a pessimistic note. Instead, dour Henry Adams ends with a sunburst of hope. Writing of the Gothic cathedral, he says, "The delight of its aspirations is flung up to the sky. The pathos of its self-distrust and anguish of doubt, is buried in the earth as its last secret. You can read out of it whatever pleases your youth and confidence; to me, this is all."[126]

One hesitates to violate the beauty of the concluding paragraph of this masterful book by adding any commentary. However, it should be remarked that, with his stress on architectural and intellectual instability, Adams introduces a note of uncertainty that indicates a retreat from the sort of prema-ture closure of the argument that flawed his novel *Democracy*. Here, all questions remain open, their answers provisional, just as they are in George Strong's discussion of the equally provisional character of science in *Esther*. Decker captures this perspective with some elegance. "What Adams regis-ters as the architecture's lack of repose materializes as his own text's restless-ness, the vagrancy of the verbal cathedral magnifying that of the stone. If art at last does not turn into history, it remains always historical, part of a con-tinuous paradoxical discourse."[127]

I also suggest that for Adams, art offers a set of social standards. We can, he seems to say, judge a society by the level of beauty it attains. Taste is an organizing principle that allows him to judge some societies as superior to others, and in this light, twelfth-century France rates high. Of course, the medieval standard he adopts in *Chartres* has little to do with history. As Kazin suggests, it is prettified and aestheticized, though this is not to denigrate Adams's achievement. Good history, after all, is not the only source of judgment. But he demonstrates a passion for his picture of the medieval world, a passion that is not often evident anywhere else in his work. Its function in his worldview is the contrast it offers to modern democratic, industrial civilization. But having said that, it is important to note that this does not entail, as some might argue, a total rejection of modern society. The modern and medieval worlds exist in tension with each other in his mind.

Adams's aestheticism is not the democratic aestheticism of which George Kateb writes.[128] The medieval dream Adams idealizes is hierarchical rather than democratic. Moreover, the democratic aestheticism Kateb describes holds that all things, though not equally beautiful, are worthy of attention, a point Adams would doubtless refuse to accept. But still, we ought not to consign Adams to the ranks of medieval reactionaries. Though the Virgin disappears after the central section of his book and is replaced by the Thomistic hierarchy, that hierarchy is unstable. More important, there is no doubt that his heart is with his heretical, anarchic heroine, whose propensity to subvert authority, not to mention her care for the downtrodden, points toward ultimately democratic sympathies.

Medieval France and Modern America

We have come to the end of a complex book, a book as elegantly poised between hope and despair as the unstable architecture and thought it describes. In the central chapters, Adams offers a kind of feminine utopia. Notice I do not say feminist, though Adams has some intellectual affinities with contemporary feminism. The title of his article "The Primitive Rights of Women," if expanded to include *Mont Saint Michel and Chartres*, says most of what needs to be said: "Henry Adams's 'Primitive Rights of Women': An Offense Against Church, the Patriarchal State, Progressive Evolution, and the Women's Liberation Movement."[129] Certainly Adams had a high regard for women in general, with the Virgin as his highest symbol, and in the *Education*, he generalizes his discussion to include her with fertility symbols from a variety of cultures. There is no doubt; for him, women speak "in a different voice," and it is a voice of unique value.[130] And there can be no doubt that Adams expresses great admiration for the strong women he writes about in "Primitive Rights." Nor is there any doubt that in the essay explicitly and in the book implicitly he lays the blame for the decline of the Virgin on the doorstep of the church. And finally, the *Education* is full of doubt about the soundness of any theory of inevitable evolutionary progress. The history of the church argues against such a view, and so does the history of politics.

But however much aid and comfort Adams might offer women, his indifference to empirical evidence precludes him from being an icon for contemporary feminists. Quite rightly, they will not accept his view of women as inherently irrational, even if he does suggest that this is a positive quality when set against the rationality of industrial capitalism. And his picture of the life of women in the medieval world is badly skewed by the focus on his utopia. Adams himself, in a brief reference to the historical world, undercuts his own argument about the beauty of the medieval world and its supposed dominance by women. He tells us, "The superiority of women was not a fancy but a fact." The role of men was to hunt, to fight, and to make love, as well as to travel in pursuit of commercial interests, so that they were frequently away from home. "The women," in contrast, "ruled the household and the workshop; cared for the economy; supplied the intelligence, and dictated taste." But then, Adams recognizes problems and introduces a flagrant contradiction of this pleasing picture. "Both physically and mentally the woman was robust, as men often complained, and she did not greatly resent being treated as a man. Sometimes the husband beat her, dragged her about by the hair, locked her up in the house; but he was always quite conscious that she always got even with him in the end."[131] This last point is hopelessly weak in view of the description that precedes it, a clear case of wishful thinking that badly weakens his case for a medieval female utopia.

At the same time, thinking back to "The Primitive Rights of Women" and including *Mont Saint Michel and Chartres*, the message sent is mixed. The feminine virtues were very powerful and much admired by Adams. Women set the standards of behavior and held the central place in the family. In fact, their great role was to hold the family together, just as Mary held medieval society together through the release of a spiritual rather than a biological energy. Strikingly, as Robert Mane remarks, "Mary of Chartres hardly appears in her role as mother; when she is maternal, it is adults whom she mothers." How could it be otherwise, he asks, "since there is so much in her of Marian Adams who never had a child?" Nor, of course, did Madeleine Lee or Esther Dudley.[132] And for all Adams's occasional references to the power of "Sex," it does not play a large role in the work. Edward Saveth writes, "As for conjugal love, the women of the thirteenth century, as Adams describes them, seemed, like Madeleine and Esther of another era, rather uninterested in it."[133] Adams was writing highly sublimated, "genteel" literature.[134] Later, to be sure, in a letter to the young poet George Cabot Lodge, he hints at the emergence of a women's movement, in spite of his earlier disdain for the cause of women's suffrage: "A branch of the sex is sure to break off as an emancipated social class."[135] But this does not help us tease much out of *Chartres* regarding politics. To do that, it is necessary to look at Mary's highly unconventional behavior as depicted in the central chapters of the book.

Writing to his close friend Charles Milnes Gaskell, Adams remarks that *Mont Saint Michel and Chartres* "is my declaration of principles as head of the Conservative Christian Anarchists; a party numbering one member. The Virgin and St. Thomas are my vehicles of anarchism."[136] Applying the anarchist label to Aquinas is quite a stretch, given Adams's recognition of his interest in preserving the stability of both the state and the church, but it makes sense when used in connection with Mary. To pair Mary and Aquinas points to the conflict between faith and reason, rationality and irrationality, the twentieth and the thirteenth centuries, which is at the heart of this book as well as of the *Education*.[137] Mary stands for faith, irrationality, and the thirteenth century. She is genuinely an anarchic figure and one who flirts with heresy; she truly is "the Virgin of Majesty and Heresy."[138] As Adams cheerfully points out, she would be very difficult for organized society to tolerate. Also quite interesting is her sympathy for society's underdogs, a sensitivity that is largely, though not entirely, missing in Adams. But aside from the warm and deep-seated feeling for Mary, there is little in *Chartres* that can explain the paradoxical idea of conservative Christian anarchy. For that, it is necessary to turn to the *Education*, where the notion is more fully developed, though not with complete clarity. What can be seen at this stage in the development of Adams's thought is an emergent, very independent radicalism — radicalism in the sense, as Marx used it, of going to the root of things.

Chartres also has implications for the vexed problem of the relation between individual and society. In spite of the fact that the book deals with medieval France, Adams's work is characteristically American. Given his heritage, this is hardly surprising. Still, there is a rambunctious quality to his thought exhibited by no one else in his family. One can also see this quality in the often violently polemical journalism and in the unabashedly pro-American, anti-British treatment of the War of 1812. Henry's unique style stands out, even if the legendarily short and explosive tempers of John and John

Quincy Adams are conceded. And while it is true that he had a mastery of European cultural history, his approach to that tradition is very American. In his provocative introduction to *Mont Saint Michel and Chartres,* Raymond Carney gives an interesting estimate of the relation of American to European culture. "America was, in its essence, the culture founded on a belief in man's personal power to escape the reigning European structures and forms of understanding and to replace them with new ones of his own creation, as substitutes for the discredited orders being left behind." He further advances his point by noting Gertrude Stein's remark that America was the first country to enter the twentieth century and cites what D. H. Lawrence called the "extremist consciousness" of Poe, Melville, Hawthorne, and Whitman. "'The European moderns,' says Lawrence, 'are all *trying* to be extreme. The great Americans I mention just were it.'"[139] Carney is attempting to locate Adams in or near the postmodernist camp. Indeed, he sees the whole tradition of American letters as being postmodernist in some sense. Given Adams's openly cavalier attitude to empirical history in *Chartres,* this makes some sense, at least for that work. But a cautionary note is needed. This is not the place to attempt to characterize the entirety of the American literary tradition, but Adams certainly does not appear to be postmodern in writing the great *History* or in his post–Civil War journalism. Those works are saturated with a moral and political critique that Adams certainly believed to be rooted in the empirical realities he saw. That he brought his own powerful imagination to the materials does not mean that he thought that another, radically different perspective would be as good. This is true, even if we recall the sense of perspective he displayed in urging on President Eliot a Harvard appointment for Henry Cabot Lodge. Surely he thought, given the histories of the two families, that he was right and Lodge wrong.

Still, Adams, as an individual who felt threatened by the encroaching rationality of industrial capitalism, makes a heroic effort to differentiate himself from the crowd by cultivating a unique self in both of his late masterpieces. As I argue later, he is not unlike Max Weber in fearing for the individual in a complex system of all-intrusive, relentlessly encroaching, bureaucratic structures. A postmodernist might associate this with the "death of the author" or the "erasure" of the individual. But the tradition of American individualism accounts just as well for the authorial personality he displays. Surely, for all of Adams's despair late in life as his close friends die and he faces death himself, he is an author who is emphatically alive and who resists the obliteration of his unique self to the end. As Carney says, Adams "refuses to accede to the nightmare erasure of the individual." Instead, he recognizes "the vocal presence of an eccentric, individual, passionate, personal author." Quite rightly he refers to the "exuberance of Adams' tone, the daring extravagance of his outlandish and inventive conceits, the puckish wit, the sly metaphorical games and puns . . . [that] are signs of an idiosyncratic, personal, authorial presence that will not be absorbed into an abstract system of signification, an ego utterly unsubdued by the reigning historical systems of analysis, an energy of personal imagination and feeling ascendant and ultimately, one may judge, supremely triumphant over all systems of understanding."[140]

All this seems to be modern rather than postmodern, the assertion of a cranky American liberal individualism. But there are ways in which Adams seems to at least flirt with postmodernism. To take only one example, I agree with Carney and Colacurcio that Adams simply imposes his own thought patterns on Saint Thomas in a way that clearly says the "real" Saint Thomas hardly matters.[141] Instead, he becomes a creature drawn from Adams's imagination. But that need not matter here, since the subject of his book is really the mind, one might say the musings, of Henry Adams more than the Angelic Doctor or any other historical figure. If we were grading Adams as a historian of ideas, as Colacurcio is to some extent, he might well receive low marks. But students of Adams can just as well express wonder at his imagination and vitality.

We cannot begin to comprehend fully the philosophy of history developed in *Chartres* until we look at it in comparison with the *Education*, its great companion volume. Here, I just call attention to the argument that has begun to emerge in this chapter. Whatever joy he takes in exploring it, Adams is not in the end a man of the thirteenth century. He certainly does not hold that history records the march of progress, but he knows that it does not run backward, so there can be no return to the age of the great cathedrals, no matter how glorious and beautiful. Nor, in spite of his frequent assertions, is he fully a man of the eighteenth century either, though the Enlightenment certainly has a powerful attraction for him. Instead, he is a man of the nineteenth century, stripped of Whiggish illusions of the inevitability of progress, who has lived on into the twentieth century. And though that century frightens him, as well it might, he is by no means ready to reject it in toto. It would be too much, I think, to say with Kazin that "Adams found [the] historic shift from religion to science utterly congenial."[142] However, he is certainly not trying to escape science and withdraw completely into a utopian, aestheticized past, though his artistic sense mattered a great deal to him. He is too much a man of his time to withdraw in that way, as can be seen most clearly in his late, and not very successful, essays toward a philosophy of "scientific" history. He is caught up in his own time and is bitterly critical of it, but he is not willing to retreat from it altogether, not least because he knows that there is no alternative to it. We cannot live in the past. What we will see in his later works is a man caught between the past and the present, between art and science, heroically trying to bridge the gap between two worlds. For this reason, I think that Samuels overstates the case to insist that Adams's attitude was one of total contempt for the modern world.[143] *Mont Saint Michel and Chartres* shows us a man in open revolt against the industrial-capitalist rationality depicted by Max Weber and against positivist history as well. But that is not all there is to this exceedingly complex mind. In the next chapter, some new dimensions will be added.

Chapter 7

History, Science, and Politics: A Lifetime's Education

More than just an autobiography, *The Education of Henry Adams* is both a tale of a lifetime of education and a theory of history.[1] It is a deeply personal book, as personal in its way as *Chartres*, and the education in question is that provided by the events of his life as filtered through his often quirky mind. Some disagree. The idea that it is less personal than its predecessor no doubt stems from the fact that Adams writes about himself in the third person, thus attempting to generate a sense of detachment from his own life.[2] Instead, I suggest that rather than being impersonal, the story of his career reveals different sides of the very complex Adams persona, more guarded and more ironic than in the utopian enthusiasm of *Chartres*. But there is no doubt that a clearly personal portrait emerges — brilliant, wry, sometimes acidic, but always a recognizable self, though perhaps not one as likable as the author of his great exploration of medieval France. "He was," as Andrew Delbanco says, "between Whitman and Mailer, the most self-conscious of our major writers, I think, defiantly asserting that the most interesting literary subject he could find was the action of his own mind."[3] Michael Rogin also notes the similarity of Adams to Norman Mailer, a comparison Adams probably would not have relished. *The Time of Our Time*, Mailer's anthology of his own work, both fiction and nonfiction, designed to tell the history of our time, may seem to be the sort of "monument to the ego" that Adams rejected, but "the *Education* did not so much 'efface the ego' (Adams's claim) as to make it the measure not just of American but of eschatological history."[4] And it is no small ego that presents its own life as history itself.[5] The story Adams tells represents not only his life but also the history of his family, his class, and indeed his country, not to mention, in his later years, the fate of the Western world. It also shifts the focus away from the "world of joy" in *Chartres* to a "world of power."[6] He explores this world as it was represented by his life, or at least a sublimated, abstracted, aestheticized version of it.

Considered as an autobiography, the book is full of twists and turns and is indeed rather odd. But Adams did not call his book an autobiography. That label was attached by the publisher after his death. This is a book that omits twenty of the most productive and, at first, happiest years of his life. Of course, the omission is due to the pain of writing about his marriage and the suicide of his wife Marian. When the narrative resumes in 1892, Adams refers to it as his "posthumous life." The book was first printed and circulated to friends in 1907. The public edition appeared after his death in 1918, with an "Editor's Preface" written by Adams but bearing the signature of Henry Cabot Lodge. In it, he treats the *Education* as the sequel to *Mont Saint Michel and Chartres* and suggests Saint Augustine's *Confessions* as a model. This obviously is no mean standard.[7]

The Education of Henry Adams offers what Adams wanted his public to think about. It is not by any means a standard autobiography. For that, it is much better to turn to the enormously voluminous and brilliantly written letters.[8] As I have suggested, what Adams had in mind was something altogether more ambitious than a mere autobiography, no matter how great, since, with no little display of ego, he took his life to be emblematic of all American history in the nineteenth and early twentieth centuries. His book is another take on his theory of American historical development, into which we have already dipped, and, running throughout but completely dominating the final chapters, his philosophy of history. The one feeds the other. And his education begins at the beginning.

Education as an Adams

Even the simple statement of Adams's birth in the famous opening paragraphs is portentous. It is clear that he saw that being an Adams conveyed both advantages and disadvantages. Born in Boston, "under the shadow of the State House," and christened by his uncle, the minister of the First Church, he could not have been more marked, or handicapped, "had he been born in Jerusalem under the shadow of the Temple and circumcised in the Synagogue by his uncle the high priest under the name Israel Cohen." A hundred years before, this heritage would have secured his future, but by 1838, the Boston associations, "so colonial—so troglodytic," posed problems for a boy required to "play the game" in the twentieth century.[9]

Education began with Henry's eighteenth-century inheritance.

The atmosphere of education in which he lived was colonial, revolutionary, almost Cromwellian, as though he were steeped, from his greatest grandmother's birth, in the odor of political crime. Resistance to something was the law of New England nature; the boy looked out on the world with the instinct of resistance; for numberless generations his predecessors had viewed the world chiefly as a thing to be reformed, filled with evil forces to be abolished, and they saw no reason to suppose that they had wholly succeeded in the abolition; the duty was unchanged. That duty implied not only resistance to evil, but hatred of it. . . . The New Englander, whether boy or man, in his long struggle with a stingy or hostile universe, had learned also to love the pleasure of hating; his joys were few.

In Massachusetts, politics was as "harsh as the climate," and, as already observed, it was simply the systematic organization of hatreds.[10]

Perhaps no other passage captures the mood of the Adams political heritage quite so well—the reformist zeal, the hatred and contempt for the opposition, the deep distrust of any form of orthodox party politics, and the conviction that moral force can improve, though not transform, the world. (It must be said that Henry Adams would come to question the last point.) The Adamses were born to be political mavericks, whether they sought office or, in the case of Henry, chose to pursue reform with the pen. He was very much a product of the education provided by this family tradition.

And, of course, at the heart of that tradition were two presidents. With great charm he tells about sitting in church in Quincy looking at the bald head of his grandfather, the sixth president, John Quincy Adams:

> It was unusual for boys to sit behind a President grandfather, and to read over his head the tablet in memory of a President great-grandfather, who had "pledged his life, his fortune, and his sacred honor" to secure the independence of his country and so forth; but boys naturally supposed, without much reasoning, that other boys had the equivalent of President grandfathers. . . . The Irish gardener once said to the child: "You'll be thinking you'll be President too!" The casuality of the remark made so strong an impression on his mind that he never forgot it. He could not ever remember to have thought on the subject; to him, that there should be a doubt of his being President was a new idea.[11]

This says a great deal. There is the well-deserved sense of familial pride; the sense of duty, if not destiny; and the seeds of disappointment when the youthful expectations were not met, a disappointment that turns into a general critique of American politics when those "obviously" best fitted to rule were unable to attain the heights of power. There is a sense of an aristocracy, perhaps even a Jeffersonian "natural aristocracy," that is central to the later generations of the Adams family. Henry explains that until 1850 and beyond, the professions ran New England. The men acted not as individuals but as representatives of their professional classes, "as though they were clergymen and each profession was a church. In politics the system required competent expression; it was the old Ciceronian idea of government by *the best* that produced the long line of New England statesmen." As a boy, he expected this system to be permanent. The system worked; even Germany wanted to try it. "England's middle-class government was the ideal of human progress." Three instruments worked for the human good: "Suffrage, Common Schools, and Press." Only Karl Marx expected radical change, as Adams so wryly remarked.[12]

It was as a boy in Quincy that Adams claims to have discovered the problem that became the center of his educational concerns and his lifelong obsession as well. It was the problem of order, but not order alone. "From cradle to grave this problem of running order through chaos, direction through space, discipline through freedom, unity through multiplicity, has always been, and must always be, the task of education, as it is the moral of religion, philosophy, science, art, politics, and economy."[13] And of course, as described earlier, he learned the power of firm, traditional, yet highly personal authority from his president grandfather, who silently marched him off to school against his will. It is also important to note that all these lessons were learned during summers in Quincy, not in Boston, which Adams came to detest, not least because it was the center of rising capitalist finance. Nor did he receive these lessons of education in school, for he believed his schooling from age ten to sixteen years to be time wasted. Pointing to the tremendous upheavals that were to come, he says, quite rightly, "Perhaps his needs turned out to be exceptional, but his existence was exceptional. Between 1850 and 1900 nearly everyone's existence was exceptional."[14]

Complexity began to enter this world of certainties when his father took twelve-year-old Henry to Washington to visit his widowed grandmother. There he made a pilgrimage to Mount Vernon. The roads were terrible, and from this he received a complete Virginia education. To a New Englander, good schools, good roads, and the like were part of the system of order. "Bad roads meant bad morals. The moral of this Virginia road was clear, and the boy fully learned it. Slavery was wicked and slavery was the cause of this road's badness which amounted to social crime—and yet, at the end of the road and product of the crime stood Mount Vernon and George Washington." Luckily, Adams tells us, boys accept contradictions as easily as their elders, or he "might have become prematurely wise." He was told, and accepted for life, that Washington stood alone, a polestar that was always steady. Jefferson, Madison, Marshall, Franklin, even John Adams could be seen in changing light, but Washington held still. "Mount Vernon always remained where it was, with no practicable road to reach it; and yet, when he got there, Mount Vernon was only Quincy in a Southern setting. No doubt it was much more charming, but it was the same eighteenth-century, the same old furniture, the same old patriot, and the same old President."[15] But still, the trip to the South introduces into the story a sense of the complexity that was to be central in Adams's thought.

Life remained fairly simple for a time. Faced with slavery, the boy simply stepped back from an eighteenth- to a seventeenth-century morality. He was more political than ever, but "slavery drove the whole Puritan community back on its puritanism." Still, he began to see that there might be some difficulty reconciling sixteenth-century principles with eighteenth-century statesmanship and nineteenth-century party organizations. Life became less simple, and old educational verities began to show signs of strain.[16]

Education at Harvard College

The early education in Quincy—since he never liked Boston—and the trip to Washington furnished Adams with the foundations of his view of the world. These ideas stayed with him, but already there is a hint that he felt that they unfitted him for the modern world in which he lived his life. The values of Quincy become a kind of lost utopia, which becomes all the more clear as he examines his Harvard education, the first of the "failures" that provide one of the main narrative lines of the *Education*.

Adams did not much like Harvard, though he thought it less hurtful than any other university of the time. The education it offered was certainly not distinguished, though it was mild and liberal and made possible a friendship with "Rooney" Lee, the son of Robert E. Lee, as well as with some of Rooney's Virginian friends. Adams liked the Virginians, but this did not stop him from looking down on them from the heights of his sense of Yankee superiority. As he puts it, "Strictly, the Southerner had no mind; he had temperament. He was not a scholar; he had no intellectual training; he could not analyze an idea, and he could not even conceive of admitting two; but in life one could get along very well without ideas, if only one had the social instinct."[17] Always assuming that Adams's recollections are accurate, one can see here the continuation of the condescension toward the prewar South that had begun in Mount Vernon and continued until after Emancipation.

Though he learned something about Southern character, Adams saw the time spent at college as largely wasted. "Harvard College was a good school, but at bottom what the boy disliked most was any school at all." He complains that he simply was not taught anything about the two writers of his time who later influenced him most; thus, he never heard the name of Karl Marx or of *Capital*, nor was there any mention of Auguste Comte. Of course, one has to say that this complaint is more than a little unfair—a case of authorial license, one might say—since the first volume of *Das Kapital* was not published until 1867, nine years after Henry's graduation, and the first English translation of Comte was not published until 1853 and popularized only in 1865 by John Stuart Mill's little book *Auguste Comte and Positivism*.[18]

In the classroom, the one saving grace seems to have been Louis Agassiz in his course on the glacial period and paleontology, which was to prove helpful later, when Adams turned his attention to the theory of evolution. More importantly, perhaps, Agassiz was to have a major influence on Adams's style of thought regarding scientific matters. Agassiz was devoutly Christian and held an antirationalist attitude toward science, which had the effect of steering Adams away from experimental and biological sciences. The religion of Agassiz never captured Adams, but when he gave up his religious heritage, it was not replaced by naturalism or scientific materialism; instead, he adopted a quasi-idealist approach to the sciences. Thus, as William Jordy says, "Adams enjoyed the vivid generalizations of science far more than its methodical investigation."[19] Certainly this may help account for the freewheeling speculation, unanchored by much real evidence, of his late attempts to apply the laws of physics to history.

Nevertheless, Harvard had its influence. The New England certainties established in childhood began to waver, if only a little. Adams "was slipping away from fixed principles; from Mount Vernon Street; from Quincy; from the eighteenth century; and the first steps led toward Concord." But "he never reached Concord, and to Concord Church he, like the rest of mankind who accepted a material universe, remained always an insect, or something much lower—a man."[20] Thus, despite his wife's close familial connections to the transcendentalists, Emerson, Thoreau, and other major intellects of his time had little impact on his thought.

So transcendentalism did not take hold, and the New England values were simultaneously weakened, though the judgmental Puritan cast of mind never disappeared. This set up a lasting tension between the certainty of moral rectitude and the growing uncertainty about the foundations of that sense of right. But still, looking back, Adams thought that his education had not even begun. So he did what any well-to-do youth might have done; he went to Europe for two years. Although being in Europe doubtless deepened his aesthetic sensibilities, there is little sign that he was provided with the ideas necessary for the tumult of the last half of the nineteenth century, let alone the early twentieth, however long he might imitate Gibbon sitting on the steps of Santa Maria Ara Coeli in Rome.[21] The next real chance for education came with the Civil War and a close-up view of international diplomacy when he served in London as his ambassador father's private secretary.

War, Diplomacy, and Education

Following the election of 1860, Adams's father, then a congressman from Massachusetts, went to Washington, accompanied by the twenty-two-year-old Henry, to be present for the looming crisis.[22] Even after forty-four years, Henry's assessment of the impending situation was clear and blunt—treason was the only word to suffice. Confronting the Southern radicals was a government that had an "air of social instability and incompleteness that went far to support the right of secession in theory as in fact; but right or wrong, secession was likely to be easy when there was so little to secede from. The Union was a sentiment, but not much more."[23] Echoing his article on the secession winter, Adams finds the secessionists "unbalanced," like victims of "hallucinations," not to mention "stupendously ignorant of the world" and "provincial to a degree rarely known." By contrast, their New England opponents, in his rather Manichaean view of the world, "were sane and steady men, well-balanced, educated, and free from meanness or intrigue."[24] In spite of any friendship he felt for Rooney Lee, Southerners as a group were to be avoided.

Of course, senators could not be avoided, but the institution they inhabited still met with Adams's withering contempt, even looking back from 1907. They were, he said, much given to "admiring in [the institution's] members a superiority less obvious or quite invisible to outsiders."[25] In this setting, the Puritan character of Representative Adams had to be supple, and though he was thick-skinned, like all the Adamses, all would have insisted "that they had invariably subordinated local to national interests, and would continue to do so, whenever forced to choose. C. F. Adams was sure to do what his father had done, as his father had followed the steps of John Adams, and no doubt thereby earned his epithets."[26] Thus, the family tradition, redolent of civic republicanism, would continue.

One thing was certain; Abraham Lincoln did not appear to be up to the job entrusted to him. In what Adams must surely have known, in retrospect, to be a bizarre misjudgment, only General Winfield Scott looked ready for the crisis. And Adams, who may have been unaware of it even as late as 1907, had misjudged Lincoln just as badly. All he could see at the Inaugural Ball was a "long, awkward figure; a plain, ploughed face; a mind, absent in part, and in part evidently worried by white kid gloves; features that expressed neither self-satisfaction nor any other familiar Americanism, but rather the same painful sense of becoming educated and of needing education that tormented a private secretary; above all a lack of apparent force. . . . No man living needed so much education as the new President . . . but all the education he could get would not be enough."[27] There is no clear sense of the famous Adams irony here. Of course, no one going into the war could have known how to cope, but Adams's lack of regard for the president, plus his own self-regard, makes it appear that at this crucial turning point in American history, Adams simply missed the significance of Lincoln.[28] Only very late in life did he offer a more positive, if brief, evaluation of Lincoln.

Certainly the important conclusion to the chapter dealing with the crisis in Washington as war fever increased gives no hint that Adams was not entirely serious in his estimate of Lincoln. Notice carefully what Adams says:

> Not a man there knew what his task was to be, or was fitted for it; everyone without exception, Northern or Southern, was to learn his business at the cost of the public. Lincoln, Seward, Sumner, and the rest, could give no help to the young man seeking education; *they knew less than he*; within six weeks they were all to be taught their duties by the uprising of such as he; and their education was to cost a million lives and ten thousand million dollars, more or less, North and South, before the country could recover its balance and movement.[29]

The familiar Adams arrogance is striking here. Certainly it is true that no one knew what to expect from the Civil War. No one foresaw the awful carnage that was to come. What is disturbing here is that Adams, while protesting his lack of education, claims to know more than the other, much more senior, much more consequential figures he mentions. This defies all probability. His views on Reconstruction provide strong evidence that he never fully grasped what was at stake in the crisis over slavery. But this is an important passage, because it is an early instance of one of the most common rhetorical strategies in the *Education*, the pose of Socratic ignorance.[30] Throughout the book Adams protests his lack of knowledge and the failure of his education. But the reader clearly is intended to understand that despite this failure, Adams grasped ideas and events better than his contemporaries. Similarly, in the Platonic dialogues, Socrates, in spite of his protests, does in fact know more than his fellow conversationalists, and he knows that he does. What is troubling here is that in this passage, it is obvious that Adams is ignorant, but it is not at all clear that *he* recognizes that fact. His assessment of the coming crisis of the Civil War shows little of his characteristic irony. For a recognition of genuine failure, a failure that really taught him something important about the difficulty of understanding human affairs, we need to look at his experience as private secretary to his father during the war. In those years, Adams came to see the difficulties of interpreting men, motives, and events, and in coming to this understanding, he developed a deep sense of the true complexity of political action.

Diplomatic service in London, even in a minor capacity, proved to be both educational and deeply disconcerting for the young secretary.[31] On May 12, 1861, things seemed simple; he thought that the British government was a friendly one, "true to the anti-slavery principles which had been their steadiest profession. For a hundred years the chief effort of his family had aimed at bringing the Government of England into intelligent cooperation with the objects and interests of America. . . . The slave states had been the chief obstacle to good understanding. As for the private secretary himself, he was, like all Bostonians, instinctively English. He could not conceive the idea of a hostile England. He supposed himself, as one of the members of a famous anti-slavery family, to be welcome everywhere in the British Islands." But on May 13, the British recognition of Confederate belligerency was announced, and Adams suddenly learned "that his ideas were the reverse of truth; that in May, 1861, no one in England—literally no one—doubted that Jefferson Davis had made or would make a nation, and nearly all were glad of it. . . . The sentiment of anti-slavery had disappeared."[32] The great goal of American policy, under these surprising circumstances, became preventing the British from extending this position and extending diplomatic recognition to the Confederacy.

At the same time, leaving other expectations to one side, Henry writes, "Thanks to certain family associations, Charles Francis Adams naturally looked on all British Ministers as enemies; the only public occupation of all Adamses for a hundred and fifty years at least, in their brief intervals [from] quarreling with State Street, had been to quarrel with Downing Street."[33] On the British side, the two principals to contend with were Lord Palmerston, the prime minister, and Lord John Russell, the foreign secretary. In private, it was taken for granted, even by his friends, that Lord Russell was a liar. Palmerston was thought to be hardly better. "Other Prime Ministers may perhaps have lived who inspired among diplomats as much distrust as Palmerston, and yet between Palmerston's word and Russell's word, one hesitated to decide, and gave years of education to deciding, whether either could be trusted, or how far." Adams did not really mind this, saying quite realistically, "Diplomatists have no right to complain of mere lies; it is their own fault, if, educated as they are, the lies deceive them; but they complain bitterly of traps. Palmerston was believed to lay traps. He was the *enfant terrible* of the British government."[34]

Ambassador Adams believed that Palmerston wanted a quarrel and that he could better trust Lord Russell than he could the prime minister. The private secretary, for his part, believed that there was nothing to choose between the two British leaders.[35] Indeed, he went so far as to ask Thurlow Weed, a consummate Albany politician who joined the embassy staff, whether he thought that no politician could be trusted; Weed advised him that a young man should not begin by thinking so. Adams thought that this simply meant that Weed believed that youth needed illusions. But later, Weed's position appeared more complex to him:

> Young men needed experience. They could not play well if they trusted to a general rule. Every card had a relative value. Principles had better be left aside. Adams knew that he could never learn to play politics in so masterly a fashion as this; his education and his nervous system equally forbade it, although he admired all the more the impersonal faculty of the political master who could thus efface himself and his temper in the game.[36]

Thus Adams had trouble taking Weed's advice. As he says, he "felt officially sure of dishonesty." But whom to distrust? Perhaps everyone? This decision depended on a knowledge of the genuine facts, which the ambassador died without knowing.[37] Charles Francis Adams went to his grave in 1886 believing Lord Russell's protestations of friendship. But in a biography of Russell, who had died in 1878, Spencer Walpole published a tale unknown to the senior Adams. By September 1862, when news of Lee's invasion of Maryland reached London, the idea of a Union in crisis was widespread. The fall of Washington or Baltimore was expected. Palmerston immediately wrote to Russell, asking whether, in such an eventuality, England and France should not intervene between North and South and suggest a separation. Had it reached the American legation, this letter would have surprised no one, given Palmerston's supposed diplomatic inclinations at the time. But, as Adams says, it is Russell's reply to Palmerston that bears careful analysis.

Russell, so trusted by Charles Francis Adams, argued that should mediation with a view to recognizing the Confederacy fail, England should indeed recognize the rebels unilaterally. "Here, then," Adams writes, "appeared in its fullest force, the practical difficulty in education which a mere student could never overcome; a difference not in theory, or knowledge, or even want of experience, but in the shear chaos of human nature. Lord Russell's course had been consistent from the first, and had all the look of rigid determination to recognize the Southern Confederacy 'with a view' to breaking up the Union." Besides having the appearance of forethought, the policy required the "deliberate dishonesty" not only of Palmerston and Russell but also of the previously unmentioned chancellor of the exchequer, William Gladstone. It would have been interesting to know the ambassador's reaction to these revelations, had he been privy to them, but, says Adams, it would have been even more interesting to know his father's response to Palmerston's reply to Russell, in which he urged caution just in case the Union forces won. Thus, "the roles were reversed. Russell wrote what was expected from Palmerston, or even more violently; while Palmerston wrote what was expected from Russell, or even more temperately." Not only was the private secretary's view wrong, but it turned out that the closest associates of the British leaders "knew little more about their intentions than was known in the Legation." Thus it emerged that only three members of the cabinet favored recognition of the Confederacy.[38]

Had these facts been known in the American embassy, there would have been great relief and a sense that the danger had passed, but this euphoria would have been mistaken. Enter William Gladstone, the Liberal leader. If there was a fixed point in the world, Adams thought, it was the British exchequer. But here, he tells us, is the education he received from observing Gladstone's actions. The chancellor indicated that he was glad to hear the prime minister's position because of the rapid progress of the Southern forces and the risk of impatience in the Lancashire mill towns, which "would prejudice the dignity and disinterestedness of the proffered mediation." This letter to Palmerston was dated September 24, but on October 3, the news of the great Union victory at Antietam and the announcement of the Emancipation Proclamation reached London. Adams remarks of Gladstone's letter to Palmerston, "Had the puzzled student seen this letter, he must have concluded from it that the best educated statesman England ever produced did not know what he was talking about, an assumption which all the world would think quite inadmissable from a private secretary—but this was a trifle."[39]

It was a mere trifle because, on October 7, in spite of his knowledge of the Union victories, Gladstone delivered an amazing address. In it he proclaimed that the North would have to take its medicine, for "there is no doubt that Jefferson Davis and other leaders of the South have made an army; they are making, it appears, a navy; and they have made, what is more than either, they have made a nation."[40]

This was a startling pronouncement. From it, Adams "drew some harsh moral conclusions: Were they incorrect? Posed bluntly as rules of conduct, they led to the worst moral practices. As morals, one could detect no shade of difference between Gladstone and Napoleon except to the advantage of Napoleon. The private secretary saw none." The evidence against Gladstone was overwhelming. One should never, says Adams, use the word "must," as Gladstone had in his speech. He knew perfectly well that the only hope for a Southern nation rested in the hands of the British. Failing British action, his position was nonsense. "Never," says Adams, rising to a great height of indignation, "in the history of political turpitude had any brigand of modern civilization offered a worse example." Even Palmerston was outraged, since he had no thought of letting the chancellor force his hand. As for Russell, he followed Gladstone in favoring British intervention, but when Russell met with Ambassador Adams, he contended that intervention was still in doubt, insisting that Gladstone had been misunderstood. In spite of Gladstone's speech, the ambassador continued to believe in Russell. The "truth," when it was revealed thirty years later, showed Russell's position to be the reverse of what he had claimed while meeting the senior Adams. In fact, as it turned out, Gladstone had drawn his position from Russell's own policy. Palmerston disavowed Gladstone, but Russell never did. For the young Adams, "the lesson was to be crucial; it would decide the law of life. All these gentlemen were superlatively honorable; if one could not believe them, Truth in politics might be ignored as a delusion."[41]

Young Henry might have been distrustful—he only later learned the truth himself—but his father's belief in Lord Russell continued, as we have seen, to his death. Without pursuing further complications relating to this matter, such as the involvement of Napoleon III in pursuit of the goals of Russell and Gladstone, Adams drew some important lessons on which we too can build. Of the principal actors, Russell was the most interesting to Adams, simply because he was the most consistent and hence "statesmanlike." His every act showed a clear determination to break up the Union. He showed persistence, "supported, as was necessary, by the usual definite falsehoods." He said one thing and "habitually" did another.

Palmerston, so distrusted in the American embassy, tried to check Russell, scolded Gladstone, and discouraged Napoleon. "Palmerston told no falsehoods;

made no professions; concealed no opinions; was detected in no double deal-ing. The most mortifying failure in Henry Adams's long education was that, after forty years of confirmed dislike, distrust, and detraction of Lord Palmer-ston, he was obliged at last to admit himself in error, and to consent in spirit— for by that time he was nearly as dead as any of them—to beg his pardon."

Gladstone was the "sum of contradictions." His confessions of 1896 "brought all reason and hope of education to a standstill." Gladstone simply confessed to "undoubted error." He even had the effrontery to assert that his statement that Jefferson Davis was making a nation was intended, though based on a "false estimate of the facts," as an act of "friendliness to all America." Doubtless out of a sense of filial piety, Adams does not comment on his father's repeated acceptance of Lord Russell's lies, which merited a more skeptical examination. There is no doubt that the senior Adams was regularly deceived.

From all these misperceptions, Adams concludes that he, the private sec-retary, had "seen nothing correctly at the time."[42] He is perhaps a little unfair to himself, since he indicates that he entertained a certain skepticism about British leadership as these events occurred. However, the situation points the way to what may be, for him, the central implication of this complex diplo-matic situation. "Forty years afterwards," reading Gladstone's reports on cab-inet meetings, "when everyone except himself, who looked on at this scene, was dead, the private secretary of 1862 read these lines with stupor, and hur-ried to discuss them with John Hay, who was more astounded than himself. All the world had been at cross-purposes, had misunderstood themselves and the situation, had followed wrong paths, drawn wrong conclusions, and had known none of the facts. One would have done better to have drawn no con-clusions at all. One's diplomatic education was a long mistake."[43]

As usual, Adams's protestations of failed education go too far. In fact, they provide important lessons for scholars, journalists, politicians, and all others who hope to understand contemporary events. One thing that can surely be learned, or relearned, is that it is necessary for decision makers to do as well as possible under the prevailing circumstances, whatever they are. And these circumstances always include incomplete information. Frequently, perhaps usually, it is not possible to wait until all the facts are in, and when they are in, precisely what they are is likely to be disputed, as is their meaning. The most direct, close-up participants are likely to be deceived by the events going on around them, yet they must act in spite of their ignorance. This is an im-portant lesson that Adams can teach.

Nor is this situation unique to the specific situation Adams was in. This is certainly part of the meaning of Tolstoy's account in *War and Peace* of the great Russian battles in the Napoleonic wars, in which he portrays scenes of incredible confusion where no one has any real knowledge of what is going on. But we need not limit ourselves to fiction. In his superb account of U.S.-Soviet relations in the immediate postrevolutionary setting, George Kennan observes something quite similar. His was the first study to go back to the original sources to try to discern what had happened. The first volume is a minutely detailed study of events from the revolution in November to the Russian withdrawal from World War I in March. Kennan's comments on his work and what he found are amazingly reminiscent of Adams's. He notes "the marvelous manner in which purpose, personality, coincidence, communication, and the endless complexity of the modern world all combine to form a process beyond the full vision or comprehension of any single contemporary." Then he concludes, "It is sobering to reflect that, imperfect as this study is, there was none of the participants in the events recounted here—indeed, there was no one alive in those years of 1917 and 1918—who knew even the entirety of what is set forth in this volume."[44] Surely this passage would have been relished by Adams, and I suggest that no serious history or any contemporary study of politics can honestly avoid similar conclusions. The methodological lessons for history and political science today are clear and profound.

One can hardly doubt that when he returned from England in 1868, Adams combined his wartime experiences and the skepticism they bred with the long-standing Adams family distrust of any orthodox party politics of the sort abundantly on display in England. With this skepticism came a growing sense of the ambiguity of agency and intention in politics. Doubtless these attitudes influenced his journalistic critiques of American politics and society, which have already been examined, as have relevant passages in the *Education*. These criticisms must be kept in mind while we consider some of Adams's other intellectual interests, not least his growing concern with scientific developments in his time, which often fed back into his conceptions of politics and history.

Darwinism and Education

Adams's interest in science carried on a long family concern, perhaps most notably in the case of John Quincy Adams.[45] But the interest goes back as far as John Adams, who perceived "laws of nature, not less without our power, than beyond our comprehension."[46] But between the first and fourth generations of the Adams dynasty, there was a significant difference.

The second president's beliefs reflected, and in turn encouraged, the socially engaged interests of a practicing statesman; the future historian's search for unalterable law reflected and encouraged his tendency to passive observation and lonely disinterestedness. The Adams trait they shared was a scientific turn of mind with a clear history for four generations—and something beyond that, an obscure love of cosmic necessity that seems to reach into the Calvinist Puritan past with its central, compelling interest in the providence of an inscrutable, omnipotent God.[47]

To be sure, Henry no longer believed in the Puritan God, but he surely held to the Puritan cast of mind, try though he did to use it to fathom the inscrutable.

That Adams should develop an interest in Darwinism in the years following the Civil War is hardly surprising. Darwinism was a rather loose body of ideas that swept the English-speaking world, particularly in the popularized form offered by Herbert Spencer and, in the United States, by William Graham Sumner. More often than not put to deeply conservative purposes as a defense of the allegedly fittest who had survived the rigors of laissez-faire competition, it could also be used by reformers to support cooperative action on behalf of the victims of unrestrained competition.[48] Adams, however, was not particularly interested in either political use. He was too critical of postwar capitalism to join with the conservatives, and his reformist sensibilities did not run in the direction of cooperative social and economic reform.

Indeed, his first response to evolutionary theory seems to have been simple curiosity:

> Unbroken Evolution under uniform conditions pleased everyone—except curates and bishops; it was the very best substitute for religion; a safe, conservative, practical, thoroughly Common-Law deity. Such a working system for the universe suited a young man who had just helped to waste five or ten thousand million dollars and a million lives, more or less, to enforce unity and uniformity on people who objected; the idea was only too seductive in its perfection; it had the charm of art.[49]

Thus, evolution attracted Adams as a possible way to reach his lifelong goal of unity, as well as providing a cosmic basis for moral intention, since Darwinism has a tendency to moralize force and necessity. But Darwinism proved not to be the answer, and he was not to reach the goal of theoretical unity by this or any other means.

Technical discussions of Adams's views on evolution need not detain us here.[50] The political and historical lessons he drew are of interest, however. On the level of scientific evidence, his brief explorations into the fossil record were not of much value to him. *Terebratula*, a kind of mollusk, proved to be uniform from the beginning of geological time, so there was no evidence of development through natural selection. Then he considered *Pteraspis*, a fish and a very early vertebrate. But he could detect no connection between *Pteraspis* and other higher vertebrates. He was untroubled by the idea that *Pteraspis* and sharks were "his cousins, great-uncles, or grandfathers." What did trouble him was that he could see no evidence of evolution from lower to higher species. "He could detect no more evolution in life since the *Pteraspis* than he could detect it in architecture since the Abbey. All he could prove was change."[51]

He elaborates this theme:

> Behind the lesson of the day, he was conscious that, in geology as in theology, he could prove only Evolution that did not evolve; Uniformity that was not uniform; and Selection that did not select. To other Darwinians—except Darwin—Natural Selection seemed a dogma to be put in the place of the Athanasian Creed; it was a form of religious hope; a promise of ultimate perfection. . . . [But Adams] felt he had no Faith; that whenever the next new hobby should be brought out, he should surely drop off from Darwinism like a monkey from a perch; that the idea of one Form, Law, Order, or Sequence had no more value for him than the idea of none; that what he valued most was Motion, and that what attracted his mind was Change.[52]

And then, shockingly for an Adams, "Henry Adams was the first in an infinite series to discover and admit to himself that he really did not care whether truth was, or was not, true. He did not even care that it should be proved true, unless the process were new and amusing. He was a Darwinian for fun."[53] This takes being playful with ideas to a considerable extreme.

But Adams fought against accepting this dangerous new thought. "From the beginning of history, this attitude had been branded as criminal—worse than crime—sacrilege. Society punished it ferociously and justly, in self-defense." This sort of relativism was a belief that annoyed his father, but it annoyed Henry no less; he had no thought of falling victim to Hamletian doubts. He wanted the dominant current of his time to be his current. "He insisted on maintaining his absolute standards; on aiming at ultimate Unity."[54]

There is a certain defiance of reason here. His mind tells him that truth

is an illusion, but he vows to cling to the illusion because it is socially useful, as when Socrates propagates the myth of the metals in the Republic, but
with this difference: Socrates remains undeceived. He knows that the myth
is a myth or, in some interpretations, an outright lie. In the case of Adams,
he too is a Socratic figure, but one trying as hard as he can to believe what
his mind tells him is no longer valid. The tension between the New England
heritage and the disruptions of modern thought and life is beginning to become extreme.

In any case, it is clear to Adams that while change is the law of life, there
is no guarantee that the direction of change will be positive. In the optimistic
nineteenth century, belief in progress was widespread, but of course, Adams
believed, as we know, that the history of the presidency from Washington to
Grant was enough to disrupt any fantasies about inevitable progress. As Levenson says, "Instead of having to deduce George Washington from the sum
of all wickedness . . . he now faced the up-to-date, inductive question of explaining" presidential and, more generally, political decline.[55]

But other, more personal, more serious events were to create further problems, further education for Adams's developing perceptions. As we have seen,
he thought that the country was in a constitutional crisis, a crisis brought
about by sheer drift, his common term to describe the policies of the Grant
administration but affecting the reformers as well. Political chaos could be
seen in the pervasive corruption he documented in his journalism. To the
reformer, it seemed that "the country might outlive it, but not he. The worst
scandals of the eighteenth century were relatively harmless by the side of this,
which smirched executive, judiciary, banks, corporate systems, professions,
and people, all the great active forces of society, in one dirty cesspool of vulgar corruption."[56]

The last lesson of education, as he called it at the time, came in 1870,
when he was called from London to his sister's bedside in Bagni di Lucca,
Italy. She had been thrown from a cab and injured. Tetanus set in. Here, genuine chaos struck the family. Before, Adams had never really seen nature —
only the "sugar-coating that she shows to youth." He remarks, "One had
heard and read a great deal about death, and even seen a little of it, and knew
by heart the thousand commonplaces of religion and poetry which seemed
to deaden one's senses and veil the horror. Society being immortal, could put
on immortality at will. Adams being mortal, felt only the mortality."[57]

He was deeply shaken. Gone are the usual cynical mannerisms, gone are
all traces of superciliousness. Instead, he emits a cry of pure existential rage
against the universe:

The usual anodynes of social medicine became evident artifice. Sto-
icism was perhaps the best; religion was the most human; but the idea
that any personal deity could find pleasure or profit in torturing a poor
woman, by accident, with a fiendish cruelty known to man only in
perverted and insane temperaments, could not be held for a moment.
For pure blasphemy, it made pure atheism a comfort. God might be,
as the Church said, a Substance, but He could not be a Person.[58]

Reading these words, it is hard to see *Mont Saint Michel and Chartres* as
a religious book. At most, it is a picture—highly partial, to be sure—of a
beautiful society inspired by what, given the outburst precipitated by Catherine's death, Adams might well have thought to be a delusion. As Levenson
says, while the earlier book confirmed the reality of the Virgin, "the other
confirmed doubt." After quoting Adams's outburst, he continues, "instead of
being about the works of love which defy reality, the *Education* is concerned
with the ultimate reality of the real world. Yet the terrifying negation in this
climax, it must be emphasized, is a turning point and not an end."[59] This is
true enough, I think, for Adams had a mind too restless to ever come to a
complete stop. But once again, the New England verities were shaken, and
one can see in this statement the themes of Adams's later years beginning to
take shape, affecting the still-to-be-written *History*, where even men conventionally called great become the mere playthings of forces beyond their
control. Drift leading to chaos begins to be a central theme in Adams's
thought. Again, Levenson is on the mark when he comments, "The discon-
tinuities of experience, which made Adams repeat so often that he had a new
world to learn, attained their ultimate form."[60]

One can see these ideas at work during Adams's brief tenure as a Harvard
University history professor. As a result of President Eliot's famous reforms,
this Harvard was much improved over the Harvard College Adams had
attended and scorned. The problem he saw as a teacher was this: "A teacher
must either treat history as a catalogue, a record, a romance, or as an evolution; and whether he affirms or denies evolution, he falls into all the burning faggots of the pit. He makes of his scholars priests or atheists, plutocrats
or socialists, judges or anarchists, almost in spite of himself. In essence inco-
herent or immoral, history had either to be taught as such—or falsified."

Adams wanted to do neither. He had no theory of evolution to teach,
and could not make the facts fit one. He had no fancy for telling agree-
able tales to amuse sluggish-minded boys, in order to publish them
afterwards as lectures. He could still less compel his students to learn

the Anglo-Saxon Chronicle and the Venerable Bede by heart. He saw no relation whatever between his students and the Middle Ages unless it were the Church, and there the ground was particularly dangerous. He knew better than though he were a professional historian that the man who should solve the riddle of the Middle Ages and bring them into the line of evolution from past to present, would be a greater man than Lamarck or Linnaeus; but history had nowhere broken down so pitiably, or avowed itself so hopelessly bankrupt, as there. Since Gibbon, the spectacle was almost a scandal. History had lost even the sense of shame. It was a hundred years behind the experimental sciences. For all serious purposes, it was less instructive than Walter Scott and Alexandre Dumas.[61]

This is a stern indictment, though anyone teaching today can certainly recognize the problem inherent in engaging students with events in the distant past, particularly at a time when a generation seems like infinity. Having repudiated the lecture system, Adams introduced the German seminar to Harvard. Characteristically, Adams certified his years at Harvard as a failure. But his own words belie him. He found the students "excellent company. Cast more or less in the same mould, without violent emotions or sentiment, and, except for the veneer of American habits, ignorant of all that man had ever thought or hoped, their minds burst open like flowers at the sunlight of a suggestion."[62] Surely in this picture there is hope for democracy. For a professor, this is not failure but success. Adams should have taken his own words to heart. "A teacher affects eternity; he can never tell where his influence stops."[63]

Twenty Years After (1892)

Here there occurs a huge break in Adams's narrative and the start of what he often referred to as his posthumous life. The break, as I have mentioned, was occasioned by Adams's inability to write about the years of his marriage to Marian Adams, who committed suicide in 1885. We largely lose any further reflections he may have had on the political and social developments in these twenty years or any thoughts supplementing his writings, including, in particular, the *History*, but also the novels so close to his heart. And also, more important from our point of view, there is a change in his concerns, not immediate but nonetheless real. Adams does not lose interest in American politics; indeed, he has a considerable fascination with the Populist movement of the 1890s. But closely connected to this, he develops a growing interest in international capitalism, particularly in its banking dimensions; he is deeply interested in geopolitics; he displays an intensifying concern with the development of technology and an equally intensifying search for a source of unity in a world whose principal attribute is multiplicity. This last, in particular, leads him into deep, if often quixotic, reflections on the philosophy of history. The consequence of this is that much of the last third of the *Education* operates on a very high level of abstraction, making it necessary to refer more often to his correspondence to establish the context for his theorizing. But in no sense does he give up his intellectual quest. His ever-active mind pursues a general theory of history and politics to the end.

It is best to begin with the politics and economics, which are closely linked in his thought. As of 1892, when the narrative of the *Education* resumes, Adams is indifferent to party; politicians are graded according to whether they are friends or enemies of reform. In either case, as he wryly puts it, his views of politics and politicians "lacked enthusiasm."[64] But, as is already abundantly clear, to banks and to the rigid orthodox adherence to the gold standard, "he was fated to make his last resistance behind the silver standard." His own interests as an investor were with gold, but, he tells us, he was more interested in the "moral standard" than in the gold standard.[65]

Then came the panic of 1893, and Adams, incorrectly fearing that he was now a beggar, returned from Switzerland to help save the family fortune.[66] Though the situation proved to be less dire than initially thought, it did set Henry thinking, partly under the influence of his younger brother Brooks, about the nefarious role of banking in politics and society. And this process lessened his faith, already shaky, in the status of orthodox economics. As Ernest Samuels says, "The Panic of 1893 opened his eyes to the larger economic and social movement. The sacred laws of laissez-faire economics no longer supplied a clear guide to political morality, especially if they meant enriching one's enemies. Perhaps the power of government should be used after all when the laws of economics no longer served one's purposes. Perhaps their political philosophy had been wrong from the start."[67] On the political side, this meant that Adams allied himself, loosely, tentatively, and temporarily, with some of the more radical forces in American politics, the aggrieved farmers from the South and Midwest. It also brought him together with Brooks, who was developing the ideas that became his major contribution to the interpretation of history, *The Law of Civilization and Decay*. Finally, and very unfortunately, it tapped into a previously buried vein of anti-Semitism, based on his association of banking with Jews. The last result of his trip home for the family emergency was a visit to the Chicago Exposition, where he was particularly fascinated by the display of dynamos, which were to play a large part in his general theory of history and the forces that made it move.[68] Chicago raised serious questions about where the nation was going; Adams professed not to know the national destination and doubted that his fellow citizens did either. But Washington raised fewer questions. Already, as discussed in chapter 4, the decision had clearly been made for a system of centralized industrial capitalism, which Adams opposed, without elaboration, to simple industrialism standing alone. In 1893, when the decision turned on the gold standard, the choice was decisively for the new capitalism and all that it entailed, the very system Adams liked least. This result, as Russell Hanson and Richard Merriman argue, certainly precluded any revival of a civic republican tradition via a return to first principles of the political system.[69] Those principles had simply been superseded. And, even granted Adams's distinction between industrialism and capitalist industrialism, it was clearly too late to return to the earlier "precapitalist" form of organization.

Though Adams comments on how easily he and his silver friends adapted to the gold standard, in fact, the fight continued into the presidential election of 1896. Adams says very little in the *Education* about his temporary flirtation with the Populists. One suspects that he considered it an unfit subject for public discussion. But Adams misdates the final triumph of the gold system, which occurred not in 1893, as his chronology suggests, but with the presidential election of 1896. A brief look into his letters suggests the complexities of Adams's position. "Although I—very doubtfully—hold that on the whole the election of McKinley will do more mischief than that of Bryan, and, as a conservative anarchist, am therefore inclined to hope for McKinley's success, while I help Bryan all I can, certainly I cannot make so very complicated a program intelligible to any party." Unexpectedly, given the huge differences between his sensibility and the Democratic candidate's, he says, "I rather like Bryan—I mean politically—and go near going over to him." This was especially true if Europe were to go politically, socially, and financially bankrupt within the next five years, in which case he would definitely support Bryan, because that would "cut us free" at once. But then he lapses into his anti-Semitic obsession. If the "Jew regime" were going to continue for ten or twenty years, so that "all the world is to be owned by Lombard Street," then McKinley would be preferable, because the tariff would be more important than free silver, which could be useful for barely ten years as a weapon against Europe.[70] This, of course, rests on the crazed assumption that the international banking system was under Jewish control and centered in London, hence the reference to Lombard Street. For a time, this notion has a place in Adams's thought, and we will have to explore it further. But for now, the politics is of particular interest.

The statement about helping Bryan refers to the fact that, at the urging of his brother Brooks, and through him as an intermediary, Adams donated money to Bryan's campaign. He seems to have thought the money well spent. Again writing to Mrs. Cameron, Adams comments, "Bryan has made quite a wonderful fight, whether beaten or not, and poor McKinley seems a very sad jellyfish beside him. But the Major has never been regarded as serious by anyone—except himself—and me."[71] Thus, as I have mentioned, crusty old Henry Adams aligned himself temporarily, using what must be called bizarre reasoning, with some of the most radical forces in American politics.[72] But Adams lacked the courage of his peculiar convictions and in the end came round to McKinley, going home in October, as he put it, "with every-one else, to elect McKinley President and to start the world anew."[73]

Adams must certainly have had mixed feelings about this new world. It is true that John Hay, his closest friend, became ambassador to Britain and later secretary of state, so that Adams stood closer to the halls of power than he had ever been. At the same time, it is even clearer now than it was in 1906 that the election of William McKinley established a new regime in Ameri-can politics that was to last until the New Deal. It was a regime of corporate domination and declining voter participation in elections, as well as a decline in the importance of political parties. Bryan had no appeal for the urban working class, and his capture of the Democratic Party narrowed the options for voters, a trend partially reversed by the New Deal, but now again one of the deepest dilemmas for American democracy. As Walter Dean Burnham writes, "The ultimate democratic purpose of issue formulation in a campaign is to give the people at large the power to choose their and their agents' options. Moreover, so far as is known, the blunt alternative to party govern-ment is the concentration of political power in the hands of those who already possess concentrated economic power." Given the weakness of par-ties, we are thrown back on "image" and "personality" voting.[74]

The existence of such a system posed serious problems for Adams. He hated corporate capitalist domination, but he hated political parties as well. A lifetime of heterodox independence left him without the institutional means to fight back. We do not know in any detail what he thought of Theodore Roosevelt's attempts to regulate the trusts, though we do know that in general terms he was contemptuous of TR. Perhaps if his serious practi-cal interest in the domestic scene had lasted longer, he would have contin-ued his flirtation with radicals such as Bryan. But even in 1896, his attention was turning toward geopolitics and the philosophy of history. And of course, his interest was always more in diagnosis than in treatment, so he was an unlikely candidate to become an activist, no matter how much he despised the status quo.

When his thinking on international developments is considered, it is also important to take note of his intellectual relationship to his brother Brooks. "Brooks Adams had taught him [Henry] that the relation between nations was that of trade."[75] Of course, this implies a need for markets, and although Henry emphatically rejected territorial empire, he certainly favored keeping international markets open as a means to the end of American economic development. Henry pithily sums up Brooks's central thesis:

All Civilization is Centralization.
All Centralization is Economy.
Therefore all Civilization is the survival of the most economical
(cheapest).[76]

But Adams does not think that capitalism can continue indefinitely. One possibility that intrigues him comes from his brother. "Among other general rules he laid down the paradox that, in the social disequilibrium between capital and labor, the logical outcome was not collectivism, but anarchism," a point he marks for study.[77] But more immediately, he sees something else. Writing in 1898, he saw Hungary as a "child of State-Socialism in a most intelligent and practical form. In principle there is no apparent limit to its application." It is a form of society that deserves attention, "especially in connection with Russia." It is a future he says he wants nothing to do with. Nevertheless, he writes, "To me it seems to demonstrate the axiom of what we are civil enough to call progress, has got to be:—All monopolies will be assumed by the state; as a corollary to the proposition that the common interest is supreme over the individual." Then Adams goes on to urge Brooks to drop the free silver campaign and move on to socialism. He adds, in a peculiarly Hegelian fashion,

Not that I love Socialism any better than I do Capitalism, or any other Ism, but I know only one law of political or historical morality, and that is that the form of Society which survives is always in the Right; and therefore a statesman is obliged to follow it, unless he leads. . . . Socialism is merely a new application of Economy, which must go on until Competition puts an end to further Economies, or the whole world becomes one Socialist society and rots out. One need not love Socialism in order to point out the logical necessity for

Society to march that way; and the wisdom of doing it intelligently if it is to do it at all.[78]

This is a striking commentary, and not completely characteristic of Adams's thinking. Here, "Adams momentarily envisioned an ideal socialism which transcended nationality and was consistent with individual energy, but a mere glimpse could not revive youthful hope or generate a practical belief in a utopia he might help to build. . . . Intellectual curiosity was more important than humane sentiment in determining the meaning of this vision. What lasted from this phase of his peregrinations was the insistence that a real choice could be made between intelligence and drift."[79] This important point should be remembered as the fatalistic theories of his last years emerge after 1910.

Along this line, as Levenson suggests, the 1898 letter to his brother shows that he had not completely given in to determinism; intelligent leadership still had a role to play. Adams's position is very much like Joseph Schumpeter's thirty-six years later. Schumpeter too believed that capitalism would not survive if it continued along its present developmental path, which he saw threatened by the New Deal. However, unlike Adams, he was distressed by the thought, since he was an admirer of the capitalist system. Still, he saw a movement much like the one Adams suggests. In the long run, the difference between capitalism and socialism would not prove to be great, he thought; however, he hoped that the dire trends he saw could be halted in time. And though he did not much care, he thought that democracy would survive under capitalism, contrary to the ideas of some free-market liberals, though it would still be what he called "more of a sham than capitalist democracy ever was."[80]

Of course, Adams too was troubled by democracy under capitalism. But he saw more grounds for hope than did Schumpeter. He believed deeply in the need for a governing elite and felt that the need to manage the new socialist system would provide the Adamses a way back into power. R. P. Blackmur neatly sums up the implications of his analysis of the dynamics of capitalism.

> Henry Adams in making out his rough socialist position was making out, as much as anything, a case for the only possible vitalization of the governing class that he could see. Every other position constituted a more or less abject surrender to the money power; a surrender upon which every president since Lincoln had battened, just as the money power had battened on presidents. Socialism as framed was meant precisely to control the money power through absorption. So far,

Socialism was the only means of control that went further than compromise. No government that was at the conspicuous mercy of the
bankers, as Grant's had been, and Cleveland's, and Roosevelt's, could
fairly be said to govern. . . . There was, in short, no such thing as political independence at home or abroad, unless there was financial
independence.[81]

This is an extreme statement of Adams's position, though it is certainly
not an illogical extension of it. In fact, however, his stance on socialism fluc-
tuated frequently. As is so often the case, there is a tension in his thought.
Reflecting this, he wrote in the *Education*, "By rights, he should . . . have
been a Marxist, but some narrow trait of the New England nature seemed to
blight socialism, and he tried in vain to make himself a convert. He did the
next best thing; he became a Comteist, within the limits of evolution."[82] But
he continued to forecast the eventual triumph of socialism in spite of his distrust, though in his view, as in Schumpeter's theory, capitalism and socialism would become virtually indistinguishable forms dominated by large-scale
organizations.

Money, Markets, and Anti-Semitism

Throughout his career, Adams had always been interested in the subject of
money, from early writings on British financial policy to his pieces "The
Legal Tender Act" and "The New York Gold Conspiracy." But, at least partially under the influence of Brooks, foreign exchange, gold, and trade became of obsessive interest to him. This phase in Adams's thought lasted from
the mid-1890s until 1906, at which point he regained some sense of proportion. But in this obsessional stage, Adams fell victim to delusions that resulted
in a vicious anti-Semitism. This does not assume a large role in *Chartres* or
the *Education*, but it is certainly there, even if not central to his theories. As
Levenson says, his anti-Semitism "disfigures, albeit inessentially, his late
masterpieces—pockmarks of a disease that can be fatal."[83] Certainly Adams
had no idea of the horrors that were to come. "As a chapter of engineered
cruelty, the genocidal programs that would come in consequence of the nineteenth century's discourse of hate far exceeded Adams's worst expectations
of the twentieth century."[84] However, his letters are filled with a poisonous
anti-Semitism. Jews, bankers, goldbugs, and usurers are mentioned more or
less interchangeably, all as synonyms of something hateful. The attitudes spill
over from monetary questions into such celebrated cases as the Dreyfus affair.
Adams saw Dreyfus as a "howling Jew" and became a bitter anti-Dreyfusard.[85]

And, bizarrely, he identified the British campaign against the Boers with the legal campaign for Dreyfus. "Both of them are Jew wars, and I don't like Jew wars."[86] For whatever reason, he does not take up this theme in the *Education*, and, as Samuels says, "Happily, in suppressing it he suppressed most other phases of his morbid anti-Semitism."[87]

But Adams did not always hold this ugly view of the world. When younger, he did not hesitate to chide Thomas Jefferson for an anti-Jewish remark, and in spite of occasional use of common stereotypes, "he had a genuine liberal's distaste for either scorn or pride of race."[88] During the years of his marriage to Marian Adams, the couple had many Jewish friends, and his much-loved sister was married to a Jew.[89] As late as 1880, as Barbara Miller Solomon writes, Jews appeared in his novel *Democracy* "as upper class Americans with no ethnic stigma."[90] In the *History*, he is almost rhapsodic about immigration to the United States and its relation to democracy, a position that seems to cover Jewish as well as other immigrants. There is no trace of ethnocentrism here:

> [The Americans] said to the rich as to the poor, "Come and share our limitless riches! Come and help us bring to light these unimaginable stores of wealth and power!" The poor came, and from them were seldom heard complaints of deception or disillusion. Within a moment, by the mere contact of a moral atmosphere, they saw the gold and jewels, the summer cornfields, and the glowing continent. The rich for a long time stood aloof,—they were timid and narrow-minded; but this was not all,—between them and the American democrat was a gulf.

Adams continues on an even more exalted, less material plane. "Every American," except for a few Federalists, "seemed to nourish the idea that he was doing what he could to overthrow the tyranny which the past had fastened on the human mind." It was easy for the sophisticated or the cynical to fail to see in this "its nobler side, to feel the beatings of a heart underneath the sordid surface of a gross humanity." Europeans could not see this nobility. They found only cause for complaint "in the remark that the American democrat believed himself to be working for the overthrow of tyranny, aristocracy, hereditary privilege, and priesthood, wherever they existed."[91]

What happened to this Adams? Digby Baltzell points out that the first mention of the word "Jew" in Adams's letters occurs in 1896.[92] Until then, there is no sign of serious derangement in his thought. But in the 1890s, the leadership positions of the upper class were threatened; the old establishment could no longer claim unquestioned authority, nor could it count on winning positions of power as a matter of right. The upper classes tended to respond by turning an aristocracy, which Baltzell thinks of as open to the talented, into a closed caste, walling itself as a matter of self-protection. Privilege without power breeds resentment and leads to the creation of a caste system, thus depriving the nation of the services of an open-ended, upper-class elite.[93] This sense of having been displaced from positions of power can also be explained by Richard Hofstadter's well-known theory of status anxiety. Both theories clearly apply to the Adamses and are abundantly evident in the pages of the *Education*.

Combined with this was the nationwide emergence of patterns of deep-seated, nativist, anti-immigration sentiment, which included but was not limited to Jews.[94] As Samuels writes, "All the antiforeignism and racism of the time against the south European immigrant and the Oriental came to a head in the Jew as the master image of the enemy to Anglo-Saxon supremacy."[95] This sentiment tapped a powerful stain of ascriptive prejudice buried in the American national character and challenging the "official" liberal ideology so well reflected in Adams's *History*.[96] The anti-Semitic version of ascriptivism was widespread and could be found in virtually all segments of American life and culture. The Jewish stereotype did not appear until the 1870s and after that spread throughout the culture. In addition to Adams it can be found in such literary luminaries as Theodore Dreiser, Willa Cather, Edith Wharton, Thomas Wolfe, and William Faulkner, not to mention the later and more egregious cases of T. S. Eliot and Ezra Pound.[97] The anti-Semitism of many of these writers was essentially cultural, with the Jew symbolizing liberal capitalist modernity without the saving grace of a Christian aristocracy that could dilute the vulgarity of capitalist society. It is also worth noting that the Jewish stereotype is based on Jews' success as immigrants to the American culture,[98] which occurred at a time when Adams saw himself as a failure, at least by the exalted standards of his family. Thus, in one of the few outbursts in the *Education* displaying his psychic disorder—one can hardly call it less—Adams cries out,

> he twisted about in vain to recover his starting point; he could no longer see his own trail; he had become an estray; a flotsam or jetsam of wreckage. . . . His world was dead. Not a Polish Jew fresh from Warsaw or Cracow—not a furtive Jacoob or Ysaac still reeking of the Ghetto, snarling a weird Yiddish to the officers of the customs—but had a keener instinct, an intenser energy, and a freer hand than he— American of Americans, with Heaven knows how many Puritans and Patriots behind him, and an education that had cost a civil war.[99]

This is certainly part of what drove Henry Adams; he simply did not like the way his America had turned out and was looking for someone to blame. Carey McWilliams writes, "Although he regarded the new dispensation as inevitable, he could not accept it because he was too deeply immersed in the older democratic culture."[100] This sense of displacement and the decline of an earlier form of democracy would still be evident, even if we leave aside the anti-Semitic excrescences. Jews serve as a scapegoat for his more general rage against the widespread corruption of American society and politics.

All these factors no doubt played a part in the eruption of Adams's irrational anti-Semitism. But one other important factor needs to be taken into account—his detestation of capitalism. It is clear from his journalism that he saw an intimate connection between capitalism and the corruption of the political system that was so destructive to his idea of democracy. But where does the anti-Semitism come from? He despised capitalism before the emergence of the Jewish stereotype in the 1870s. Of course, anti-Semitism in general has an ancient and dishonorable pedigree. But the connection between Judaism and capitalism goes back before Adams; in fact, none other than Karl Marx—an example of that peculiar creature, the anti-Semitic Jew— gives an early statement of the theme in his 1843 pamphlet *On the Jewish Question*. Writes Marx, "What is the profane base of Judaism? *Practical* need, *self-interest*. What is the worldly cult of the Jew? *Huckstering*. What is his worldly god? *Money*."[101] Almost immediately he goes on, "In the final analysis, the emancipation of the Jews is the *emancipation* of mankind from *Judaism*." And then, sounding very like Adams lamenting the presumed international power of Jews, he adds, quoting Bruno Bauer, " 'The Jew, who is merely tolerated in Vienna, for example, determines the fate of the whole Empire by his financial power.' "[102]

Though it is extremely doubtful that Adams could have known these early works of Marx, they have the tone he was to adopt, a tone that became widespread in American culture and in other cultures as well. There is the same paranoid distrust of bankers and the same tendency to list a set of disparaging terms associated with the word *Jew*: in the case of Marx, self-interest, huckster, and the like. And yet, as already mentioned, Adams did not turn his disgust with capitalism into anti-Semitism until the 1890s. Perhaps this cannot be adequately explained short of psychoanalysis. There simply may be no fully rational explanation for the irrational. It can be said that the anti-Semitic stereotype was not available to Adams when he began his biting critique of capitalism. But in 1893, when the Adamses' financial fortunes took a downturn, perhaps the new vocabulary seemed plausible to him. It is also important to remember the political aspects of McWilliams's interpretation. Deep down, what may have bothered Adams the most was the decline of the democratic forms he believed in and their subversion by capitalism.

The anti-Semitism never entirely disappeared, but the obsession with markets and money did, and with it, the virulence of his ethnic hatred declined also. In 1906, probably reflecting the final stages of his work on the *Education*, he wrote to Brooks, "But please give up the profoundly unscientific jabber of the newspapers about MONEY in capital letters. What I see is POWER in capitals also. You may abolish money and all its machinery, the Power will still be there, and you will still have to trapeze after it in the future just as the world has always done in the past. On the whole, our generation has suffered least of any. The next can run its own machine."[103] Certainly Adams was fully aware of money as a major source of power, so he could not have meant to deny that. But by that time, technology was on his mind as a force to be reckoned with, as was mass democracy. Just possibly, there may have been hopeful moments in which he believed that, in a better world, democratic public opinion might regain some degree of power and become a force for positive change. Commenting on Theodore Roosevelt's approach to the trusts, he said that the problem was that "the public had no idea what practical system it could aim at, or what sort of men could manage it. The single problem before it was not so much to control the Trusts as to create the society that could manage the trusts." The new American must be either the child of the new forces or a sport of nature.[104] He must adapt to the new realities of the modern political economy and all that went with it. The import of this is not altogether clear. The distinction between control and management is muddy, to say the least. As someone who feared centralization, perhaps he hoped that society would replace centralized control with a revolutionary change in the public perception of the trusts. This would, as McWilliams suggests,[105] involve a transformation of values of major dimensions. Did Adams have any real hope that such a thing could happen? Probably not, but today we might, though there are certainly no particular grounds for optimism.

The Problem of Technology

When he visited Chicago for the Exposition of 1893, Adams was forcefully struck both by the city and by the power of technology. Putting aside his usual scorn for the Midwest, Adams was almost rhapsodic, though also quizzical. "The Exposition itself defied philosophy. One might find fault till the last gate closed, one could still explain nothing that needed explanation. As a scenic display, Paris had never approached it, but the inconceivable scenic display consisted in its being there at all—more surprising, as it was, than anything else on the continent."[106] Unlike Niagara Falls and the Yellowstone geysers, these were man-made creations, which made them especially remarkable. It seemed as if the Parisian school of the beaux arts had been transferred to the shore of Lake Michigan. Was it possible that it "could be made to seem at home there? Was the American made to seem at home in it? Honestly, he had the air of enjoying it as though it were all his own; he felt it was good; he was proud of it." And he goes on: "For the moment he [Adams] seemed to have leaped directly from Corinth and Syracuse and Venice, over the heads of London and New York, to impose classical standards on plastic Chicago. . . . All trader's taste smelt of bric-a-brac; Chicago tried at least to give her taste a look of unity."[107] Could this be real, Adams wonders, saying that his own personal universe depended on the answer, "for if the rupture was real and the new American world could take this sharp and conscious twist towards ideals, one's personal friends would come in as winners in the great American chariot-race for fame." Artists and architects like Hunt, Richardson, St. Gaudens, McKim, and Stanford White would be talked about when their "politicians and millionaires were otherwise forgotten." The artists themselves were not optimistic, but perhaps there was hope.[108] For Adams, this is a remarkable statement. It suggests a degree of optimism—cultural, in this case—a note not often heard in his late writings and one that ought to be remembered amidst the general gloom about the direction of his country, its culture, and indeed all of world history.

But of course what intrigued Adams even more than the architectural wonders of Chicago was the technology on display at the exposition. This is the force that began to move to the center of his thinking about the dynamics of history and that sent his historical imagination into overdrive. "One lingered long among the dynamos," he tells us, "and they gave to history a new phase."[109] Combined with his amazement at the fact of Chicago itself, the new technology posed vast problems for him to consider:

> Chicago asked in 1893 for the first time the question whether the American people knew where they were driving. Adams answered, for one, that he did not know, but would try to find out. On reflecting sufficiently deeply, . . . he decided that the American people probably knew no more than he did; but that they might still be driving or drifting unconsciously toward some point in thought; as their solar system was said to be drifting toward some point in space; and that,

possibly, if relations enough could be observed, this point might be fixed. Chicago was the first expression of American thought as a unity; one must start there.[110]

Washington was another expression of American unity, and here the picture is much less attractive. At this point, Adams launches into the lament, already discussed, that in 1893 the American majority decisively declared itself in favor of capitalism, thus joining forces with the banks and creating the form of society and government that Adams liked least. Thus, says Adams, at this point, "education in domestic politics stopped."[111]

Unfortunately, this is largely true, though Adams continues to speculate on the domestic scene in his letters. We are left, it seems to me, with cultural hope in Chicago, though not without some uncertainty, and political gloom regarding Washington. Though he was well placed to do so, Adams has little to say about the efforts of the Progressive movement, however inadequate, to come to grips with the corporate capitalism he detested. Perhaps his distaste for Theodore Roosevelt held him back. In any case, he does nothing to explore his suggestion that what was needed was a society that could manage the trusts rather than a government that could control them. Instead, he largely leaves the American scene aside in order to explore the dynamics of world history.

At this point, we return to the world of the Virgin of Chartres. The year 1900 found Adams at an exposition again, this time the Great Exposition in Paris. He continues to mull over education, saying that nothing in it is "so astonishing as the amount of ignorance it accumulates in the form of mere facts." He had seen most of the art collected in the museums of the world but could not understand the art in Paris, and he had assiduously studied Marx and found his lessons inapplicable to Paris.[112] What *was* of interest were the giant electric motors. As he grew accustomed to the gallery of machines, he began to feel them as a moral force, much as the early Christians saw the cross. By the end, he began to pray to them.[113] To him, they were like an occult mechanism. "Between the dynamo in the gallery of machines and the engine-house outside, the break of continuity amounted to abysmal fracture for a historian's objects." At the same time, he sees, quite presciently, the force revealed by the discovery of radium: "The force," Adams notes, "was wholly new."[114]

Thinking about the nature of these new forces and technologies, Adams began to reconsider the nature of history, both as a substantive analysis of what had happened in the past and as a mode of disciplined inquiry. He tells us, "Historians undertake to arrange sequences, —called stories, or histories—

assuming in silence a relation of cause and effect. These assumptions, hidden in the depths of dusty libraries, have been astounding, but commonly unconscious and childlike; so much so that if any captious critic were to drag them to light, historians would probably reply, with one voice, that they had never supposed themselves to know what they were talking about." Looking back on his own work, Adams recalls that he had published a dozen volumes of American history just to satisfy himself that facts arranged in a rigorous way could establish a "necessary sequence of human movement."[115] One may doubt that this was the reason, or at least the primary reason, for writing the history of the Jefferson and Madison administrations, but Adams still expressed dissatisfaction with the result, pointing out that when he presented his sequence, others saw something quite different. Of course, that others saw the same facts differently does not disprove Adams. These critics may only have looked at the facts from a different perspective. But, as Susan Haack has pointed out, "Truth is not relative to perspective; and there can't be incompatible truths. . . . But there are many different truths—different but compatible truths—which must somehow fit together." More importantly, Haack adds, "Although what is true is not relative to perspective, what is accepted as truth is; although incompatible statements cannot be jointly true, incompatible claims are frequently made."[116] And one might add, in good Millian fashion, that the conflict between differing perspectives can further the search for truth. Adams seems to have seen this; remember his suggestion to President Eliot of Harvard that he appoint Henry Cabot Lodge as a conservative counterbalance to his own radical democratic position. But still, Adams, for all his greatness as a historian, gives up too soon. The sequence of men leads to nothing, he concludes, and the sequence of society cannot go further, while the time sequence is artificial and the sequence of thought mere chaos. He therefore turns dramatically to the "sequence of force; and thus it happened that, after ten years' pursuit, he found himself lying in the Gallery of Machines at the Great Exposition of 1900, with his historical neck broken by the sudden irruption of forces totally new."[117]

This, he thought, was something very new. The discoveries of Copernicus and Galileo had broken professorial necks in about 1600, and a hundred years before that, Columbus had turned the world upside down, "but the nearest approach to the revolution of 1900 was that of 310, when Constantine set up the Cross."[118] A totally new education was required to deal with this almost unprecedented situation. The comparisons that leaped to his mind are interesting and important in the context of his thought. "The force of the Virgin was still felt at Lourdes, and seemed to be as potent as X-rays;

but in America neither Venus nor Virgin ever had value as force—at most as sentiment. No American had ever been truly afraid of either."[119]

Returning to a theme that goes as far back as his paper "The Primitive Rights of Women," Adams comments:

> The Woman had once been supreme; in France she seemed potent, not merely as a sentiment but as a force. Why was she unknown in America? . . . When she was a true force she was ignorant of fig-leaves, but the monthly magazine-made American female had not a feature that would be recognized by Adam. The trait was notorious, and often humorous, but anyone brought up among Puritans knew that sex was sin. In any previous age, sex was strength. Neither art nor beauty was needed. Everyone, even among the Puritans, knew that neither Diana of the Ephesians nor any of the Oriental goddesses was worshiped for her beauty. She was a goddess because of her force; she was the animated dynamo; she was reproduction.[120]

The key here is clearly not sexual activity as such, but reproduction. It was the power to reproduce that made woman the central force in the family and thus the center of society as a whole. This was the source of woman's energy. Again returning to an earlier theme, this time from *Chartres*, he says, "On one side, at the Louvre and at Chartres, as he knew by the record of work actually done and still before his eyes, was the highest energy ever known to man, the creator of four-fifths of the noblest art, exercising vastly more attraction over the human mind than all the steam-engines and dynamos ever dreamed of; and yet this energy was unknown to the American mind. An American Virgin would never dare command; an American Venus would never dare exist."[121]

Here Adams steps back from the centrality of motherhood for a moment and asks questions about sex and its representation in American culture. Adams wants to know whether any American artist ever insisted on the power of sex, as the classics had always done. In general, the answer to the question was no. The major exception was Walt Whitman, who could hardly be more different from Adams. He also mentions Bret Harte, who wrote sympathetically of gamblers and prostitutes, and one or two unnamed painters.[122] For the rest, he says, sex was mere sentiment.

Adams is even critical of his friend, the sculptor Augustus St. Gaudens, claiming that as an American, his art was starved from birth, while Adams admits that his own instincts were "blighted from babyhood." For Adams, the Virgin of Amiens became a symbol of force, while for St. Gaudens, she was merely a model of taste. Even Adams began to feel the Virgin's force only in 1895, and even then, not everywhere. "At Chartres—perhaps at Lourdes—possibly at Cnidos if one could still find there the divinely naked Aphrodite of Praxiteles—but otherwise one must look for force to the goddesses of Indian mythology." Artists complained that the power of, say, a railroad train could never be captured. But Adams could see that "all the steam in the world could not, like the Virgin, build Chartres."[123] Adams therefore decided to pursue the mystery of this force, thus leading him to write *Mont Saint Michel and Chartres*, remarking wryly that the problem could scarcely be more complex than radium. The Virgin would be easier to handle, Adams thought, though he was later forced by his never-ending curiosity to consider radium and other aspects of the new science. And the specter of controlling force begins to be raised. "Forty-five years of study had proved to be quite futile for the pursuit of power; one controlled no more force in 1900 than in 1850, although the amount of force controlled by society had enormously increased."[124] The issue starts to become whether we can control the forces being unleashed by the new science and technology. The difficulty was that the world was growing more and more confusing and required more and more intellectual energy to cope with it. Looking at everyday life, he expresses his thought—his dilemma—with moving clarity:

> In all this futility, it was not the magnet or the rays or the microbes that troubled him, or even his helplessness before the forces. To that he was used from childhood. The magnet in its new relation staggered his new education by its evidence of growing complexity, and multiplicity, and even contradiction, in life. He could not escape it; politics or science, the lesson was the same, and at every step it blocked his path whichever way he turned. He found it in politics; he ran against it in science; he struck it in everyday life, as though he were still Adam in the Garden of Eden between God who was unity, and Satan who was complexity, *with no means of deciding which was truth.*[125]

Gone are the old New England certainties; this is a genuinely open and perplexed mind. This is no dogmatist, but rather a questing spirit casting doubt on the means of discovering truth and, by extension, truth itself. We may not like the results of the search, but we can only respect the intensity and tenacity with which it is carried out. Adams is not one to give in to despair, in spite of appearances. The search goes on.

And here his thoughts begin to turn again to politics, though on a very high level of abstraction. Politics and science begin to merge. "All one's life,"

Adams tells us, "one had struggled for unity, and unity had always won. The National Government and the national unity had overcome every resistance, and the Darwinian evolutionists were triumphant over all the curates; yet the greater the unity and the momentum, the worse became the complexity and the friction."[126] Adams has to deal with these complexities with no sure sense of the nature of truth. However much he loves the image of the woman and the Virgin, deep down, Adams senses that it is too late for them to be of much help. One can contrast the twentieth century with the beauties of medieval France, all to the advantage of the latter, yet Adams knows that he has no choice but to live in the very different world of American modernity. Recall also that he lacks the faith so eloquently portrayed in *Chartres*. And, to look ahead, it is by no means as clear as is commonly believed that Adams completely rejects the modern American world. He is always a divided and ambivalent thinker.

Another Try at Political Education

In 1901, Adams visited the Wagner Festival in Bayreuth, where, with the dark strains of *Götterdämmerung* sounding in the background, he began to explore his notion of conservative Christian anarchy. Though he does not use the term there, the idea of a form of anarchism is explored earlier in *Chartres*; if anything, there is more anarchy displayed there than in the *Education*. Though he briefly cites Saint Thomas as one source, that seems entirely implausible, but, given his probably heretical portrait of the Virgin, she clearly qualifies for the label anarchist. In his image, Mary is distrustful of authority, is concerned with the victims of injustice, cares for the poor, and is at home with ordinary people. In conventional modern terms, however we may label Adams, his heroine is definitely positioned on the Left. Adams cannot have been unaware of this. In the larger context of his political thought, what does this mean? It is possible only to speculate, because Adams gives us very little to go on. As I have already suggested, a close reading of *Chartres* suggests more sympathy for modern complexity or multiplicity than Adams usually allows. And, more speculatively, if my reading of Adams on multiplicity is correct, his picture of the Virgin might be a somewhat indirect way to introduce a critical leftist position into the complex discussions of modern politics. This is, as I suggest, pure speculation; I know of no direct textual support, other than the guarded defense of socialism he offers in his letter to his brother on Hungary, presenting it as the best in an array of bad choices provided by modern politics. Of course, there is also the Virgin's disdain for authority and her tendency to support the underdog, both characteristic positions of the Left.

But, if this is not Adams's specific intent, are contemporary readers justified in using his work as a platform to explore such ideas anyway? I think the answer is yes, if they are cautious. Obviously, we are not entitled to make past political thinkers say any old thing we want them to say. Plato cannot be read as a modern democrat, and Marx is no partisan of capitalism beyond its "necessary" position along the road to socialism. But it is not uncommon or improper to discover hidden meanings in a text or to discern implications of a line of reasoning that the author may not have seen or intended or fully worked out. Once ideas reach the public, they take on a life of their own. If they are good and fruitful, they may stimulate others to take them beyond their initial boundaries. This is one way that traditions of thought grow. Perhaps it is possible to use Adams in this way,[127] though it is important not to claim that Adams read in this way is the historical Adams.

In any event, these implications are not so clear when Adams turns to conservative Christian anarchism. There he admits to having "played with anarchy; though not with socialism."[128] He tells us that his branch of the anarchist's party consists of two members, himself and Bay Lodge, the son of Henry Cabot Lodge. The role of each is to denounce the other as "unequal to his lofty task and inadequate to grasp it. Of course, no third member could be so much as considered, since this great principle of contradiction could be expressed only by opposition; and no agreement could be conceived, because anarchy, by definition, must be chaos and collision, as in the kinetic theory of a perfect gas." This law of contradiction was a kind of agreement, a limitation of personal liberty, but the continuous contradictions could lead to a still larger contradiction. "Thus the great end of all philosophy—the 'larger synthesis'—was attained, but the process was arduous, and while Adams, as the older member, assumed to declare the principle, Lodge necessarily denied both the assumption and the principle in order to assure its truth."[129] Of course, Adams is playing games with Hegel as well as with his readers, though one has to doubt that, given his aversion to metaphysics, he was seriously influenced by the great German. It is much more likely that what is at work here is his intellectual playfulness and his sheer contrariety.

But the game continues for a time, though I think that for Adams, it is more than just a game. What he calls the "last synthesis" is a recurrent theme in his late work, including the correspondence. The synthesis reached concludes that, order and anarchy were one, but that unity was chaos. As anarchist, conservative and Christian, he had no motive or duty but to attain the end; and, to hasten it, he was bound to accelerate progress; to concentrate energy; to accumulate power; to multiply and intensify forces; to reduce friction, increase velocity and magnify momentum, partly because this was the mechanical law of the universe as science explained it; but partly also in order to get done with the present which artists and some others complained of, and finally—and chiefly—because a rigorous philosophy required it, in order to penetrate the beyond, and satisfy man's destiny by reaching the largest synthesis in its ultimate contradiction.[130]

The major conclusion is that order and unity are contradictory, that the paradoxical fact is that order and chaos are synonymous. Moreover, these conclusions are validated for Adams not by Hegel's dialectic but, more importantly, by the findings of modern science as they emerged in the early twentieth century. Finally, it is important to keep in mind the analysis of *Chartres*, in which the conclusion is that unity may not be superior to multiplicity after all. With the exception of the last point, all these ideas become frequent motifs of Adams's thought, most notably in his late thinking about the nature of history. The prose may be playful, but the ideas are serious.

Adams is much too astute not to recognize the obvious objection to his formulations, namely, that they are neither conservative nor Christian nor anarchic. On the face of it, it seems like not a bad objection to say that the whole notion appears self-contradictory, but Adams is rather airily dismissive of this response. The "untaught critic," he says, should begin his education "in any infant school in order to learn that anarchy which should be logical would cease to be anarchic."[131] Prevailing anarchist doctrines were either innocent, sentimental derivations from Russian culture, such as those of Kropotkin, or the ideals of French workers "diluted with absinthe," leading to a bourgeois "dream of order and inertia." Both doctrines had simply inherited their conceptions of the universe from "the priestly class to which their minds obviously belonged." A mind that followed nature, as Adams's did, had no more in common with them than with socialists, communists, and collectivists. They all needed to go back to the twelfth century, where their ideas had enjoyed a reign of a thousand years. The conservative Christian anarchist must rest on "the nature of nature" itself. This hardly even needed proof, he says. "Only the self-evident truth that no philosophy of order—except the Church—had ever satisfied the philosopher reconciled the conservative Christian anarchist to prove his own."[132]

Blackmur offers an analysis of Adams's rather murky conservative Christian anarchism that is interesting and without Adams's flippancy. He admits that Adams gives us only a "primitive and ambiguous sketch." But, he suggests, "We can say that the point of view behind it is *conservative* because it holds hard to what survives in man's mind, *Christian* because it must encompass in a single piety even the most contradictory of the values which survive, and *anarchic* because all the values and every act of encompassment are products of an order of forces that are beyond the scope of the mind to control and that are perhaps alien and ultimately destructive to it."[133] This is a reasonable interpretation, though I think only the comment on anarchism is wholly plausible. The interpretation of "conservative" is fairly close to the mark, though what survives in man's mind is by no means beyond debate, and one must ask whether encompassing contradictory values is particularly Christian; one might even say that Christianity often tries to exclude contradictory values. Still, this is an interesting effort that captures a sense of Adams's attempt to contain enormous turbulence within the framework of a deeply challenged tradition.

J. C. Levenson offers a simpler reading of conservative Christian anarchism. He considers it a term born from confusion that means the same thing as the conservative anarchism Adams mentioned in 1896. Here the term refers to someone who resists centralization "but anticipates (often with morbid glee) his own defeat with a general cataclysm to follow." Levenson sees this meaning as essentially frivolous, leading to Adams's facetious party of two. To find a serious meaning, we must go back to *Chartres*. Recall the formulation there in which Adams states that absolute liberty is the absence of restraint but that responsibility equals restraint, so that in an ideally free world, the individual is responsible to himself. Levenson reads this to mean that Adams is willing to accept that this is a world in which religion and society no longer control individual conduct. "Within that world he chose, on his own responsibility, to conserve the liberal values among which he had lived for as long as he could remember and, ultimately, the Christian values of which he had acquired a personal memory after great pains."[134]

This reading is, I think, closer to the mark than Blackmur's. It accommodates the point I made in the previous chapter that Adams's formulation skips over the liberal theory of responsibility and substitutes anarchism for it. The case for Adams's anarchism, and for the Virgin's, is compelling, though Adams goes much beyond the conception of anarchy advanced by Levenson. Further, the idea of conserving liberalism is central to the American political tradition of which Adams is a part.[135] It is also important to remember that Adams's self-identification is as a liberal. However, it needs to be stressed that Adams's "Christianity" is entirely secular, paradoxical though that may be. The discussion of Christianity may have helped him recall a Protestant, Puritan code of conduct that supported his moral sense. His Christianity is certainly not Catholic. Adams, even if he had wished it, was not ready or able to embrace Roman Catholicism, as Levenson is well aware. As Adams wrote in 1915, referring to a priest with whom he was in correspondence, "Father Fay is no bore—far from it, but I think he has an idea that I want conversion, for he directs his talk much to me, and instructs me. Bless the genial sinner! He had best look out that I don't convert him, for his old church is really too childless for a hell in this year of grace."[136] On this, Levenson comments, "Except as his historical imagination carried him back to the high Middle Ages, he remained a stoic: God existed for him in the realm of essence and historical existence, perhaps, but not in the realm of present reality."[137] This is an odd sort of Christianity, I think.

Adams drops his arrogant tone almost immediately, admitting that, at the time, there was deep darkness. He could not even affirm, he says, that the "larger synthesis" would definitely turn out to be chaos, since, contrarian to the end, "he would equally be obliged to deny the chaos." The rapid growth of industrial power and technology "drowned rhyme and reason." At least the conservative Christian anarchists saw light in the darkness.[138]

The political party that Adams describes is a strange sort institution. Of course, it is not a party at all, except in a metaphorical sense, but rather a facet of Adams's philosophy of history. He is disturbed by the pace of social change. As he writes to Brooks, "Either our society must stop or bust." And in the same letter he says, "I rather incline to think that the situation is new, not contemplated by nature, as hitherto constituted on this planet, and that God Almighty couldn't guess what will or won't happen. This being my view of it, I am not disposed to put my fingers into the machinery. Today, no doubt, this sounds rather mad. Ten years hence, who knows? . . . *We know so little, and our power is so great.*"[139] One might read this as an expression of a conservative temperament distrustful of all efforts toward institutional reform. But I think the matter is more complex. By the time Adams wrote the *Education*, he clearly thought that nature was deeply involved in the dynamic of social change and that an adequate theory of history needed to take that fact into account. However, the other themes persist. He continues to believe in the absolute newness of the situation, and he continues to adopt a rather passive, let nature take its course, position. There is a deep-seated pessimism in his thought, though it is important to keep in mind the occasions when a glimmer of hope rises to the surface. The pessimism is evident in a letter to the poet Bay Lodge, where he writes with perhaps a little more than his usual acerbity, "Also you know that Conservative Christian Anarchy, since Cain's time, has seemed somewhat to lack popular approval. Although Christ came personally down from God the Father to set things straight, he seems to have failed, like most other poets."[140]

And yet, amidst the gloom, there are outbursts of hope, not least about America, which he continues to see, for better or worse, as being well in advance of all other nations. To Americans' great advantage is this fact:

> In America all were conservative Christian anarchists; the faith was national, racial, geographic. The true American had never seen such supreme virtue in any of the innumerable shades between social anarchy and social order as to mark it for exclusively human and his own. He never had known a complete union either in Church or State or Thought, and had never seen any need for it. The freedom gave him courage to meet any contradiction, and intelligence enough to ignore it.[141]

Here and elsewhere, it seems that at least as late as 1907, Adams was not ready to give up on America, whose saving grace seems to be an almost Whitmanesque ability to contain multitudes. What is troubling is his unwillingness to turn his mind toward meaningful reforms. This is not so much conservatism as an inclination to a passive determinism fostered by his understanding of science, sometimes tinctured by hope, but that proved, I argue later, to be a limiting factor on his political theory. And, of course, his flippant remarks about throwing his weight to whatever side would hasten the collapse of the system he loathed are totally irresponsible and potentially dangerous if acted upon. To see the danger, one need only consider the fate of the German communists who failed to confront the Nazis, thinking that the triumph of Hitler would lead to a rapid collapse, after which the Left would pick up the pieces.

In spite of this unwillingness to resuscitate his interest in reform, Adams remained an interested and interesting observer of politics.[142] Foreign policy was a matter of great concern to him, and he used his connection with John Hay to influence it as much as possible. But he was not always successful, and he opposed the sudden emergence of the American empire. Still, at the time in his life when, on the surface, he should or could have been very influential, he was not. He did not like what he called McKinleyism. Washington was needed to control the new power in the land, but, though "amusing," the capital was interesting mainly for its distance from New York. "The movement of New York had become planetary—beyond control—while the task of Washington, in 1900 as in 1800, was to control it. The success of Washington in the past century promised ill for its success in the next."[143] After the death of McKinley, Adams might have tried to use his influence with his friends President Theodore Roosevelt and Henry Cabot Lodge, now a senior and very influential senator from Massachusetts. However, the young president was a problem rather than a solution. The trouble with Roosevelt was a basic character flaw. "Power when wielded by abnormal energy is the most serious of facts, and all Roosevelt's friends know that his restless and combative energy was more than abnormal." Wryly, Adams compares himself with Seneca, saying that Seneca "must have remained in some shade of doubt what advantage he should get from the power of his friend and pupil Nero Claudius, until, as a gentleman past sixty, he received Nero's filial invitation to kill himself. Seneca closed the vast circle of his knowledge by learning that a friend in power was a friend lost."[144] An instinct of self-preservation kept him from the White House. "Power is poison," he reflected.

> Its effect on Presidents had been always tragic; chiefly as an almost insane excitement at first, and a worse reaction afterwards; but also because no mind is so well balanced as to bear the strain of seizing unlimited force without habit or knowledge of it. . . . Roosevelt enjoyed a singularly direct nature and honest intent, but he lived naturally in restless agitation that would have worn out most tempers in a month, and his first year of Presidency showed chronic excitement that made a friend tremble. The effect of unlimited power on limited mind is worth noting in Presidents because it must represent the same process in society, and the power of self-control must have limit somewhere in face of the control of the infinite.[145]

More might have been expected from Hay and Lodge than from Roosevelt, but if Adams had expected it, he was disappointed. Hay was tired and sick, and Lodge was in an impossible position. "He could not help himself, for his position as the President's friend and independent statesman at once was false, and he must be unsure in both relations." But beyond this, Adams thought that Massachusetts was an impossible state to represent, a state with a fragmented political culture that Adams knew would emerge everywhere. Already in Massachusetts there were simply too many forces at work: State Street and the banks; the Congregational clergy; Harvard; immigrants, especially the Irish; and even a new socialist class. In another of his startlingly prescient analyses, Adams comments, "New power was disintegrating society, and setting independent centers of force to work, until money had all it could do to hold the machine together. No one could represent it faithfully as a whole."[146]

Give such leadership, it would not be surprising for Adams to despair of his hope of creating a society that would not merely control the trusts but manage them. As McWilliams says, for that to work, it would be necessary to place values ahead of programs.[147] Since ideally, programs are based on values, this would doubtless be healthy. A transformation of values obviously implies a need for fresh thought, a theme that runs throughout the late work of Adams. However, what that new thought might entail is left more than a little unclear. Still, there may be a hint in a letter from Adams to Brooks. Theodore Roosevelt's famous distinction between good and bad trusts is useless, Adams says. *"It gives away our contention that they have no right to exist."* But this does not really take us anywhere, because "our society has chosen its path beyond recall." It is too late for reform. All that can be done is to "vapor like Theodore" about honesty, law, and decency. Adams damns all this as useless. The result is that all we can do is "make the machine run without total collapse in a catastrophe" until it suffers its inevitable breakdown.[148] Thus, by 1910, the hope extended in the *Education* seems to have been lost in a fit of despair, though the point that the trusts had no right to exist is a clue to his deeper feelings.

This does not imply that the failure to produce a society with the values and programs Adams would have preferred leads him to abandon democracy as a hope, even if it is not a reality. Nor are his concerns limited to the United States. When the Roosevelt administration privately negotiates a Far Eastern peace settlement, he complains, "About five hundred million people were waiting with their lives and money at stake, to hear what these two jackasses said, and nobody ever suggested that the 500,000,000 should be anyhow consulted. I'm going to die, soon—thank God."[149] But aside from this generalized and perhaps atypical concern, Adams continues to have faith in the ultimate good sense of the American people, in spite of his disgust with Theodore Roosevelt. As late as 1905, he writes, "As yet nothing is broken. Our people are quick and practical and have not yet lost their heads."[150]

It is not hard to understand why Adams was disturbed by the politics of his time. After all, it was much like our own. There is a certain symmetry between the beginning of the twentieth century and the beginning of the twenty-first. There *was* a great deal of corruption. Capital *did* at times seem out of control. And while Theodore Roosevelt was a better president than

Adams thought, there was good reason to fear his volatile temperament. Of course, the problems were structural and institutional, not just products of the president's flamboyant personality. And in spite of his worries, through all this, Adams maintained faith in the American people. Just as in the War of 1812, he saw that the problems of the nation were much more the fault of the political and economic leadership than of the people. Adams did not subscribe to a theory of the "degradation of the democratic dogma." This is the title his brother Brooks gave to the posthumous collection of his papers aimed at a scientific theory of history. Indeed, Brooks probably read his own views into the title. Characteristically, "Brooks, when President Eliot mildly observed to him after an address at the Law School that he apparently did not overcherish democracy, responded abruptly in his harsh, full-carrying voice: 'Do you think I'm a damned fool?' "[151] This is not Henry's style. It is worth noting that when the scientific essays were reissued ten years after their first appearance, they were shorn of Brooks's title and his lengthy introduction as well. The new title was *The Tendency of History*, a much more suitable label.[152] As for Henry, while it is abundantly clear that he was not some precursor of the participatory democracy of the 1960s, he was still committed to the theory and practice of representative democracy. President Eliot of Harvard was quite mistaken, I think, when he said after reading the *Education*, "I should like to be saved from loss of faith in democracy as I grow old and foolish. I should be very sorry to wind up as the three Adamses did. I shall not unless I lose my mind." It is equally mistaken for Samuels to follow this point by suggesting that Adams repudiated democracy in his late work.[153] But it is also clear that democracy as well as much else was threatened by corporate capitalism, by the dramatic growth of technological power, and by the science that made technological power possible.

Chapter 8

The End of Education

In the early twentieth century, it was easy to see the emerging problem of a threat to democracy stemming from the development of technology, the science that supported it, and the growing concentration of economic power they contributed to. Adams's philosophy of history emerged from his reflections on these large themes, both in the United States and around the world. It is important to look more closely at this set of powerful forces, starting with the impact of technology.

Technology and the Virgin

The most striking glimpse Adams offers into the new world of technology is the contrast between the Virgin and the dynamo. So far, all that has been considered in this regard is the Virgin as a force so great as to provide the impetus to build the great medieval cathedrals. There is no doubt that Adams was right, up to a point. In religiously saturated Europe, the Virgin was a great spiritual power that stimulated an explosion of artistic expression—an explosion equaled, perhaps, but not surpassed in the history of Western art. But it is also important to remember that although the cathedral builders may have been inspired by Mary, the buildings themselves were among the most important engineering feats of their time. I have no wish to detract from Mary's spiritual inspiration, but this last point must be considered, for Adams, in his idealization of the Middle Ages, tends to ignore it. This fact cannot be explained by ignorance or lack of interest in the topic, since in writing of the War of 1812, for example, he devotes a good deal of space to celebrating American inventive technological genius in critical areas such as gunnery and shipbuilding. Lynn White, Jr., goes some distance in narrowing the gap between the spiritual and the material that Adams suggests. He asks what we see when we visit Beauvais or Laon. What we see are "structures which are the greatest engineering feats in human history up to the time of their building. The technicians of the twelfth and thirteenth centuries, far from being traditionalists, were creating an entirely new concept of architecture, dynamic rather than static. In their cathedrals we see a sublime fusion of high spirituality and advanced technology. "[1]

This is not intended to discount Adams's idealization of the Virgin, nor to alter the exalted place of women in Adams's thinking. What White suggests instead is that "the Virgin and the dynamo are not opposing principles permeating the universe; they are allies. The growth of medieval power technology, which escaped Adams's attention, is a chapter in the conquest of freedom." It is perhaps too much to say that Adams paid no attention to medieval technology, but his emphasis is certainly different from White's. Moreover, White adds, this growth in humanitarian technology is part of the history of religion; it shows that technology can be put to humane use. It is not rooted in the economic necessity that is part of every society. But it has found expression only in the West, nourished, White contends, by Western theology. The labor-saving power machines of medieval Europe "harmonized with the religious assumption of the infinite worth of even the most seemingly degraded human personality," because of a repugnance "toward subjecting any man to monotonous drudgery which seems less than human." Thus, contends White, we have been too easily impressed by Adams's striking symbols.[2] Implicit in his view is the thought that Adams's spiritual and technological concerns can be reconciled, though White overestimates Adams's dislike for technology and thus fails to see Adams's guarded approval of the technological revolution of his own time and overestimates the need for reconciliation. Nor is it clear that he sees Adams as providing an aesthetic standard for political and social as well as artistic achievement.

Of course, this possible resolution of the tension between Virgin and dynamo does not invalidate Adams's amazingly far-seeing concerns about the potential impact of modern technology, concerns that long antedated the revolutionary developments at the turn of the twentieth century. In 1862, in a much quoted letter to his brother Charles, he writes, "I tell you these are great times. Man has mounted science, and is now run away with. I firmly believe that before many centuries more, science will be the master of man. The engines he will have invented will be beyond his strength to control. Some day science may have the existence of mankind in its power, and the human race commit suicide by blowing up the world." He adds, along with more fanciful things, that one day man will cruise in space.[3] Then, much later in life, thinking about his theory of the accelerating pace of history, he writes to his former student, the historian Henry Osborn Taylor:

The assumption of unity which was the mark of human thought in the middle-ages has yielded very slowly to the proofs of complexity. The stupor of science before radium is a proof of it. Yet it is quite clear, according to my score of ratios and curves, that, at the accelerated rate of progression shown since 1600, it will not need another century or half century to tip thought upside down. Law, in that case would disappear as theory or *a priori* principle, and give place to force. Morality would become police. Explosives would reach cosmic violence. Disintegration would overcome integration.[4]

Understandably, passages like this often lead to the conclusion that Adams was an antimodernist with powerful technophobic leanings. It is certainly true that he had a genuine fear of the technological future. And it is equally certain, as more and more of his predictions come true, that these fears were not groundless. But for all that, Adams was not a technophobe. He was perhaps as attracted to the new technology as he was frightened by it, and he maintained an intense interest in the natural sciences on which technological development was based. Like many of us today, he adopted a bemused but welcoming attitude to the everyday uses of technology. "A world so different from that of my childhood or middle-age can't belong to the same scheme. . . . Out of a medieval, primitive, crawling infant of 1838, to find oneself a howling, steaming, exploding, Marconiing, radiumating, automobiling maniac of 1904 exceeds belief."[5] Along with the amazement, the wry tone cannot conceal the note of pleasure, even of delight.

A more general case for Adams's endorsement of technology can be made. Of course, he was deeply skeptical about the notion of moral and material progress, but, as Cecilia Tichi argues, he "looked to the example of the engineer for the potential redemption of the wayward culture." This is a theme that appears frequently in his work.[6] Tichi's analysis supports many of the points I have made about Adams's interest in technology. One should recall his enthusiasm for the technological ingenuity of the average American in the administrations of Jefferson and Madison. And surely the "new type of man" that Adams hopes can build the society that will bring the trusts to heel would have to be a product of the technological age. Of course, Adams is fully aware of the dangers of modern technology. He understands the new capacity to blow up the earth, and he is also fully aware of the threat of environmental degradation. On his way to Saint Louis to attend the 1904 Exposition, he notices that "agriculture had made way for steam; tall chimneys reeked smoke on every horizon, and dirty suburbs filled with scrap-iron, scrap-paper, and cinders, formed the setting of every town. Evidently cleanliness was not to be the birthmark of the new American."[7] But the often deeply buried hope is still there; we must not lose sight of the modernist in Adams.

Tichi suggests that one example of that hope is his close friend Clarence King. Discussing the *Education*, she points out that Adams sees King as an exemplary figure, in fact, the type of figure Adams believed was needed for the American future. Professionally, King was an outstanding geologist and mining engineer. He knew art and America, especially the West; he knew politics; and "he knew even women; even the American woman; even the New York woman, which is saying much."[8] It was such active-minded men that Adams thought could rescue civilization.[9] Of course, this may all be merely a dream, but it makes an interesting counterpoint to the more frequent outpourings of gloom in Adams's later writings. And it is worth pointing out that King provides an example of the sort of man needed for the intellectual elite Adams thought was required to run the socialist economy that he privately discussed with both hope and fear in his correspondence with his brother Brooks.

Adams's thoughts on technology reveal an exceedingly complex intellect at work. He was much too intelligent to become a Luddite, partly because he knew that the genie was already out of the bottle and that technological development could not be stopped, but also because he could see the advantages of the new technologies. The result was that he was deeply ambivalent about his observations, even as he recognized their frightening dimensions. And ambivalence seems to be absolutely the appropriate response. George Kateb writes, "It is plain that so much of the spirit of the West is invested in modern technology. We have referred to anger, alienation, resentment. But that cannot be the whole story." The other considerations include virtuosity and skill for their own sake, a desire to make nature "beautiful or more beautiful," and the reckless exhilaration of discovery and the overcoming of obstacles. "All these considerations move away," Kateb says, "from anger, anxiety, resentment, and so on. The truth of the matter, I think, is that the project of modern technology, just like that of modern science, must attract a turbulence of response. The very passions and drives and motives that look almost villainous or hypermasculine simultaneously look like marks of the highest human aspiration, or, at the least, are not to be cut loose from the highest human aspiration."[10] I think Henry Adams has some such sense, a sense captured by Daniel Bell when he refers to Adams's "strange mingling of exultation and dismay."[11]

Again, this seems exactly the right response, for us as well as for Adams, and it is this mix that drives Adams to attempt to develop a scientific theory of the trajectory of history, a project begun in the *Education* and continued in a series of puzzling essays.

Toward a Dynamic Theory of History

In Adams's mind, the concluding chapters of the *Education* are linked to the concluding chapters of *Chartres*. While commenting on what he saw as the inadequacies in the literary form of both books, he wrote, "The volume on Chartres is involved in the same doubt, for both go together, the three last chapters of the Education being the Q.E.D. of the three last chapters of Chartres."[12] And to William James, he wrote, "Weary of my own imbecility, I tried to clean off a bit of the surface of my own mind, in 1904, by printing a volume on the twelfth century, where I could hide, in the last hundred pages, a sort of anchor in history. I knew that not a hundred people in America would understand what I meant, and these were all taught in Jesuit schools, where I should be a hell-born scorpion."[13]

In these chapters he tries to account for an observation made earlier in the *Education*. "In plain words," he writes, "Chaos was the law of nature; Order was the dream of man." The church had continued to insist that anarchy was not order, but "suddenly, in 1900, science raised its head and denied."[14] For Adams, there was nothing to do but to accept the findings of science; in this he was a modernist, even when that stance made him uncomfortable. All around him, he could see the signs of disorder and chaos as men engaged in a constant, Sisyphean struggle to maintain order. A child born in 1900 would inevitably be brought into a world characterized by multiplicity rather than unity. Adams goes on, brilliantly assessing the never-ending struggle between order and disorder:

> He could not deny that the law of the new multiverse explained much that had been most obscure, especially the persistently fiendish treatment of man by man; the perpetual effort of society to establish law, and the perpetual revolt of society against the law it had established; the perpetual building up of authority by force, and the perpetual appeal to force to overthrow it; the perpetual symbolism of a higher law, and the perpetual relapse to a lower one; the perpetual victory of the principles of freedom, and their perpetual conversion into principles of power; but the staggering problem was the outlook ahead into the despotism of artificial order which nature abhorred.[15]

Though Adams tries to cast his theory in scientific terms, it is rapid technological development made possible by science that is the driving force whose impact Adams wants to address. And he must try to achieve this end, recognizing at the same time that "the historian must not try to know what is truth, if he values his honesty; for, if he cares for his truths, he is certain to falsify his facts. The laws of history only repeat the lines of force or thought. Yet though his will be iron, he cannot help now and then resuming his humanity or simianity in face of a fear."[16] What Adams seems to be trying to say is that the truth *is* that the laws of history "only repeat the lines of force or thought." In any case, he apparently sees truth as multiple in the world of the practicing historian.

This analysis suggests that Adams was in the grip of a serious theoretical dilemma. He has already come close to the denial of any truth at all, but he shrinks back at the last instant and embraces a salutary myth that truth indeed exists, even though, on a purely intellectual level, he does not really believe it. In the preceding statement, he says that the historian must avoid seeking truth, for fear that commitment to his "truths" will compromise his honesty and cause him to falsify facts. This is Adams's statement of the fact-value distinction so central to much twentieth-century social science, which holds, properly enough, that the social scientist must try not to allow his values to influence his empirical conclusions. Put differently, Adams is saying that historians become committed to their discoveries in such a way as to blind them to contrary evidence. Of course, this is an ever-present danger for other social sciences as well. The argument is like the classic liberal position that no judge should preside over his own case. Thus Adams is theoretically debarred from seeking truth but is required by his understanding of the welfare of society to deny this prohibition, and so he "pretends" to seek truth anyway. Conversely, the fact-value distinction is impossible for him to abide, because his human nature requires him to cling to his values, his "truths," no matter what, even if they are without foundation. This is a very convoluted argument, though in the end, he falls back on the values and sense of reality that go with his instincts rather than with what his scientific rationalism teaches him to believe. Perhaps this is a source of his celebration of "irrationalism" in *Chartres*.

In spite of this seriously unsettled state of mind, Adams presses the case for a scientific philosophy of history. The first general foray is in his essay "The Tendency of History," a paper written in 1894 as a substitute for a formal presidential address to the American Historical Association, a message surely intended to tease its members. This is the most sober of his efforts along these lines, and it deals, in its fashion, with the problems inherent in relating truth and values just discussed. "The Tendency of History" can best be seen as a prolegomenon to the dynamic theory of history Adams began to develop in the *Education*. This paper is essentially a warning to historians that if they are genuinely scientific, they will discover unsettling truths that may well cause them to run afoul of the authorities. Suppose, for example, that scientific analysis leads to the conclusion that the triumph of socialism is inevitable. Even if we assume that American universities would permit their professors to announce these findings, he questions whether Europe would be as liberal. "Would property, on which the universities depend, allow such freedom of instruction? Would the state suffer its foundation to be destroyed? Would society as now constituted tolerate the open assertion of a necessity which should affirm its approaching overthrow?" Or suppose we assume that the world would continue on its present course for another thousand years. No one would listen to that with satisfaction. Or lastly, suppose that science were to discover that there must be a reversion to the church and revealed religion; this would mean the suicide of science. If the world continues as it has for another fifty years, the hopes of labor would be destroyed. If society goes communist, it places itself in conflict with "the entire fabric of our social and political system." The outlook is bleak. "If [the world] goes on, we must preach despair. If it goes back, it must deny and repudiate science. If it goes forward, round a circle which leads through communism, we must declare ourselves hostile to the property that pays us and the institutions we are bound in duty to support."[17]

These are not foolish concerns. Scholars often court trouble when they challenge the status quo. But then it is just as likely that they will be ignored as suffer retribution. And the range of choice that Adams offers, given the seemingly rigid determinism of his speculations, seems very limited. Of those choices, continued drift along current lines of development seems the most likely. Any observer of the history of the twentieth century knows that the results of such a development can be terrible, though not infrequent, although Adams seems to think this the least likely of the possibilities he suggests. In truth, though his warning is worth hearing, there is not much substance to this paper.

The dynamic theory itself, as developed in the *Education*, is considerably more interesting. As a historian, Adams continues to be preoccupied with change. He argues that a dynamic theory of history requires two forces, man and nature, acting and reacting on each other. This process is unending.[18] "Man's function as a force of nature was to assimilate other forces as he assimilated food. He called it the love of power."[19]

Adams skips lightly, though interestingly, over the history of the Western world until 1600. Here, Francis Bacon—Lord Bacon, as Adams likes to call him—enters the scene. Bacon made a simple, revolutionary proposal. Sounding like Marx turning Hegel upside down, "He urged society to lay aside the idea of evolving the universe from a thought, and to try evolving thought from the universe. . . . As Galileo reversed the action of earth and sun, Bacon reversed the relation of thought to force. The mind was henceforth to follow the movement of matter, and unity must be left to shift for itself."[20] Paradoxically, in the interest of mastery through the exercise of mind, the mind becomes subordinated to material forces.

Humans began to depend on forces not their own, and the results were exceedingly dramatic.

> The microscope revealed a universe that defied the senses; gunpowder killed whole races that lagged behind; the compass coerced the most imbruted mariner to act on the impossible idea that the earth was round; the press drenched Europe with anarchism. Europe saw itself, violently resisting, wrenched into false positions; drawn along new lines as a fish that is caught on a hook; but unable to understand by what force it was controlled. The resistance was often bloody, sometimes humorous, always constant. Its contortions in the eighteenth century are best studied in the wit of Voltaire, but all history and all philosophy from Montaigne and Pascal to Schopenhauer and Nietzsche deal with nothing else; and still, throughout it all, the Baconian law held good; thought did not evolve nature, but nature evolved thought.[21]

The results of Bacon's method are obviously remarkable. In its wake came an almost spontaneous influx of new forces. "As Nature developed her hidden energies, they tended to become destructive. Thought itself became tortured, suffering reluctantly, impatiently, painfully, the coercion of new method. Easy thought had always been movement of inertia, and mostly mere sentiment; but even the processes of mathematics measured feebly the needs of force."[22] The result of the entry of these new ideas into society was deeply troubling. "In the earlier stages of progress, the forces to be assimilated were simple and easy to absorb, but, as the mind of man enlarged its range, it enlarged the field of complexity, and must continue to do so, even unto chaos, until the reservoirs of sensuous or supersensuous energies are exhausted, or cease to affect him, or until he succumbs to their excess."[23]

The great danger is the accelerating development of this new power. This brings us to the heart of Adams's theory of history. He returns again to the theme that his great concern is motion, but now he is interested in measuring it. He attempts this by examining the world's coal output, which he tells us doubled every ten years between 1840 and 1900, with each ton of coal yielding three times as much power in 1900 as it did in 1840.[24] Similar technological developments can be seen everywhere. What is at work is "a law of acceleration, definite and constant as any law of mechanics, [which] cannot be supposed to relax its energy to suit the convenience of man."[25] Fifty years before, he explains, no scientist believed that this rate of change could last. But they were wrong.

> Two generations, with John Stuart Mill, talked of this stationary period, which was to follow the explosion of new power. All the men who were elderly in the forties died in this faith, and other men grew old nursing the same conviction, and happy in it; while science, for fifty years, permitted, or encouraged, society to think that force would prove to be limited in supply. This mental inertia of science lasted through the eighties before showing signs of breaking up; and nothing short of radium fairly wakened men to the fact long since evident, that force was inexhaustible. Even then the scientific authorities vehemently resisted.

"Nothing so revolutionary had happened since the year 300." And Adams ominously adds the frightening thought that "impossibilities no longer stood in the way."[26]

The huge forces at work and the rapidity with which they changed created major problems even for the scientists. If current scientific notions of the universe were sound, men like Galileo, Descartes, Leibnitz, and Newton should have stopped scientific progress before 1700, assuming they were honest in their professed religious convictions. "In 1900 they were plainly forced back on faith in a unity unproved and an order they themselves had disproved. They had reduced their universe to a series of relations to themselves. They had reduced themselves to motion in a universe of motions, with an acceleration, in their own case, of vertiginous violence."[27]

In 1909, Adams wrote a paper "The Rule of Phase Applied to History," explicitly conceived as a supplement to the *Education*, which attempted to make this line of thought more precise. In it he draws an analogy between the phases of a substance in chemistry—for instance, ice, water, and water vapor—and Auguste Comte's phases of history.[28] With his usual good sense, J. C. Levenson suggests that we forget about the chemistry and focus on the analogy,[29] though as a metaphor, the rule of phase has some use. Comte had defined three phases: the theological, the metaphysical, and the positive. Adams proposed to discard these labels while keeping the idea of phase. As always, he was interested in motion, that is, a change of direction that was equivalent to a change in form. These changes are caused by acceleration and an increase in volume or concentration.[30] For Adams, the phase to start with was the great age of Bacon, Descartes, Galileo, and Columbus. Between 1500 and 1700, there was a definite change in the direction of the history of the Western world. This new phase embodied so great a change that it had no direct relationship to what preceded it. Society followed along the lines laid down in the early modern era until about 1840. The acceleration of change in this period was remarkable. And by focusing on the condemnation of Galileo in 1633, Adams suggests that this period might be dated roughly from 1600 to 1900, a time that he calls the Mechanical Phase.[31] Adams then considers the problem of defining the boundaries of the earlier phase. Most historians would be inclined to pick the year 500 as a starting point because of the establishment of monotheism and of the Christian and Muslim faiths, though Adams is not sure that these events really entailed a change in direction. Indeed, from a scientific point of view, there was probably no significant change of phase from the beginning of history until Galileo was condemned. Through calculations later in the article, Adams concludes that this earlier Religious Phase, as he calls it, occupied no less than 90,000 years.[32]

Adams then raises the question of when the Mechanical Phase ended. He believes that a change began around 1870 as the invention of the dynamo started to suggest a new era. The new generation trained after 1900 in the physics of electromagnetism and radiation might see that date as the beginning of a new period. The discovery of radium was as startling to the physicists grounded in classical mechanics as the discoveries of Galileo were to the church. This was the dawn of the Electric Phase, which, since the Mechanical Phase had lasted 300 years, had an expected life of about 17.5 years—the square root of 300. It is something of a mystery where the use of the square root comes from, since Adams does not explain it, but it probably derives from chemist Willard Gibbs's work on the rule of phase. The succeeding phase, the Ethereal, would last for the square root of 17.5, or about 4.2 years, which would "bring Thought to the limit of its possibilities in the year 1921." Adams adds, "It may well be!" Nothing, he says, is beyond probability. Even if the previous phase were to last another hundred years, in the long panorama of history, the difference would be negligible. Then the Ethereal Phase would last until about 2025.[33] This is obviously wildly speculative, but the central idea that the phases of historical development are being radically shortened seems more plausible.

If taken literally, much of this is manifestly nonsense, most obviously the notion that thought would reach its limit in 1921. It is hardly a cause for wonder that the *American Historical Review* refused to publish the paper when Adams submitted it. Nor does it add much to Adams's chapter on the law of acceleration in the *Education*. Certainly the article inadvertently illustrates the sheer silliness of trying to quantify huge historical changes with such a degree of specificity. But the article is not useless, in spite of these flaws. It helps capture something of the decisive change that occurred in early modern Europe and swept through the New World. As Levenson says, "Henry Adams insisted that men do die, that the Middle Ages were dead, and that the modern era was flirting with catastrophe, but he also argued that society had hitherto been immortal and could maintain itself now by a new leap of mind."[34] Not the least striking of Adams's conclusions, and Levenson's, is that the Middle Ages are in some sense beside the point and that *Chartres* is therefore, in the grand scheme of Adams's thought, almost irrelevant, a beautiful memorial and a great work of art, but unfortunately of limited earthly use in the twentieth century. At most, it constitutes an aesthetic recoil from twentieth-century scientism. But "The Rule" and the concluding chapters of the *Education* show how much a part of the twentieth century Adams was, in spite of all his aesthetic protestations to the contrary. After all, he insists on pressing a scientific worldview. As usual, his thought exists in a state of high internal tension. Perhaps the most important implication of Adams's article is that there may be a limit to the human capacity to comprehend rapid change in time to be able to assert control over it. He was certainly not wrong to raise the question. It is, for example, not clear today that we truly understand the enormous changes, both social and technological, going on around us. Perhaps, like Adams, we must learn to embrace our uncertainties as we struggle to comprehend our own rapidly changing world.

However, before we return to the concluding pages of the *Education*, Adams's last major work, "A Letter to American Teachers of History," written in 1910, must be considered. Like "The Rule of Phase," it remained unpublished until after his death in 1918, when his brother Brooks brought these two papers together, along with "The Tendency of History," and released them to the public under the unfortunate and misleading title *The Degradation of the Democratic Dogma*. About this long essay it is harder to find positive things to say. Here Adams is even more insistent that history must be treated as if it were a physical science and that the ruling physical law is the second law of thermodynamics, which holds that all the energy of the universe is slowly being dissipated. Again, if taken literally, the "Letter" arguably brings out the worst in Adams, except for his anti-Semitism. Even a sympathetic critic like Levenson writes, "The scientific figure he now elaborated had a tenor of its own which brought to expression the most desperate and perverse aspect of his personality." His thinking had long flirted with despair, but until 1910, he had kept his worst fears private, being "more concerned with the dynamic theory of history than with a thermodynamic theory of calamity. The letter writer, on the other hand, was full of dire predictions that the world was going to smash."[35] In this essay, Adams the historian comes perilously close to abdicating the field to physicists. Harking back to the fears expressed in "The Tendency of History," he says that if Lord Kelvin's second law is true, "the American professor who should begin his annual course by announcing to his class that their year's work would be devoted to showing in American history 'a universal tendency to the dissipation of energy' and degradation of thought, which would soon end in making America 'improper for the habitation of men as he is now constituted,' might not fear the fate of Giordano Bruno, but would certainly expect that of Galileo. . . . The University would have to protect itself by dismissing him."[36]

Though Adams grabs halfheartedly at some straws, he suggests that there is no real possibility of escape: "Man and beast can, at the best, look forward only to a diversified agony of twenty million years."[37] Conceding the worst, Adams says, "Science has shut and barred every known exit. Man can detect no outlet except through the loophole called Mind."[38] But then, in the last sentence, Adams holds out the dim hope for "another Newton" to find a way out.[39] This last appeal to the possibility of a new Newton suggests that even in the deep gloom of the "Letter," Adams never quite gives in to an entirely deterministic position; he continues to look for, or at least hope for, some escape route. In this sense, the "loophole" has some significance. Adams is never entirely willing to give up on mind.

These stirrings of hope are only signs of desperation, looking back to earlier times when Adams hoped that new thought would help save the nation and the world. Adams, unlike so many nineteenth-century thinkers, was never a historical optimist, but the near total despair in the late scientific essays runs counter to the ideas he expressed throughout most of his career, at least in his published work. But in "The Rule," and even more in "A Letter," these fleetingly hypothesized ways of escape run directly counter to the logic and the rhetoric of the main argument. Adams suppressed "The Rule," which was published only after his death, and "A Letter," which was privately printed and circulated to historians, was read by very few. One who did was William James. Writing to his old friend virtually from his deathbed, his comments were devastating.

> "To tell the truth, it doesn't impress me at all save by its wit and erudition; and I ask you whether an old man soon about to meet his Maker can hope to save himself from the consequences of his life by pointing to the wit and learning he has shown in treating a tragic subject. No, sir, you can't do it, can't impress God in that way." James conceded the inescapability of the second law "in the present state of scientific conventions and fashions" but protested the "interpretation . . . of the great statistical drift downwards of the original high-level of energy. . . . To begin with, the *amount* of cosmic energy it costs to buy a certain distribution of fact which humanly we regard as precious, seems to me to be an altogether secondary matter as regards the question of history and progress." A dinosaur's brain may have been as good an exchanger of physical energy as man's but it could not "issue proclamations, write books, describe Chartres Cathedral, etc." "*The second law is wholly irrelevant to 'history'*—save that it sets its terminus." There was therefore "nothing in physics to interfere with the hypothesis that the penultimate state might be the millennium."[40]

No one has ever stated the case against the "Letter" better. The only thing possible to add is that when we consider the twenty million years Adams gives us, it is appropriate to remember Lord Keynes's immortal quip that in the long run we are all dead. And the long run Adams concedes us is very long indeed. The folly of simply giving in to determinism in a time frame that covers twenty million years needs no further comment. Still, it should be remarked that by addressing his thoughts to historians, Adams was writing to a group, many of whose members were Darwinians, only too ready to give in to *that* form of determinism, a mode of thought Adams had decisively rejected.

The best line of defense Adams had against critics was to pass the whole thing off as a joke or as an attack on socialism. He admitted to Charles Milnes Gaskell that he did not really know if our energy was declining and alluded to the thought that the larger subject of the "Letter" was socialism. There are other similar suggestions in the correspondence, but this argument is not very convincing. As William Merrill Decker writes, "The book becomes an antisocialist tract only through such generalized reading—or, to cite a practice traditionally deplored by the Adamses, such loose construction—as must render unimportant the terms and argumentative lines that Adams did adopt."[41]

The idea that the book was a joke was also somewhat feeble. The "fun" was that his colleagues could not understand it, and Adams admits that even he probably would not have seen "the joke myself if I were not its author."[42] More plausibly, one must suppose that these essays were a general assault on evolutionary theorists who still thought in terms of inevitable progress. On this level, Adams's position is eminently defensible, as much of his earlier work shows. It is a pity that, as Perry Miller wrote, "These essays incarnate those elements of perversity, affectation, parade of erudition, assumption of intellectual superiority, and downright irresponsibility which make Adams both fascinating and exasperating. . . . They constitute the furthest any American went toward erecting against the evolutionary and pragmatic idea a rigid system within which the heavens themselves might be confined. . . . The intention . . . is to demolish the overeasy optimism which lies at the heart of most varieties of Darwinism."[43] Read in this light, Adams's paper can be seen as a critique of the idea of inevitable progress that is both valuable and important.

These late essays obviously present a major interpretive problem. Taken literally, they are very weak. But it is important to remember Adams's love of irony. If we read them in this light, it must be said that the irony is heavy-handed and obscure. A joke that has to be explained after the fact even to close friends well versed in the eccentricities of the teller is not a very good joke. If Adams's intent was humorous, one must say that it is possible to ridicule the fallacies of a rigid determinist philosophy more clearly and with a lighter hand. Consider Mark Twain's hilarious essay "The Turning Point of My Life," also published in 1910, two months before the author's death. In it, he explains how he became a writer and constructs a web of determining forces that extends back to Adam and Eve. The satire, unlike Adams's, is impossible to miss.[44]

It is not possible to rate the dynamic theory of history as a success. But it *is* necessary to admire Adams's desperate attempt to come to grips with the enormous importance of modern science. Science is so much a part of our world that it cannot be ignored. The quest that Adams began so early still goes on. Consider a recent essay by William McNeill:

> During the twentieth century the physical sciences converged with biology in transforming the Newtonian world machine governed by eternal, universal, and mathematical laws into an evolving—indeed exploding—cosmos where uncertainty prevails, and human efforts at observation affect what is observed. This brings the mathematical sciences closer to the social sciences, and turns history into another kind of black hole from which no branch of knowledge can escape.[45]

Adams might well have written these words, and his effort to come to terms with such problems while clinging to his humanistic inclinations can only be called admirable — even intellectually heroic — in spite of the fact that the attempt is ultimately a failure.

I argue that the essays collected in *Degradation of the Democratic Dogma* are only loosely connected to the main body of Adams's work, the connecting link being his lifelong interest in science and his unsuccessful attempt to find unity in history. They are steeped in a rigid determinism that Adams flirted with, but tried to resist, throughout his career. Thus 1910 marks a turning point; prior to then, "the much vaunted pessimism of Henry Adams found expression in his personal correspondence rather than what he wrote for circulation."[46] It is true that in his late letters he was depressed, self-pitying at times, and often bitter. But his friends knew how to discount for his hyperbole,[47] and contemporary commentators would do well to follow their lead. The hope that keeps breaking out in his published work through the *Education* is better expressed — somewhat offhandedly, to be sure — in a 1911 letter to Brooks saying that he "looked forward with consternation to the possibilities of a pessimistic America. Pessimism without ideas, — a sort of bankrupt trust, — will be the most harrowing form of ennui the world has ever known."[48] Adams desperately wants to hold on to his sense of this essentially American optimism in spite of himself. The papers published in *Degradation of the Democratic Dogma* are his last works, but the true climax of his career is the *Education*.[49] The late essays are essentially a reductio ad absurdum of his long-standing interest in science expressed there and elsewhere. It is therefore appropriate to return to that book and move toward a summary discussion of Adams's work.

The Meaning of an Education

Adams's letters to William James and Whitelaw Reid would lead one to expect the final chapter of the *Education* to be closely connected to the dynamic theory of history and to the concluding chapter of *Chartres*. But this is not the case. The concluding chapter has a valedictory quality captured in its title — "*Nunc Age*," now go. It is not really about his scientific philosophy of history at all. He now tells us that dispute about the dynamic theory is idle; "it would verify or disprove itself within thirty years." However annoying it might be to those players still in the game, "it tended to encourage foresight and to economize waste of mind," even if it was "profoundly unmoral and tended to discourage effort." Though it was not itself education, "it pointed out the economies necessary for the education of the new American. There, the duty stopped."[50] Adams comments briefly on the problem of controlling the trusts, as we have already seen, and then on the physical decline and death of John Hay. He lauds Hay for having solved nearly every problem in American statesmanship, but he cannot resist yet another dig at the Senate, which held up a dozen treaties "like lambs in a butcher shop." Forgetting his dire warnings about a coming European crisis, he claims that due to the efforts of Hay, "for the first time in fifteen hundred years a true Roman pax was in sight." The only alternative to Hay's scheme was world war.[51] (Whether or not the Hay peace had a chance, it was, of course, the catastrophe rather than the peace that occurred.)

Alluding to Hamlet, Adams sighs, "the rest is silence." Shortly after their last meeting, Hay died. For Adams, it is the end of an age. As his chapter title suggests, he feels that it is time to go. But he allows himself one last wistful hope, a fantasy. Thinking of Hay and Clarence King, both now dead, he writes:

> Education had ended for all three, and only beyond some remoter horizon could its values be fixed or renewed. Perhaps some day—say 1938, their centenary—they might be allowed to return together for a holiday, to see the mistakes of their own lives made clear in the light of the mistakes of their successors; and perhaps then, for the first time since man began his education among the carnivores, they would find a world that sensitive and timid natures could regard without a shudder.[52]

But of course, the dream could never have come to pass. The year 1938 turned out to be a very bad one indeed, and much worse was to come. It was not his faint hopes but the catastrophes he foresaw that engulfed the world. And of course, Adams's restless mind was not yet ready to declare education to be entirely at an end. The scientific essays were still to come. The product might not have been very satisfying, but the mind continued to work. But if Adams was not quite ready to go, he was ready for those who cared to be his students to build on his education and become leaders in a rapidly changing world. This didactic purpose was clearly stated in his preface to the *Education*, where he lays down the goal of all good teachers and explains what he hopes for from his students. "At the utmost, the active-minded young man should ask of his teacher only the mastery of his tools. The young man himself, the subject of education, is a certain form of energy; the object to be gained is economy of his force; the training is partly the clearing away of obstacles, partly the direct application of effort. Once acquired, the tools and models may be thrown away."[53] This seems to be another meaning of the "Now Go" injunction, this time addressed to those who were willing to be taught by him.

What then did Adams hope to teach? Like T. S. Eliot, his end was in his beginning. The wistful fantasy of a return to a better world in 1938 is, according to Ernest Samuels, "a deliberate return to the mood of the first chapter, to the idealization of Quincy." This is the basic moral of the *Education*. "Not the coarse and predatory immoralism of the financial districts but the idealism of Quincy would delight the sensitive nature with which he was born and which he liked to think was shared by his two closest friends."[54] It is also worth noting that for all the pull of determinism in Adams's thought, a determinism to which he appears to surrender almost completely in the "Letter," in his last truly *major* statement, he ends on a hopeful note, however wan it may be. Whatever the temptation, Adams could never quite surrender his mind to any scheme of absolute determinism. Perhaps no determinist ever does. Consider the case of Marx: If revolution is preordained, why take the trouble to be a revolutionary? It would surely be easier to sit back and wait for the inevitable to happen. But of course, even determinists tend to believe, with Mr. Justice Holmes, that the mode by which the inevitable comes to pass is through effort.

Naturally, the question arises as to the extent to which Adams's readers will be educated by his autobiographical reflections. I think that we can easily dismiss the recurring idea that Adams's own education was a failure. In fact, the whole work stands as impressive testimony to the possibility of a lifelong education, constantly adjusting to ever-changing conditions. One can disagree with many things he has to say, but no one could possibly miss the fact that Adams was supremely well educated, by life and by study. The frequently adopted pose of Socratic ignorance was just that—a pose. Like Socrates, he was well aware that few readers would be able to challenge him on his own level. Thus, among his contemporaries, it took a William James to offer the most penetrating comments on the privately circulated edition of the *Education*.

Adams was fully aware of the difficulties his book presented. Writing to Barrett Wendell, he establishes the standard he sets for himself and suggests the nature of the formal experiment he has undertaken. "When I read St. Augustine's *Confessions*, or Rousseau's, I feel certain that their faults, as literary artists, are worse than mine. We have all three undertaken to do what cannot be successfully done—mix narrative and didactic purpose and style.

The charm of the effort is not winning the game but in playing it. . . . And I found that a narrative style was so incompatible with a didactic or scientific style, that I had to write a long supplementary chapter to explain in scientific terms what I could not put into narration without ruining the narrative."[55] Here, while putting his finger on a serious problem, Adams attempts to pre-empt criticism by noting the failure of other, even greater writers to accomplish what he set out to do. It may also be useful to note the supreme arrogance with which in assessing this "failure" he asserts his superiority to both Augustine and Rousseau. Some failure!

The basic problem in Adams's approach is beautifully captured by William James in a letter to Adams that, according to Samuels, caused Adams some misgivings. Again, James is one of Adams's most searching critics. His deserves to be quoted at length:

> The boyhood part is really superlative. It and the London part should become classic historic documents. . . . There is a hodge-podge of world-fact, private fact, philosophy, irony, (with the word "education" stirred in too much for my appreciation!) which gives a unique cachet to the thing and gives a very pleasant *gesamt-eindruck* of H. A.'s *Self*. A great deal of the later diplomatic history is dealt with so much by hint and implication, that to an ignoramus like W. J. it reads obscurely. . . . I don't follow or share your way of conceiving the historical problem as the determination of a curve by points. I think that applies only to what is done and over. . . . But unless the future contains genuine novelties, unless the present is really creative of them, *I don't see the use of time at all.* Space would be a sufficient theatre for these statistically determined relations to be arranged in.[56]

For all the genuine praise, the last point, if sound, is a truly damning criticism, for without time, there can be no history, and Adams's perpetual stress on motion would be seriously undermined. The point also continued to worry James, for in 1909 he returns to it in an appendix to *A Pluralistic Universe* called "The Notion of Reality as Changing." His general point is that "remoter effects are seldom aimed at by causal intentions." He then turns to Adams, though not mentioning him by name.

> A friend of mine has an idea, which illustrates on such a magnified scale the impossibility of tracing the same line through reality, that I will mention it here. He thinks that nothing more is needed to make history "scientific" than to get the content of any two epochs (say the end of the thirteenth and the end of the nineteenth century) accurately

defined, from the one epoch into the other, then accurately to define
the nature of the change that led from the one epoch into the other,
and finally to prolong the line of that direction into the future. So pro-
longing the line, he thinks, we ought to be able to define the actual
state of things at any future date we please. We all feel the essential
unreality of such a conception of "history" as this, [but if a pluralistic
universe of the sort Bergson, Peirce, and I believe in really exists], every
phenomenon of development, even the simplest, would prove equally
rebellious to our science should the latter pretend to give us literally
accurate instead of approximate, or statistically generalized, pictures
of the development of reality.[57]

This is a very serious criticism of an allegedly "dynamic" theory of history. Interestingly, it does not seem to apply to the historical account of the
Jefferson and Madison administrations, which is characterized by such rich
detail and so intense a focus on events that move in directions not intended
by the actors, who are caught up in forces beyond their control and who do
not achieve the ends aimed at by their causal intentions, that it seems easily to surmount James's strictures on the dynamic theory and the projection
from the unity of *Chartres* to the multiplicity of the *Education*. But what
will work for a sixteen-year period will not work over many centuries. Thus,
as history, it is Adams's earlier masterpiece that is far more successful than
his late speculations.

This does not mean, however, that the comparison between the twelfth
and twentieth centuries is of no value for Adams, or necessarily for us. As I
have noted, Adams is willing deliberately to suppress much history in order to
create what is essentially a utopian aesthetic vision of medieval order. In this
context, a reader might or might not find the utopia attractive. Roman
Catholics might find it heretical, as Adams well knew. But for all that, some
see Adams as a hidebound conservative. I repeat that the Virgin's sympathy
for ordinary people and the victims of injustice and her distrust of authority
might well find a sympathetic hearing on the Left, though I certainly do not
claim that this is Adams's intended audience or that he himself should be
placed on the left of the political spectrum. In fact, his intent, particularly
when *Chartres* and the *Education* are assessed together, as he insisted they
should be, is not altogether clear. The two works seem to be in some significant tension with each other, a tension that once again reveals deep ambiguity within Adams's thought.

It may be that he hoped to reconcile these ambiguities in the *Education*,
but if so, he did not succeed. First of all, in *Chartres*, there is his flamboyant

disregard of mere fact, which might testify to what Samuels calls "his fundamental quarrel with science."[58] It certainly testifies to a powerfully developed
aesthetic sense that resulted in a book of great beauty and reads as a challenge to positivist history. And yet the Virgin, who stands for Adams's ideals in
that volume, disappears in the last three chapters, on which Adams placed
so much emphasis. The conclusion points to a beautiful but unstable equilibrium in which science, fostered even by Thomas Aquinas, has achieved
the upper hand in a world in which the church, by Adams's lights, is already
dead. Aside from this, it is hard to read the late "scientific" papers and accept
the idea that Adams saw them as simply a joke, no matter what defenses he
threw up in his letters. They express a commitment to science, even if that
commitment is based only on the frequent theme of swimming with the current of one's own time; thus, in the *Education* and after, Adams adopts a scientific view of the world. But at the same time, Adams does not renounce
Chartres and insists that the two great masterpieces stand together. It will not
do to let the later book simply displace the former. This tension is the mark
of a divided thinker in dialogical conflict with himself. This complex relationship can be resolved only in a more general conclusion, which must
await a further assessment of the *Education*.

As for the *Education*, it is interesting to reflect further on the relation of its
conclusion to Adams's preface.[59] The fact that the text itself was privately circulated in 1907, eleven years before its first public appearance following
Adams's death in 1918, suggests that it was open to debate up to that time,
and I suggest that it still should be read as if it were a tentative rather than a
dogmatic document, though it was not revised prior to its posthumous publication. The concluding chapters of the book suggest resignation before
forces beyond his control, but the early chapters stress the reformist impulses
that Adams shared with his whole family. As Decker puts it, "If the *Education* reflects the lifelong disabusal of Henry Adams, it does so against the
depiction of his own bygone youthful attitude that the world exists to be
reformed." He remains "more or less" sympathetic to youth. The preface can
be read as a countermove to the bleakness of the dynamic theory of history, a
"statement of faith: an afterword that breaks with the overwhelmingly deterministic logic of the dynamic theory, that affirms youthful effort in the face
of a denuded, dehumanized, de-creating cosmos."[60] In this light, it is possible to see the preface as an invitation to pick up the cause of reform, in spite
of the dynamic theory and in spite of his own refusal to do so. Here, as in his
rather feeble appeal for a new Newton, Adams seems to suggest that what we
need is imaginative new thinking to match the dramatic new ideas and

events of the early twentieth century. The implication is that theory is logically prior to policy and that, as Hannah Arendt used to argue, it is necessary to stop and think what we are doing.

But Decker, giving due recognition to the complexity of Adams's mind, argues that there is another possible reading of the 1907 preface. He observes that in his correspondence Adams shows little faith in the ability of future generations to learn from him; he does not, in fact, have much hope of finding an audience. Read this way, Decker sees the preface as a "belligerent" statement to what Adams was sure would be an uncomprehending audience. However, I do not read the tone of the preface as belligerent, but rather as something that challenges his readers to learn what they can, acquire the tools of analysis, come to an understanding of history, and then strike off on their own to struggle against the forces Adams identifies. He may feel that the challenge will not be accepted or, if it is accepted, that those who do so will succumb in the end to the superior forces of modern society. But still, a positive reading of the preface is consistent with Adams's refusal, down to the last paragraph of the *Education*, to surrender completely to the dynamics of the rapidly changing society.

Decker is certainly right that there is a tension here, and elsewhere in Adams's work as well. As his letters show, Adams was aware of this problem in the *Education*, most notably in the conflict between his narrative and didactic purposes. Although many have argued the contrary, the book is not well unified, a reflection perhaps of the loss of unity and the rise of twentieth-century multiplicity.[61] Nor do "The Rule" or "A Letter" help very much. Next to the *Education*, they are rigid and intellectually negligible, a minor appendix to Adams's work. All they can do is indicate that part of his complex mind was filled with a powerful, if in the end not very useful, scientific component. But as Decker suggests, that "irresolution" makes the "book all the more dynamic, all the more insistently a reader's book."[62] The conflicts within Adams's work invite a variety of responses. Like all major writers, he stimulates a wide range of reflections. The interpretive problem is similar to that encountered in discussing the possibility that he can be read as sympathetic to a critical leftist position, one not completely resistant to twentieth-century multiplicity. Once again, this should not be taken to mean that any interpretation of the *Education* will suffice. No one can make Adams a proponent of modern mass democracy or a celebrant of unfettered technological development. But it does mean, as Decker says, that "any committed reading of the work should aspire to some purpose and unity on its own terms, along the lines of the reader's preference." Adams himself gives a certain license to his interpreters, saying, "No one means all he says, and yet very few say all they mean, for words are slippery and thought is viscous."[63] I agree with Decker's preferred reading, which "finds the book's nihilism decidedly mitigated."[64] This is an example of a fruitful interpretation built on a palpable tension in Adams's thought. And my own reading aspires to a unity that paradoxically stresses the ultimate lack of unity in Adams.

With all this in mind, we still have a great deal to learn, not only from the *Education* but from all of Adams's work. But particularly in the *Education*, he does not make it easy for the reader, as William James so rightly observed. Adams himself is clearly aware of the problem, which stems, at least in part, from the difficulty of integrating his dual commitments to both narrative and didactic purposes. The first two-thirds of the book are not too problematic in this respect. However, the argument of the remainder tends to move by fits and starts. Personal history is often interrupted by theoretical reflections, with the result that neither seems quite complete.[65] It is frequently necessary to factor out the theory and the autobiography into separate parts, so that in this case, it can be a virtue to lift arguments out of their *immediate* context in pursuit of a clear presentation of ideas in a *larger* context. It is rather like trying to piece two jigsaw puzzles simultaneously, with the additional complication that the two are closely linked. I have been focusing on the puzzle presented by the philosophy of history. But now I return to his interpretation of American history, politics, and society, out of which the philosophy grows.

History and Politics in the Education

The *Education* is certainly an invitation to revisit and rethink the course of American history, though for this purpose, it needs to be read in conjunction with his history of the Jefferson and Madison administrations and the journalism as well. The invitation may seem to come from on high, and in this day and age, it may seem to be insufferably elitist, not least because at times it is. Still, Adams is a learned and well-placed guide with a unique perspective matched, perhaps, only by one of his intellectual mentors, Alexis de Tocqueville. I think we must learn to set aside his elitist tone and instead attend carefully to what he has to say. It is his attainments and arguments and not his upper-class background that earn him the right to be heard, even if, as with any writer, we need to discount for the obvious and sometimes troubling biases that stem from his background.

Levenson makes a sweeping claim. "Henry Adams offers to his fellow

Americans the richest and most challenging image of what they are, what they have been, and what they may become."[66] This may seem a bit much, but probably only Tocqueville is a real rival to this claim. James Bryce's *American Commonwealth* is wonderfully descriptive but lacks theory, and since it is so heavily descriptive, it is dated. Among modern works, Louis Hartz's *Liberal Tradition in America* is theoretically brilliant but arguably too narrowly focused, and it lacks historical detail. Richard Hofstadter's large body of work has the detail and offers powerful middle-range theories, but he lacks the historical sweep of Hartz, a fact that makes Hofstadter's early death all the more tragic, since we were denied his projected three-volume magnum opus. Many have tried to displace Hartz, but no one has succeeded beyond forcing modifications of his theory of a hegemonic liberalism. In any event, no one can say that his theory is not rich and challenging. As for Tocqueville, he is more theoretically coherent than Adams, but Adams has the advantage of seventy more years of the American experience on which to base his observations. Thus he saw the rise of machine politics, the explosion of industrial and financial capitalism, and the dramatic growth of science and technology that came after Tocqueville's brief visit to America.

Adams sees most of these developments as either unhealthy or ambiguous in their impact, and therefore problematic. He looks at the urban machine in much the same negative light as did the reformers of the Progressive movement, though he does not comment directly on their reforms. His discussion of machine politics is marred by his inability to see the positive contributions political parties can make to modern democracies, since Adams, with three generations of family party irregularity behind him, had no talent for partisan politics and no understanding of the function of party in a mass democracy.

In addition, the corruption of politics was closely associated in his mind with the rapid development of modern capitalism after the Civil War. This development was subversive of any decent democracy as Adams understood the term, a development that more than fulfilled Tocqueville's warning of the rise of a harsh aristocracy of manufacturers.[67] To Tocqueville's fears, Adams added his own hatred of banking and high finance. He was right to identify these as powerful and dangerous forces but horribly misguided in identifying them with an imaginary Jewish menace. But, as I have said, his noxious anti-Semitism came late in life, long after his intense dislike of capitalism emerged. This dark stain cannot be ignored, but his critique of capitalism is largely independent of it. It is also important that Adams identified a link between corrupt economic and political forces that has proved to be endemic in the United States. It may be salutary to look at contemporary

American politics in this light. Political and economic corruption may be more subtle in contemporary America than in the nineteenth century, but it is no less in evidence.[68] It begins to look like a permanent condition of American politics rather than some sort of passing aberration. One must seriously consider the possibility that it is deeply embedded in the economy, politics, and culture of the United States, in which case the relevance of Henry Adams to our condition is all the more clear. We are confronted with a need, in the terms of Michael Walzer, to find a way to separate the legitimate spheres of money and politics so as to reduce the influence of political money, a separation that is necessary for the achievement of a just society.[69]

Adams is also prescient on the problems of technology. It is positively eery that as early as 1862 he raised the possibility that we would have the capacity to blow up the world. But of course, this may have been just a lucky shot in the dark. Nevertheless, it is technology, undergirded by science, that is the driving force of much of the dynamic theory of history. Again, Adams has a divided mind. On the one hand, he finds technology amazing, amusing, and enjoyable. On the other, he sees the danger that it may go out of control. This situation has changed little since Adams wrote. Enormous numbers of people have had their lives improved, or in fact saved, by technological advances. At the same time, equally enormous numbers have had their lives threatened by, for example, environmental degradation. And the dangers of nuclear weapons have only recently receded into the background; they could easily come to the fore again. The Senate's defeat of President Clinton's nuclear test agreement only makes this more likely. And the great political issue remains unsolved. How are we to exert human control over the forces unleashed by technology? Technocratic elites are often effectively in charge, though without the education Adams wished for the new American, an education oriented not only toward science and technology but also toward humanistic systems of controlling them. The need is for a politics of technology, a politics that can impose human authority on technological development.[70] These problems open up larger questions that can best be addressed in the context of an overview of the whole corpus of Adams's work.

A Complex Mind in a Complex World

One of the most insistently sounded themes in the *Education* is Adams's labeling of his education, and indeed his whole career, as a failure. Can this self-assessment stand? Or is it merely a rhetorical ploy on Adams's part? By any reasonable standard, it must be the latter.[71] The only way to classify

Adams as a failure is to accept the exalted standards of the Adams family, which, as Adams knew from boyhood, suggested the possibility of his becoming president. But one can hardly call him a failure for not achieving what he never attempted. Of course, given his personality, he probably would have failed as a politician had he tried, but that is a separate issue, as is the question of whether he would have been successful in the office. Probably Adams's own sense that he was unfit for politics is correct, though a high diplomatic position might well have been appropriate for him. For the rest, if we look at what he did accomplish, failure is anything but the right term; in fact, the alleged failure is simply a "myth,"[72] a myth that suits Adams's analytical purposes. In making this point, William Dusinberre takes an unusual tack, contending that there is a considerable falling off of Adams's powers after 1890, a decline of "mental vigor," as he puts it.[73]

Dusinberre's judgment strikes me as too harsh. I believe *Chartres* to be almost flawless on its own terms, though I do accept that the last third of the *Education* is, for the reasons I have suggested, less successful than what goes before. But Dusinberre's reading has the considerable advantage of calling attention to the greatness of the monumental study of Jefferson and Madison, which he considers to be Adams's finest achievement and certainly the greatest American work of history.[74] Of course, as he recognizes, over a hundred years of new research and the development of new interpretive perspectives inevitably undermine some of Adams's conclusions. However, its mixture of art and science, its masterful use of primary sources, its portrait of Jefferson, its analysis of a critical period in the early history of the United States, and its well-defined, if complex, critical position make it a tremendous masterpiece. However great the more famous *Education*, the *History* and *Chartres* are Adams's most perfectly realized works.[75] To this day, as I suggested at the outset, the *History* illustrates Judith Shklar's argument that "narrative history, informed by philosophical and social analysis and a critical spirit, remains our likeliest route to political understanding."[76] A hint of its utility is suggested in a fascinating study by Richard Neustadt and Ernest May. Their book is an outgrowth of a course the two taught together for many years at Harvard, in which historical case studies were used for the analysis of decision making by political leaders. Classing the *History* with books "by writers who were primarily historians but whose experience or observation were enough to give them something of an insider's perceptiveness," they place Adams in a category with Machiavelli, Macaulay, and Arthur Schlesinger, Jr., and call the *History* a study from which men in power might benefit.[77] Adams certainly belongs on this list, though one must say that the omission of Thucydides is inexplicable. One could also add Tocqueville. But the general point is certainly valid.

Granting that only the application of an extremely high standard can justify calling Adams a failure, how can we sum up his contribution? What is his place in the history of American thought? Given the complexity of his ideas and the sometimes indirect, unsystematic way they are expressed, it is difficult to pin a label on him. In fact, perhaps one of his virtues is that the range of his thought is so wide and his imagination so fertile that he transcends the standard categories. Perhaps we should say that, like Walt Whitman, he contains multitudes.

Let us consider some of the possibilities somewhat more fully than we did earlier.[78] It is clear that Adams, so often treated as a conservative, is not a Federalist, the most conservative party in the early years of the Republic about which he wrote so much. The Federalists, after all, were based in New England, with a strong outpost in New York, and were the hated enemies of the Adams family. However great the reservations Henry Adams had about Thomas Jefferson, he certainly thought that Jefferson was at least superior to Alexander Hamilton.[79]

In the early national period, the principal alternative to the Federalists was the Republican Party of Thomas Jefferson. However, Adams cannot be said to have seized that alternative either. There is no doubt that Jefferson and Adams shared deep personal and characterological affinities: shyness, refinement, intellectual brilliance, a love of speculation, and a certain distaste for the rough and tumble of politics, though Jefferson often managed to rise above that distaste in ways that Adams found disreputable. Adams is at his most sympathetic to democracy in the 1880s when he was writing the *History* and his novel *Democracy*. In the former, it is Jefferson who is the spokesman for democracy.[80] But in spite of this, it is necessary to point out again that Adams was a constitutional purist and a strict moralist who believed that Jefferson betrayed his principles in not seeking a constitutional amendment to support the Louisiana Purchase. In addition, the embargo was a policy disaster that greatly increased national power in such a way as to subvert Jefferson's decentralist principles. So in spite of his sympathy, Jefferson was too flawed for Adams to join the ranks of his supporters. Yet Adams is quite clear that his model American statesman is that eminent Jeffersonian Albert Gallatin, so perhaps it is the leader rather than the abandoned principles that is at fault.

There are also certain affinities with the Whig Party, notably, support for internal improvements, but Adams has little to say about them, and there is no evidence to put him into that camp.

He should have been a Lincolnian Republican, but he was not. Lincoln's policy of slow strangulation of slavery by refusing to allow its expansion was very close to the policy of Charles Francis Adams, but it appears that sheer prejudice against Lincoln's midwestern origins and his alleged lack of the social graces, along with his willingness to play patronage politics, poisoned Adams's mind against him. Only late in life did he quietly recognize Lincoln's greatness.[81]

By rights, he should also have been part of the Progressive movement. His journalism following the Civil War was one of the first great muckraking efforts, which were part of the foundation on which the movement was built. And it is worth noting that Brooks Adams, so close to Henry, was also very close to Theodore Roosevelt. But Adams was scornful of Roosevelt, thinking he displayed far too much energy in proportion to the thought behind his policies. And he failed to develop his implied, but very briefly stated, critique of Roosevelt's trust policy. The trust crisis passed "when J. P. Morgan seized the initiative from Roosevelt, efficiently mobilized his Wall Street satellites, and rescued the securities markets, giving Adams arresting evidence of the accelerating concentration of economic power and of his fatalistic theory that Roosevelt's trust-busting tactics were worse than useless." From this, in the end, he drew the bizarre conclusion that McKinleyism was the "most beneficent evil" and that "tinkering was no substitute for root and branch measures."[82] Finally, by the time the Progressives took power, Adams was well into the pursuit of his gloomy theory of historical dynamics, which left little time for politics, except insofar as his energies went into attempts to influence John Hay's foreign policy when the time seemed propitious; not much time was left for domestic issues. Given his hatred of the trusts, his failure to engage with the Progressives must be counted as a lost opportunity.[83]

This covers most of the more organized political possibilities with which Adams might have had an affinity. He did flirt briefly with the Populists in 1896, and one might have expected him to admire William Jennings Bryan's Cross of Gold speech, whose rhetoric on the subject of banks was as flamboyant as his own. But the Populist flirtation did not survive past 1896.

Nor, in spite of his glorification of women in *Chartres*, in "The Primitive Rights of Women," and in his correspondence, could Adams identify himself with feminism in any modern sense. The place for women, in his view, was not in the voting booth but in the home, where they could be the heart and soul of the family, imparting their superior moral wisdom to their husbands and children. While there are contemporary feminists who might accept the claim of the moral superiority of women, none would be prepared to give up the right to vote, and none, I am sure, would accept the idea that women are by nature irrational, even if their thought patterns are revealed to be different from those of men. Perhaps the feminist theorists closest to Adams would be those who, like Jean Elshtain, place the strong family at the center of their thought.[84]

Modern conservatives have also paid little heed to Adams. It is true that Russell Kirk liked his work, but as I have said, he seems to have been misled by Brooks Adams's title *The Degradation of the Democratic Dogma*. Among other modern conservative thinkers, Leo Strauss admired him, but his student Allan Bloom dismissed him as a "crank,"[85] and one does not often see his views reflected in the writings of other conservative thinkers. On the other side of the political equation, Adams has appealed to some on the Left, including the journalist Carey McWilliams, who entitled his autobiography *The Education of Carey McWilliams*, and the communitarian participatory democrat John Schaar.[86] Both engage in a moral critique of contemporary capitalist democracy. But in the end, Adams is simply too complex to be adopted with ease by any political movement, and least of all by most contemporary conservatives, who are, for the most part, in thrall to the capitalism Adams despised.

Perhaps the historical category that comes closest to explaining Adams is, as Russell Hanson and William Merriman suggest, the civic republicanism discovered in the founding period by Bernard Bailyn and Gordon Wood, and most fully theorized by J. G. A. Pocock.[87] This classification has real plausibility and is the most successful attempt to date to place Adams in the general context of American political thought. Civic republicanism is based on the idea that the foundation of the good society and political system is the active, virtuous citizen led by virtuous public officials. Virtue is defined as the willingness to subordinate private to public interests. Corruption is the antithesis of virtue, the readiness to pursue private interests at the expense of what is objectively best for the public. Civic republicanism is not an individualistic theory; the focus is on the community and its well-being as a whole. In contemporary debates over the origins of American politics, it is often viewed as the antithesis of liberalism. The distinction has been stated concisely, if too formulaically, by Harvey Mansfield, Jr. "Civic humanism," he tells us, "is the republican virtue of citizens participating in rule," while liberalism, in contrast, "favors rights over community, liberty over duty, representation over participation, and interest over virtue."[88]

Adams fits at least parts of this formula. Considering the above antitheses, he would embrace the idea of community, the stress on duty, and virtue as the antithesis of corruption, but he would not be so enthusiastic about the republican theory of participatory democracy. What he hopes is that under the leadership of enlightened representatives and writers like himself, citizens would choose public-spirited men to look after their fortunes. His is a deferential theory of representative democracy. It is this form of democracy that he believed was threatened by the widespread corruption accompanying the explosive development of late-nineteenth-century capitalism. But as was the case with the disasters in the War of 1812, the fault lay more with political and economic elites than with the people, who, he believed, were still sound, in spite of the disastrously bad representatives they had placed in office. In the desperation of his late years, this faith was to decline, but it was still evident in his major works, and it sometimes resurfaced in his letters.

It is also important to bear in mind that Adams's own self-identification, early and late, is as a liberal, not as a conservative. Remember that at the start of his career he listed Tocqueville and Mill as his patron saints, though at the end he despaired of this form of liberalism. Thus his lament is for the unrealized ideals of the nineteenth-century liberalism of his mentors. There is an obvious paradox here. Adams is attached to orthodox, liberal, capitalist market economics through much of his career. Partly this is due to fear of paternalism and the strong state, but it is also due to his belief in the essential soundness of the market system. The paradox lies, of course, in the similar attachment of the capitalists Adams despised to that same orthodoxy, an intellectual prison that contributed so much to the destruction of all that Adams loved. Markets are indispensable institutions for economic decision making, but unregulated markets raise the specter of oligopoly or monopoly and of the worst sort of factionalism and corruption in the strict republican sense of self-interest subversive of any meaningful public interest. Adams understood this but was unable to act on his perception.

In sum, Adams clung to the old republican component of his ideals longer than most, but like many American political intellectuals, going back to the Framers of the Constitution, his ideas in the end were a none too consistent mixture of civic humanism, liberalism, and, in his case, a residual Puritanism. It is also worth noting the now conventional position that, based on James Madison's theory of the role of faction in the Constitution, the document underwrote the very factions that led to self-interested politics. Again, given Adams's constitutional purism, there is irony here, all the more so because the nationalism Adams favored virtually required a governmental framework with geographic and institutional separation that almost guaranteed faction. Thus Adams is, at best, a highly imperfect exemplar of the liberal consensus described by Louis Hartz.[89] Hartz sees the American tradition as having skipped feudalism to arrive at an essentially middle-class, egalitarian, Lockean consensus in which, he claimed (following Tocqueville), Americans were "born equal" without having to become so, dedicated to rights and to what he refers to as atomistic social freedom. This is a brilliant but flawed theory; it is too simple, overlooking the nonliberal aspects of the Puritan tradition and, above all, the point that the central fact of American history is the Civil War, an event exceedingly difficult to explain within the framework of an all-embracing consensus. What it can best explain, and what I think was one of Hartz's major interests, is the relatively low level of class conflict and the virtual absence of any serious socialist tradition when American politics is considered in a comparative perspective.[90]

Adams fits into this framework, but only loosely. Unlike Locke, he is silent on the contractual origins of the state, as well as the theory of individual rights.[91] We can infer from his hatred of slavery that there *were* some rights that could not be violated, but there is nothing specific as to what they are, unless his devotion to the early Constitution can be assumed to extend to the Bill of Rights.

Still, even though Adams does not see a liberal consensus in the same way as Hartz, and even though he sees more conflict between the Federalists and the forces of democracy than does Hartz, there is a strong sense in the *History* that the new American nation was something special and unique, a middle-class country leaving European feudal traditions far behind. This much is entirely consistent with the Hartz thesis, which begins by arguing that America simply skipped over the feudal stage of history and became from the start a bourgeois, middle-class society. This seems to be what Adams sees in the *History*—the emergence of a unique American nationalism or sense of national identity, as Melvin Lyon calls it, based on the clever inventiveness of the people. William Jordy too asserts that "the theme of the *History* is American nationalism."[92]

This sense of identity is based on the acceptance of a liberal or democratic dream according to which American democracy is something new under the sun. For Adams, it is an experiment. The content of the dream is best expressed in the sixth chapter of volume one of the *History*, the discussion of "American Ideals." The heart of the dream, shared by "every American, from Jefferson and Gallatin down to the poorest squatter, seemed to nourish an idea that he was doing what he could to overthrow the tyranny which the past had fastened on the human mind." This, Adams says, could appear to outsiders as so pompous or silly that it was hard to see its "nobler side," but it was there nonetheless. Europeans tended not to see it but instead complained that "every American democrat believed himself to be working for the overthrow of tyranny, aristocracy, hereditary privilege, and priesthood, wherever they existed."[93] The other great part of the dream was to lift the common man to a social and intellectual level on a par with the "most favored."[94] Ordinary people could not have articulated this ideal, so Jefferson became its principal spokesman, although, partly because he feared his own reputation as a visionary, his "writings may be searched from beginning to end without revealing the whole measure of the man."[95]

In spite of his reputation as an antidemocrat, Adams clearly is sympathetic to this vision and to Jefferson as its spokesman. This view is related to the theory of American exceptionalism, the idea that Americans were a unique people with a unique national destiny. Adams would became more skeptical of this theory as he saw his country caught up in the dynamics of the capitalist industrialization sweeping the Western world. His complaints about Jefferson stem from his belief that Jefferson betrayed his principles, as in the case of the Louisiana Purchase and his surrender to nationalist centralization.[96] But these failings of Jefferson were more personal than theoretical. Adams's sympathy for the theory remains, though that sympathy was incomplete and increasingly bruised and battered by the debaucheries of late-nineteenth-century political economy. But it threatened to give way entirely only in the unfortunate coda to Adams's career, primarily as expressed in Adams's letters after he ceased writing for publication in 1910.

The emergence of what Adams called McKinleyism—the capitalist world economy later brilliantly theorized by Karl Polanyi and named by the contemporary sociologist Immanuel Wallerstein—did terrible damage to the fabric of democratic politics and, at the intellectually sad end of his life, seriously undermined Adams's democratic commitments.[97] As discussed in the previous chapter, by the early part of the twentieth century, Adams had pretty much abandoned reform, though he continued to hope that new thought patterns would emerge to energize the forces of change. We can only speculate why Adams was so doubtful about the possibility of any alterations for the betterment of society beyond the limited palliative of civil service reform. It may be that, given his social position, he simply had no significant contact with those most damaged by the new political economy—the working class and the small independent farmers. He perceived their plight only in distant, macroscopic terms; he could see structural but not individual problems.

Thus, in 1894 and 1895, he wrote to his close English friend Charles Milnes Gaskell that "Europe and Asia are used to accepting disease and death as inevitable, but to us the idea is a new one. We want to know what is wrong with the world that it should suddenly go to smash without visible cause or possible advantage. Here in this young, rich continent, capable of supporting three times its population with ease, we have had a million men out of employment for nearly a year, and the situation growing worse rather than better." As for agriculture, "The tiller of the soil is always being exploited by the trader and the money lender."[98]

Adams could see the underlying problems quite clearly, but he could not bring himself to support concrete reform actions after his brief Populist period. This reflects a peculiar characteristic of Adams's thought, a tendency to await a catastrophe in the hope that something better would emerge from the ruins, a position that is at best pointless and at worst one of the surest ways to bring about a true catastrophe with disastrous consequences. Of course, this view also reflects his growing sense that the world's political economy was in the grip of forces beyond the power of anyone to control.

This raises the question of the nature of Adams's determinist beliefs. As I have already suggested, it is only in the late scientific papers that these beliefs really seem to take over Adams's thought, and even there, he clings to his desperate hope for a new Newton to forestall the inevitable. But until the very end, Adams found it difficult to accept determinist theories. In general, he would enter a qualification to his worst fears, just as he often found the American people to be the saving grace for democracy. But the pull of deterministic science was still strong, driven, as it was, by his ceaseless quest for unity. In turn, in spite of his insistence that his was an eighteenth-century mind ill suited to the world of his own time, the commitment to science was part of the legacy of the eighteenth century to the modern world. It is surely no accident that modern science is often labeled the Enlightenment project, so that Adams's eighteenth century is closely linked to his twentieth-century scientific concerns.

While many would trace the origins of modernity to Thomas Hobbes or perhaps to Machiavelli, for Adams, the stress falls not on a political theorist but on a philosopher of science, Francis Bacon, and sometimes on Descartes or Galileo (though it must be observed that Hobbes was also powerfully influenced by mathematics and the scientific discoveries of the seventeenth century).

Adams's commitment to science is much less grudging than might appear to be the case, even when *Mont Saint Michel and Chartres* is taken into account. He did not like what he believed science told him, but he tried heroically, if foolishly, not to escape from its intellectual power but rather to face up to the world as he saw it. This explains why he wrote essays such as "The Rule" and "A Letter." At the same time, this belief in science did not preclude his intellectual journey into twelfth-century France. His mind was too restless to stay tied to a single perspective on his intellectual problems. It should also be added that in making his pilgrimage to the medieval world, he spoke for more than just himself. In spite of the fact that he never connected directly with domestic progressivism, it can be argued that his "wistful yearning for the Virgin was the inner voice of the movement. More or less desperately, Progressives were seeking some way of *comprehending*, as well as *controlling*, the energies in the 'power house' of industrial civilization."[99] Like his great German contemporary Max Weber, Adams saw the "disenchantment of the world," the decline of religious faith, and its replacement by scientific rationalism.[100]

Though he knew the cause to be hopeless, Adams turned to the Virgin Mary as a possible source of the "charismatic authority" that might provide a release from the domination of science, which existed in profound tension with his powerful humanistic instincts. The Weberian concept of charisma fits the Virgin exactly; hers is the "authority of the extraordinary and personal gift of grace."[101] But Adams's sense of the presence of this authority, this glimpse of utopia, did not last even the length of *Chartres*. The Virgin disappears in the last three chapters, and her church is pronounced dead when she does. Saint Francis is a partial stand-in for her, but Aquinas gets the last word, however unstable his Church Intellectual may be, and Adams cannot even repress his affection for the superrational Abelard. At the same time, he surely would have agreed with Weber, who, quoting Tolstoy, tells us, "Science is meaningless because it gives us no answer to our question, the only question important for us: 'What shall we do and how shall we live?' "[102]

But in spite of his praise for the irrationality of the Virgin—here understood as a defense against the scientific, instrumental rationality described by Weber—Adams could not embrace her faith, much as he might have wished to. Science has its limits, which cannot be transcended, but for Adams, it is all there is left to us in the twentieth century. His friend the painter John La Farge said to him, "Adams, you reason too much," to which he could only reply, "the mind resorts to reason for want of training."[103] No picture of Adams as an irrationalist, whatever his longings, can really be supported. Even *Chartres*, for all its wonderful exuberance, is very carefully reasoned and structured. Once again, had he known Weber's work, the great

German could have spoken for him. "To the person who cannot bear the fate of the times like a man, one must say: may he rather return silently, without the usual publicity build-up of renegades, but simply and plainly. The arms of the old churches are opened widely and compassionately for him. After all, they do not make it hard for him. . . . If he can really do it, we shall not rebuke him."[104] Adams, the reluctant, critical modernist, would certainly have agreed. And yet, in the end, what remained as the last best hope was mind.[105]

Thus, as Samuels says, Adams is "modern man writ large." And, in a nice characterization, he dismisses his "cultivated misanthropy" and says, "He shows himself as infinitely aware of the underlying sadness of life, yet infinitely zestful of living; fearful of showing compassion, yet consumed with the desire for the good society."[106] But I think Samuels is wrong to stress as often as he does Adams's "fundamental quarrel with modern science." Adams is queasy about the results of his scientific pursuits and fully aware that science, and the technology it breeds, creates terrible dangers on a planetary scale. Yet he is also deeply intrigued and sees no alternative to accepting science as the path to knowledge. He is so committed, in fact, that in the late essays he pushes the argument to a point where, if taken literally, it threatens to slide into absurdity. But still he remains a scientific modernist. For this reason, I think that Jackson Lears's often brilliant analysis of Adams as an anti-modern modernist is just slightly off the mark.[107] It seems to me that the better label is critical modernist. He is fully aware of the dangers of modernity and is more than willing to discuss them, but he does not reject the sources of the dangers, nor does he see a realistic alternative to them. He asks only that we be cognizant of the possible dangers that lie ahead.

Here Adams diverges somewhat from that other critical modernist, Max Weber. As John Patrick Diggins writes, "For Weber, science meant rationalization, the development of more complex institutions of organization and control; for Adams, science meant acceleration."[108] And what drove acceleration was technology. This raises the vexed question of technological determinism. Adams fits into a broader tradition of American literature, including many of the greatest American writers, whose idea was of an Edenic garden being invaded by the machine, though it has to be said that, whatever his feelings about technology, Adams was no pastoralist. But Leo Marx, in his book exploring this theme, is right to claim that "a sense of the transformation of life by technology dominates *The Education* as it does no other book."[109]

But having said this, Marx, like so many others, exaggerates the extent of Adams's dislike of technology. Quite rightly, he points to the antitheses within which Adams works: Virgin and dynamo, the "clash between past and present, unity and diversity, love and power."[110] These points are all there, but a careful reading suggests that the dichotomies are not so Manichaean as Marx suggests. In discussing *Chartres*, I have argued that in writing of the Virgin, Adams reveals a little-noticed sympathy for diversity, without giving up the pursuit of unity. Similarly, the dynamo has a fascination for Adams that prevents him from unequivocally taking the part of the Virgin. And he sees enough science in Thomas Aquinas to blur the divide between past and present, though of course there is a deep, nostalgic melancholy when he reflects on the lost world of Quincy. These tensions in Adams's thought are important, and I want to insist that he is more divided between these opposing concepts than is often recognized. His sympathies do not automatically lean toward the earlier of the dichotomous choices Marx notes. Adams dreams of unity, but he does not quite succeed in finding it in his own mind. He is engaged in a constant dialogue with himself.

This is not to deny the powerful belief in technology as a driving force that, as Marx says, permeates Adams's thought. Nor is it to deny his uneasiness with the powerful forces he discusses. Certainly, from an early age, at least part of his mind anticipated technological disaster. But at the same time, he seems to delight in taking advantage of new technological developments. It is necessary to take into account both aspects of his complex and divided mind.

The immediate problem is whether technology can be controlled, or whether it takes on a life of its own.[111] The question is whether technology is autonomous.[112] On one level, this is not a very useful question. George Kateb tells us, "Fear and hate of the machine are among the stalest and most pervasive emotions of modern life." Moreover, the idea that machines can take on lives of their own and control their masters, like Frankenstein's monster or the sorcerer's apprentice, is a little strange. As Kateb says, "It is hard to say just what is to be done with this idea except to translate it into the less dramatic assertion that machines may exact the cost of unpleasant alterations in human life in exchange for the immense benefits they bestow, and may at times seem to be leading men to do things that serve no purpose but an endless, useless refinement of mechanical proficiency." However, "the real danger," he states, "is not that the increasingly subtle and potent machines of modern technology will develop a will of their own (whatever that may mean) but that they are and will continue to be used in the service of evil human wills."[113] This seems just about right, though it is well to remember that much modern technology is, in fact, controlled if not by men with evil wills then by men who may not have the well-being of society fully in mind or, less ominously, be unclear about the effects of the enormous forces they command. In brief, this brings us back to the modern corporation, the modern state, and the need to control both.

This means that we need a politics of technology control. Like Adams, Weber is a critical modernist who is at one with him on a central political issue. "It is utterly ridiculous to see any connection between the high capitalism of today . . . with democracy or with freedom in any sense of these words. Yet this capitalism is an unavoidable result of our economic development. The question is: how are freedom and democracy in the long run at all possible under the domination of highly developed capitalism? Freedom and democracy are only possible where the resolute will of a nation not to allow itself to be ruled like sheep is permanently alive."[114] But Weber differs politically from Adams, the proponent of civil service reform, when he writes, "The American workers who were against the 'Civil Service Reform' knew what they were about. They wished to be governed by parvenus of doubtful morals rather than by a certified caste of mandarins. But their protests were in vain."[115] The difference between Adams and Weber is that Weber had a grasp of what party politics is all about. There was no reason that reform and democratic politics could not have been accomplished so that such a divide was unnecessary. However, Adams was too deeply opposed to the party system to see this, and the tension noted by Weber bore fruit in the antiparty legislation of the Progressive period, legislation that turned out to be of little use in fostering democracy. The Adams who was sensitive to power relationships in international politics was so put off by the sheer messiness of the domestic scene that he was rendered helpless, unable to make use of the key political institutions that offer the only hope of controlling the economic structures that so rightly troubled him. He was a powerful diagnostician and critic but not much good at treatment, particularly late in his career, as deterministic fancies took a larger place in his mind. He could only chide those who foolishly believed in automatic progress.

Of course, Adams is not alone in his distrust of political action. In his very interesting book on the political theory of technology, Langdon Winner is uneasy about the routines of ordinary political conflict. In one orientation toward politics, "the focus comes to rest on matters of risk and safeguard, cost and benefit, distribution, and the familiar interest-centered style of politics." Even the new, sometimes apparently radical movements pursuing ecological issues, such as Naderism, public interest science, and technology assessment, fit into this framework. They offer little that is new. "What one finds here is the utilitarian-pluralist model refined and aimed at new targets."[116] Winner is right to be worried, insofar as Adams and Weber are correct about the domination of politics by corporate interests incompatible with democracy. Under these conditions, interest-group politics is dangerous, but however unfortunate that may be, it is the only game in town if one wants to engage in politics seriously. Where Adams is handicapped is in his inability to see beyond his legitimate structural concerns about the economy and into the necessity of building coalitions with groups he does not quite trust or understand. Anyone wishing to build on Adams's theory of history must start with his diagnosis but go beyond him into a world of new alliances. This will not be easy and may prove impossible, but it is necessary for those concerned with the drift of modern technological politics to make the effort.

On an abstract and speculative level, Winner is more stimulating. Whereas we have been considering the problem of technological control through legislation, Winner suggests that we consider technology *as legislation.* "*Different ideas of social and political life,*" he tells us, "*entail different technologies for their realization.*" Unwittingly, we can build technologies that are incompatible with "autonomous, self-determining individuals in a democratic polity."

> If, for example, some perverse spirit set out deliberately to design a collection of systems to increase the general feelings of powerlessness, enhance the prospects for the dominance of technical elites, create the belief that politics is nothing more than a remote spectacle to be experienced vicariously, and thereby diminish the chance that anyone would take democratic citizenship seriously, what better plan to suggest than to keep the systems we already have?[117]

This sounds very much like a theory of autonomous technology and is subject to the same criticisms as any other, but it *is* a tolerably accurate sketch of American politics today. The question is, how much of this picture derives from technology as such, and how much from the organized institutions that create and control the applications of technology. Perhaps there is a mixture. Perhaps there are some technologies that are so appealing to so many people that they might just as well be autonomous. And some innovations—the Internet is the common example today—may have a liberating capacity by making information widely available to a potentially aroused citizenry. However, the increasing concentration in the field of technology symbolized by, to take just two examples, the proposed mergers of AOL with Time Warner and of AT&T with MediaOne does not bode well, since this may lead to constriction rather than expansion of information sources. Nor should one overlook the mounting concern over the technological potential for the invasion of privacy. In such circumstances, to control technology requires the control of enormous economic institutions, so we are again brought back to the basic problem of finding democratic means to control large and growing concentrations of economic power. In the world of industrial capitalism, there is no escaping the central issues of a politicized economy.

Winner offers some hope for a decentralized politics, having in mind such historical examples as the Paris communes of 1793 and 1871, nineteenth-century utopias, Spanish anarchism, and worker and community counsels.[118] But the history of such organizations does not provide much hope for the present. However interesting they may be, Winner is well aware of their difficulties, so he does not devote space to proposing panaceas based on them. Instead, he lays down a set of general rules: technology should be comprehensible to nonexperts, it should be flexible and mutable, and dependency should be avoided. More generally still, he proposes a rule of what he calls "epistemological Luddism." The original Luddites argued that if new techniques do not improve the quality of the product or the quality of work, they should not be allowed. Pursuant to this, he suggests that we need to consider "the connections of the human parts of modern social technology."

> To be more specific, it would try to consider at least the following: (1) the kinds of human dependency and regularized behavior centering upon specific varieties of apparatus, (2) the patterns of social activities that rationalized techniques imprint upon human relationships, and (3) the shapes given everyday life by the large-scale organized networks of technology. Far from any wild smashing, this would be a meticulous process aimed at restoring significance to the question, What are we about?[119]

All this is largely unexceptionable, but it does not really deal with the political problem. Almost inevitably, the large state will be involved in any attempt to control technology. And that will bring us back to the issue of the economic domination of politics seen a century ago by Adams and Weber, though of course, not only by them. At best, it may be, as Michael Walzer suggests, that although the state will not wither away, it can be hollowed out.[120] This would involve the democratization of institutions below the level of the state—universities, corporations, unions, and the like—along with a more general decentralization of the political system. There are some signs that this may be part of our future, though not all of it, and one ought to be very cautious about seeing such a development as a permanent trend. In fact, it may well be that some issues can best be handled locally, while others invite global intervention. It is almost certainly the case that no single level or size of governmental unit is well adapted to deal with all problems. We may see some decentralization in some policy arenas and considerable centralization in others. Doubtless there will be a period of flux as governments and citizens try to adjust to rapid change.[121] It is hard to say whether Adams would approve of democratic decentralization. His focus is on the state, which he distrusts, and the control of its power. I have argued that in spite of his complaints against democracy, deep down (sometimes very deep down), late in life, Adams is still a democrat. Of course, the democracy he avows is clearly representative democracy. A more participatory form of democratic rule is not part of his ideal, though if he believed that democratization at this level could help contain the corporation (which seems unlikely, at present), he might be interested. Thus, how he would feel about "hollowing out" the state is by no means clear.

Still, his real fears about democracy were activated by what he saw as the failings of a representative system. Kateb argues that representative democracy fosters certain desirable moral qualities. At its best, representative democracy leads to a certain independence of spirit, as well as to a continuous "incitement to claim the status of citizen." Another result—in some ways, I think, the most interesting—flows from the partisan nature of the electoral system. Representative democracy entails a system in which a partial group temporarily stands for the whole. Associating authority with partisanship promotes a sense of "moral indeterminacy,"[122] a sense that can counter the dogmatism that is potentially fatal to a democratic polity. Adams himself certainly had great independence of spirit, though how much he would have welcomed it in the electorate of a modern mass democracy is unclear. And, given the mass basis of citizenship, it is far from certain that he would have been an enthusiast for ordinary citizens claiming their citizenship rights beyond voting. He might also have been perplexed by Kateb's last point. Surely, given his detestation of partisan politics, he would not have been happy to see the part stand for the whole, unless, perhaps, he himself happened to stand with that temporary majority. On the subject of moral indeterminacy, his views were decidedly mixed. Philosophically, he could easily accept this position, but temperamentally, he could not. Nor did he believe moral indeterminacy to be good for society. So his residual Puritan moral code took hold and led him to make absolute judgments on the failings of his time, even when his philosophical commitments told him that he had no warrant to do so. Here, as always, Adams does not fit conveniently into conventional categories.

What Adams hoped for was a version of representative democracy based on the classical theory of rule by the best, which, in the context of a democratic society, requires a deferential electorate. But the time for deferential voting had long since passed, and Adams personally had no legitimate claim to expect preference on the basis of the contribution of his distinguished family, as he sometimes seemed to believe. But his animadversions against the politics of his time were not entirely unjustified. The "best," whoever they might be, were arguably not chosen during much of his lifetime, anymore than they are today. It may be that he thought the ordinary citizen incapable of making sound electoral choices. At the same time, it is important to recall that his most savage attacks were reserved for the political and economic elites. It is equally important to remember that he continued to believe, for all his occasional hyperbole indicating the contrary, that the people were still basically sound. What they needed was better leadership, leadership that could gain the necessary authority by being able and willing to offer plausible justifications for their policies, as Jefferson signally failed to do in the debates on the Louisiana Purchase.

It is unfortunate that Adams never codified his melange of ideas about politics into a single, coherent political theory. This may be a product of the sort of mind he had. Here again, the similarity to Weber may be worth a brief comment. Like Adams, Weber was deeply interested in politics and was tempted to give up academic life to pursue those interests. He also wrote an enormous amount about politics, even more than did Adams. And yet, as Sheldon Wolin points out, "Weber never set down a coherent political theory comparable to the great theories of the tradition of political theory. That inability may well be the meaning of social science."[123] Of course, Adams was not a social scientist in the same sense as Weber. But he clearly identified himself as a scientific historian, which is surely close enough to make comparison fruitful. Wolin argues that theory is political in the sense that it lays down rules or principles that, "when legitimated," become the potential basis for a society—in other words, a master science in the Aristotelian sense, one "that legislates for the good of the whole."[124] But this is something science has not been able to accomplish. Instead, even great social scientists like Weber turn their attention to methodology. But scientific methodology, as Weber well knew, cannot legitimate the values that are the foundation of a society or a political system. Thus they cannot convert power into right. As Wolin sums up, "Having undermined religious, moral, and political beliefs, the forces of rationalization had finally exposed the meaning of meaninglessness to be power without right."[125] It was this intellectual crisis that prevented Weber from moving beyond historical sociology into political theory as it had been conceived historically.

Henry Adams was caught in the same intellectual vise. He too saw the grounds of his deepest beliefs undermined. Religion was long since dead; the Constitution had, in his view, been subverted; and economic barons of dubious morality dominated not only the economy but also the political system. But increasingly, Adams clung to his scientific commitment, even though his scientific competence was doubtful, and even though it led him to discover chaos rather than the unity he sought. On one level, his intellectual courage must be admired; he had the strength of mind to face up to his conclusions without retreating to positions he felt were no longer tenable. But his pursuit of scientific answers led him close to absurdity, at least if we read him literally, so that he was left with no possible way to follow his strong theoretical bent in an attempt to repair the eroded foundations of legitimate authority in American politics. Late in life, the inveterate reformer abandoned politics just when reform was most needed.

Instead of attempting to reconstruct the theoretical foundations of the American republic, Adams, leaving the *History* aside, became a political and social critic; although this is a fine and noble calling, from a mind of the stature of Adams's, one might have hoped for more. His criticism often took on a cynical form, a term that, in his circumstances, I do not intend as pejorative. William Chaloupka defines cynicism as "the condition of lost belief" and suggests that it is not necessarily the case that we are always better off without cynics.[126] Cynicism may be inadequate as the only response to a situation, but there are times when it is almost necessarily *part* of a response. It is certainly often well suited to the role of a social critic. And in the Gilded Age, there was much to be cynical about.

The question of lost belief is very important. The composer and performance artist Laurie Anderson is also concerned with this condition, drawing, in her most recent work, on Herman Melville. She quotes the conclusion of Father Mapple's sermon in *Moby Dick*: "So what is a man if he outlives the lifetime of his God?" And Anderson adds, "Yes, really. What do you do when you no longer believe in the things that have driven you? How do you go on?"[127] I think Adams was very much in the situation Chaloupka and Anderson describe. He never had religious faith, however tempted he might have been, and in his later years, his belief in the efficacy of democracy and the Constitution was sorely tried. As he withdrew from politics, unity became his great white whale, and he turned to science to help him find it. At the very end of his career, this led him to a deeply troubling theory of history. He became preoccupied with disaster or the imagination of disaster as his irony threatened to spin out of control. And yet, in spite of the pessimism of his historical theory, his late professions of faith in the people still stand, as does the great *History*. Even during World War I, his harsh rebuke to Henry Cabot Lodge when he attacked President Wilson showed that he had not quit the discussion of American democracy and that, as Levenson says, he "could not [do so] without withdrawing his *History* from circulation." It is there that Adams "presents the American democrat in whose mock heroic figure we glimpse the shape of greatness."[128] That monument remains and should be one of the foundation stones for anyone trying to build on Adams's work. There, it is possible to revisit the early idealism of American politics. Surely it would be of great value for students of American political development to return to the deep questions raised at the end of the last volume on James Madison and make a systematic attempt to answer them.

A major theme of this study has been the deep divisions within Adams's mind. I have also alluded to the parallels between Adams and Leo Tolstoy, particularly as the latter's *War and Peace* is discussed by Isaiah Berlin.[129] The similarities between Adams and Berlin's Tolstoy are quite striking. To be sure, there are differences, but the similarities are more important. Thus, there is no debt to Rousseau in Adams's work, as there was in Tolstoy's, and although the master novelist did not deny the truths of physics, he thought, unlike Adams, that they were essentially trivial because they could not give us answers to the genuinely important questions about politics and society and, above all, to the question of how we should live. One can only regret that Adams did not pursue such questions, but at the end of his life, he had given up on them and had come close to unconditional surrender to the second law of thermodynamics. Both Adams and Tolstoy believed that men, even great men, are caught up in forces they cannot control. And each, on the evidence of Tolstoy's novel and Adams's *History* and journalism, had a vivid, almost overwhelming sense of the enormous complexity of life.

Here Berlin's famous dichotomy dividing hedgehogs and foxes comes into play. The categories are based on the saying of the ancient Greek poet Archilochus that the fox knows many things but the hedgehog knows one big thing. According to Berlin, Tolstoy's tragedy was that he was a fox who wanted to be a hedgehog. But his sense of the complexity of human life was too rich for him to achieve this end. "His sense of reality was until the end too devastating to be compatible with any moral ideal which he was able to construct out of the fragments into which his intellect had shivered the world, and he dedicated all his vast strength of mind to the lifelong denial of this fact."[130]

Adams also wanted to be a hedgehog. This is the meaning of his search for unity. But all his relentlessly active mind could discover was multiplicity. Even near the end of his long life, when he almost completely surrendered his intellect to the demands of physics, all he could find was the dissipation of energy leading to the ultimate in disorder. Order, he said, was the dream of man, and chaos the law of nature. His attempt to find a unifying device in the laws of physics was a total failure, at least as far as politics is concerned. The words with which Berlin describes Tolstoy also apply to Adams, "a desperate old man, beyond human aid, wandering self-blinded at Colonus."[131]

But it is not fair to Adams to leave him in this way. No one could ever achieve unity on the desperate terms he imposed on himself at the end of his career. Let us instead celebrate and remember Adams the fox, the greatest of all American historians. The richness of his *History* is a wonderful legacy. In his own peculiar way, this is his testament to American democracy and its potential. It is a foundation on which others can build, even if his own work turned down another road. In *Chartres* and in the first two-thirds of the *Education*, there is also much to draw on. The *Education* in particular remains tremendously important, despite its flawed structure, not only because of its obvious brilliance but also because it is Adams's most general statement of his views. The heritage Adams left us is very rich, despite his occasional wrongheadedness. No great American thinker is so exasperating. He is a deeply ambivalent writer, and it is impossible not to be ambivalent about him. As Lionel Trilling said, it is hard to identify ourselves with him for very long. Some of what Adams wrote near the end is nearly useless except as metaphor, and some of it is profoundly dangerous, though one must always keep in mind his love of hyperbole and be prepared to discount it. But I think Trilling is right to say, "We shall be wrong, we shall do ourselves a great disservice, if ever we try to read Adams out of our intellectual life. I have called him an issue—he is even more than that, he is an indispensable element of our thought, he is an instrument of our intelligence. To succeed in getting rid of Adams would be to diminish materially the seriousness of our thought. . . . Nothing can be more salutary for the American intelligence than to remain aware of Adams and to maintain toward him a strict ambivalence, to weigh our admiration and affection for him against our impatience and suspicion."[132]

It is not surprising that Trilling admired Adams. A recently published collection of Trilling's work is entitled *The Moral Obligation to Be Intelligent*, an obligation that Adams surely felt and fully met. And since, in the end, Adams was part of the liberal tradition, he was a liberal of the type who was aware of the qualities Trilling celebrates: "variousness and possibility, which implies the awareness of complexity and difficulty."[133] This sense of complexity is all-important. Adams had the "ability to keep two, perhaps three, ideas in mind at the same time."[134] This is the reason he is so difficult to fit into the standard ideological categories and is one of his greatest strengths. He is truly a multivalent thinker.[135] At one and the same time, he can embrace science and religion, liberalism and civic republicanism, political economy and philosophy, art and culture, history and theory. The enormous range of Adams's mind, along with his sense of the sheer contrariety of the world, is the source of much that is valuable in his thought.

Adams can tell Americans a great deal about who they are. In many ways, he reads like our contemporary. His is an enormous legacy that we ignore at our peril, for to a startling extent, his problems remain our problems. We too worry about the condition of American democracy, and many hope for a revival of its early idealism. We too worry about the rapid development of technology and its seemingly infinite capacity to shape our lives, though like Adams, we welcome its benefits. And many worry about the power of American business and the tendency for politics to be dominated by money, which is so central to both the problem of democracy and the problem of rapid technological development. It can be very useful to return to thinkers who raised contemporary problems early on. Such analyses of problems at their onset sometimes have a clarity that later statements lack. In this perspective, Henry Adams's work stands as a lost treasure waiting to be unearthed, not least because of his recognition of complexity and his unwillingness to settle for easy answers.

NOTES

Abbreviations of Frequently Cited Sources

WORKS BY HENRY ADAMS

Chartres	In *Novels, Mont Saint Michel and Chartres, The Education of Henry Adams*, ed. Ernest Samuels (New York: Library of America, 1986).
Degradation	*The Degradation of the Democratic Dogma*, ed. Charles Hirschfeld, with an introduction by Brooks Adams (New York: Harper Torchbooks, 1969).
Democracy	In *Novels, Mont Saint Michel and Chartres, The Education of Henry Adams*, ed. Ernest Samuels (New York: Library of America, 1986).
Education	*The Education of Henry Adams*, ed. Ernest Samuels and Jayne Samuels (Boston: Houghton Mifflin, 1963).
Esther	In *Novels, Mont Saint Michel and Chartres, The Education of Henry Adams*, ed. Ernest Samuels (New York: Library of America, 1986).
Great Secession Winter	*The Great Secession Winter of 1860–61 and Other Essays*, ed. George Hochfield (New York: Sagamore Press, 1958).
History I	*History of the United States During the Administrations of Thomas Jefferson*, ed. Earl N. Harbert (New York: Library of America, 1986).
History II	*History of the United States During the Administrations of James Madison,*

	ed. Earl N. Harbert (New York: Library of America, 1986).
Letters	*The Letters of Henry Adams*, ed. J. C. Levenson, Ernest Samuels, Charles Vandersee, and Viola Hopkins Winner, vols. 1–3 (Cambridge: Harvard University Press, 1982), vols. 4–6 (Cambridge: Harvard University Press, 1988).
Life of Gallatin	*The Life of Albert Gallatin* (New York: J. B. Lippincott, 1879).
Randolph	*John Randolph*, ed. Robert McColley (Armonk, N.Y.: M. E. Sharpe, 1996).

SECONDARY SOURCES

Literary Vocation	William Merrill Decker, *The Literary Vocation of Henry Adams* (Chapel Hill: University of North Carolina Press, 1990).
Major Phase	Ernest Samuels, *Henry Adams: The Major Phase* (Cambridge: Harvard University Press, 1964).
Middle Years	Ernest Samuels, *Henry Adams: The Middle Years* (Cambridge: Harvard University Press, 1958).
Mind and Art	J. C. Levenson, *The Mind and Art of Henry Adams* (Stanford, Calif.: Stanford University Press, 1957).
Scientific Historian	William Jordy, *Henry Adams: Scientific Historian* (New Haven, Conn.: Yale University Press, 1952).
Young Henry Adams	Ernest Samuels, *The Young Henry Adams* (Cambridge: Harvard University Press, 1948).

Introduction

1. Richard Hofstadter, *The Progressive Historians: Turner, Beard, Parrington* (New York: Alfred A. Knopf, 1968), 4. Alfred Kazin makes a similar point but from a different perspective. "History exerts its power as literature, not because a book has literary distinction, but because the magisterial pattern it weaves is felt to shape us, to change us, to embody our ideas and image of collective experience. History then

becomes a memory of the race." And later he adds, "The historical thinkers we read over and again, because their books *are* the history we have, are those whom we believe even if we do not accept their argument. Our image of history is not even obtained directly from their books; it is passed from mind to mind in the excited discovery that this is how history 'works.'" Kazin, *An American Procession* (New York: Vintage Books, 1985), 281, 282.

2. Judith Shklar, "*The Education of Henry Adams* by Henry Adams," in *Redeeming American Political Thought* (Chicago: University of Chicago Press, 1998), 80–90, and "Learning Without Knowing," in *Political Thought and Political Thinkers* (Chicago: University of Chicago Press, 1998), 114–16.

3. Russell L. Hanson and W. Richard Merriman, "Henry Adams and the Decline of the Republican Tradition," *American Transcendental Quarterly* (September 1990), 161–83.

4. Henry Kariel, "The Limits of Social Science: Henry Adams' Quest for Order," *American Political Science Review* 50 (December 1956), 1074–92.

5. Though a historian, John Patrick Diggins has many of the concerns of historically oriented political theorists. On Adams, see *The Lost Soul of American Politics* (New York: Basic Books, 1984), and *The Promise of Pragmatism* (Chicago: University of Chicago Press, 1994).

6. Michael Walzer, *Interpretation and Social Criticism* (Cambridge: Harvard University Press, 1988), and *The Company of Critics* (New York: Basic Books, 1988).

7. Decker, *Literary Vocation*, 3. An interesting anecdote illustrates Adams's intense patriotism. One evening at dinner during World War I, Adams's former student Henry Cabot Lodge attacked Woodrow Wilson. Though no fan of the president, Adams said, "Cabot! I've never allowed treasonable conversation at this table and I don't propose to allow it now" (quoted in Levenson, *Mind and Art*, 165). Wilson Carey McWilliams points out that Adams must have enjoyed the irony here, since Lodge was attacking Wilson for being insufficiently patriotic (personal communication). It may be worth noting that Adams and his wife were both very critical of their friend Henry James for his protracted periods of exile in Britain, as well as for his preference for English ways. See introduction to *The Correspondence of Henry James and Henry Adams: 1877–1914*, ed. George Monteiro (Baton Rouge: Louisiana State University Press, 1992), esp. 5–6. Still, it must be mentioned that Adams himself was a notable traveler, though Washington remained his base. He worked against success by publishing his novels anonymously or pseudonymously and by circulating *Chartres* and the *Education* privately to his friends. Neither was published until years later.

8. *Education*, 382.

9. Henry Adams to Charles William Eliot, March 2, 1877, in *Letters* 2:301. See also his letter to another student, Henry Osborn Taylor, a medieval historian. "To me, accuracy is relative. I care very little whether the details are exact, if only my *ensemble* is to scale" (Adams to Taylor, January 17, 1905, in *Letters* 5:628). This is in reference to his much later book *Mont Saint Michel and Chartres*.

10. Clive Bush, *Halfway to Revolution: Investigation and Crisis in the Work of Henry Adams, William James, and Gertrude Stein* (New Haven, Conn.: Yale University Press, 1991), 460 n. 1.

11. Austin Warren, *The New England Conscience* (Ann Arbor: University of Michigan Press, 1967), 3–28, quotes at 5 and 28.

12. For a classic account of the Jeremiad, see Perry Miller, *The New England Mind: From Colony to Province* (Boston: Beacon Press, 1961), esp. 27–39.

13. For a sketch of the importance of the tradition of the Jeremiad in American political thought, see James P. Young, *Reconsidering American Liberalism: The Troubled Odyssey of the Liberal Idea* (Boulder, Colo.: Westview Press, 1996), 19–21, and the literature cited therein.

14. Hofstadter, *Progressive Historians*, 12–20, quote at 17.

15. Ibid., 20–29, esp. 27–28.

16. J. C. Levenson, "Henry Adams," in *Pastmasters: Some Essays on American Historians*, ed. Marcus Cunliffe and Robin Winks (New York: Harper and Row, 1969), 49.

17. Søren Kierkegaard quoted in Clifford Geertz, *After the Fact* (Cambridge: Harvard University Press, 1995), 166.

18. Ibid., 166.

19. Richard Taruskin, *Mussorgsky: Eight Essays and an Epilogue* (Princeton, N.J.: Princeton University Press, 1993), 36. Taruskin has a great deal to say about the hermeneutical problems involved in the analysis of tradition. After all, the study of music, like political theory, is very much involved with a canonical tradition. See Taruskin, *Text and Act: Essays on Music and Performance* (New York: Oxford University Press, 1995), esp. 90–155. In Taruskin's work, the analogies between the history of music and the history of political theory seem very strong.

20. Judith Shklar, *Montesquieu* (Oxford and New York: Oxford University Press 1987), 126.

21. Any consideration of Tolstoy's theory of history requires notice of Isaiah Berlin's seminal essay "The Hedgehog and the Fox," in *Russian Thinkers*, ed. Henry Hardy and Aileen Kelly (New York: Viking Press, 1978), 22–81.

22. Ernest Samuels, *The Young Henry Adams, Henry Adams: The Middle Years*, and *Henry Adams: The Major Phase* (Cambridge: Harvard University Press, 1948, 1958, 1964). There is also a one-volume version of the Samuels biography that takes advantage of the completion of the Harvard edition of the Adams letters. However, it devotes much less attention to the works than does the original. See also Edward Chalfant, *Both Sides of the Ocean: A Biography of Henry Adams: His First Life, 1838–1862* and *Better in Darkness: A Biography of Henry Adams: His Second Life, 1862–1891* (Hamden, Conn.: Archon Books, 1982, 1994). Chalfant's work is massive and detailed, but it lacks focus and cannot match that of Samuels.

23. For a fine study that focuses on the relation of Adams as a writer to his family, see Earl N. Harbert, *The Force So Much Closer Home: Henry Adams and the Adams*

Family (New York: New York University Press, 1977). See also Paul Nagel, *Descent from Glory: Four Generations of the John Adams Family* (Cambridge: Harvard University Press, 1999).

24. On the letters, see William Merrill Decker, *Epistolary Practices: Letter Writing in America before Telecommunications* (Chapel Hill: University of North Carolina Press, 1998), 176–228, and Decker, *Literary Vocation*, 91–100. On the possibility that Adams thought his letters might be published, see Decker, *Literary Vocation*, 96. See also Joanne Jacobson, *Authority and Alliance in the Letters of Henry Adams* (Madison: University of Wisconsin Press, 1992).

25. Henry Adams, *History of the United States During the Administrations of Thomas Jefferson*, ed. Earl N. Harbert (New York: Library of America, 1986), 188. Along with its companion volume, *History of the United States During the Administrations of James Madison*, ed. Earl N. Harbert (New York: Library of America, 1986), this will no doubt become the standard edition of Adams's great *History*. These volumes began to circulate privately at the end of 1884. The first public publication came in 1889–1891 in a total of nine volumes. The Harbert edition presents the text of the 1903 version containing the last of Adams's many revisions.

26. Brooks D. Simpson, *The Political Education of Henry Adams* (Columbia: University of South Carolina Press, 1996), 145. The use of the word "distorted" suggests the relentlessly hostile character of Simpson's discussion, which is of interest but must be used with at least as much caution as Adams's own account of his life.

1. Foundations of the Early Republic

1. In spite of my decision to begin with a brief look at some of Adams's youthful thoughts on the Civil War, I generally approach his interpretation of the course of American history according to the chronology of the history rather than the chronology of Adams's writing. This seems to be the best way to capture the full sweep of Adams's assessment of the American experiment.

2. Henry Adams, "The Great Secession Winter of 1860–61," in *Great Secession Winter*, 4. This collection, edited by Hochfield, includes almost all of Adams's important journalism.

3. Ibid., 30.

4. Henry Adams to Charles Francis Adams, Jr., July 8, 1864, in *Letters* 1:442. There is a useful selection of Adams's Civil War correspondence in *The Real War Will Never Get in the Books: Selections from Writers During the Civil War*, ed. Louis P. Masur (New York: Oxford University Press, 1993), 3–17.

5. Henry Adams to Charles Francis Adams, Jr., November 25, 1864, 1:458.

6. Henry Adams to Charles Francis Adams, Jr., May 10, 1865, in *Letters*, 1:495–96.

7. Andrew Delbanco, "The Seer of Lafayette Square," *New Republic* (October 16, 1989), 36. Delbanco's brief article is very insightful.

8. Henry Adams to Charles Francis Adams, Jr., March 27, 1863, in *Letters*, 1:339.

9. Henry Adams, *The United States in 1800* (Ithaca, N.Y.: Cornell University Press, 1955). For the estimate of their readership see Levenson, *Mind and Art*, 149. For the only major critical assessment of these opening chapters, see Noble Cunningham, Jr., *The United States in 1800: Henry Adams Revisited* (Charlottesville: University Press of Virginia, 1988). See also William R. Taylor, "Historical Bifocals on the Year 1800," *New England Quarterly* 23 (1950), 172–86. Cunningham notes that as of 1986, the Cornell paperback had gone through seventeen printings and had sold 131,000 copies (*Adams Revisited*, 3). The book is still in print.

10. *History* I, 5, 7.

11. Ibid., 20.

12. Ibid., 15. On other primitive conditions, see Taylor, "Historical Bifocals," 179.

13. Quoted in ibid., 13.

14. Ibid., 9.

15. Ibid., 7, 9.

16. Ibid., 47–53, quote at 49.

17. Ibid., 47.

18. Ibid., 52–53.

19. Ibid., 11.

20. Ibid., 31.

21. Ibid., 54–55.

22. Ibid., 57.

23. Ibid., 59. One popular answer to every democratic idea was simply, "Look at France!" which became a "monomania with the New England leaders." Such ideas have recently been revived in the remarkable diatribe by Conor Cruise O'Brien, *The Long Affair: Thomas Jefferson and the French Revolution, 1785–1800* (Chicago: University of Chicago Press, 1996).

24. Fisher Ames and George Cabot quoted in *History* I, 59–60.

25. Alexander Hamilton quoted in ibid., 61.

26. Ibid.

27. Ibid. Whatever the deficiencies of Jefferson, these "High Federalists" were as bad or worse. At their worst, these Federalists were, in the pungent terms of Richard Hofstadter, "crazed vendettists and reckless conspirators" (*The Progressive Historians: Turner, Beard, Parrington* [New York: Alfred A. Knopf, 1968], 32). Adams would no doubt have agreed.

28. *History* I, 67.

29. Ibid., 72–75, quotes at 72, 74.

30. Ibid., 76–77.

31. Ibid., 78.

32. Ibid., 79–80. It should be remembered that the alliance Adams discusses was in fact the founding of what is now the Democratic Party.

33. Ibid., 80.

34. Ibid., 81.

35. Ibid., 90.

36. William Ellery Channing quoted in ibid., 92.

37. Ibid., 93–95.

38. Henry Adams to Charles Francis Adams, Jr., September 5, 1862, in *Letters* 1:309–10.

39. *History* I, 95–96.

40. Ibid., 99. There is no doubt that in some sense Adams sees Jefferson as a great man, but he also appears so deeply flawed as to raise the question whether Adams accepted the "admitted standards."

41. On Jefferson and happiness, see John Schaar, ". . . And the Pursuit of Happiness," in *The Legitimacy of the Modern State* (New Brunswick, N.J.: Transaction Books, 1981), 231–50.

42. *History* I, 100–101.

43. John Adams to Thomas Jefferson, September 3, 1816, in *The Adams-Jefferson Letters*, ed. Lester J. Cappon (Chapel Hill: University of North Carolina Press, 1959), 487.

44. *History* I, 101–2.

45. Ibid., 102–6. Adams's brief discussion of the young John C. Calhoun in 1800 is interesting. He is portrayed as cold and rigid but a fervent Jeffersonian with little affection for slavery. "A radical democrat, less liberal, less cultivated, and much less genial than Jefferson, Calhoun was the true heir to his intellectual succession; stronger in logic, bolder in action" (ibid., 106). Adams refrains from discussing where the thought of the mature Calhoun was to take him as his zeal for democracy lessened and his support for slavery increased and he helped take his region down the road to the secession that Adams despised.

46. Ibid., 120.

47. Ibid., 107–8; emphasis added.

48. Ibid., 108–9, quotes on 109. In writing of the new man, did Adams have in mind Hector St. John de Crevecoeur?

49. Ibid., 109–19. On bourgeois radicalism, see Isaac Kramnick, *Republicanism and Bourgeois Radicalism* (Ithaca, N.Y.: Cornell University Press, 1990).

50. *History* I, 121.

51. Ibid., 122–23. Without mentioning his name, Adams uses his own great-grandfather John as support for his theory of upward mobility, pointing out that the incumbent president in 1800, who, with Benjamin Franklin, had signed the peace treaty with Britain, was the son of a small farmer and had been a schoolteacher in his youth.

52. Ibid., 125.

53. Richard Hofstadter, *America at 1750* (New York: Alfred A. Knopf, 1971), 4; Cunningham, *Adams Revisited*, 4–5.

54. Cunningham, *Henry Adams Revisited*, 7.

55. Ibid., 10.

56. Ibid., 17–19.

57. I disagree sharply with Cunningham's suggestion that Adams may have devoted excessive attention to sectionalism. See ibid., 57.

58. Ibid., 25–43; on the South, see Eugene Genovese, *The Political Economy of Slavery* (New York: Vintage Books, 1967). Genovese's work is controversial. For a brief assessment and a guide to the literature, see James P. Young, *Reconsidering American Liberalism: The Troubled Odyssey of the Liberal Idea* (Boulder, Colo.: Westview Press, 1996), 111–12, and the literature cited there. Cunningham points out that Adams has little to say about slavery except that it depressed the South. This is a major point of Genovese's.

59. At the same time, it is worth stressing that the sort of history Adams was writing in these introductory chapters was something quite new and that he did go to some lengths to give his sources a critical evaluation, though the evaluation might be inadequate by twentieth-century standards and, of course, relevant data and secondary studies are now more accessible.

60. Cunningham, *Adams Revisited*, 45–46.

61. Ibid., 51.

62. On the last point, see Merrill Peterson, *The Jefferson Image in the American Mind* (New York: Oxford University Press, 1960), 285–86.

63. Cunningham, *Adams Revisited*, 52.

64. On Jefferson's ambiguity, see Young, *Reconsidering American Liberalism*, 81–91, 108–9.

65. Jefferson to Spencer Roane, September 6, 1819, quoted in Cunningham, *Adams Revisited*, 51. For a full-scale effort to take Jefferson seriously on this point, see Daniel Sisson, *The American Revolution of 1800* (New York: Alfred A. Knopf, 1974).

66. *Life of Gallatin*, 170.

67. Ibid., 199.

68. Ibid., 211. Adams even resorts to the use of Jefferson's own language to describe aspects of the tense situation, though he does concede some exaggeration. See ibid., 206.

69. It is striking how much of Adams's argument is echoed by Hofstadter in *America at 1750*, 131–79. It might be thought that this title is an homage to Adams, but Hofstadter's widow, who edited the posthumous publication of this fragment of his intended magnum opus, says that it was modeled on Halevy's *England in 1815*.

70. For a similar point, see Hofstadter, *America at 1750*, 132–33.

71. Henry James, *Hawthorne* (1879), in *Essays on Literature, American Writers, English Writers*, ed. Leon Edel (New York: Library of America, 1984), 351–52.

72. *History* II, 1344.

73. Hofstadter, *America at 1750*, 132–33.

74. See Gordon Wood, *The Radicalism of the American Revolution* (New York: Alfred A. Knopf, 1991), and Joyce Appleby, *Inheriting the Revolution* (Cambridge: Harvard University Press, 2000). In another recent book, Jon Butler pushes these modernizing tendencies back to 1680 and argues that even in the colonial period,

the territory that was to become the United States was the most modern in the world, including Britain. This too points to an exceptionalist thesis. However, Gordon Wood contends that Butler misconceives the nature of early American modernity, since he focuses on ethnic and religious diversity rather than on the idea of equal and independent citizens for whom authority had to be earned and consented to. See Jon Butler, *Becoming America: The Revolution Before 1776* (Cambridge: Harvard University Press, 2000), and Gordon Wood, "Give Me Diversity or Give Me Death," *New Republic* (June 12, 2000), 34–39. For Wood's discussion of Appleby, see "Early American Get-up-and-go," *New York Review of Books* (June 29, 2000), 50–53.

75. Wood, "Early American Get-up-and-go," 50. Some, including Appleby, might argue that this theory is an intellectually constructed myth, but Wood contends that it was "rooted in the lives of many ordinary Americans" (53). Much of Appleby's analysis seems to bear him out, though it is clear that much of the emerging consensus applies better to the North than to the South. In particular, she stresses the rapidly emerging differences between North and South, a view to which Adams could fully subscribe. Also, Wood admits that the new social history of the past generation raises questions about the tendency of the consensus theory to overlook race, slavery, the poor, the immigrants, and the victims of persecution.

76. William Ian Miller, *Humiliation* (Ithaca, N.Y.: Cornell University Press, 1993), 209.

77. Henry Adams to Charles Francis Adams, Jr., May 1, 1863, in *Letters* 1:350.

78. Alexis de Tocqueville, *Democracy in America*, trans. George Lawrence (Garden City, N.Y.: Anchor Books, 1969), 509.

79. Louis Hartz, *The Liberal Tradition in America* (New York: Harcourt Brace, 1955).

2. The Jeffersonian Foundation

1. Robert W. Tucker, *Empire of Liberty: The Statecraft of Thomas Jefferson* (New York: Oxford University Press, 1990), 3.

2. *History* I, 117.

3. Martin Diamond quoted in Joyce Appleby, "Jefferson: A Political Reappraisal," *Democracy* (fall 1983), 140.

4. Adams's great *History* has been discussed primarily in relation to his philosophy. While I do not neglect this topic, I want to consider the work as part of a theory about the course of American history, which gradually flows into his more general philosophical concerns.

5. A disclaimer is in order. I cannot hope to establish the historical validity of Adams's view of Jefferson, though it is sometimes necessary to consult the literature on the Master of Monticello. My interest lies in what that view tells us about Adams. Jefferson will continue to remain a mystery, though so too may Adams. For my own brief attempt to sketch Jefferson, see James P. Young, *Reconsidering American Liberalism:*

The Troubled Odyssey of the Liberal Idea (Boulder, Colo.: Westview Press, 1996), and the works cited there. The literature on Jefferson's thought is huge. For two divergent but interesting studies, see Richard K. Matthews, *The Radical Politics of Thomas Jefferson: A Revisionist View* (Lawrence: University Press of Kansas, 1984), and Lance Banning, *The Jeffersonian Persuasion: Evolution of a Party Ideology* (Ithaca, N.Y.: Cornell University Press, 1978). For a comprehensive, though now dated, consideration of the vast body of literature on Jefferson, see Merrill Peterson, *The Jefferson Image in the American Mind* (New York: Oxford University Press, 1960). A more recent, detailed work on Jefferson's constitutional theory is David N. Mayer, *The Constitutional Thought of Thomas Jefferson* (Charlottesville: University of Virginia Press, 1994). Recent literature on Jefferson has often been very critical. See Peter Onuf, *Jefferson's Empire: The Language of American Nationhood* (Charlottesville: University of Virginia Press, 2000), and Peter Onuf, ed., *Jeffersonian Legacies* (Charlottesville: University of Virginia Press, 1993). In the latter, the papers by Joyce Appleby and Gordon Wood are particularly well balanced. Much of the criticism revolves around the deep conflict between Jefferson's natural rights principles and his ownership of slaves. See Jan Ellen Lewis and Peter Onuf, eds., *Sally Hemings and Thomas Jefferson* (Charlottesville: University of Virginia Press, 1999). In spite of his hostility to slavery, the tension between Jefferson's beliefs and actions on this subject are not part of Adams's discussion.

6. Merrill D. Peterson, "Henry Adams on Jefferson the President," *Virginia Quarterly Review* (spring 1963), 190.

7. Samuels, *Middle Years*, 387.

8. Jordy, *Scientific Historian*, 73.

9. Henry Adams to Henry Cabot Lodge, May 15, 1876, *Letters* 2:263. In a letter to Henry Cabot Lodge, he comments that "much as I want to read your Hamilton, the subject repels me more than my regard for you attracts" (quoted in Jordy, *Scientific Historian*, 67). Wilson Carey McWilliams points out that Adams's dislike for Hamilton goes back to the political enmity between John Adams and Hamilton, the latter having supported Jefferson in the close election of 1800; moreover, Adams detested Hamilton's sexual morals.

10. Peterson, *Jefferson Image*, 285. Peter Shaw gives a useful brief survey of the interpretive situation. He forcefully supports the position that the *History* presents a scathing indictment of the Jeffersonians and a defense of the Adams family against them. The analysis is useful and stimulating, but I cannot entirely agree. See Peter Shaw, "Blood Is Thicker than Irony," *New England Quarterly* (June 1967), 163–87. There is reason to think that the *History* might be even more pro-Jefferson had it not been for the intervention of Adams's older brother Charles Francis Adams, Jr. In commenting on the privately printed draft manuscript, Charles was ever watchful for signs that Henry was soft on Jefferson. Henry frequently gave in to Charles's criticisms. See Samuels, *Middle Years*, 390–97. See also Peter Shaw, "The War of 1812 Could Not Take Place: Henry Adams's History," *Yale Review* (June 1973), 544–56. For a com-

mentary on some recent literature dealing with the period that is critical of Adams's scholarship or interpretations, see William Dusinberre, *The Myth of Failure* (Charlottesville: University Press of Virginia, 1980), 147–57. On the whole, Dusinberre tends to support Adams's interpretations.

11. *History* I, 188.

12. Ibid., 100–101.

13. Ibid., esp. 58–59. One finds the same hysteria to this day; Jefferson still stirs enormous passion in all parts of the political spectrum. See, in this instance, Conor Cruise O'Brien, *The Long Affair: Thomas Jefferson and the French Revolution, 1785–1800* (Chicago: University of Chicago Press, 1996). This is one of the most intemperate assaults on Jefferson ever; it links him with even Pol Pot and Timothy McVeigh (who was found guilty of bombing the Federal Building in Oklahoma City), not to mention the Ku Klux Klan. Of course, Jefferson did admire France, but for a more sober view, see William Howard Adams, *The Paris Years of Thomas Jefferson* (New Haven, Conn.: Yale University Press, 1997). Earl Harbert perceptively notes that Adams "seems to attribute greatness of mind, not to any Adams but to Thomas Jefferson" (Earl N. Harbert, *The Force so Much Closer Home: Henry Adams and the Adams Family* [New York: New York University Press, 1977], 90).

14. *History* I, 99–100.

15. One observation on Jefferson's principles is of interest. Henry's father, Charles Francis Adams, wrote in a Fourth of July letter to Charles Francis Adams, Jr., "Had they [our ancestors] then consented to follow Thomas Jefferson to the full extent of the first draught of the Declaration, they would have added little to the seven years severity of their struggle and would have entirely saved the present trials from their children" (quoted in Levenson, *Mind and Art*, 11). Of course, the reference is to Jefferson's early proposal to end slavery. Jefferson's position on this question is characteristically more ambiguous than the senior Adams makes it. See Joseph Ellis, *American Sphinx: The Character of Thomas Jefferson* (New York: Alfred A. Knopf, 1997), 51–53.

16. *Life of Gallatin*, 491–92. Note the high place assigned to Gallatin in this assessment.

17. For the full text of the address, see Thomas Jefferson, *Writings*, ed. Merrill Peterson (New York: Library of America, 1984), 492–96.

18. *History* I, 135.

19. Thomas Jefferson quoted in ibid., 136.

20. Ibid.

21. Ibid., 137.

22. Thomas Jefferson, paraphrased from ibid., 138–39. The phrase "entangling alliances," often attributed to Washington in his Farewell Address, was actually coined by Jefferson. See Ellis, *American Sphinx*, 181.

23. *History* I, 139.

24. Ibid.

25. Ibid., 97–99, 140. For the text of the Virginia Resolution, see *The Mind of the Founder: Sources of the Political Thought of James Madison*, ed. Marvin Meyers (Indianapolis: Bobbs Merrill, 1973), 297–349. Madison, working closely with Jefferson, was the author of the Virginia Resolution. For the Kentucky Resolution, which Jefferson authored, see Jefferson, *Writings*, 449–56.

26. Jefferson, *Notes on Virginia*, in *Writings*, 241.

27. *History* I, 140–41, 175–76.

28. Ibid., 141. This raises an interesting question. How are we to judge so contradictory a figure as Jefferson? His private opinions were frequently more radical than his public statements and actions. Which standard do we adopt? Perhaps the real Jefferson, in spite of his inflammatory private rhetoric, was a cautious compromiser who liked to give vent to his dreams in his voluminous correspondence. The "real" Jefferson is elusive, but this remains one of the possibilities. To the extent that Adams is like his protagonist, perhaps he shares in this ambiguity.

29. Ibid., 142.

30. On the preference for agriculture over manufacturing and the dislike of cities, see Jefferson, *Notes on Virginia*, 290–91.

31. *History* I, 142–43.

32. Ibid., 143.

33. Ibid., 144.

34. Thomas Jefferson quoted in ibid., 146–47.

35. Ibid., 147. As can be seen today, the use of economic power to achieve foreign policy ends is a persistent theme in American history. It might also be observed that it frequently meets with as little success today as it did in the days of Jefferson and Madison.

36. For background on the Jefferson presidency, see Dumas Malone, *Jefferson the President: First Term, 1801–1805* (Boston: Houghton Mifflin, 1970) and *Jefferson the President: Second Term, 1805–1809* (Boston: Houghton Mifflin, 1974) for a favorable account. For a critical view, see Forrest McDonald, *The Presidency of Thomas Jefferson* (Lawrence: University Press of Kansas, 1976). For a slightly more theoretical account, see Forrest McDonald, *The American Presidency: An Intellectual History* (Lawrence: University Press of Kansas, 1992), 245–74. For a political scientist's analysis of Jefferson's presidency see Stephen Skowronek, *The Politics Presidents Make: Leadership from John Adams to George Bush* (Cambridge: Harvard University Press, 1993, 62–85). See also the notes, 457–63 for further bibliography. Skowronek classifies Jefferson as a reconstructive president who emerged from opposition to the previous regime. Not being a historian, I do not try to settle the historiographical disputes surrounding Jefferson and Madison. My interest is in Adams's ideas about them as a key to the understanding of his thought. On occasion, I suggest other accounts to supplement Adams's.

37. *History* I, 177, 186–87.

38. Thomas Jefferson, quoted in ibid., 175.

39. Ibid., 189, 202. Not until four years before his death, in a letter to W. T. Berry, did Jefferson call for this radical democratic reform (quoted in ibid., 176). For Adams's detailed account of the judiciary debate, see ibid., 174–77, 186–90, 193–202. One wonders whether Adams would really have favored an elected judiciary. It seems doubtful.

40. Alexander Hamilton quoted in ibid., 188–89. It should be remembered that Hamilton's remark occurs in his famous letter to Senator Bayard, in which he swung his support to Jefferson against Aaron Burr during the struggle to settle the tied election of 1800.

41. Ibid., 180.

42. Ibid., 180. For a fuller discussion, see 180–83.

43. John Marshall quoted in Edward S. Corwin, *The President: Office and Powers*, 3d ed. (New York: New York University Press, 1948), 20. Adams also quotes this passage, but only the prediction that Jefferson would weaken the office of president, without citing Marshall's sense of the dynamics of the situation (see *History* I, 179).

44. *History* I, 362.

45. Thomas Jefferson quoted in ibid., 363.

46. Ibid.

47. Ibid., 366. The first Adams family member to note the reliance on implied powers and the abandonment of republican principles in the Louisiana Purchase was John Quincy Adams, writing in his diary (quoted in Harbert, *The Force so Much Closer Home*, 90–91). The diary notation is brief, and Henry deserves full credit for developing it. Like his grandson, John Quincy Adams had ambivalent feelings about Jefferson. Consider his comment on the relation of John Adams and Jefferson: "The mutual influence of these *two mighty minds* upon each others a phenomenon, like the invisible and mysterious movements of the magnet in the physical world, and in which the sagacity of the future historian may discover the solution of much of our national history not otherwise easily accountable" (quoted in Ellis, *American Sphinx*, 123; emphasis added). Charles Francis Adams was more critical: "He did not always speak exactly as he felt, either towards his friends or his enemies. As a consequence, he has left hanging over a part of his public life a vapor of duplicity" (quoted in ibid., 124).

48. *History* I, 378–79; emphasis added. For a full discussion of the congressional debate, see ibid., 366–79.

49. Ibid., 380–81. This is one of the few direct references to a family member Adams allows himself.

50. Ibid., 381–82.

51. Ibid., 383.

52. Ibid., 384.

53. Ibid., 385–86. Jefferson's bitter enemy John Marshall concurred, with what Adams sarcastically refers to as his "characteristic wisdom," when the issue reached the Supreme Court in *American Insurance Company and Others v. Canter*, saying, "The right to govern may be the inevitable consequence of the right to acquire territory.

Whatever may be the source whence the power is derived, the possession of it is unquestioned" (see ibid., 386).

54. Ibid., 386.

55. Ibid., 387.

56. Ibid., 388.

57. Thomas Jefferson to John Breckinridge quoted in ibid., 359.

58. Ibid., 359–60. Not until the midpoint of the Civil War did *nation* begin to replace *Union* in constitutional language. See James M. McPherson, *Abraham Lincoln and the Second American Revolution* (New York: Oxford University Press, 1990), viii.

59. This interpretation anticipates Sheldon Wolin's stimulating work *The Presence of the Past* (Baltimore: Johns Hopkins University Press, 1987).

60. *History* I, 388.

61. Ibid., 388–89, quote at 389. For a brief but spirited defense of Jefferson's actions, see Ellis, *American Sphinx*, 211–13. The defense is couched in terms of practicality. Debate over an amendment, Ellis contends, would have raised troublesome questions about slavery, the slave trade, Spanish land claims, and other issues. He even defends the "arbitrary and despotic" provisional government established over Louisiana on the grounds of the size and ethnic diversity of the territory. He also correctly points out that on issues such as the debt and the embargo, Jefferson held fast to his principles, "despite massive evidence that they were at odds with reality." For Ellis, the key to Jefferson's actions was his sense that the West was America's future. What Frederick Jackson Turner later called a "safety valve" was for Jefferson "a self-renewing engine that drove the American republic forward. The West was the place where his agrarian idyll could be regularly rediscovered." He saw the West the way some modern optimists see technology. He was startlingly nonchalant about whether all the territory remained within the American Union. Though it became the dominant issue of the next half century, he had little interest in the long-term fate of the territory. One might add that Adams slights Jefferson's almost mystic vision of westward expansion as a means to preserve his ideal republic. This may be due to a certain provincial distaste for the West.

62. On this point, see Judith N. Shklar, "Redeeming American Political Thought," in *Redeeming American Political Thought* (Chicago: University of Chicago Press, 1997), 92.

63. Earl Harbert suggests that in the *History* Adams attempts to show that the "political disasters" of 1800 to 1816 derived from the Southern failure to carry out Jefferson's program. But this implies that Adams thought the Jeffersonian program was right. I argue that Adams accepted the substantive results of the program, while regretting the unprincipled way the ends were achieved. This judgment applies only to the Louisiana Purchase and not to the events of Jefferson's second term. See Harbert, *The Force so Much Closer Home*, 119.

64. Harbert, *The Force so Much Closer Home*, 126–29. Harbert notes that Jeffer-

son's policies made protection from foreign enemies difficult, but Adams, like Jefferson, makes the near doubling of the nation's size the key to the entire *History*. This suggests that Adams had a Jeffersonian sense of importance, though Adams by no means ignored foreign affairs. Harbert notes that with his protestations that he was an eighteenth-century man living in the twentieth century, Adams proclaimed his own obsolescence, but one must take Adams's penchant for dissimulation into account here. J. C. Levenson notes that Adams had "a more than casual relationship with the founders of pragmatism," including Chauncey Wright, Charles Sanders Peirce, and, perhaps most important, William James (see *Mind and Art*, 130). John Diggins comments, "Adams did not have to wait until the pragmatists came along to advise Americans to reject all ideas that cannot be translated into action" (*The Promise of Pragmatism* [Chicago: University of Chicago Press, 1994], 75).

65. Levenson, *Mind and Art*, 132. At the same time Adams wished for theory, he also thought it important to avoid framing issues so technically and legally that a large society could not comprehend them (*History* II, 300). Levenson's outstanding work guided me to this passage.

66. See Russell L. Hanson and W. Richard Merriman, "Henry Adams and the Decline of the Republican Tradition," *American Transcendental Quarterly* (September 1990), 161–83.

67. *Education*, 11; Diggins, *Promise of Pragmatism*, 55.

68. For a theory of authority of this type, see Carl J. Friedrich, "Authority, Reason, and Discretion," in *Authority* (Cambridge: Harvard University Press, 1958), 28–48. It follows from this that no special person or class can lay claim to authority. It must be earned. See Norman Jacobson, "Knowledge, Tradition, and Authority: A Note on the American Experience," in ibid., 112–25. Consider also Michael Walzer's argument that in a just democratic society, political power rightfully goes to the contestants who make the best arguments for their positions (*Spheres of Justice: A Defense of Pluralism and Equality* [New York: Basic Books, 1983], esp. 303–6). Used in this sense, political power is closely linked to authority.

69. *History* I, 471.

70. Ibid., 437.

71. Ibid., 210.

72. Ibid., 438.

73. Ibid., 439.

74. Ibid., 299. On the absolute centrality of peace in Adams's interpretation, see Peterson, *Jefferson Image*, 287–90.

75. *History* I, 525.

76. Ibid., 1020.

77. Ibid., 929–46, passim.

78. Ibid., 1021.

79. Ibid., 1040.

80. Ibid., 1040–44.

81. Ibid., 1045–47.

82. Ibid., 1048; emphasis added.

83. Ibid., 1115.

84. Ibid., 1116.

85. Ibid., 1117. Adams notes that in the end, Jefferson believed that the embargo had no "claim to respect" as an economic policy (see ibid., 1116).

86. Ibid., 1117–18.

87. Ibid.

88. Ibid., 1118.

89. Levenson points out that Adams was less militaristic than such passages make it appear. His interest in military affairs "grew from studious reflection on the nature and possibility of peace," and developed out of his concern with Jefferson's pacifism (see *Mind and Art*, 174). Jordy also plays down the thought that Adams was a militarist, while making interesting comments on this passage (see *Scientific Historian*, 110).

90. *History* I, 1118–21.

91. Ibid., 1121.

92. Ibid., 1122–25.

93. Ibid., 1126.

94. Ibid.

95. For an exhaustive recent survey of the abundant literature on American exceptionalism, see Seymour Martin Lipset, *American Exceptionalism: A Double-edged Sword* (New York: W. W. Norton, 1996).

96. Diggins, *Promise of Pragmatism*, 76.

97 *History* II, 354, 467.

98. Mayer, *Constitutional Thought of Jefferson*, 213–18, quote at 215.

99. Joyce Appleby, *Capitalism and a New Social Order: The Republican Vision of the 1790's* (New York: New York University Press, 1984), 103.

100. Ibid., 104.

101. The last paragraph owes a great deal to comments by Wilson Carey McWilliams, who helped me clarify the issues at stake.

102. Peterson, *Jefferson Image*, 285–86.

3. The Madisonian Continuation

1. Perhaps it should also be suggested that Madison suffers because his greatest contributions were his role in drafting the Constitution and then defending it in the Federalist Papers and his equally large part in drafting the Bill of Rights. All this work falls outside the scope of Adams's study. Since Madison was undoubtedly superior to Jefferson as a theorist, it is unfortunate that Adams did not need to come to grips with these writings. Adams certainly gives every sign of admiring the Constitution Madison did so much to create.

2. *History* I, 129.

3. *History* II, 216–17.

4. Ellis, *American Sphinx*, 123.

5. Samuels, *Middle Years*, 264.

6. *History* II, 7–8.

7. Ibid., 12. For other assessments of the Madison administration that are generally less harsh than Adams's, see Robert Rutland, *The Presidency of James Madison* (Lawrence: University Press of Kansas, 1990), and Ralph Ketcham, *James Madison: A Biography* (Charlottesville: University Press of Virginia, 1990). See also Marcus Cunliffe, "Madison as Commander-in-Chief," in *In Search of America* (New York: Greenwood Press, 1991), 115–38.

8. *History* II, 14–15.

9. Ibid., 16.

10. Ibid., 19.

11. Ibid., 110.

12. Francis Jackson quoted in ibid., 150.

13. On Madison's distrust of unrestricted commerce and his continuing attachment to "peaceable coercion," see *History* II, 148–49, 205. These ideas were a persistent thread throughout the history of his administration until the outbreak of war in 1812.

14. Ibid., 118.

15. Ibid., 447. In general, Adams thinks that the issue of impressment was not well understood. The great majority of those impressed were, in fact, British subjects, and American ships were frequently manned by foreign nationals whose services the United States volunteered to do without, an act not without cost. See, for example, *History* II, 595, 612.

16. For an interesting perspective on this point that has helped me here, see Shaw, "The War of 1812 Could Not Take Place," 544–56. Shaw's title is obviously a little overheated. It would have been better to say that Adams believed that it should not have taken place, at least not when it did.

17. On French policy on the high seas, see *History* II, 22–32; 101–9, esp. 109; 173–82. Nowhere is Adams's hatred of Napoleon more clear than in his discussions of French maritime policy. He notes that the emperor did not act "according to the rules of ordinary civilization" (26) and later gives a more extended assessment of his character:

> Napoleon could seize without notice ten million dollars worth of American property, imprisoning the American crews of two or three hundred vessels in his dungeons, while at the same instant he told the Americans that he loved them, that their commerce was within the scope of his policy, and as a climax avowed a scheme to mislead the United States government, hardly troubling himself to use forms likely to conceal his object; yet the vast majority of Americans never greatly resented acts which seemed to them like the

exploits of an Italian brigand on the stage. Beyond doubt, Napoleon regarded his professions of love and interest not as irony of extravagance, but as adapted to deceive. (Ibid., 181–82)

18. Ibid., 447–49.

19. Ibid., 573. It might be noted that the extremists probably needed little persuasion to convince themselves of this absurd point.

20. Ibid., 905–6.

21. Shaw, "The War of 1812," 547.

22. *History* II, 1221–22.

23. Ibid., 1109.

24. Ibid., 1112.

25. Ibid., 1114.

26. Ibid., 1114–15.

27. For the full text of the proposed amendments, see "Report and Resolutions of the Hartford Convention," January 4, 1815, in *Great Issues in American History: From the Revolution to the Civil War, 1765–1865*, ed. Richard Hofstadter (New York: Vintage Books, 1958), 241. The bias of the amendments is so evident that Madison is said to have laughed aloud when he read them (Rutland, *Presidency of Madison*, 186).

28. *Boston Centinal* and Gouverneur Morris quoted in *History* II, 1116. The approval of the militant Morris and Pickering was important. Pickering approved because he believed the Union to be already dissolved (see ibid., 1116).

29. Ibid., 1120–21.

30. George Ticknor quoting John Adams in ibid., 1122.

31. Ibid.

32. Ibid., 1123.

33. On the dissenting Federalists, see Linda K. Kerber, *Federalists in Dissent: Imagery and Ideology in Jeffersonian America* (Ithaca, N.Y.: Cornell University Press, 1970); James T. Banner, *To the Hartford Convention: The Federalists and the Origins of Party Politics in Massachusetts* (New York: Alfred A. Knopf, 1969); David H. Fischer, *The Revolution in American Federalism: The Federalist Party in the Age of Jeffersonian Democracy* (New York: Harper and Row, 1965). For a more specialized study quite critical of Adams, see David H. Fischer, "The Myth of the Essex Junto," *William and Mary Quarterly*, 3d ser. (April 1964), 191–235. Another important study from the perspective of the Adams family is a very analytic work by political scientist Manning J. Dauer, *The Adams Federalists* (Baltimore: Johns Hopkins University Press, 1968).

34. *History* I, 1019.

35. Ibid., 1020.

36, *History* II, 1342.

37. Ibid., 1336–41. Adams undertakes an extensive analysis of each of the major naval battles and in each case gives a detailed discussion of the gunnery on each side,

invariably demonstrating the superiority of the American performance. Levenson is helpful on these matters; see *Mind and Art*, 176–80.

38. *History* II, 1273–74.

39. Ibid., 1299–1300.

40. *Jordy, Scientific Historian*, 95.

41. Shaw, "The War of 1812," 554. William Anders Smith also sees the hero of the entire work to be the American people (see "Henry Adams, Alexander Hamilton, and the American People as a 'Great Beast,'" *New England Quarterly* [June 1975], 225). He suggests that, like Tocqueville, Adams believed that the future of the world was tied to democracy.

42. *History* II, 1237.

43. John Adams quoted in Shaw, "The War of 1812," 549. Shaw sees John Quincy Adams's view as less favorable to Madison, though that evaluation is not obvious (see ibid.).

44. *History* II, 585–86; emphasis added.

45. Shaw, "The War of 1812," 553. Ernest Samuels reads this passage more literally so that it emerges as praise for Madison (see *Middle Years*, 398).

46. Even if the practice was abandoned, the principle was not. As Wilson Carey McWilliams reminds me, Adams knew full well that the principle could not be abandoned, both because the British thought that it was just, since American ships *did* shelter British deserters and nationals, and because it was potentially important to manning their fleet.

47. *History* II, 1331.

48. Ibid., 1332.

49. John Patrick Diggins, *On Hallowed Ground: Abraham Lincoln and the Foundations of American History* (New Haven, Conn.: Yale University Press, 2000), 99.

50. *History* II, 1287–94.

51. Ibid., 1300.

52. Ibid., 1317.

53. Ibid., 1330.

54. It is striking how little Adams was interested in the American Renaissance of the midcentury. The discussion is similar to Tocqueville's, but unlike his mentor, Adams lived to see the full flowering of American literature. That it made so little impression on one so sensitive is more than a little perplexing.

55. *History* II, 1245.

56. Ibid., 1302.

57. Ibid., 1304.

58. Ibid., 1305–6.

59. Ibid., 1309.

60. Ibid., 1309–12.

61. Ibid., 1312–13. Jefferson quoted at 1312.

62. Ibid., 1313.

63. Ibid., 1314–16. Taylor wrote to answer John Adams's *Defense of the Constitutions of the United States*, which, by the logic of Henry's reasoning, he must also have considered obsolete.

64. *History* II, 1331. The reference to uniformity may well owe something to the influence of Tocqueville.

65. Ibid., 1331–32.

66. Ibid., 1332.

67. Ibid., 1332–35.

68. Ibid., 1334–35.

69. Ibid., 1336. Tocqueville, of course, had a brighter view of American political capacity.

70. Ibid., 1342–43.

71. Ibid., 1345.

72. Levenson, *Mind and Art*, 187.

73. *History* II, 1345. Samuels is inclined to see these questions as purely rhetorical (see *Middle Years*, 352–53), and they are in form. However, I argue below that they are of real substance for the development of American democracy.

74. Henry Adams to Charles Francis Adams, Jr., April 11, 1862, in *Letters* 1:290.

75. Henry Adams to Charles Francis Adams, Jr., October 3, 1863, in *Letters* 1:395–96.

76. Samuels alludes to this comparison, though he does not dwell on it (see *Middle Years*, 349–50, 353). Like anyone concerned with Tolstoy's theory of history, I owe a huge debt to Isaiah Berlin's great essay "The Hedgehog and the Fox," in *Russian Thinkers* (New York: Alfred A. Knopf, 1978), 22–81.

77. Leo Tolstoy, *War and Peace* (Baltimore: Penguin Books, 1957), vol. 2, epilogue, pt. 2, chap. 1, 1402–3.

78. Henry Adams to Samuel J. Tilden, January 24, 1883, in *Letters* 2:491. For Decker's comments on this theme, see *Literary Vocation*, 202–3.

79. Decker, *Literary Vocation*, 183.

80. See Berlin, "Hedgehog and Fox," 81. For a fuller discussion, see chapter 8.

81. *History* I, 907. Samuels notes that in his draft, Adams claimed that in 1808 Congress could have doubled its proportions of tailors and swindlers if it could have lessened the number of "gentlemen." Reading the draft, his brother Charles persuaded him to change "gentlemen" to "conspirators" (Samuels, *Middle Years*, 378–79).

4. Secession, Capitalism, and Corruption

1. *Education*, 325. This statement may suggest that Lincoln had a greater significance for Adams than his rather cursory remarks suggest.

2. Henry Adams, "Von Holst's 'Administration of Andrew Jackson,'" in *Sketches from the North American Quarterly*, ed. Edward Chalfant (New York: Archon Books, 1986), 139–46. Later, Adams gave to von Holst's extended analysis a detailed treat-

ment that reveals a great deal about his assessment of American political and constitutional history.

3. Ibid., 141.

4. Ibid., 142.

5. Ibid., 144.

6. Henry Adams, "Von Holst's History of the United States," in *Great Secession Winter*, 285.

7. *Randolph*, 37.

8. Ibid., 51–52.

9. See Robert McColley's introduction to *Randolph*, 16.

10. *Randolph*, 52.

11. Ibid., 53.

12. Ibid., 178.

13. Ibid., 179, 189.

14. *Education*, 98–109.

15. *Life of Gallatin*, 635–36.

16. Samuels, *Young Henry Adams*, 95.

17. Charles Francis Adams quoted in ibid., 78.

18. On Adams's political career, see Brooks D. Simpson, *The Political Education of Henry Adams* (Columbia: University of South Carolina Press, 1996). This useful study is a good guide to Adams's political writings following his return from England in 1868. It is also very helpful in searching the letters of this period. Simpson has a real mastery of the sources, though I find the book to be marred by the author's hostility to his subject.

19. *Education*, 7.

20. Samuels, *Young Henry Adams*, 79–80.

21. For a discussion of Lincoln's position, see James P. Young, *Reconsidering American Liberalism: The Troubled Odyssey of the Liberal Idea* (Boulder, Colo.: Westview Press, 1996), and the literature cited therein. See especially Harry V. Jaffa's important book *Crisis of the House Divided* (Garden City, N.Y.: Doubleday, 1959).

22. Henry Adams, "The Great Secession Winter of 1860–61," in *Great Secession Winter*, 20. On the difficulty of destroying slavery without violence, see Young, *Reconsidering American Liberalism*, 120–23 and the literature cited.

23. George Fredrickson, *The Inner Civil War: Northern Intellectuals and the Crisis of the Union* (New York: Harper Torchbooks, 1968), 171–72; Henry Adams to Charles Francis Adams, Jr., May 16, 1862, in *Letters* 1:299.

24. Simpson, *Political Education of Adams*, 25–26.

25. Henry Adams to Charles Francis Adams, Jr., quoted in ibid., 25.

26. Judith N. Shklar, "The Education of Henry Adams by Henry Adams," in *Redeeming American Political Thought*, ed. Stanley Hoffman and Dennis F. Thompson (Chicago: University of Chicago Press, 1998), 83. She adds, "The Civil War

appeared as an inexplicable, accidental destruction of the old America into which he had been born" (ibid.). Against this should be set Adams's denunciations of the slave power.

27. *Education*, 235.

28. Ibid., 253–54.

29. Ibid., 237. Perhaps the influence of Tocqueville's *Democracy in America* can be seen here.

30. Barrington Moore, Jr., *Social Origins of Dictatorship and Democracy: Lord and Peasant in the Making of the Modern World* (Boston: Beacon Press, 1966), 111–55.

31. On this development, see the massive ongoing study of constitutional change by Bruce Ackerman, *We the People I: Foundations* (Cambridge: Harvard University Press, 1991), 82 and passim, and *We the People II: Transformations* (Cambridge: Harvard University Press, 1998), passim. See especially *We the People II*, 113–15, for a brief discussion of whether the South was to be treated as a conquered province, an argument central to the Reconstruction plans of Republican radicals.

32. Robert Wiebe, *The Search for Order: 1877–1920* (New York: Hill and Wang, 1967).

33. Howard Mumford Jones, *The Age of Energy: Varieties of American Experience, 1865–1915* (New York: Viking Books, 1971), xii. For a fuller statement, see 104.

34. Sidney Fine, *Laissez Faire and the General-Welfare State: A Study of Conflict in American Thought, 1865–1901* (Ann Arbor: University of Michigan Press, 1956), 23–24.

35. *Education*, 245–46.

36. Ibid., 260.

37. Ibid., 260–61.

38. Ibid., 262.

39. Ibid.

40. Ibid., 263.

41. Ibid., 263–67.

42. Ibid., 267. On this point, see note ibid., 619 n. 28. In fact, the number of years to meet the goal was about thirty.

43. Ibid., 249.

44. Henry Adams, "The New York Gold Conspiracy," in *Great Secession Winter*, 159.

45. *Education*, 247. Of course, one may be permitted to doubt the truth of Adams's claim that he was not worthy of credit. State Street refers to the center of the Boston banking industry.

46. Henry Adams to Hugh Milnes Gaskell, March 7, 1870, in *Letters* 2:65. The article in question was based on work done by his friend Francis Walker, but to protect Walker, who had become census superintendent, Adams assumed full authorial responsibility. See Samuels, *Young Henry Adams*, 192. In one of the running themes of *The Political Education of Henry Adams*, Brooks Simpson contends that Adams often undercut his effectiveness by the violence of his polemical style.

47. Henry Adams, "The Legal Tender Act," in *Great Secession Winter*, esp. 142.

48. Ibid., 145.

49. Ibid., 134.

50. Ibid., 134–35.

51. Ibid., 148–49.

52. If *McCulloch v. Maryland* had not already done the job, then certainly "the constitutionalization of paper money was one of the achievements of Republican Reconstruction" (Ackerman, *Foundations*, 167). See also *The Legal Tender Cases*, 79 U.S. (12 Wall.) 457 (1871).

53. Ackerman, *Foundations*, 150.

54. William Pitt Fessenden quoted in ibid., 151.

55. On Adams's faith in laissez-faire economics, see Samuels, *Young Henry Adams*, 193. Samuels comments, "For a devotee of the Constitution he was uttering more dangerous doctrine than he knew, as the arguments of the higher law had already cost a civil war and could more properly be asserted by non-idolaters." The opinion recalls Adams's 1861 comment that it was futile for the stonemasons' union to strike for the nine-hour day, as such matters are "regulated by rules which are beyond the just range of mere enacted law" (quoted in ibid., 194).

56. Adams quoted in *Great Secession Winter*, 61, editor's note. On the question of reaching cultivated minds, Adams writes, "The difference is slight, to the influence of an author, whether he is read by five hundred readers, or by five hundred thousand; if he can select the five hundred, he reaches the five thousand" (*Education*, 259).

57. Henry Adams, "The Session, " in *Great Secession Winter*, 64. For Theodore Lowi, see *The End of Liberalism*, 2d ed. (New York: W. W. Norton, 1979).

58. Adams, "The Session," 65–66.

59. Ibid., 67–68.

60. Ibid., 70.

61. Ibid., 71.

62. Massachusetts Bill of Rights quoted in Henry Adams, "Civil Service Reform," in *Great Secession Winter*, 97.

63. Ibid., 98–99.

64. Ibid., 102.

65. Ibid. Interestingly, though one can hardly think of Lincoln as a weak president, Adams says that it was in his administration that Congress first assumed that local patronage was its right (ibid., 103).

66. Ibid., 104.

67. Ibid., 113.

68. Ibid., 125.

69. Ibid., 127.

70. Adams, "New York Gold Conspiracy," 162–63.

71. Ibid., 164.

72. Ibid., 159.

73. *Education*, 269–70.

74. Ibid., 271. For a brief but highly readable account of the scandal, see Matthew Josephson, *The Robber Barons* (1934; reprint, New York: Harvest Books, 1962), 141–48.

75. Adams, "New York Gold Conspiracy," 189.

76. Charles E. Lindblom, *Politics and Markets* (New York: Basic Books; 1977), 356.

77. *Education*, 292. Adams points out that the article on the gold conspiracy was also "instantly pirated on a great scale" (ibid.).

78. Henry Adams to Charles Milnes Gaskell, December 19, 1870, in *Letters* 2:95.

79. Henry Adams, "The Session, 1869–1870," in *Great Secession Winter*, 193–94.

80. Ibid., 195–99.

81. Ibid., 202. Adams notes again the corruption of the great cities and the growth of corporate power (ibid., 205).

82. Ibid., 205, 222.

83. Gustav von Holst quoted by Adams, "Von Holst's History of the United States," 260–61.

84. On Constitution worship, see the exhaustive recent study by Michael Kammen, *A Machine that Would Go of Itself* (New York: Alfred A. Knopf, 1986). On the closeness of original ratification, see Norman Jacobson, "Parable and Paradox; In Response to Arendt's *On Revolution*," *Salmagundi* (spring/summer 1983), 135, and Richard J. Ellis, "The Persistence of Anti-Federalism After 1789," in *Beyond Confederation: Origins of the Constitution and American National Identity*, ed. Richard Beeman, Stephen Botein, and Edward C. Carter II (Chapel Hill: University of North Carolina Press, 1987), 295–314.

85. Adams, "Von Holst's History of the United States," 262–64, quote at 264.

86. Ibid., 265.

87. Ibid., 266–67, 270.

88. Ibid., 271–75, Adams quote at 275. Von Holst's history concludes with 1833.

89. Ibid., 275.

90. Alexander Hamilton quoted in ibid., 276.

91. Ibid., 279–80.

92. Ibid., 280–81.

93. Ibid., 285–86.

94. Ibid., 286. Interestingly, a similar point is made about the War of 1812. That war was deservedly popular, says Adams, not because of military glory or even naval glory. Rather, "it showed that there is such a thing as self-respect in a nation," and "it did more to strengthen the national feeling than all the twenty-five years that had preceded it." Moreover, just as with the South, "New England learned then, once and for all, not to trifle with the Constitution and with the Union" (ibid., 284).

95. Ibid., 258. Adams cannot resist a dig at von Holst's German perspective. Noting von Holst's tendency to patronize American history and statesmen, and alluding

to Bismarck, Adams suggests that "however bad an institution Tammany Hall may be, it at least did not corrupt our American universities, nor pervert the moral sense of our historians" (ibid., 282).

96. Ibid., 287.

97. Henry Adams, "The 'Independents' in the Canvass," in *Great Secession Winter*, 291–92.

98. Ibid.

99. Ibid., 292–93.

100. Ibid., 301, 324. Still, he was surely, if perhaps sadly, right that "the South will in the future be left to work out its own destiny undisturbed by national interference" (ibid., 303).

101. Ibid., 293–94.

102. Ibid., 298–301.

103. Ibid., 306–7.

104. Ibid., 307–8.

105. Ibid., 327–30, quote at 330. Here it seems that Adams had the British civil service in mind.

106. Ibid., 326–27.

107. Ibid., 322–23. Adams's position offended the Republican Party orthodoxy of the publishers of the *North American Review*, so he had to give up his position as editor, though he was no doubt ready to do so anyway. See Samuels, *Young Henry Adams*, 286.

108. Adams, "'Independents' in the Canvass," 319. The phrase "forms and formalities" is Harvey Mansfield's (see *America's Constitutional Soul* [Baltimore: Johns Hopkins University Press, 1991], 193–208).

5. Democracy and Empire

1. For a discussion of who is represented by the characters in the novel, see Samuels, *Middle Years*, 84–97.

2. *Democracy*, 25. This intense "Americanness," if that is the proper term, is very like Marion "Clover" Adams, Henry Adams's wife. Henry James said, "Clover Adams is the incarnation of my native land" (quoted in Eugenia Kaledin, *The Education of Mrs. Henry Adams* [Amherst: University of Massachusetts Press, 1994], 13). Always clear-headed, Clover notes this remark and adds that this is "a most equivocal compliment coming from him. Am I then vulgar, dreary, and impossible to live with. . . . Poor America! She must drag on somehow without the sympathy & love of her denationalised children. I fancy she'll weather it" (quoted in ibid., 18). Kaledin's study is notable as a biography of Mrs. Adams; as an illustration of how difficult it was for a woman of outstanding ability to find an outlet for her intelligence in nineteenth-century America; and, not least, for its insights into the work of Henry Adams.

3. *Democracy*, 2–8, 39. Other less central but still striking aspects of Madeleine's

character include the fact that "she herself had not entered a church in years; she said it gave her unchristian feelings," and "she was something more than republican—a little communistic at heart" (ibid., 11, 149). Her thoughts on religion link Madeleine to the title character in *Esther*.

4. The summary is that of Denis Donoghue, "Henry Adams' Novels," in *Nineteenth Century Fiction* (September 1994), 188–89.

5. *Democracy*, 17.

6. Ibid., 37.

7. Ibid., 38.

8. Ibid., 40. As William Decker points out, Gore's views are confirmed by Adams in the chapter "American Ideals" in the *History*. See Decker, *Literary Vocation*, 152.

9. *Democracy*, 40–41.

10. Irving Howe, *Politics and the Novel* (New York: Meridian Books, 1987), 181; Samuels, *Middle Years*, 86. On occasion, Adams liked to boast (or perhaps tease) that he enjoyed striking a "blow at democracy." But I think it is right to note of the novel, along with Samuels, that "violent as the satire was, it reflected a mind eager to amend democracy." Not knowing who the anonymous author was, a friend wrote to Mrs. Adams, "The author seemed to me profoundly convinced that America had made the only solution worth having of the problem of government" (Samuels, *Middle Years*, 84).

11. Levenson, *Mind and Art*, 93.

12. Henry James quoted in Kaledin, *Education of Mrs. Adams*, 13.

13. Howe, *Politics and the Novel*, 179–80.

14. *Democracy*, 42–44.

15. Ibid., 53.

16. Ibid., 80–81.

17. Ibid., 151.

18. For an outstanding modern treatment of this problem, see Michael Walzer, "Dirty Hands," in *War and Moral Responsibility*, ed. Marshall Cohen (Princeton, N.J.: Princeton University Press, 1974), 85–103.

19. *Democracy*, 54.

20. Ibid., 55.

21. Ibid., 173–76.

22. Ibid., 182, 168.

23. Michael Colacurcio, "*Democracy* and *Esther*: Henry Adams's Flirtation with Pragmatism," *American Quarterly* (spring 1967), 53–70.

24. Ibid., 60.

25. *Democracy*, 89.

26. Colacurcio, "Adams's Flirtation," 60–61. There is an interesting alternative reading of the conclusion of *Democracy*. Fuehrer suggests that Madeleine Lee's sister Sybil strikes a balance between idealism and realism that Adams approves of. She too is an idealist, but she is quite willing to conspire with Nathan Gore to provide her

sister with documentary evidence that Ratcliffe is guilty of bribery in order to induce her to turn down his proposal. This suggests that she is willing to play "hardball" politics in order to further her idealistic ends. Thus, she is willing to go beyond mere moralizing in pursuit of her political goals, without abandoning her moral distaste for Ratcliffe and, more generally, her dislike of the endemic corruption of late-nineteenth-century politics. As Fuehrer says in her conclusion, Sybil "assures that it is possible to employ the darker elements of political power in the service of idealism." Perhaps Adams intended us to come away with this lesson. See Natalie Fuehrer, "The Landscape of Democracy," *Legal Studies Forum* 4 (1998), 627–39, quote at 639. However, Sybil is a relatively minor character in the novel, and this interpretation does not square with Adams's withdrawal from active politics. However, to see this aspect of the book's arguments shows the richness of Adams's thinking on the problem of the relationship of politics to morality.

27. On the Mugwumps, I have been influenced by Richard Hofstadter, *The Age of Reform* (New York: Alfred A. Knopf, 1955), 137–43, and Martin Shefter, *Political Parties and the State: The American Historical Experience* (Princeton, N.J.: Princeton University Press, 1994), 72–75. One need not fully endorse Hofstadter's well-known though controversial theory of status anxiety to see that it has an uncanny power to explain Henry Adams.

28. Hofstadter, *Age of Reform*, esp. 140–43. Hofstadter's remarks on the ineffectuality of the reformers should be qualified a little. Elections during the period tended to be quite close, so the Mugwumps often held the balance of power. Thus they were instrumental in securing passage of the Pendleton Act. However, this achievement did little to alter the course of politics as the century drew to a close. See Shefter, *Political Parties and the State*, 74.

29. For a good brief summary of the party system of the time, see Gerald M. Pomper, *Passions and Interests: Political Party Concepts of American Democracy* (Lawrence: University Press of Kansas, 1992), 70–84. On financial corruption, see the brilliant chapter in Richard Hofstadter, *The American Political Tradition*, 25th anniversary ed. (New York: Alfred A. Knopf, 1973), 162–82. For a fuller treatment, see the still classic account by Matthew Josephson, *The Robber Barons* (1934; reprint New York: Harvest Books, 1962).

30. An important treatment that is also a classic in sociological theory is Robert K. Merton, "The Latent Functions of the Political Machine," in *Social Theory and Social Structure* (Glencoe, Ill.: Free Press, 1957), 72–82.

31. For similar views, see Howe, *Politics and the Novel*, 180, and Decker, *Literary Vocation*, 149–52.

32. Adams quoted by Ari Hoogenboom, "Henry Adams and Politics," in *Henry Adams and His World*, ed. David R. Contosta and Robert Muccigrosso (Philadelphia: American Philosophical Society, 1993), 29. It is worth noting that the sentiments quoted here were written in an 1869 letter; he made many more enthusiastic pronouncements on democracy in the mid-1880s.

33. On the dangers of premature closure in political theory, see Sheldon S. Wolin, "On the Theory and Practice of Power," in *After Foucault; Humanistic Knowledge; Postmodern Challenges*, ed. Jonathan Arac (New Brunswick, N.J.: Rutgers University Press, 1988), esp. 198–99.

34. On the letters as a guide to Adams's views on foreign policy I relied heavily on David R. Contosta, "Henry Adams and the American Century," in *Adams and His World*, 36–47. There is no way I could surpass Contosta's thorough job of mining the primary sources in the letters, so I followed his research here.

35. Characteristically, Adams played down his influence on Hay; see *Education*, 366. Per contra, see Samuels, *Major Phase*, 409, and Contosta, "Adams and the American Century," 39.

36. Henry Adams to John Hay, December 16, 1900, in *Letters* 5:180.

37. Hofstadter, *Age of Reform*, 91. He names Brooks and Henry Adams, Theodore Roosevelt, Henry Cabot Lodge, John Hay, and Albert J. Beveridge as Mugwumps.

38. Contosta, "Adams and the American Century," 43–47. Contosta provides a guide to the primary sources as found in the letters. He is right to note how Adams subdues his long-standing Anglophobia in what he took to be the interests of peace.

39. *Education*, 423.

40. Samuels, *Major Phase*, 246–47; *Education*, 417.

41. Contosta, "Adams and the American Century," 41–42.

42. Woodrow Wilson, *Congressional Government*, introduction by Walter Lippmann (1885; reprint, Cleveland: Meridian Books, 1956); James Bryce, *The American Commonwealth* (Indianapolis: Liberty Press, 1995). The balance of power between the legislative and executive branches established by the Constitution was clearly nondefinitive. Lippmann suggests that there is a cyclical alteration of power (see Wilson, *Congressional Government*, 7–8). Wilson described the executive end of this tension in his 1908 book *Constitutional Government*.

43. Hoogenboom, "Adams and Politics," 37. Hoogenboom's article is a fine brief summary of Adams's political efforts. On the limitations of the Pendleton Act, see Stephen Skowronek, *Building a New American State: The Expansion of National Administrative Capacities, 1877–1920* (Cambridge and New York: Cambridge University Press, 1982), 78–84.

44. *Education*, 343–45.

45. This is a very complex debate that need not be fully explored here. For a sharp contrast between an analysis focused on the context in which institutions operate and one in which institutions are said to have much greater independent force, see Robert A. Dahl, *A Preface to Democratic Theory* (Chicago: University of Chicago Press, 1958), and Harvey Mansfield, Jr., *America's Constitutional Soul* (Baltimore: Johns Hopkins University Press, 1991), esp. 137–62.

46. George Fredrickson, "Nineteenth Century," in *Imagined Histories: American Historians Interpret the Past*, ed. Anthony Molho and Gordon Wood (Princeton, N.J.: Princeton University Press, 1998), 177.

47. See Jack Rakove, *Original Meanings: Politics and Ideas in the Making of the Constitution* (New York: Alfred A. Knopf, 1996), and *Interpreting the Constitution: The Debate over Original Intent* (Boston: Northeastern University Press, 1990). For a lively, if brief, argument against originalism, see Don Herzog, "Approaching the Constitution," *Ethics* (October 1988), 147–54.

48. This view persisted until after the midpoint of the twentieth century. The path-breaking studies that began the great sea change in perception were Kenneth Stampp, *The Era of Reconstruction* (New York: Alfred A. Knopf, 1965), and Eric McKitrick, *Andrew Johnson and Reconstruction* (Chicago: University of Chicago Press, 1960). The standard work today is Eric Foner, *Reconstruction: America's Unfinished Revolution* (New York: Oxford University Press, 1988). For recent surveys of the historiography of Reconstruction, see Eric Foner, "Slavery, the Civil War, and Reconstruction," In *The New American History* (Philadelphia: Temple University Press, 1990), 73–92, and Fredrickson, "Nineteenth Century," 173–84.

49. The classic account of this is C. Vann Woodward, *Origins of the New South: 1877–1913* (Baton Rouge: Louisiana State University Press, 1951), 23–50. For a fully detailed statement, see C. Vann Woodward, *Reunion and Reaction: The Compromise of 1877 and the End of Reconstruction* (1951; reprint, New York: Oxford University Press, 1991).

50. On the nineteenth-century origins of Progressivism and the welfare state, see Fine, *Laissez Faire and the General-Welfare State*, 167–369, and Eldon Eisenach, *The Lost Promise of Progressivism* (Lawrence: University Press of Kansas, 1994), esp. 31–40. For Adams on Marx, see chapter 6. Unlike Henry, his brother Charles did get deeply involved in the regulation movement. For a discussion, see Thomas K. McGraw, *Prophets of Regulation* (Cambridge: Harvard University Press, 1984), 1–56.

51. Perhaps the most powerful statement of this position was Hegel's. For a brilliant discussion, see George Armstrong Kelly, "Hegel's America," in *Hegel's Retreat from Eleusis* (Princeton, N.J.: Princeton University Press, 1978), 184–223, and Skowronek, *Building a New American State*, 6–10. Skowronek broadens his analysis to include Tocqueville and Nietzsche.

52. Skowronek, *Building a New American State*, ix.

53. Hofstadter, *Age of Reform*; Skowronek, *Building a New American Society*, 304. See also Christopher Lasch, "The Moral and Intellectual Rehabilitation of the Ruling Class," in *The World of Nations: Reflections on American History, Politics, and Culture* (New York: Alfred A. Knopf, 1973), 80–99.

54. The issue briefly outlined here has been the subject of extensive discussion. The major source of the idea of liberal domination is Louis Hartz, *The Liberal Tradition in America* (New York: Harcourt Brace, 1955). The republican theory owes most to Bernard Bailyn, *Ideological Origins of the American Revolution* (Cambridge: Harvard University Press, 1967); Gordon Wood, *The Creation of the American Republic* (Chapel Hill: University of North Carolina Press, 1969); and J. G. A. Pocock, *The Machiavellian Moment* (Princeton, N.J.: Princeton University Press, 1975). For a

strong critique, see Isaac Kramnick, *Republicanism and Bourgeois Radicalism* (Ithaca, N.Y.: Cornell University Press, 1990). See also J. G. A. Pocock, "Virtue and Commerce in the Eighteenth Century," *Journal of Interdisciplinary History* (summer 1972), 119–34. For further discussion, see James P. Young, *Reconsidering American Liberalism* (Boulder, Colo.: Westview Press, 1996), and the literature cited therein. Here I leave aside the vexed question of the current vitality of the liberal consensus.

55. Russell L. Hanson and W. Richard Merriman, "Henry Adams and the Decline of the Republican Tradition," *American Transcendental Quarterly* (September 1990), 161–83. This is the best work done by any political theorists on Adams. Though we differ on how early the decline of republicanism began, the general outlines of our positions are close, and I have learned a great deal from this piece. In the following discussion of Adams and republicanism, I have drawn heavily on it. On the broader setting of their argument, see Russell L. Hanson, *The Democratic Imagination in America* (Princeton, N.J.: Princeton University Press, 1985). For my comments on this fine study, see my review in *Political Theory* (May 1987), 265–69.

56. Hanson and Merriman, "Adams and the Decline of Republican Tradition," 167.

57. Ibid., 169. One is reminded of the opening of Karl Marx's Eighteenth Brumaire of Louis Napoleon.

58. This should not be taken as an endorsement of the republican argument. That is another topic I leave open here. For an interesting and skeptical discussion of the republican revival, see Don Herzog, "Some Questions for Republicans," *Political Theory* (August 1986), 473–91.

59. Russell Kirk, *The Conservative Mind*, 3d ed. (Chicago: Gateway Books, 1960), 402–14.

60. Henry S. Commager, *The American Mind* (New Haven, Conn.: Yale University Press, 1950), 132–40; Arthur M. Schlesinger, Jr., *The Disuniting of America*, 2d ed. (Boston: Houghton Mifflin, 1998), 175–77, and *The Cycles of American History* (Boston: Houghton Mifflin, 1986); Alfred Kazin, *An American Procession* (New York: Vintage Books, 1985), 3–21, 277–309.

61. Martin J. Sklar, "Disaffection with Development: Henry Adams and the 1960s 'New Left,'" in *The United States as a Developing Country* (Cambridge: Cambridge University Press, 1992), 197–208. Note that Sklar does not regard himself as a New Leftist but rather as "an extremely old left thinker, a socialist, and an historian." By this he means to convey "a rootedness in the Enlightenment and nineteenth-century rationalism, humanism, and evolutionism" (197). Adams might well have been pleased or at least stimulated.

6. Religion, History, and Politics

1. *Education*, 34. See also the remark shortly after. "The children reached manhood without knowing religion, and with the certainty that dogma, metaphysics, and

abstract philosophy were not worth knowing. So one-sided an education could have been possible in no other country or time, but it became, almost of necessity, the more literary and political" (35). It may be that the novel *Esther* is Adams's justification for the cessation of his churchgoing. See Samuels, *Middle Years*, 235.

2. *Education*, 85.

3. Ibid., 353.

4. *Chartres*, 523.

5. Henry Adams, "Primitive Rights of Women," in *Great Secession Winter*, 332–60.

6. *Education*, 442.

7. Samuels, *Young Henry Adams*, 261–62.

8. Adams, "Primitive Rights," 346.

9. Ibid., 343.

10. Ibid., 358.

11. Samuels, *Young Henry Adams*, 263.

12. Adams, "Primitive Rights," 358–59. Note that vindictiveness is treated as a positive quality. Adams concedes that some relief came with the Protestant Reformation, though he seems not to notice that the revolution against religious and political absolutism was accompanied by new forms of absolute authority (ibid., 360).

13. Samuels, *Young Henry Adams*, 260–61.

14. Clive Bush, *Halfway to Revolution: Investigation and Crisis in the Work of Henry Adams, William James, and Gertrude Stein* (New Haven, Conn.: Yale University Press, 1991), 54.

15. Decker, *Literary Vocation*, 206.

16. All the same, on one of his more exotic subjects, the Norse legends, Adams looks fairly sound. In medieval Iceland, women suffered some legal disabilities, but whether single or married, they had substantially more property rights than in other Scandinavian countries or on the Continent. Rules governing divorce were complex and related more to natal kin than to the marriage grouping, but they were relatively egalitarian. See William Ian Miller, *Bloodtaking and Peacemaking: Feud, Law, and Society in Saga Iceland* (Chicago: University of Chicago Press, 1990), 27, 149–50.

17. Joan Wallach Scott and Natalie Zemon Davis quoted in Eugenia Kaledin, "Henry Adams's Anthropological Vision," in *Henry Adams and His World*, ed. David R. Contosta and Richard Muccigrosso (Philadelphia: American Philosophical Society, 1993), 66. Somewhat more debatably, Kaledin also suggests affinities with the interpretive anthropology of Clifford Geertz (ibid., 60).

18. Frances is a feminine version of Francis, an old family name, while Snow and Compton suggest Adams's bleak Comtean outlook. See Levenson, *Mind and Art*, 199, and Decker, *Literary Vocation*, 214.

19. Henry Adams to Elizabeth Cameron, February 6, 1891, in *Letters* 3:409.

20. For a discussion of the real-life sources of the characters in the novel, see Samuels, *Middle Years*, 238–44, and Levenson, *Mind and Art*, 200–201.

21. Clarence King was a very close friend of the Adamses and a member of their inner social circle. On this group, see the fine book by Patricia O'Toole, *The Five of Hearts* (New York: Ballantine Books, 1990). In addition to the Adamses and King, the other two members were John Hay and his wife Clara. O'Toole likens them to the Bloomsbury group or Gertrude Stein's circle in Paris. The Hearts "had a genius for befriending everyone worth knowing" (xii). For O'Toole's reading of *Esther*, see 133–39.

22. *Esther*, 196.

23. For James on Clover Adams, see the previous chapter.

24. *Esther*, 199–200. This passage parallels one in the *History*, so that Esther's character is seen as parallel to the national character. Decker points to the brilliant chapter in the *History* on the glories of the privateering schooner in the War of 1812; see *Literary Vocation*, 211–13. Decker's interpretation of *Esther* is one of the finest readings of the novel. Wharton's comment that Esther has never read a book does not apply to Marian Adams, who read voraciously.

25. *Esther*, 234.

26. Ibid., 263.

27. Ibid., 200. The observation that Esther is in no way medieval is interesting, in view of Adams's foray into medievalism in *Mont Saint Michel and Chartres*, where the Virgin Mary has characteristics markedly similar to Esther's and, by extension, to Marian Adams.

28. Ibid., 270, 200.

29. Levenson, *Mind and Art*, 201.

30. For an outstanding discussion, see Samuels, *Middle Years*, 227–35. For Samuels's interpretation of the novel, see 236–58.

31. *Esther*, 190.

32. Ibid., 191, 193.

33. Ibid., 294–95.

34. Ibid., 221.

35. Ibid., 281.

36. Ibid., 284–86; emphasis added.

37. Ibid., 296.

38. Ibid., 289.

39. Ibid., 330.

40. Ibid., 329. See also Michael Colacurcio, "*Democracy* and *Esther*: Henry Adams' Flirtation with Pragmatism," *American Quarterly* (spring 1967), 65.

41. See Colacurcio, "Flirtation with Pragmatism," 66; Samuels, *Middle Years*, 255; William James, "The Will to Believe," in *Writings: 1878–1899*, ed. Gerald E. Meyers (New York: Library of America, 1992), 457–79.

42. *Esther*, 333.

43. Ibid., 335.

44. Levenson, *Mind and Art*, 199.

45. *Esther*, 320.

46. For a similar argument, see Millicent Bell, "Adams' *Esther*: The Morality of Taste," in *Critical Essays on Henry Adams*, ed. Earl N. Harbert (Boston: G. K. Hall, 1981), 108.

47. Colacurcio, "Flirtation with Pragmatism," 69–70.

48. *Education*, 435.

49. *Chartres* is more personal, Michael Colacurcio suggests, than Adams's (somewhat peculiar) autobiography. See Colacurcio's "The Dynamo and the Angelic Doctor: The Bias of Henry Adams' Medievalism," *American Quarterly* (winter 1965), 697. I have been much influenced by this article as well as by Alfred Kazin, "American Gothic," *New York Review of Books* (November 23, 1989), 45–46. It should be added that the *Education* has its own decidedly personal quirks.

50. *Chartres*, 343. In addition to the Library of America edition, which I used, there is an excellent version published by Penguin Classics. It has good notes, a useful glossary of architectural terms, and a stimulating introduction by Raymond Carney that takes Adams to the brink of postmodernism but not beyond. See Henry Adams, *Mont Saint Michel and Chartres*, ed. and with an introduction by Raymond Carney (Baltimore: Penguin Books, 1986).

51. William James quoted in Samuels, *Major Phase*, 306.

52. John P. McIntyre quoted in Robert Mane, *Henry Adams on the Road to Chartres* (Cambridge: Harvard University Press, 1971), 195. Though I disagree with some of his interpretations, Manes provides an important guide to *Chartres*.

53. Edward N. Saveth, "The Heroines of Henry Adams," *American Quarterly* (fall 1956), 231–42.

54. Kazin, "American Gothic," 46.

55. Samuels, *Major Phase*, 283.

56. Ibid., 281. Samuels adds, "So far as art and architecture reflected the history of the time, it reflected the loves and hates, the alliances and rivalries, the trusts and treacheries of a small class of kings and queens, nobles and prelates."

57. *History* I, 227, 605.

58. *Chartres*, 536, 549.

59. Interestingly, if we are looking for a fixed starting point, the eleventh century seems, on Adams's own account, to be deficient. He admits that while the movement of the twentieth century is fast and furious enough to make us giddy, the eleventh "moved faster and more furiously still." He cites the Norman Conquest and the first crusade. The unity came with the energy with which Europe "flung itself on the East" (*Chartres*, 371).

60. Levenson, *Mind and Art*, 270. For a somewhat different view, see Colacurcio, "Dynamo and Angelic Doctor."

61. *Chartres*, 343.

62. Colacurcio, "Dynamo and Angelic Doctor," 705. Colacurcio refers to J. P. McIntyre, "Henry Adams and the Unity of Chartres," in *Twentieth Century Literature* (1962).

63. R. P. Blackmur, *Henry Adams*, ed. and with an introduction by Veronica A. Makowsky, foreword by Denis Donoghue (New York: Harcourt Brace Jovanovich, 1980), 178.

64. *Chartres*, 579. Of course, the "biographical" literature is the twelfth- and thirteenth-century literary treatments of the Virgin and, even more, the major monuments of medieval art.

65. Robert Spiller writes, "The trail from Esther to the Virgin of Chartres, is a long and intricate one but it is straight" (quoted in Mane, *Road to Chartres*, 196).

66. *Chartres*, 586, 598.

67. Ibid., 424.

68. Ibid.

69. Ibid., 431–32.

70. Ibid., 432–33.

71. Ibid., 434.

72. Ibid., 434–36.

73. Ibid., 503. In this connectrion, it is interesting to note that *Chartres* ends with Aquinas and therefore the reception of Aristotle, which indicates what Adams laments as the displacement of the Virgin in Catholic theology.

74. Ibid., 581.

75. Ibid., 586.

76. Ibid., 600.

77. Ibid., 596.

78. Ibid., 596–97.

79. Ibid.

80. Ibid., 582.

81. Ibid., 582–83.

82. Ibid., 583–84; emphasis added.

83. Decker, *Literary Vocation*, 245.

84. *Chartres*, 571–72.

85. Samuels, *Major Phase*, 283–84.

86. *Chartres*, 619.

87. Ibid., 622–23.

88. Ibid., 623–24.

89. Ibid., 632. Adams goes on to note that Bernard and Lord Bacon arrive at the same conclusion starting from opposite points.

90. Blackmur, *Henry Adams*, 210. See Adams's harsh biography of Randolph. But could Adams not also be described as an irritant, an innovator, and a rebellious anarchist? Certainly this comes close to his own self-description.

91. Ibid., 211.

92. *Chartres*, 610–11.

93. Mane, *Road to Chartres*, 214–15. Decker too sees Adams as sympathetic to Abelard and draws the parallel to Jefferson (*Literary Vocation*, 251).

94. *Chartres*, 640.

95. Ibid., 650.

96. Ibid., 656–57.

97. Ibid., 657.

98. Ibid., 657–58.

99. Ibid., 659.

100. Samuels, *Major Phase*, 278, 301. Mane suggests that "the fall of the House of Mary corresponds to what was, for this fourth-generation Adams, the Fall of the House of Adams" (*Road to Chartres*, 238).

101. *Chartres*, 663–64.

102. Manes, *Road to Chartres*, 210–11.

103. Henry Adams to Charles Milnes Gaskell, July 27, 1900, in *Letters* 5:141. Surely this must be the only time Saint Thomas has ever been called droll. The choice of this adjective says a lot about Adams's underlying attitudes.

104. Adams quoted in Colacurcio, "Dynamo and Angelic Doctor," 698.

105. Mane, *Road to Chartres*, 219.

106. *Chartres*, 666. Adams analyzes only one of Thomas's proofs.

107. Ibid., 667.

108. Colacurcio, "Dynamo and Angelic Doctor," 701.

109. *Chartres*, 669.

110. Ibid., 692–93.

111. Colacurcio, "Dynamo and Angelic Doctor," 704.

112. *Chartres*, 438.

113. Adams, quoted in Colacurcio, "Dynamo and Angelic Doctor," 700.

114. *Chartres*, 670.

115. Ibid., 685.

116. Ibid., 684–85.

117. Ibid., 686–87.

118. Ibid., 681, 693.

119. Ibid., 693.

120. Ibid.

121. Ibid., 692–93.

122. Ibid., 442. Adams does not mention the collapse of the crossing tower at Beauvais, which would have made direct comparison with Chartres "too obvious" (Levenson, *Mind and Art*, 282).

123. Blackmur, *Henry Adams*, 221.

124. *Chartres*, 694–95.

125. Ibid., 522.

126. Ibid., 695.

127. Decker, *Literary Vocation*, 257.

128. George Kateb, "Aestheticism and Morality: Their Cooperation and Hostility," *Political Theory* (February 2000), 5–37. Kateb argues that aestheticism, whether demo-

cratic or not, is inescapable and that it accounts for much that is great in human existence. At the same time, he fears that there is a risk that aesthetic values will be placed above moral concerns. For an argument that beauty conduces to justice, see Elaine Scarry, *On Beauty and Being Just* (Princeton, N.J.: Princeton University Press, 1999). Scarry's book is itself beautiful, though I cannot comment here on whether it is convincing. She mentions Chartres Cathedral as an instance of the beautiful but does not elaborate (see 49).

129. David Partenheimer, "Henry Adams's 'Primitive Rights of Women': An Offense Against Church, the Patriarchal State, Progressive Evolution, and the Women's Liberation Movement," *New England Quarterly* (December 1998), 635–42.

130. See Carol Gilligan, *In a Different Voice* (Cambridge: Harvard University Press, 1982).

131. *Chartres*, 524.

132. Mane, *Road to Chartres*, 200–201.

133. Saveth, "Heroines of Henry Adams," 239.

134. Mane, *Road to Chartres*, 202.

135. Henry Adams to George Cabot Lodge quoted in Samuels, *Major Phase*, 287.

136. Henry Adams to Charles Milnes Gaskell, December 20, 1904, in *Letters* 5:618. Adams's first mention of his strange form of anarchism seems to be in a letter to Elizabeth Cameron, October 23, 1899, in *Letters* 5:50.

137. See Mane, *Road to Chartres*, 194.

138. Samuels, *Major Phase*, 270.

139. Carney, introduction to *Mont Saint Michel and Chartres*, xviii–xix. Lawrence is quoted from *Studies in Classic American Literature*.

140. Carney, introduction, xxv. Later, Carney, referring to the treatment of Saint Thomas, remarks on "the outrageousness, the extravagance, the outright nuttiness (at times) of these passages" (xxvi). He uses such adjectives throughout.

141. For Carney on Adams's treatment of Aquinas, see ibid.

142. Kazin, "American Gothic," 45.

143. Samuels, *Major Phase*, 266.

7. History, Science, and Politics: A Lifetime's Education

1. I want to use the *Education* much less as a clue to the life of Henry Adams than as a source of ideas on his political and social thought. Like most such books, Adams tells us what he wants us to know about his life with relatively little regard for the actual events. Nevertheless, we can learn something about the period itself, as well as his philosophy, from his observations.

2. Colacurcio argues, "The work which seems to be a history turns out to be a good deal more personal than the one which seems to be an autobiography" (Michael Colacurcio, "The Dynamo and the Angelic Doctor: The Bias of Henry Adams'

Medievalism," *American Quarterly* [winter 1965], 697). Robert Manes agrees (*Road to Chartres*, 238).

3. Andrew Delbanco, "Henry Adams and the End of the World," in *Required Reading* (New York: Farrar, Straus, and Giroux, 1997), 98. I disagree with Delbanco's argument that Adams's corrosive irony was meant to dissolve the self. However, this is a fine essay.

4. Michael Rogin, "Christian v. Cannibal," *London Review of Books* (April 1, 1999), 19.

5. Alfred Kazin, *An American Procession* (New York: Vintage Books, 1985), 278; see also 294. One is reminded of the famous quip about Winston Churchill's history of World War I: "Winston has written a three volume work about himself and called it *The World Crisis*."

6. Levenson, *Mind and Art*, 289.

7. For a somewhat overinterpreted account of the publishing history of the book, see Edward Chalfant, "Lies, Silence, and Truth in the Writings of Henry Adams," in *Henry Adams and His World*, ed. David R. Contosta and Robert Muccigrosso (Philadelphia: American Philosophical Society, 1993), 8–22. The Samuels edition of the *Education* contains a useful editorial selection from Adams's letters bearing on his intentions as the author (507–18).

8. Kazin, *American Procession*, 146.

9. *Education*, 3–4.

10. Ibid., 7.

11. Ibid., 15–16.

12. Ibid., 32–33.

13. Ibid., 12.

14. Ibid., 38.

15. Ibid., 47–48.

16. Ibid., 48–49.

17. Ibid., 54–58; quote at 57–58.

18. Ibid., 60, 560, editor's nn. 9, 10. Adams had a copy of the Marx dated 1887.

19. Samuels, *Young Henry Adams*, 17; Jordy, *Scientific Historian*, 91, 179 n. 51. Or, as Samuels puts it, "Henry continued to subordinate science to conventional metaphysics as did Agassiz himself" (*Young Henry Adams*, 165).

20. *Education*, 63.

21. Ibid., 70–97.

22. For Henry's detailed contemporaneous account, see the title essay in *Great Secession Winter*.

23. *Education*, 99.

24. Ibid., 100–101.

25. Ibid., 102.

26. Ibid., 104–5.

27. Ibid., 107.

28. Adams made belated amends to his slighting of Lincoln when he contributed an introduction to the letters and selections from the diary of John Hay, prepared with Mrs. Hay. In international politics, Adams wrote, "the hand is the hand of Hay, but the temper, the tone, the wit and genius bear the birthmark of Abraham Lincoln." As Samuels remarks, this comes with "sudden grace," while it also suggests reservations about Hay's achievements (*Major Phase*, 408). Herbert Croly recalled to Edmund Wilson a meeting with Adams to discuss the possibility of his writing a biography of Hay. "By the time he left Adams' presence, Croly had been made to feel that he would not for anything in the world undertake the biography of Hay. Though Adams' ostensible role had been that of a friend of the family who was trying to provide a memorial for an old and valued friend, he had constantly betrayed this purpose by intimating in backhanded but unmistakable fashion his conviction that Hay was a mediocre person, that it would be impossible to write truthfully about him, and to satisfy the family at the same time, and that no self-respecting writer ought to think of taking on the job" (Edmund Wilson, introduction to Henry Adams, *The Life of George Cabot Lodge*, in *The Shock of Recognition*, ed. Edmund Wilson [New York: Modern Library, 1955], 743–44). This runs very much counter to the opinion of Hay expressed in the *Education*.

29. *Education*, 109; emphasis added.

30. On Socratic ignorance in this instance, see *Education*, 574, editor's n. 21. Samuels also comments on the "widening embrace of the metaphor of 'education.' Education becomes an omnibus term for knowledge of cause and effect in every area of human experience, especially history and politics." Adams, Samuels also notes, felt that he could assume that they knew less than he because they were unaware of *their* ignorance. One must doubt that this was the case with Lincoln. Finally, Samuels suggests that Adams implies that soldiers on the battlefield would teach their leaders what was at stake and what needed to be done. Perhaps. One might add that if so, there is a certain similarity to Tolstoy's *War and Peace* here. This is true, I think, in other aspects of Adams's work, though it seems less clear here.

31. There is no clue as to how close to the inside Henry got in his post or whether he participated as an adviser in the decision-making process. There is the precedent of his grandfather John Quincy Adams, who held responsible positions as a teenager. Henry was twenty-three when he went to London.

32. *Education*, 114–15.

33. Ibid., 116.

34. Ibid., 128, 132, 133.

35. Ibid., 135.

36. Ibid., 148.

37. Ibid., 149, 151.

38. Ibid., 153–54.

39. Ibid., 155. In fairness to Gladstone, it should be noted that his communication to Palmerston was dated before the news from Antietam, so that on this point, he

looks less foolish than Adams suggests. However, Gladstone was soon to give Adams more ammunition after he was in full possession of the facts.

40. William Gladstone quoted in *Education*, 156.

41. Ibid., 156–59.

42. Ibid., 163–65.

43. Ibid., 161–62. Gladstone's notes are bizarre and are clearly designed to make both Russell and Palmerston look bad.

44. George F. Kennan, *Soviet-American Relations, 1917–1920, I, Russia Leaves the War* (Princeton, N.J.: Princeton University Press, 1956), viii. It is interesting to reflect on the similarities between Adams and Kennan. The latter, while not of Adams's class background, was still anxious to serve his country and was sometimes vilified for his pains. He can be highly critical and at the same time movingly patriotic in the best sense of the word, that is, by trying to serve and reserving the right to criticize.

45. Much of Brooks Adams's long introduction to his brother's posthumously published collection of essays directed toward a "science" of history is devoted to John Quincy Adams. See "The Heritage of Henry Adams," in *Degradation*, 1–122.

46. John Adams, *Discourses on Davila*, quoted in Levenson, *Mind and Art*, 27.

47. Levenson, *Mind and Art*, 27, citing Yvor Winters.

48. After over fifty years, the outstanding work on the subject is still Richard Hofstadter, *Social Darwinism in American Thought*, rev. ed. (1944; Boston: Beacon Press, 1955). For a brief summary, see also James P. Young, *Reconsidering American Liberalism* (Boulder, Colo.: Westview Press, 1996), 127–36 and the literature cited there.

49. *Education*, 225–26.

50. For those interested in a more technical discussion, see Jordy, *Scientific Historian*, esp. 172–88, and Samuels, *Young Henry Adams*, 161–67. Jordy and Samuels disagree on some of the technical aspects of Adams's writing on evolution, particularly his review of Sir Charles Lyell's *Principles of Geology*. See Jordy, *Scientific Historian*, 178–79 n. 51.

51. *Education*, 230.

52. Ibid., 231.

53. Ibid., 231–32.

54. Ibid., 232.

55. Levenson, *Mind and Art*, 319.

56. *Education*, 271–72.

57. Ibid., 287–88.

58. Ibid., 288–89.

59. Levenson, *Mind and Art*, 323.

60. Ibid., 321. Yet, as Levenson points out, in *Chartres*, Adams tells us that we may choose between Saint Francis's embrace of death and the complexities of Saint Thomas. This, he says, is as close as Adams came to saying, with Dylan Thomas, "Do not go gentle into that good night." Adams, "fully conscious of how fragile were the works of man, chose the less simple solution" (ibid., 324; for the *Chartres*, see 661).

61. *Education*, 300–301.

62. Ibid., 301.

63. Ibid., 300. Adams was doubtless right that he could teach students nothing (ibid., 306). Students really teach themselves, but they can be guided, and by all accounts, Adams was brilliant in that role.

64. Ibid., 321, 325.

65. Ibid., 335, 336.

66. As it turned out, Adams, being a more prudent investor, was in less danger than his brothers Brooks and Charles. As Brooks says, "Henry was not the least affected by our indiscretions" ("The Heritage of Henry Adams," in *Degradation*, 90).

67. Samuels, *Major Phase*, 124.

68. *Education*, 342.

69. Russell L. Hanson and W. Richard Merriman, "Henry Adams and the Decline of the Republican Tradition," *American Transcendental Quarterly* (September 1990), 175. They suggest that since one way to return to first principles to revive civic virtue is to write history, this may explain Adams's abandonment of traditional history. Perhaps this is so, though it is just as possible that Adams, with his interest in sweeping generalizations, merely wanted to expand his horizons. Recall that he wrote that between them, he and John Hay had written most of the American history worth writing. Hanson and Merriman are certainly right that at this point in the nineteenth century, a return to republican principles was too late. For comments on this fine interpretation of Adams, see chapter 5.

70. Henry Adams to Elizabeth Cameron, July 27, 1896, in *Letters* 4:404, 406.

71. Henry Adams to Elizabeth Cameron, October 19, 1896, in ibid., 433.

72. Brooks Adams was also delighted by Bryan's performance, particularly since he had refused to be bought off by Wall Street money. However, he feared that the moneyed interests would seize the government if Bryan won (Samuels, *Major Phase*, 169).

73. *Education*, 355. It should be remembered that since he resided in the District of Columbia, Adams could not vote there. Moreover, he did not maintain a Massachusetts voting address. Perhaps he felt that, given the state of the parties, there was no point in voting.

74. Walter Dean Burnham, "The Changing Shape of the American Political Universe," in *The Current Crisis in American Politics* (New York: Oxford University Press, 1982), 51, 25–55. This is an important article for understanding the crisis of both Adams's time and our own; indeed, the two are part of the same movement.

75. *Education*, 360. On Brooks Adams and his relation to Henry, I found the following to be helpful: Charles A. Beard, introduction to Brooks Adams, *The Law of Civilization and Decay* (1896; reprint, New York: Alfred A. Knopf, 1943), 3–53; Daniel Aaron, *Men of Good Hope* (New York: Oxford University Press, 1951), 252–80; Samuels, *Major Phase*, 17–155; and, above all, R. P. Blackmur, "Henry and Brooks Adams: Parallels to Two Generations," *Southern Review* (autumn 1939), 308–34.

76. Henry Adams to Brooks Adams, April 2, 1898, in *Letters* 4:557. Adams goes on

to add a second formula to the effect that, given centralization, Asia is cheaper than Europe, so that Asia tends to survive and Europe to perish (ibid., 558).

77. *Education*, 339.

78. Henry Adams to Brooks Adams, May 7, 1898, in *Letters* 4:586–87.

79. Levenson, *Mind and Art*, 292–93.

80. Joseph A. Schumpeter, *Capitalism, Socialism, and Democracy*, 3d ed. (New York: Oxford University Press, 1950), esp., 64–163; quote at 302.

81. Blackmur, "Henry and Brooks Adams," 321–22.

82. *Education*, 225. Adams did follow developments in Marxist theory. Brooks sent him a copy of the German edition of Eduard Bernstein's *Evolutionary Socialism*. Saying that he took Marxism to be the foundation of Brooks's ideas, Henry added, "The assertion of the law of economy as the law of history is the only contribution that the socialists have made to my library of ideas, and I am curious to get their best statement" (Henry Adams to Brooks Adams, October 31, 1899, in *Letters* 5:54–55). A few days later, he responded in more detail. After noting that Bernstein is Jewish and that his writing style is impossible, Adams states, "He seems to prove that he is very much in my intellectual condition. He throws up the sponge in the whole socialist fight. Absolutely nothing is left of Karl Marx except his economical theory of history in its crudest form. . . . Bernstein not only argues, but proves, that the Marxian theory of a social cataclysm has been abandoned, and that the socialist has no choice but to make himself a petit bourgeois, with all the capitalistic machinery and methods. He preaches the bankruptcy of the only idea that our time has produced." He adds that the capitalists have abandoned their teachers and principles and that there is no reason why the capitalist "should not become a socialist functionary" (Henry Adams to Brooks Adams, November 5, 1899, in ibid., 56). This is an early statement of the convergence theory so much discussed two to three decades ago. The influence of Comte is most clear in an essay called "The Rule of Phase Applied to History," discussed in the next chapter.

83. Levenson, *Mind and Art*, 226.

84. Decker, *Literary Vocation*, 98.

85. Henry Adams to Elizabeth Cameron, January 13, 1898, in *Letters* 4:522–25; Henry Adams to Elizabeth Cameron, September 5, 1899, in *Letters* 5:26.

86. Levenson, *Mind and Art*, 223–24; Henry Adams to Elizabeth Cameron, September 5, 1899, in *Letters* 5:26. Levenson notes that Adams's virulence tapered off when the Dreyfus affair came to an end and he turned to more constructive work. "The latter explanation is the one hopeful aspect of a story which is disagreeable in itself and necessarily alarming to a world that has witnessed antisemitism as a catastrophic social event rather than as, in Adams's case, a datum of personal psychology like insomnia or an addiction to privacy. One consequence of the episode is the occasional use of the word 'Jew' which disfigures, albeit inessentially, his late masterpieces—pockmarks of a disease that can be fatal" (*Mind and Art*, 226).

87. Samuels, *Major Phase*, 358.

88. Levenson, *Mind and Art*, 224. Samuels is comprehensive in his coverage of Adams's anti-Semitism; see *Major Phase*, esp., 129–30, 356–58.

89. Eugenia Kaledin, *The Education of Mrs. Henry Adams* (Amherst: University of Massachusetts Press, 1994), 121–22.

90. Barbara Miller Solomon quoted in E. Digby Baltzell, *The Protestant Establishment: Aristocracy and Caste in America* (New York: Vintage Books, 1964), 91.

91. *History* I, 119–20. Levenson comments that this indicates a profound commitment to American democracy. "The scion of presidents, not the first of his family to be accused of blood-pride, made steerage immigrants, malarial frontiersmen, and lower-class inventors his heroes alongside the Virginia aristocrat to whom he gave his qualified allegiance" (*Mind and Art*, 148).

92. Baltzell, *Protestant Establishment*, 91. This date might be subject to correction if one searched the now standard Harvard edition of the letters, which was not available to Baltzell when he wrote. He used the Cater edition. However, the date is surely approximately correct.

93. Ibid., 93. For Baltzell's more general theory, see 7–10.

94. The classic study of this subject is John Higham, *Strangers in the Land* (New York: Atheneum, 1963).

95. Samuels, *Major Phase*, 357.

96. See the massive study by Rogers Smith, *Civic Ideals* (New Haven, Conn.: Yale University Press, 1997). Smith is mainly interested in the problems of African Americans and women. Somewhat strangely, there is no index entry for Jews or antiethnic prejudice generally. Henry Adams is quoted briefly without reference to the subject.

97. Carey McWilliams, *A Mask for Privilege* (Boston: Little, Brown, 1948), 179–81.

98. Ibid., 164.

99. *Education*, 238.

100. McWilliams, *Mask for Privilege*, 70. In spite of this observation, Adams, in an excess of self-pity combined with a seeming failure of self-knowledge, claims that he "found no fault with his time" and that he was no worse off than the buffalo or the Indians, but he did insist that "he himself was not at fault" (*Education*, 238).

101. Karl Marx, *On the Jewish Question*, in *The Marx-Engels Reader*, 2d ed., ed. Robert C. Tucker (New York: W. W. Norton, 1978), 48; emphasis in original.

102. Ibid., 49; emphasis in original. It is interesting to note that at the time, the German word *Judentum* had, as its secondary meaning, commerce (ibid., 50, editorial note).

103. Henry Adams to Brooks Adams, April 12, 1906, in *Letters* 6:13.

104. *Education*, 500–501. Cf. Carey McWilliams, *The Education of Carey McWilliams* (New York: Simon and Schuster, 1979), 323.

105. McWilliams, *Education of McWilliams*, 323.

106. *Education*, 339.

107. Ibid., 340.

108. Ibid., 340–41.

109. Ibid., 342.

110. Ibid., 343. To this day, Chicago seems the quintessentially American city that Adams suggests it is, as well as an architectural marvel.

111. Ibid., 344.

112. Ibid., 379.

113. In fact, Adams wrote a prayer to the dynamo in the form of a poem included in a longer prayer to the Virgin of Chartres. One verse seems to hint at the possibility that he sees technology as a neutral force:

> We know not whether you are kind
> Or cruel in your fiercer mood;
> But be you Matter, be you Mind,
> We think we know that you are blind,
> And we alone are good.

"Prayer to the Dynamo," in *Novels, Mont Saint Michel and Chartres, The Education of Henry Adams*, ed. Ernest Samuels (New York: Library of America, 1986), 1204. See also David E. Noble, *The Religion of Technology: The Divinity of Man and the Spirit of Invention* (New York: Alfred A. Knopf, 1997).

114. *Education*, 380–81.

115. Ibid., 382.

116. Susan Haack, "Staying for an Answer: The Untidy Process of Groping for the Truth," *Times Literary Supplement* (July 9, 1999), 13.

117. *Education*, 382. The comment about Adams giving up too soon on conventional history does nothing to undermine the importance of his work pursuant to the impact of the dynamos.

118. Ibid., 383.

119. Ibid. Notice the parallel between the force of the Virgin and the power of X-rays, as Adams tries to assimilate the latest science to his thinking.

120. Ibid., 384.

121. Ibid., 384–85.

122. For a discussion of Whitman and Adams, see William H. Jordy, "Henry Adams and Walt Whitman," *South Atlantic Quarterly* (April 1941), 132–45.

123. *Education*, 387–88.

124. Ibid., 389.

125. Ibid., 397; emphasis added.

126. Ibid., 398.

127. The closest approach to such a reading is Martin J. Sklar, "Disaffected with Development: Henry Adams and the 1960's 'New Left,'" in *The United States as a Developing Country* (Cambridge: Cambridge University Press, 1992), 197–208. Sklar calls himself an *"extremely* old leftist" who believes in the Enlightenment and nineteenth-century rationalism, humanism, and evolutionism. Sklar sees the 1960s

radicals as miniature Adamses, caught in a period of transition between capitalist industrialism and socialism—a socialism that does not look very different from the capitalism it is trying to supplant.

128. *Education*, 405. Note that this is eight years after his speculations on Hungarian socialism in his letter to Brooks Adams.

129. Ibid., 406.

130. Ibid., 406–7.

131. Ibid., 407.

132. Ibid.

133. R. P. Blackmur, *Henry Adams*, ed. Veronica A. Makowsky, foreword by Denis Donoghue (New York: Harcourt Brace, 1980), 154.

134. Levenson, *Mind and Art*, 296. Perhaps the point is not as frivolous as Levenson claims. Wilson Carey McWilliams suggests to me that Adams's teaching is not unlike Matthew Arnold's "Dover Beach," where "ignorant armies clash by night."

135. Louis Hartz, *The Liberal Tradition in America* (New York: Harcourt Brace, 1955).

136. Henry Adams to Elizabeth Cameron, January 22, 1915, in *Letters* 6:681.

137. Levenson, *Mind and Art*, 271.

138. *Education*, 408. However, in his late "Letter to American Teachers of History," he succumbs to chaos; see the next chapter.

139. Henry Adams to Brooks Adams, May 7, 1901, in *Letters* 5:251; emphasis added.

140. Henry Adams to Bay Lodge, December 1, 1904, in *Letters* 5:616. Note that Bay Lodge had just written a poem about Cain.

141. *Education*, 408.

142. In working through the complexities of Adams's thought on politics early in this century, particularly as expressed in his letters, I relied heavily on Levenson, *Mind and Art*, esp. 289–304.

143. *Education*, 436.

144. Ibid., 417.

145. Ibid., 418. It is no wonder that Roosevelt was not enthusiastic about the *Education*. Adams's comments there are mild compared with his abuse of Roosevelt in his private correspondence.

146. Ibid., 418–19. In time, Adams came to be disdainful of Lodge. In 1900 he wrote, "Cabot more and more makes me sea-sick. His senatorial atmosphere has become unendurable" (Henry Adams to Elizabeth Cameron, April 16, 1900, in *Letters* 5:121). Earlier the same year, he wrote, "As usual, the Senate makes trouble; and you know that to me the Senate means practically Cabot; and you know Cabot; and you don't know that Cabot is ten times more *cabotin* than ever. The word was made to describe him, and it fits as though it were a Sargent portrait" (Henry Adams to Elizabeth Cameron, February 19, 1900, in ibid., 94). According to an editorial note, *cabotin* means a "second-rate strolling actor; hence, political showman."

147. McWilliams, *Education of McWilliams*, 323.

148. Henry Adams to Brooks Adams, September 20, 1910, in *Letters* 6:369; emphasis added. As I suggest later, 1910 marked a crucial turning point for Adams, and not a turning point for the better.

149. Henry Adams to Elizabeth Cameron, August 27, 1905, in *Letters* 5:710.

150. Henry Adams to Elizabeth Cameron, in ibid., 486. Earlier in the same letter, in one of his moods where he seems to hope that catastrophe will usher in a dramatically different system, Adams says, "Only I fear that, with their confounded practical common-sense, our people will soon realize [what is happening], and invent some practical working system" (485).

151. Blackmur, "Henry and Brooks Adams," 316. Blackmur observes that Henry's sophistication overrode his candor and that Brooks's candor sometimes triumphed over his sophistication. During World War I, Brooks was elected to the Massachusetts constitutional convention, where he astonished the delegates with his "totalitarian proposals to save society." He believed that democracy would perish without Draconian measures. In spite of this, he attacked what he saw as Wilson's "dictatorial methods," saying that they were not "the right foundation for an authoritarian society." His hatred for the president was so great that "in an agony of frustration he wildly exhorted Lodge, 'Kill Wilson!'" While Henry was by this time as critical of the failures of democracy as Brooks, "he was as skeptical of the prescriptions of the radical Right as of those of the radical Left—and, for that matter, of every other point of the political compass" (Samuels, *Major Phase*, 567–68).

152. See Charles Hirschfeld, introduction to *Degradation*, vii.

153. Charles William Eliot quoted in Samuels, *Major Phase*, 369. For Samuels's view, see ibid. It is true that after his final published work, Adams was bitterly critical of democracy in his letters, but his published work held, sometimes tenuously, to his belief.

8. *The End of Education*

1. Lynn White, Jr., *Dynamo and Virgin Reconsidered* (Cambridge, Mass.: MIT Press, 1971), 62–63. Beauvais Cathedral seems a strange choice, since as Adams subtly points out, that structure was unsound. White notes that these great buildings, instead of being built by slaves, were built by free and in fact unionized labor. Moreover, the churches displayed not only gifts from the aristocracy but also chapels, windows, and the like donated by merchants and craftsmen's guilds. This points to a "social revolution closely connected with the technological revolution."

2. Ibid., 72–73.

3. Henry Adams to Charles Francis Adams, Jr., April 11, 1862, in *Letters* 1:290.

4. Henry Adams to Henry Osborn Taylor, January 17, 1905, in *Letters* 5:627.

5. Henry Adams quoted in Samuels, *Major Phase*, 320. Adams neglects to mention his Kodak.

6. Cecilia Tichi, *Shifting Gears: Technology, Literature, Culture in Modernist*

America (Chapel Hill: University of North Carolina Press, 1987), 137–68, quote at 137. On this point, it is interesting to compare Adams with Thorstein Veblen, *The Engineers and the Price System* (New Brunswick, N.J.: Transaction Books, 1982).

7. *Education,* 466; cf. Tichi, *Shifting Gears,* 158.

8. *Education,* 311; cf. Tichi, *Shifting Gears,* 167–68.

9. Tivhi, *Shifting Gears,* 168.

10. George Kateb, "Technology and Philosophy," *Social Research* (fall 1997), 1245.

11. Daniel Bell, *The Coming of Post-Industrial Society,* anniversary ed. (New York: Basic Books, 1999), 169.

12. Henry Adams to Whitelaw Reid, September 13, 1908, in *Letters* 6:179.

13. Henry Adams to William James, December 9, 1907, in *Letters* 6:91–92.

14. *Education,* 451–52.

15. Ibid., 458.

16. Ibid., 457.

17. Henry Adams, "The Tendency of History," in *Degradation,* 130–31. One could suggest that it would be more difficult to proclaim the inevitable triumph of socialism in the United States than in Europe.

18. *Education,* 478.

19. Ibid., 475.

20. Ibid., 484.

21. Ibid., 485.

22. Ibid., 486.

23. Ibid., 487.

24. Ibid., 489–90.

25. Ibid., 493.

26. Ibid., 493–94.

27. Ibid., 495.

28. For a time, Comte had a good deal of influence in American social thought. See Gillis J. Harp, *Positivist Republic: Auguste Comte and the Reconstruction of American Liberalism, 1865–1920* (University Park: Pennsylvania University Press, 1995). It is interesting to note that Harp's book does not contain an index entry for Henry Adams, though he does refer to Charles Francis Adams, Jr.

29. Levenson, *Mind and Art,* 360. For Levenson on "The Rule," see 358–66. Adams requested J. Franklin Jameson, the editor of the *American Historical Review,* to commission Henry Andrew Bumstead, a Columbia University physicist, to review "The Rule." Bumstead "praised the ingenuity of Adams's analogical applications but left no doubt in the historian's mind that he possessed no knowledge, let alone mastery, of the language of scientific thought" (Decker, *Literary Vocation,* 72; see also Samuels, *Major Phase,* 449). The most devastating account of Adams's scientific deficiencies is Jordy, *Scientific Historian,* 131–255.

30. Henry Adams, "The Rule of Phase Applied to History," in *Degradation,* 286.

31. Ibid., 286–93.

32. Ibid., 293–97, 305. Following Levenson, I omit discussion of the calculations.

33. Ibid., 308. Carey McWilliams points out to me that if we date the changes from the condemnation of Galileo, we arrive at 1933, a most important year. This is a coincidence, no doubt, but interesting to contemplate.

34. Levenson, *Mind and Art*, 364.

35. Ibid., 366, 369.

36. Henry Adams, "A Letter to American Teachers of History," in *Degradation*, 189–90.

37. Ibid., 185.

38. Ibid., 191.

39. Ibid., 263.

40. William James quoted in Samuels, *Major Phase*, 490; emphasis added. James also points out that "history is the course of things *before* that terminus" (Andrew Delbanco, *Required Reading* [New York: Farrar, Straus, and Giroux, 1997], 96). Delbanco comments that the "wonderfully sanative" response of James has "the effect of making Adams seem a brooding misanthrope, but one should resist the indictment. In his own courageous way, Adams was driven by the peculiar spirit that has always both inspired and afflicted the greatest American writers: by an unembarrassed willingness to express the child's horror at the ubiquity of death, by the urge, as if in bedside prayer, to speak directly with God" (ibid., 97). I can agree that Adams was more than a misanthrope; that characteristic was a mask, another of his poses. But given his deep agnosticism, his desire to speak with God must have been limited, handicapped by the fact that though he wished for faith, he never achieved it.

41. Decker, *Literary Vocation*, 89–90.

42. Ibid., 91.

43. Perry Miller quoted on the cover of the Harper Torchbooks edition of *Degradation*.

44. Mark Twain, "The Turning Point of My Life," in *Collected Tales, Sketches, Speeches, and Essays: 1891–1910*, ed. Louis J. Budd (New York: Library of America, 1992), 929–38.

45. William McNeill, "A Short History of Humanity," *New York Review of Books* (June 29, 2000), 9.

46. Levenson, *Mind and Art*, 369.

47. See Samuels, *Major Phase*, 363. Samuels points to the contradiction between the "obsessive pose of pessimism and the lurking residue of optimism" in Adams's work. This was part of the "habitual rhetoric of the idealist of the forlorn hope." Even Adams says that he "had enjoyed his life amazingly" (ibid., 362, 363).

48. Henry Adams quoted in Samuels, *Major Phase*, 520.

49. I leave out of consideration his biography of the poet George Cabot (Bay) Lodge, which is politically insignificant and, in my view, otherwise uninteresting as well.

50. *Education*, 501.

51. Ibid., 503.

52. Ibid., 505.

53. Ibid., xxx.

54. Samuels, *Major Phase*, 363.

55. Henry Adams to Barrett Wendell, March 12, 1909, in *Letters* 6:237–38. Of course, Adams alludes here to his late theorizing on scientific history.

56. William James, writing to Adams, quoted in Samuels, *Major Phase*, 340–41; emphasis in original. Wilson Carey McWilliams suggests to me that this may say as much about James as about Adams, but that is another story. In a further exchange of letters, James assures Adams that his education was anything but a failure, but instead a "superlatively precious achievement." He ranks the *Education* with *Faust* as the "pride" of his library (ibid.).

57. William James, *A Pluralistic Universe*, in *Writings: 1902–1910*, ed. Bruce Kucklick (New York: Library of America, 1987), 814, 816. Of William James, "set up," Adams says, as "our last thinker," he writes, "I never could master what he thought" (Henry Adams to Charles Milnes Gaskell, September 22, 1910, in *Letters* 6:371).

58. Samuels, *Major Phase*, 387.

59. In what follows, I was much helped by Decker, *Literary Vocation*, esp. 53–63. Decker is very sensitive to the tensions in Adams's work I have been discussing.

60. Ibid., 59.

61. For a useful survey of views that find unity, see ibid., 293–94 n. 21.

62. Ibid., 57.

63. *Education*, 451.

64. Decker, *Literary Vocation*, 60.

65. On this problem, see Levenson, *Mind and Art*, 357–58.

66. Ibid., 1.

67. Alexis de Tocqueville, *Democracy in America*, trans. George Lawrence (New York: Harper, 1988), vol. 2, pt. 2, chap. 20, 555–58.

68. The literature on contemporary corruption is vast. For a careful account, particularly as it is revealed in campaign finance, see Elizabeth Drew, *The Corruption of American Politics: What Went Wrong and Why* (Secaucus, N.J.: Birch Lane Press, 1999). Also useful is Ronald Dworkin, "The Curse of American Politics," *New York Review of Books* (October 17, 1996), 19–24.

69. Michael Walzer, *Spheres of Justice* (New York: Basic Books, 1983).

70. Langdon Winner, *Autonomous Technology: Technics-out-of-Control as a Theme in Political Thought* (Cambridge, Mass.: MIT Press, 1973).

71. For the contrary position, see Judith Shklar, "The Education of Henry Adams by Henry Adams," in *Redeeming American Political Thought* (Chicago: University of Chicago Press, 1998), 90. For Shklar, Adams's confession of his failure redeemed him. She admits, somewhat grudgingly, that there is much to learn from Adams.

72. William Dusinberre, *Henry Adams: The Myth of Failure* (Charlottesville: University Press of Virginia, 1980).

73. Ibid., 217.

74. Winters agrees, as he heaps scorn on *Chartres* and the *Education* but places the *History* above even Gibbon's *Decline and Fall of the Roman Empire*, calling it the "greatest historical work in English" (Yvor Winters, "Henry Adams or the Creation of Confusion," in *Defense of Reason* [Denver: Allan Swallow, 1947], 415).

75. Dusinberre has an interesting suggestion. He would like to see a scholar do an annotated edition of the *History*, as J. B. Bury did of Gibbon's *Decline and Fall* in the nineteenth century. There, in footnotes, the text could be corrected, supplemented, and challenged on the basis of later research. See Dusinberre, *Myth of Failure*, 161. Since Dusinberre wrote, we have the Harbert edition from the Library of America, which, though annotated, is not a critical edition in Dusinberre's sense. Although Dusinberre's suggestion is a good one, the resulting work would probably be too long to win a wide readership. It would also be helpful to have a substantial abridgment with a similar critical apparatus. There have been two abridgments, but they were too truncated to gain a real sense of Adams's achievement.

76. Judith Shklar, *Montesquieu* (New York: Oxford University Press, 1987), 126.

77. Richard E. Neustadt and Ernest R. May, *Thinking in Time: The Uses of History for Decision Makers* (New York: Free Press, 1986), 266. Apropos the problem of length, Neustadt and May say that in spite of its huge size, "it is such lively reading that it seems too short."

78. What follows owes a good deal to questions and, in a few instances, hints of answers posed by Tom Dumm on the basis of an early draft of this study.

79. For the most part, documentation for this point and most of what follows has already been presented.

80. This point is most clearly stated in Melvin Lyon, *Symbol and Idea in Henry Adams* (Lincoln: University of Nebraska Press, 1970), 65.

81. See chapter 7, note 28.

82. Samuels, *Major Phase*, 412.

83. I do not want to suggest here that the Progressive movement was an enormous success in its trust policy, but that Adams might have been a useful influence. Against this is the fact that Theodore Roosevelt was not friendly toward him. This is small wonder, given what Adams said of him in the *Education*, which TR had read in the privately circulated version.

84. Jean Elshtain, *Public Man, Private Woman* (Princeton, N.J.: Princeton University Press, 1981), and *The Family in Political Thought* (Amherst: University of Massachusetts Press, 1982). See also Christopher Lasch, *Haven in a Heartless World* (New York: Basic Books, 1977).

85. See Leo Strauss, *The Rebirth of Classical Political Rationalism*, ed. Thomas L. Pangle (Chicago: University of Chicago Press, 1989), 76, and Allan Bloom, *The Closing of the American Mind* (New York: Simon and Schuster, 1987), 55.

86. See John H. Schaar, *Legitimacy in the Modern State* (New Brunswick, N.J.: Transaction Books, 1981), esp. the title essay.

87. Bernard Bailyn, *Ideological Origins of the American Revolution*, enlarged ed.

(Cambridge: Harvard University Press, 1992); Gordon Wood, *The Creation of the American Republic* (Chapel Hill: University of North Carolina Press, 1969); J. G. A. Pocock, *The Machiavellian Moment* (Princeton, N.J.: Princeton University Press, 1975). For a discussion of the complex relations between republicanism and liberalism, see James P. Young, *Reconsidering American Liberalism* (Boulder, Colo.: Westview Press, 1996), esp. 41–54, 66–71, and the literature cited therein.

88. Harvey Mansfield, Jr., review of *The Machiavellian Moment, American Political Science Review* 71 (1974), 1151.

89. Louis Hartz, *The Liberal Tradition in America* (New York: Harcourt Brace, 1955).

90. For an extensive exploration of the Hartz thesis and the peculiarities of the liberal tradition, see Young, *Reconsidering American Liberalism.*

91. It might be said that the charming story Adams tells about being marched off to school without his consent by John Quincy Adams suggests skepticism about the contractual theory of rights and the origin of authority.

92. Lyon, *Symbol and Idea*, see 58–77; Jordy, *Scientific Historian*, 81.

93. *History* I, 119–20.

94. Lyon, *Symbol and Idea*, 61–62.

95. *History* I, 122.

96. Lyon, *Symbol and Idea*, 65.

97. Karl Polanyi, *The Great Transformation* (Boston: Beacon Press, 1957). Immanuel Wallerstein is much influenced by Polanyi. The best way into Wallerstein's work is through *The Modern World System* (New York: Academic Press, 1974) and *Historical Capitalism* (London: Verso, 1983). Wallerstein also looks forward to a socialist world system or world government; see "The Rise and Demise of the World Capitalist System: Concepts for Comparative Analysis," in *The Capitalist World-Economy* (Cambridge: Cambridge University Press, 1979), 1–36. Adams would have been repulsed by the idea of a socialist world government but might have feared that it would come to pass. It is no doubt fortunate that this idea is clearly a fantasy. Wallerstein gives up no hostages by predicting when his projection would come to pass.

98. Henry Adams to Charles Milnes Gaskell, April 28, 1894, and February 16, 1895, in *Letters* 4:185, 259. See Decker, *Literary Vocation*, 32–33.

99. Wilson Carey McWilliams, "Standing at Armageddon: Morality and Religion in Progressive Thought, in *Progressivism and the New Democracy*, ed. Sidney M. Milkis and Jerome M. Mileur (Amherst: University of Massachusetts Press, 1999), 109. On the more general fascination of New England intellectuals with the medieval world, see Alfred Kazin, "American Gothic," *New York Review of Books* (November 23, 1989), 46.

100. Max Weber, "Science as a Vocation," in *From Max Weber*, ed. Hans Gerth and C. Wright Mills (New York: Oxford University Press, 1958), 155, 129–56 passim. John Patrick Diggins makes a very interesting comparison between Weber and Adams in

The Promise of Pragmatism: Modernism and the Crisis of Knowledge and Authority (Chicago: University of Chicago Press, 1994), 22–54.

101. Weber, "Politics as a Vocation," in *From Max Weber*, 79.

102. Leo Tolstoy quoted in Weber, "Science as a Vocation," 143.

103. John La Farge quoted in Samuels, *Major Phase*, 377.

104. Weber, "Science as a Vocation," 155.

105. On this, see Kazin, "American Gothic," 46.

106. Samuels, *Major Phase*, ix.

107. Jackson Lears, *No Place of Grace: Antimodernism and the Transformation of American Culture: 1880–1920* (New York: Pantheon Books, 1981), 262–97. Lears offers an outstanding reading of Adams, though for my purposes, it is a little too psychoanalytical in orientation.

108. Diggins, *Promise of Pragmatism*, 45.

109. Leo Marx, *The Machine in the Garden: Technology and the Pastoral Idea in America* (New York: Oxford University Press, 1964), 345.

110. Ibid., 347.

111. There is an arguably deeper problem that Adams does not consider. "If the difficulties caused by technology are, in fact, only problems—say, for example, the problem of unintended side effects—we are certainly well-advised to be looking for solutions. But what if the difficulties attending technology are both integral to its very being and inseparable from its benefits—like the other side of a coin? This would make technology more like a tragedy that begs for understanding and endurance than like a problem that calls for a solution. To put the point starkly: to formulate the question about technology as the *problem* of technology is itself a manifestation of technological thinking—of the desire to knock down all obstacles, even if only in the mind. To ask about the *problem* of technology, in fact, *exemplifies* it." Leon R. Kass, "Introduction: The Problem of Technology," in *Technology in the Western Political Tradition*, ed. Arthur M. Melzer, Jerry Weinberger, and M. Richard Zinman (Ithaca, N.Y.: Cornell University Press, 1993), 9–10.

112. For a provocative survey of this literature, see Winner, *Autonomous Technology*.

113. George Kateb, *Utopia and Its Enemies* (New York: Schocken Books, 1972), 108–9. Kateb adds that this last point seems to be a truism. He attributes this statement about danger to Norbert Wiener.

114. Max Weber quoted in Gerth and Mills, introduction to *From Max Weber*, 71.

115. Ibid. Apropos Adams's alleged anti-intellectualism, he and the other Mugwumps were ridiculed as intellectual, antidemocratic snobs because of their adherence to civil service reform. See Richard Hofstadter, *Anti-intellectualism in American Life* (New York: Alfred A. Knopf, 1963), 180–85. In fact, Adams had one of his rare periods of popularity when alienated intellectuals took him up during the 1920s (ibid., 409).

116. Winner, *Autonomous Technology*, 317–19.

117. Ibid., 325; emphasis in original.

118. Ibid., 324.

119. Ibid., 325–31, quote at 331.

120. Michael Walzer, *Radical Principles* (New York: Basic Books, 1980), 46.

121. On these matters, see Alan Ehrenhalt, "Demanding the Right Size Government," *New York Times*, national ed., October 4, 1999, A31. Following Daniel Bell, Ehrenhalt argues that in the twenty-first century the most important issues will be global or national. He is particularly struck by the ineffectuality of Congress. Here he may be overestimating the importance of a situation rooted in the peculiar politics of the 1998 elections. On the problem of finding the optimal unit size for governmental action, see Robert A. Dahl and Edward R. Tufte, *Size and Democracy* (Stanford, Calif.: Stanford University Press, 1973).

122. George Kateb, "The Moral Distinctiveness of Representative Democracy," in *The Inner Ocean* (Ithaca, N.Y.: Cornell University Press, 1992), 39–40.

123. Sheldon S. Wolin, "Max Weber: Legitimation, Method, and the Politics of Theory," *Political Theory* (August 1981), 405. Much of Wolin's powerful analysis of the dilemmas of Weber can also be applied to the thought of Adams (see ibid., 401–24).

124. Ibid., 402.

125. Ibid., 422.

126. William Chaloupka, *Everybody Knows: Cynicism in America* (Minneapolis: University of Minnesota Press, 1999), xiv–xv. Chaloupka's analysis does not extend back to the nineteenth century, but I think Adams clearly fits the category. I owe the reference to Chaloupka to Tom Dumm. The discussion of cynicism is suddenly a new trend in political theory. See Chase Madar, "Dog Days," *Lingua Franca* (October 1999), 25–28. I cannot comment beyond the limited use I have made of it here.

127. Laurie Anderson, program notes for her brilliant *Songs and Tales from Moby Dick*, University Musical Society, Ann Arbor, Mich., September 30, 1999, 6. She also writes, "I fell in love with the idea that the mysterious thing you look for your whole life will eventually eat you alive" (ibid.). It was Anderson who led me to Melville, whose work is very suggestive in dealing with Adams. It should be noted that where she writes "outlives," Melville writes "lives out." I think he intends the same thing she does, but if not, then what she says fits the case of Adams very well.

128. Levenson, *Mind and Art*, 188–89.

129. See Isaiah Berlin's brilliantly provocative essay "The Hedgehog and the Fox," in *Russian Thinkers*, ed. Henry Hardy and Aileen Kelly (New York: Viking Press, 1978), 22–81.

130. Ibid., 81.

131. Ibid.

132. Lionel Trilling, "Adams at Ease," in *A Gathering of Fugitives* (Boston: Beacon Press, 1956), 118–19.

133. Lionel Trilling, *The Moral Obligation to Be Intelligent: Selected Essays*, ed.

Leon Wieseltier (New York: Farrar, Straus, and Giroux, 2000); Lionel Trilling, *The Liberal Imagination* (Garden City, N.Y.: Anchor Books, 1957), xii.

134. Irving Howe, *A Margin of Hope* (New York: Harcourt Brace Jovanovich, 1982), 322. In this passage, Howe refers particularly to his friend Richard Hofstadter and also to Lionel Trilling. It seems to me that this understanding of intellectual capacity can readily be applied to Adams as well.

135. I owe the term *multivalent* to a personal communication from William Merrill Decker.

INDEX

Abelard, Pierre, 145, 146
Abolitionists, 83
Absolute authority, 98
Adams, Abigail, 129
Adams, Brooks, 7, 115, 122, 180, 182, 183, 185, 203
Adams, Catherine, 177–78, 186
Adams, Charles Francis, 7, 82–83
  ambassador to England, 167, 169, 170, 172
Adams, Charles Francis, Jr., 7, 24
  and freedmen as soldiers, 84
Adams, Henry (1838–1918)
  on Alexander Hamilton, 32
  ambivalence in thought, 55
  on art, 154–55, 191
  on balance of power, 115
  biographies, 7, 252nn22,23
  character, 2, 8, 158–59
  as civic republican, 2, 45, 121, 167, 231–32
  on Civil War, 85
  and Constitution, 53–54, 117–18, 232–33
  as critic, 2–3, 5, 45, 95, 98, 99, 102, 106, 204
  and democracy, 5, 9, 14, 15, 27, 48–49, 54, 184, 189, 203, 226, 232
  and empire, 116, 200
  on Europe, 14, 23–24, 27
  family, 7, 83, 162–65, 177–78, 228
    (see also individual names)
  as father's private secretary, 167, 169, 173

  as historian, 1, 3, 5, 6, 8, 41, 78, 114, 120–23, 159–60, 166, 178–79, 191–92, 199, 209–13, 215, 222, 245, 246
  as humanist, 6–7, 218, 232
  idealism, 84, 109, 220
  irony, 81, 217
  journalism, 13, 89, 90, 122, 230, 253n2
  letters, 13, 115, 162, 183, 218
  as liberal, 247
  medievalism, 137, 138, 155, 156, 204, 205
  on Midwest, 189
  as nationalist, 7, 43, 104
  on North, 13–14, 32, 57
  and political parties, 113, 163, 174
  and politics, 33, 44, 83, 91, 117, 163, 179–80, 194–95, 200–201, 239
  pseudonym (see Compton, Frances Snow)
  and Reconstruction, 85, 118–19
  and religion, 127, 128, 137, 166, 199
  schooling, 164, 165–66
  and science and technology, 2, 6–7, 8, 63, 73, 114–15, 133, 152–53, 166, 174–79, 190–92, 197, 204–8, 217, 218, 236–40
  sister (see Adams, Catherine)
  on slavery, 13, 14, 20, 21, 23, 79, 84–85, 165
  and socialism, 14–15, 183–84, 207
    (see also Capitalism)

303